GRAHAM GREENE

GARLAND REFERENCE LIBRARY
OF THE HUMANITIES
(VOL. 923)

GRAHAM GREENE
A Character Index and Guide

Robert Hoskins

GARLAND PUBLISHING, INC. • NEW YORK & LONDON
1991

HOUSTON PUBLIC LIBRARY

Library of Congress Cataloging-in-Publication Data

Hoskins, Robert.
    Graham Greene : a character index and guide / Robert Hoskins.
        p.   cm. — (Garland reference library of the humanities ; vol.
923)
    Includes bibliographical references and index.
    ISBN 0–8240–4111–9
    1. Greene, Graham, 1904–1991—Characters. 2. Greene, Graham, 1904-1991
—Stories, plots, etc. I. Title. II. Series.
PR6013.R44Z63348   1991
823'.912—dc20   91–2714
                                                                        CIP

Printed on acid-free, 250-year-life paper
Manufactured in the United States of America

For Betty, Lane, and David

CONTENTS

PREFACE

The death of Graham Greene earlier this year brought to a close a remarkable literary career and left many of his readers and admirers with a sense of loss. As a writer Greene was a meticulous craftsman who understood the need to entertain as surely as he felt the need to express profound questions at the heart of human experience--questions of faith and doubt, of love and hate, of fear and suffering and hope. It has been a pleasure to discover through many years of teaching that Greene's novels seem to appeal even more strongly to my students now than they did two decades ago. I hope that the appeal will endure, and that students and other interested readers may find in this volume a useful companion to the study of a rich and varied body of imaginative writing.

This book, then, is a character index and guide to Graham Greene's fiction and drama. All of the novels and entertainments are included along with the *Collected Stories*, the *Collected Plays*, and the final volume of short stories *The Last Word*. The two early novels *The Name of Action* and *Rumour at Nightfall*, though long suppressed by the author, have been included here because they represent a significant stage of his artistic development even though they seem manifestly inferior to the other novels. Similarly, the unusual story "The Bear Fell Free," though it does not appear in the *Collected Stories,* is included because its experimental quality reveals a direction Greene's work might have taken but did not.

Within the guide, novels are presented in chronological order; stories and plays are presented in the order in which they appear in the collections mentioned above. Characters, historical and literary allusions, place names, and foreign phrases likely to be of special interest are presented alphabetically under each title. Unnamed relatives are listed with the name of the character with whom they are associated; that character's first or last name is used in accordance with Greene's practice in the narrative: thus, *Bendrix's* father, but *Marie's* mother. Unless otherwise indicated, all parenthetical citations refer to pages in the work under discussion. British spelling has been preserved in quotations; American spelling has been used elsewhere. Dates provided for novels identify the year of first publication; for plays, the year of first performance. For short stories, parenthetical dates are those provided by the author; bracketed dates identify the date of first publication for stories to which the author did not append a date. The General Index is an alphabetized list of all entries in the guide together with the number of the entry and an indication of the work from which that entry is taken.

ACKNOWLEDGMENTS

For generous assistance in the completion of this work I am grateful to the James Madison University Program of Sponsored Research for two summer grants which enabled me to pursue my interest in Graham Greene's writing; and to the Faculty Assistance Program for a semester of academic leave in which to complete much of the preparation of this index.

I would also like to thank the publishers and agents who have given permission to quote from Mr. Greene's works: Simon and Schuster, for *Monsignor Quixote, Dr. Fischer of Geneva,* and *The Tenth Man;* International Creative Management, for the Collected Edition of the novels, the *Collected Plays,* and the *Collected Essays;* and Viking-Penguin, a division of Penguin Books U.S.A., for the *Collected Stories* (Copyright 1935, 1941, 1942, 1946, 1947, 1949, (c) 1955, 1956, 1957, 1962, 1965, 1966, 1969, 1970, 1972 by Graham Greene).

A list of the many people who offered advice and information during my work on this project would be too lengthy for inclusion here, but I thank all of them and would like especially to express my gratitude to the following: to Robert F. Geary, who in his tenure as head of my department was an unfailing source of encouragement and support; to Michelle Crotteau, who proofread the manuscript and made many helpful suggestions; to Louise White and Cindi Dixon, who tolerated with good humor my daily invasion of their office space; to my sons Lane and David, for their patient understanding during a long period of closed study doors; and most of all to my wife Betty, for her interest, help, and wise criticism.

Graham Greene

CHAPTER ONE: INTRODUCTION

Few twentieth-century English writers have been as versatile or durable as Graham Greene, whose career spanned six decades and included distinguished achievements in drama, biography, the short story, the essay, and the travel book. His youthful poetry was negligible, but his film criticism for *The Spectator* and *Night and Day* was among the best of the day. Yet from his first book, *The Man Within* (1929) to his final one, *The Last Word* (1990), Greene was best known as a novelist, and his novels seem certain to be regarded in the future, as they are now, as his most important achievements. For that reason this brief introduction to his imaginative writing will focus attention primarily on the novels, with references to the stories and plays as they help to clarify the direction of his work and thought.

Greene's three earliest novels might best be regarded as apprentice works. Reflecting strongly the young author's boyhood love of romantic adventure stories, they have been compared with the fiction of his cousin Robert Louis Stevenson. The first of these, *The Man Within* (1929), is the best and retains interest even today for its psychological probing of the divided self in the protagonist Andrews. *The Name of Action* (1930), a Ruritanian adventure reminiscent of the fiction of Anthony Hope, moves at a sprightly pace but lacks plausibility and depth of character. It was suppressed by the author along with *Rumour at Nightfall* (1931), which has a remote historical setting like the first book but lacks the clarity and ease of style of that novel. The turgid prose

3

and murkily conceived action of *Rumour* make it the least
readable of these early works. The early short story "I Spy"
(1930) more closely resembles the manner of the later fiction than
do any of these apprentice novels.

The Man Within received favorable reviews (Aldous Huxley
thought it better than *To the Lighthouse*), sold well, and earned
advances and high expectations from Greene's publishers. The
next two novels were neither popular nor well-received, however,
and Greene, who had resigned his position as sub-editor for *The
Times* in order to devote himself to fiction, was faced with a
sinking career and rising debt. His fortunate recovery came about
in 1932 with the publication of the first of his "entertainments,"
Stamboul Train, a book through which Greene discovered both his
audience and some of his most important strengths as a writer.
Still highly readable, *Stamboul Train* displays many of the qualities
that would make its author successful: a fast pace; a
contemporary setting; vivid presentation of character and event in
an energetic, nervous style; a line of action which sets characters
against a background of international events worthy of news
headlines. "Headline" events--in this case a failed revolution in
Belgrade--are prominent throughout Greene's fiction but especially
so in the work of the thirties: the outcome of a murder trial
following the Hyde Park riots is central to his next book *It's a
Battlefield* (1934); a political assassination sets the plot in motion
in *A Gun for Sale* (1936); a holiday murder in a seaside resort
city begins *Brighton Rock* (1938). Greene, who had been a
promising journalist himself, often drew material from the
newspapers, and he used journalists as prominent characters in
every novel from *Rumour* through *Brighton Rock*, with the
exception of *A Gun for Sale*, which is nevertheless full of
headlines and is set in "Nottwich," the Nottingham where Greene
spent a year working on the *Nottingham Journal* (1925-26).

The entertainments which followed *Stamboul Train* continued
to provide income and allowed Greene to work on projects he
considered more important. They were distinguished from the
novels primarily by their faster pace and their tendency to
subordinate character and theme to action; it is a distinction easily
exaggerated, however, for Greene's attention to the psychology of
character in these works makes them superior to most examples
of the spy and detective genres, and in any case Greene himself

dropped the distinction between novel and entertainment when he began preparation of his works for the Collected Edition. The dubious nature of the distinction became apparent with *Brighton Rock*, which was conceived and begun as an entertainment but later became a novel.

Brighton Rock represented a turning point for Greene; his best work up to that point, it remains one of his major achievements, the beginning of what has often been called the "Catholic cycle" of four novels on religious themes (including *The Power and the Glory*, 1940; *The Heart of the Matter*, 1948; and *The End of the Affair*, 1952). These books more than any others would establish his critical reputation. His first two plays, *The Living Room* (1955) and *The Potting Shed* (1957), also center around Catholic characters and themes, but in the later works of both fiction and drama the emphasis usually rests upon social, political, and personal themes rather than religious ones. Obvious exceptions to this general direction are the play *Carving a Statue* (1975) and the late novel *Monsignor Quixote* (1982).

By the time he had reached middle age in the 1950's (b. 1904), Greene enjoyed an enviable commercial and critical success. Endlessly restless, he continued to travel the world in pursuit of adventure and material for his writing, displaying a remarkable affinity for regions where political turmoil had already erupted or was about to so do: Indo-China, Cuba, the Congo, Haiti, Argentina, Paraguay, Panama. The English (especially London) settings so familiar to the work of the thirties are largely displaced by these and other exotic locations. The protagonists become older, closer in many respects to their creator, and more likely to be revealed through first-person narrative. And like the author, they are more prosperous: when Greene does return to the London setting, briefly in *Our Man in Havana* (1958), extensively in *The Human Factor* (1978), it is not the seedy Warren Street and Soho of the thirties but the comparatively elegant region of St. James's and Piccadilly; these two works and the play *The Return of A.J. Raffles* (1975) place characters in the exclusive chambers of Albany, where Greene himself lived for several years in the 1950's and '60's.

The essential setting for Greene's work, of course, does not change: it is a territory of the mind which projects itself upon the external world no matter how vividly and accurately that external world is represented. It is a region of doubt, failure, and betrayal, redeemed only through occasional acts of love and quixotic heroism. It is the world largely unchanged from the earlier fiction, but now rendered with the style more subdued and the melodrama transmuted into various shades of comedy from the absurd to the farcical. Greene first introduces the comic mode in his entertainments in the diverting *Loser Takes All* (1955); in his plays it appears first in *The Complaisant Lover* (1961). There are delightfully humorous stories such as "When Greek Meets Greek" (1941) in the earlier short fiction, but the first collection in which the prevailing mode is comic is *May We Borrow Your Husband* (1967). Among the novels Greene's serious comedy emerges more gradually and is first easily recognized in *The Comedians* (1966).

Although a lengthy survey of Greene's work is beyond the scope of this introduction and, in any case, has been done ably in many other books, the following paragraphs may serve as an introduction to some of his major characteristics and the works in which those can be most readily observed. Rather than follow a strict chronology, I have used rubrics drawn from the author's own titles and intended here to suggest topics under which the works can conveniently be considered.

1. "The Basement Room"

The 1936 short story "The Basement Room" is not only one of Greene's finest stories but one of the most representative of his prewar works. It concerns a nine-year-old boy, Philip Lane, whose parents go away for a holiday, leaving him with the butler Baines and Baines's horrible wife. Philip's passage through the green baize door separating the servants' quarters from the rest of the house proves to be a traumatic passage from the secure world of childhood to the troubled one of adulthood. In a short time he is drawn into a pattern of deceit and betrayal as he discovers Baines in a teashop with a young woman, promises Baines he will not reveal the secret, and then accidentally does just that under pressure from Mrs. Baines. Later, after Mrs. Baines is killed in a quarrel with her husband, Philip betrays Baines, once more unwillingly, to the police; his fear of entering the room where she died and where he assumes she still lies reveals to the detectives that Baines has moved the body to make the death appear

accidental. The Baines whom he has idolized is incriminated, and
Philip is so traumatized by the events that he never opens himself
to life but remains withdrawn, neither loved nor loving, until the
end of his life.

"The Basement Room" embodies many of the distinctive
characteristics of Greene's fiction of the period. It is seriously
concerned with the psychology of its protagonist; it presents
dramatically the pattern of deceit and betrayal which for the
author is deeply rooted in our flawed human nature; it uses a
symbolic border (a familiar occurrence in Greene, seen here in the
green baize door) to emphasize the rite of passage from innocence
to experience; it exposes the torment of an unhappy marriage,
with the submissive husband's longing for escape and adventure.
Most important of all, it gives an essentially romantic conception
of childhood a modern psychological twist and thereby presents
one of Greene's most memorable versions of "the lost childhood."

We know from Greene's own testimony in *A Sort of Life*
(1971) and elsewhere that his own unhappy experience in his
father's Berkhamsted boarding school lay behind many of the
versions of unhappy children in his fiction. Actually "the lost
childhood" (a phrase from the title of one of Greene's essays)
takes two forms in his writing: more commonly, it involves
children deprived of happiness and/or innocence, often forced
prematurely, like Philip, into the world of adult experience; less
frequently it involves the recollection of adults whose memory of
childhood happiness and innocence is juxtaposed against joyless
conditions of their adult lives. Else Crole in *The Confidential
Agent* (1939) and Coral Fellows in *The Power and the Glory*
(1940) are, like Philip, representative of the former, but more
memorable than any of these cases are the youthful murderers
James Raven (*A Gun for Sale*, 1936) and Pinkie Brown (*Brighton
Rock*). In these very similar characters the lost children become
psychological grotesques, and the theme of lost childhood merges
with more public concerns of social justice. Both Raven and
Pinkie display a horror of life which they transmute into hatred
and aggression; both are victims of childhood trauma: Raven,
disfigured by a harelip, found his mother's body in the kitchen
where she had cut her throat, and grew up in an orphanage where
brutality rather than kindness was the guiding principle; Pinkie,
who as a small boy was exposed to the sexual activity of his

parents in their impoverished one-room flat, would rather murder a whole world than submit to the intimacies of ordinary adult life. At the opposite extreme is Arthur Rowe, protagonist of *The Ministry of Fear* (1943), whose childhood memories are of mothers and aunts, garden teas and church bazaars, all peaceful, happy images of an idyllic Edwardian past set against the horror of adult life in which he is guilty of murder (the mercy-killing of his wife) and the London he has known is being destroyed by the blitz. Together these and other accounts of "the lost childhood" bear the uncomfortable suggestion of a terror of life itself in which growing up may be the only thing worse than not growing up at all.

2. "The Religious Sense"

By the late 1930's Greene's typical methods and subjects--his adaptations of familiar crime and detective genres, his cinematic narrative techniques, his evidence (notably in *It's a Battlefield*, 1934, and *A Gun for Sale*) of a troubled social conscience, and his memorable versions of the lost childhood mentioned earlier--would presumably have assured his continued success. Yet it is unlikely that they alone would have led to the sustained critical interest and the international following he was to acquire.   Those achievements can be traced, I think, to the change of direction his work took in 1938 with *Brighton Rock*.

As a Catholic convert since 1926 Greene had by his own accounts been persuaded intellectually rather than emotionally to the faith.   It was apparently something perceived rather than something felt, a condition which may account for the fact that although occasional references to religion and a few Catholic characters appear (Minty, in *England Made Me*, is the most significant), no sustained treatment of religious themes occurs in the writings of his first nine years. If specific events or conditions brought about the change that took place, Greene was typically reticent about them, but the likelihood that his work might follow the direction it did may be implied in his critical comments on Henry James in essays published in 1933, 1936, and 1945.

In his 1936 essay, "Henry James: The Religious Aspect," Greene argued that "the ruling fantasy which drove [James] to write" was "a sense of evil religious in intensity."   James's

greatness, according to Greene, lay in his determination to render
even evil characters "the highest kind of justice":

> . . . it is in the final justice of his pity, the completeness of an
> analysis which enabled him to pity the most shabby, the most
> corrupt, of his human actors, that he ranks with the greatest
> of creative writers. He is as solitary in the history of the
> novel as Shakespeare in the history of poetry.[1]

In 1945 Greene wrote that after the death of James the "religious
sense" disappeared from the English novel,

> . . . and with the religious sense went the sense of the
> importance of the human act. It was as if the world of fiction
> had lost a dimension: the characters of such distinguished
> writers as Mrs. Virginia Woolf and Mr. E.M. Forster wandered
> like cardboard symbols through a world that was paper-thin.
> Even in one of the most materialistic of our great novelists--in
> Trollope--we are aware of another world against which the
> actions of the characters are thrown into relief.[2]

Clearly, Greene wanted his own characters to exist in that extra
dimension, and he found in the Catholic faith, once grasped
emotionally as well as intellectually, a bold and compelling
framework for his examination of contemporary life.

In *Brighton Rock* Greene first set forth in its full horror his
vision of the fallen world as a place of violence, extortion, murder,
and twisted sexuality. Brighton itself becomes the apt symbol of
the completely secular world, incarnated in the well-meaning but
ultimately merciless paganism of Ida Arnold, who drives the reader
into the unlikely but unavoidable state of sympathy with Pinkie,
the first of Greene's sinners who are paradoxically close to the
heart of God. Ida's superstitions, including her ouija board and
her often-mentioned belief in "ghosts," are counterpointed against
the Catholic faith of Pinkie and Rose and against the ministry of
the Holy Ghost recalled by the Pentecost holiday on which the
novel begins; and Ida's insistence upon "justice" is inadequate
alongside the Christian concept of mercy. A hunted man, a
heartless murderer, a lost child, Pinkie is Greene's creation of a
character worthy of hell whose fate in the end is nevertheless left

uncertain: the old priest who has the last word on Pinkie insists upon the folly of trying to understand the mystery of God's mercy. Left to mourn Pinkie is Rose, the child-bride (both are seventeen) who loves him profoundly in spite of his manifest evil; she is the first of Greene's characters who perform memorably the imitation of Christ through their ability to love someone who is unlovable by ordinary human beings.

Like *Brighton Rock, The Power and the Glory* employs the device of pursuit and discovers holiness where it might not be expected. The Whisky Priest is like Pinkie an outlaw, although his only serious crime is that of being a priest in a Mexican province where the government is destroying the priesthood. As in the earlier novel, there is once more a sharp contrast between the sacred and the secular, although the latter is given a more compelling voice in this novel. The Marxist lieutenant who relentlessly pursues the priest articulates with both reason and passion his desire for a just world in which no children will suffer in poverty as he did (another echo of the lost childhood). His vision of an empty, cooling, meaningless universe sets the faith of the priest in sharp relief, just as his cry for social justice brings about what may have been inevitable in Greene's work: a confrontation between the awakened social conscience and the faith, or the dialogue between Marxism and Catholicism which appears again in *The Comedians* (1966), *The Honorary Consul* (1971), and most notably in *Monsignor Quixote* (1982).

The Heart of the Matter again deals with a hunted man, although Scobie, unlike Pinkie and the Priest, does not know until very late that he is being pursued. Scobie, a Deputy Police Commissioner, is a good man of unquestioned reputation whose pity for the wife he no longer loves leads him through a series of skillfully plotted events into lies, dishonesty, abuse of his own office, and ultimately blasphemy and suicide. More rigorously than any of Greene's other novels, *The Heart of the Matter* employs plot as a kind of trap, an infernal machine wherein what might ordinarily be considered Scobie's virtue--his unwillingness to cause others to suffer--becomes a weakness which destroys him. He borrows money from Yusef, unwisely, to finance a vacation for the unhappy Louise; while she is away he visits the survivors of a shipwreck and comforts a dying child, praying to God that He end the child's suffering and give her peace even if it means the taking away of Scobie's own peace forever. The prayer seems answered: the child dies, and Scobie soon afterward begins the love affair with Helen Rolt, a young widow. He is discovered by Yusef, blackmailed, compromised; rather than risk Louise's unhappiness that would result from her discovery of his affair, he receives the sacraments when he has not confessed. Believing finally that his life is an affront to God and a source of pain for the two women he cares for, he chooses to die rather than to continue causing them suffering and unhappiness.

Sarah, in *The End of the Affair*, and Father William Callifer, in *The Potting Shed*, are brought to suffering through prayers similar to Scobie's prayer for the suffering child. Sarah, believing her adulterous lover Bendrix dead after a bomb strikes the house where they have been together, offers to a God she does not fully believe in the only thing she values--her love affair itself--if He will let Bendrix live. Father William, discovering the suicide of his younger brother James, offers that which he values most in life--his faith--in exchange for his brother's resurrection. Both prayers are granted, and both petitioners begin a period of prolonged suffering. Sarah's ends only with her death; William's ends when his brother's recovery of the truth and, consequently, happiness rekindles the priest's dead faith. *Brighton Rock, The Power and the Glory*, and especially *The End of the Affair* all suggest very powerfully the way in which human love prepares the heart for divine love. The theme is most emphatic in the last of these, where the experience of physical love enables Sarah to accept more readily the idea of God's existence in the human body of Christ.

Greene's Catholic works all link faith with suffering; all involve characters who suffer for others and in doing so pose the question of the possibility of sainthood in a secular world. In addition, all involve one of the main characters in the choice of death over life: Scobie, James Callifer (though he is restored to life), and Rose Pemberton (in *The Living Room*, 1955) are suicides; Pinkie's leap over a cliff into the sea to escape the police is arguably a suicide; the Whisky Priest, who has reached safety across the border, knows that when he returns to aid the dying murderer Calver he is choosing certain death; and Sarah invites her death by going out into the rain when she is already ill. The intersection of faith and worldly life seems inevitably to bring a tragic result, although the resolutions after the unhappy death become generally more positive in the later works.   Bendrix, after Sarah's death, displays such convincing evidence of weakening resistance that he seems certain to be drawn into belief, as Sarah was, before long; Teresa Browne, after the death of her niece Rose Pemberton, regains a sufficient measure of hope in God's mercy that she reopens the closed-off rooms of the family home; James Callifer discovers the truth of his mysterious past as well as the falseness of his late father's atheistic pose, and looks hopefully toward a reconciliation with his wife.   None of these works, however, offers the tranquility and acceptance of life to be found in the much later *Monsignor Quixote.*

3.   "The Human Factor"

In a central action in *The Heart of the Matter* Major Scobie, on his visit to the dying girl, pauses to reflect upon the ironic contrast between the beauty of the night and the tragic sense of life which arises from the situation he must contemplate:

> The lights inside would have given an extraordinary impression of peace if one hadn't known, just as the stars on this clear night gave also an impression of remoteness, security, freedom . . . . If one knew, he wondered, the facts, would one have to feel pity even for the planets?   If one reached what they called the heart of the matter?[3]

The lines echo, perhaps more than anything else in Greene's writing does, the "eternal note of sadness" heard beneath the calm, moonlit night in Arnold's "Dover Beach."[4] By pressing on to "the heart of the matter," Scobie's meditation on pity exposes a universe of suffering and implicitly summarizes the author's concern for injustice and treachery, for innocent victims of war and illness and death, for lost children and betrayed friends and lovers.   Scobie's question, of course, has no answer.   It may be transcended by the saintly characters--Rose Wilson, Sarah, the Whisky Priest, those whose selfless love, unlike Scobie's pity, can resolve itself in action.   But Greene the novelist knew all too well that few individuals can achieve saintly transcendence.   The best most of us can hope to achieve is that paradox of loyalty and

disloyalty which one of the later novels calls the human factor.
Again the attitude is akin to that in "Dover Beach," where human
fidelity is celebrated as consolation for the uncertainties of life in
the world at large:

Ah love, let us be true
To one another! for the world, which seems
To lie before us like a land of dreams,
So various, so beautiful, so new,
Hath really neither joy, nor love, nor light,
Nor certitude, nor peace, nor help for pain;
And we are here as on a darkling plain
Swept with confused alarms of struggle and flight,
Where ignorant armies clash by night.[5]

Greene's human factor is the unpredictable element--love,
compassion, divided loyalty--that makes a rather ordinary and
unheroic intelligence officer like Maurice Castle betray his country
(and the Western alliance) to the Soviets out of a sense of
obligation to Communists who helped his African wife to escape
from prison years ago. Castle is not an ideologue: he does not
act in order to promote Marxism. Nor is he a believer. He is
simply a flawed human being whose love for his wife and child
and, through her, her people, is a factor overlooked in the steely
machinations of agency chiefs. (They suspect and execute the
wrong man.) Castle practices what Greene has elsewhere called
the "virtue of disloyalty"--he values individuals more than states
and doctrines, human love more than abstractions or ideologies.

Castle fails the official, legal test of loyalty in order to pass
the private, personal one--in Greene's world, the only one that
matters. This kind of test, though it does not always take such a
dramatic form, is so central to Greene's writing that the story in
which it does not appear is the exception rather than the rule. In
the first published novel, *The Man Within*, Andrews betrays the
saintly Elizabeth, whom he genuinely loves, out of first lust and
then cowardice. The betrayal is fatal to both: she kills herself
rather than submit to violation by the smugglers, and Andrews
takes his own life because he cannot bear to go on living once he
has failed this vital test.

To trace the theme of betrayal through Greene's works would involve an examination of virtually all of them and would repeat much of what has been written often by his critics. A few examples should suffice: in *The Name of Action*, the next novel, Anne-Marie's betrayal of her husband Paul Demassener, and Chant's betrayal of her confidence, bring about the fall of the dictatorship and Chant's disillusionment. Crane's death in *Rumour at Nightfall* results from betrayal by his best friend Chase; Raven in *A Gun for Sale* goes "soft on a skirt" and trusts Anne Crowder, who betrays him to the police; Sarah Miles, Mary Rhodes, Clara Fortnum, and Martha Pineda are among the many wives whose betrayal of their husbands is central to the plots in which they appear; Fowler betrays his "innocent" best friend Pyle to certain death; the Mestizo who betrays the Whisky Priest is depicted from his first appearance onward as the archetypal Judas.

It is because our flawed humanity makes these characters both frequent and credible in Greene's works that instances of loyalty emerge not merely as memorable but as Greene's version of heroic action. Loyalty, of course, is synonymous with love: Rose loves Pinkie so completely that she prefers to suffer damnation with him rather than salvation alone; Sarah loves Bendrix so passionately that she offers the only thing of value in her life--her relationship with him--in order to preserve his life; William Callifer sacrifices his own faith to restore his younger brother's life. On a more ordinary scale Charley Fortnum loves the unfaithful Clara with generosity and forgiveness that win from her an affection likely to be much more durable than passion; Maurice Castle and the Captain (in *The Captain and the Enemy*) are similarly capable of absolute fidelity. Such forms of self-sacrificing love and loyalty, it might be added, are the implied models against which characters like Brown and Plarr measure themselves, discover their shortcoming, and thereby attain a measure of redemptive humility.

4. "The Comedians"

The title of *The Comedians* points to the comic element that characterizes much of Greene's later work, a comedy that is often highly serious in its willingness to confront the possibility that life is ultimately absurd. This 1966 novel involves three characters caught up in serious actions which spring from absurd premises:

Brown, the protagonist, who operates a resort hotel in a country
with no tourists; Smith, who travels to Haiti to promote
vegetarianism in a country where people cannot afford to eat
meat; and Jones, whose braggadocio traps him in the leadership
of guerrilla soldiers even though he has never done military
service. Behind all lurks the sinister figure of "Papa Doc"
Duvalier, whose brutal regime is a grim reminder of Dr.
Hasselbacher's observation in *Our Man in Havana* that political
life in our century is too horrible to be contemplated. Brown's
conclusion that God, if He exists, must be a joker is consistent
with the novel's dark humor and its ironic conclusion in which
Brown affirms his own spiritual deadness by becoming, at the
novel's end, an undertaker.

   Brown, educated by Jesuits who believed that the boy might
have a vocation, is one of Greene's many versions of failed priests
in a line that includes Pinkie (who once wanted to be a priest,
and is also named Brown), Father William Callifer, and León
Rivas in *The Honorary Consul* (1972). Like *The Comedians*,
Consul blends serious themes and characters with an absurd comic
situation: terrorists who hope to win the release of political
prisoners in Paraguay by kidnapping an American ambassador in
Argentina kidnap the wrong person the alcoholic English "honorary
consul" Charley Fortnum, who is so unimportant that no one in
power is interested in bargaining for his release. Only the
Argentine Dr. Eduardo Plarr tries actively to help Fortnum, and
Plarr's position in the matter is rendered absurd, first because he
has assisted the guerrillas in planning their action, and second
because he is carrying on an affair with Fortnum's wife. Father
Rivas, leader of the guerrillas and Plarr's friend, is a priest turned
political activist out of his conviction that God takes no interest in
the political affairs of humankind. Rivas has abandoned the
priesthood but not belief; he sees God as having both a good and
a dark side, and argues that human actions are involved in the
evolution of God--a thoughtful answer to Brown's view of God as
joker.

   It might be said that Greene's comedy in the later works also
has a bright side as well as a dark. Two of the novels--*Travels
with my Aunt* and *Monsignor Quixote*--are among the happiest
and funniest of all of his works. *Travels* records the delayed
awakening to life of a retired bank manager, Henry Pulling, under

the tutelage of his septuagenarian Aunt Augusta, whose zest for
adventure and love are affirmative even if somewhat anarchical.
Through the comic spirit the novel posits a reconciliation with life,
an acceptance of its joys and surprises, a love of adventure, a
sexuality untroubled by guilt, a love unburdened by demands. It
is perhaps also a kind of self-justification of the wandering life
the author has long pursued.

   Monsignor Quixote offers a more philosophical, less exuberant
form of reconciliation and acceptance. Carrying forward the
dialogue between Marxism and Catholicism begun at least as early
as *The Power and the Glory*, this novel presents a blending of
faiths as the philosophical Father Quixote accepts doubt as a
condition of faith on the only terms we can experience it in our
human condition. He also acknowledges the goodness of Marx,
and he displays a Christlike love for humanity with all its faults.
His good-willed companion Sancho is moved by Quixote's example
to doubt his own dogmatic Marxist faith and open himself to the
possibility of Christian belief. Together they demonstrate
memorably the simple joys of friendship, trust, good wine, and a
gentle heart. *Monsignor Quixote* is the most serene of Greene's
works and, although he published two additional novels after it
appeared, the most obvious choice for a conclusion to his long
and distinguished work.

CHAPTER TWO: THE NOVELS

THE MAN WITHIN (1929)

1 Absalom
Third son of King David, killed by Joab for his rebellion against
the king (II Samuel). By introducing himself to Mr. Farne as
"Absalom," Andrews expresses his desire to rebel against the spirit
of his own father.

2 Andrews, Francis
The self-divided, cowardly young protagonist, whose brutal, abusive
father provided him a good education and then forced him to join
the gang of smugglers the father led. Desiring justice and a
higher life as well as revenge against his father, Andrews betrays
his fellow smugglers to the excisemen and runs away. He is
sheltered by Elizabeth, whose affection and trust appeal to his
higher self and give him courage to testify against the gang at
their trial in Lewes; but upon their acquittal he loses both his
courage and his resolve and betrays Elizabeth twice, first by
sleeping with Lucy and later by failing to defend Elizabeth against
the smugglers. After her death he realizes that his real quarrel
has been with his father, not Carlyon. He confesses, falsely, to the
murder of Elizabeth in order to protect Carlyon, then exorcises
the spirit of his father by taking his own life.

3 Andrews' father
Andrews' father was a large, brutal, domineering man "with a quick cunning brain and small eyes" (69). He beat his son and his wife. For his bravery and strength he was always held up as a model to his son, a model the boy could not live up to, and so the son hated him. He died in a battle at sea, but young Andrews cannot escape his shadow, for he feels that the father's spirit lives on in him.

4 Andrews' mother
Andrews recalls his mother as "incurably romantic," a "quiet pale woman who loved flowers" and used to collect them and press them in albums which her brutal husband destroyed (69). Her son attributes her death to a broken will.

5 Bill
An "elderly, benevolent man" (127) in the witness room who taunts Andrews as an informer and slaps him in the face. Because the man is old, Andrews refuses to fight.

6 Bottom
Under questioning from Braddock, Andrews smiles at the memory of Bottom the weaver in *A Midsummer Night's Dream* and recalls the line "I will roar you as gently as any sucking dove" (I, ii). Shakespeare's character is comically ignorant and conceited, confident that he can do anything better than anyone else.

7 Braddock, Mr.
Defense attorney, "a large man with an apoplectic face which might well have been formed by an undue consumption of contraband liquor" (132). In court he is sometimes bullying, sometimes friendly and insinuating. He accuses the gaugers of lying.

8 Butler, Mrs.
The old woman who cleans Elizabeth's cottage. Upon seeing Andrews there she concludes that he and Elizabeth are lovers. Her belief that such is the case--and that Elizabeth lied to her--leads the defending lawyer Braddock to assert that Andrews spent only one night in the cottage, not a week as Elizabeth said.

9 Carlyon
Present leader of the gang of smugglers, loved and feared by
Andrews, who betrays him.   Carlyon's dual nature--he resembles
an ape but has an aesthetic sensibility and a sentimental romantic
imagination--parallels the self-division in Andrews.

10 Cockney Harry
One of the smugglers who escapes capture. Andrews sees him in
the courtroom but does not betray him. After the trial he warns
Andrews that Carlyon and the others will give Elizabeth a "fright"
and will expect to trap Andrews at her cottage.

11 Collier, Joe (Elephantine Joe)
One of the smugglers, "a fat, big, clumsy, stupid creature, a prize
bull of a man" (70). When he tortures Elizabeth to get her to
reveal Andrews' whereabouts, she takes her own life in order to
avoid betraying her lover.

12 customs officer
Andrews wrote to the customs officer at Shoreham, notifying him
of where and when the smugglers' cargo (spirits from France)
would be delivered.

13 Duke of Northumberland
See Grey, Jane.

14 Elizabeth
Saintly, innocent, brave young woman of eighteen who shelters
Andrews, hides him from Carlyon, and offers him friendship and
love. Her appeal to his higher nature gives him the courage to
testify in court against the smugglers, and he falls in love with her;
but when, following the acquittal, they come after him, he runs
away for help instead of staying to protect her. When he returns,
she has killed herself with his knife.

15 Elizabeth's father
His actual fate is unknown, but Elizabeth believes that he must
have died or left her mother.

16 Elizabeth's grandfather
A farmer, wealthy by local standards, who provided whatever
money Elizabeth's mother had.

17 Farne
A small, respectable, religious man who meets the drunken
Andrews in a tavern, suspects him to be one of the smugglers and
takes him to Sir Henry Merriman, with whom Farne shares a
serious concern for justice.

18 Gadarene swine
Jesus healed two Gadarene demoniacs by driving the devils out of
their bodies and into swine, which then rushed into the sea and
drowned (Matthew 8:28-34). Andrews, fearing for his life as he
hides from Carlyon at Elizabeth's cottage, feels that time is rushing
past like the Gadarene swine.

19 gardener
Andrews dreams of the old gardener from his childhood home
who dragged one foot behind him.

20 Garnet, Mrs.
Elizabeth's mother. Braddock says it is not known whether she
was ever married.

21 gaugers
Revenue officers who inspect bulk goods subject to import duty.

22 George
A potman at the Goat Inn in Lewes.

23 *Good Chance*
Carlyon's ship.

24 Grey, Jane (c. 1537-1554)
Henry VII's great-grand-daughter whose nine-day reign as Queen
of England in 1553 resulted from the unsuccessful attempt of her
father-in-law, the Duke of Northumberland, to transfer the
succession away from the Tudors and into his own family, the

Dudleys. Sir Henry Merriman, in defeat, compares himself to Northumberland.

25 Hake
A large, bearded member of the gang who threatens both Andrews and the jury in the courtroom, accuses Tims of having killed Rexall, and denies having been present at the scene of the crime.

26 Hassocks
Town in West Sussex.

27 headmaster
The headmaster of the school Andrews attended beamed with pleasure when the boy told his father that he was happy studying Sophocles and Horace.

28 Hilliard, Thomas
Officer in command of the revenue post at Shoreham for over four years. He has not made successful arrests in the past three years. In the trial, Braddock contends that Hilliard and his men, fearful of losing their jobs, arrested the six known smugglers in their homes, not at the shore.

29 Jennings
Lodger who took over the farm from Mrs. Garnet and raised Elizabeth as his daughter. Braddock says many people in the countryside think Elizabeth is both his daughter and his mistress.

30 Jonah
The biblical character who tried to flee from the presence of God by embarking upon a ship to Tarshish but was swallowed by a whale; hence, a person whose presence brings misfortune to his companions. Tims, the half-wit upon whom the smugglers are willing to blame the murder of Rexall, is described as an "unwanted Jonah."

31 Lewes Assizes
Assizes are court sessions held periodically in each of the counties
of England and Wales for the trial of criminal or civil cases.
Lewes is a town in West Sussex.

32 Lucy
Young, pretty, well-dressed mistress of Sir Henry Merriman for
three years. Bored with Sir Henry's work and expectant that he
will turn away from her eventually, she fears that with him she will
grow old too quickly (apparently through lack of sexual activity):
"When all's sad there's only one amusement while one's young"
(118). She behaves seductively but then rejects Andrew's advances
on the night of their meeting, yet sells herself for the following
night for the price of his testimony against the smugglers--causing
Andrews to do the right thing for the wrong reason.

33 Merriman, Sir Henry
The prosecuting attorney, whose weariness in efforts to stop
smuggling through the courts is exacerbated by the acquittal of
Carlyon's gang. He doubts whether juries will ever be trustworthy
in such cases. He offers to help Andrews with protection, money,
and introductions in London to enable Andrews to escape the
danger and influence of the gang of smugglers.

34 Parkin, Sir Edward
The judge at Lewes, a short, plump, fastidious man whose
snobbery, conceit, and verbosity Sir Henry believes likely to
alienate honest jurors and work to the advantage of the prisoners.

35 Petty, Mr.
Clerk of the Arraigns, a somnolent officer at the trial of the
smugglers who conveys intense boredom with the entire
proceeding. He testifies to the court that Tims is not capable of
making his own defense.

36 priest
Performs at Jennings' funeral a "mechanic ritual less conscious
than the act of brushing teeth" (31).

37 Rexall, Edward
A gauger killed in the capture of the smugglers.   Braddock
attempts to prove that his murder resulted from a private quarrel,
not a battle with smugglers.

38 Shoreham
Shoreham-by-Sea, coastal town in East Sussex.

39 "There's another man within me that's angry with me."
The novel's epigraph is from Sir Thomas Browne's *Religio Medici*
(1642).

40 Tims
Youngest of the smugglers, a "wizened half-witted youth" (70) who
had been Andrews' father's personal servant and thus (because he
was bullied) the only member of the crew who did not worship
the senior Andrews.   Once he realized that the son was not like
the father, he became friendly to him as a fellow victim.

41 unjust steward
Elizabeth describes how Jennings, upon hearing her read the
parable of the unjust steward (Luke 16:1-10), confessed that as a
clerk in the Customs he had accepted bribes from seamen whose
undeclared cargo he would not report.   Jennings felt that the
parable vindicated that period of his life.

42 Venus
Roman goddess of love and beauty.   Andrews sees Elizabeth as
a Venus-like figure, a "goddess" with white birds around her
(doves were sacred to Venus).

43 woman, fat
Buys Andrews a whisky at the Goat and encourages him to draw
a picture of Elizabeth.

44 "Ye have been fresh and green. . . ."
Andrews recalls the first stanza of Robert Herrick's "To
Meddowes" (1648), which he associates with Carlyon and their
shared love of poetry.

THE NAME OF ACTION (1930)

45 Adolph
A lodger in the house next to Kapper's who laughs in the night
when he wakes and thinks of something funny. His laughter
alarms Chant on the night the policeman is murdered.

46 Baptist's head, the
When John the Baptist was beheaded at the request of Salome,
his head was brought to her upon a platter.

47 barge-keeper
The elderly owner of the barge *Rhine Maiden* retrieves the
policeman's body from the river.

48 "Between the conception / And the creation"
The novel's epigraph is from T.S. Eliot's "The Hollow Men"
(1925).

49 Chant, Oliver
A wealthy young Londoner whose boredom with upper class social
life and his longing for romantic adventure lead him to journey to
Trier to join the revolutionaries attempting to overthrow the
dictatorship of Paul Demassener.   Chant purchases arms and
smuggles them into the country, and he is willing to fight in the
streets if necessary, but his resolve weakens when he falls in love
with Demassener's wife Anne-Marie, as he was disposed to do
already, having seen her photograph in London.   Her
disillusioning rejection of him is ironically the catalyst for successful
revolution: in his anger he betrays her confidence by revealing to
Kapper that her husband is impotent. Kapper's verses bring about
Demassener's humiliation and fall from power, but Chant, who
now regards Demassener with both pity and respect, befriends the
fallen dictator as both journey toward London on the train.

50 Crane
American engineer in Coblenz who deals in illegal or covert
weapons sales. He sells guns to Chant, as he had done to
Demassener in the past.

51 Croesus (d. c.547 B.C.)
Ancient king of Lydia, a man of legendary wealth who allied his
country with Babylonia and Egypt in a failed struggle against the
Persians under Cyrus the Great. In regarding Chant as a modern
Croesus, Mrs. Meadmore probably has in mind both Chant's
idealism and his wealth.

52 Demassener, Anne-Marie
The dictator's beautiful, unsatisfied wife of five years, Anne-Marie
is the object of her husband's genuine affection and Chant's
romantic fantasy. After a brief flirtation and a sexual encounter
with her, Chant believes that she loves him and might return to
London with him, but she rejects him so coldly, revealing that she
has merely used him to satisfy her physical desire, that he
determines to stay in Trier and work against her husband. Her
infidelity with Chant is a double betrayal of Demassener, for she
reveals to her lover the secret of her husband's impotence.

53 Demassener, Paul
The dictator of Trier, a quiet, somewhat weary man of intelligence
and refined manners whose repressive rule seems less intended to
exercise raw power than to impose a rigid morality upon his
people. Opposed to freedom because it means freedom for the
animal in human nature, he has closed the brothels, imposed a
strict curfew, and forbidden anyone to bear arms. Demassener's
sexual impotence, once revealed, exposes him to public ridicule
and brings about his downfall, and he flees the country.

54 Fritz (dog)
The barge-keeper's dog which sees the policeman's body and pulls
it to the barge.

55 Fritz (man)
Fritz and Karl, two of Kapper's supporters, are large, heavy,

somnolent men who bar the door to Herr Lintz's inner room while Kapper interrogates Chant about his second visit to the palace.

56 Gruner, Frau
An old woman who interrupts Chant's visit with the Demasseners by coming to beg for the body of her recently executed son, whom she wants to give a Catholic burial. Demassener gives her permission to bring a priest to the funeral.

57 Kapper, Bertha
Joseph Kapper's wife, who is sent by Chant and her husband to cover with red meat the bloodstains from the body of the murdered policeman.

58 Kapper, Joseph
Poet and revolutionary leader to whom Chant is sent by Kurtz. Though he does not hesitate to murder a policeman to save Chant from arrest, Kapper maintains steadfastly his belief in the superior power of the pen over the sword, a belief that appears sustained when his verses lampooning Demassener as an impotent cuckold destroy the dictator's power by exposing him to public ridicule. Ultimately vain and cruel, lacking the romantic imagination Chant expected in him, Kapper is less admirable to Chant in the end than the dictator himself.

59 Karl
See Fritz.

60 Kraft, Captain
Head of police in Trier, a man of rigid bearing and movements so mechanical that they remind Chant of a clockwork toy. His many scars indicate a history of duelling.

61 Kurtz
Exiled patriot from the Palatinate Republic who persuades Oliver Chant to assist the effort to overthrow the dictatorship there. Ironically, the dictator Demassener has a high regard for Kurtz.

62 Lintz, Sebastian
An old shoemaker, the contact in Trier who introduces Chant to
the conspirators Kapper and Torner.

63 Mann
Passport officer whose interest in talking to Chant as someone
familiar with Tottenham Court Road in London makes it difficult
for Weber to offer Muller, the customs officer, a bribe.

64 Marlowe
Prior to meeting Kapper and Torner, Chant imagines them as
corresponding to his romanticized images of poet and painter
respectively: the poet Christopher Marlowe, the painter Peter
Paul Rubens.

65 Mayfair
Fashionable district in the West End of London, associated with
high society.

66 Mazzini
Guisseppe Mazzini (1805-72), Italian patriot and revolutionary
leader, advocate of an Italian republic. Mrs. Meadmore regards
Kurtz as her Mazzini, perhaps chiefly because Mazzini, like the
fictional Kurtz, spent several years of exile in London.

67 Meadmore, Mrs.
London society hostess whose interest in European politics leads
her to befriend the exiled Kurtz and encourage him to seek
financial help from Oliver Chant. Chant meets Kurtz at her house
and thus begins his adventure.

68 Muller
Customs officer at Cochem, on the Moselle River, who has
regularly accepted bottles of wine as a bribe for allowing his friend
Weber to smuggle wine into the Palatinate.   He becomes
suspicious when Chant, eager to prevent him from opening the
crates containing the guns, offers too large a bribe, but he is
persuaded by Weber to allow the shipment to pass uninspected.

69 Otranto Castle
A castle on the river near Cochem reminds Chant of Horace
Walpole's Gothic novel *The Castle of Otranto* (1765).

70 Palatinate
Two adjacent regions in western Germany, the names of which
are derived from their control by the Count-Palatine Conrad,
brother to Holy Roman Emperor Frederick I.   Trier, center of
action in the novel, is in the lower or Rhenish Palatinate.

71 police officer
A young police officer who pursues Chant through the streets of
Trier when Chant violates the curfew is killed by Kapper, who
will not risk having Chant deported.

72 Remnant, Peter
London friend with whom Chant often has lunch.

73 Rubens
See Marlowe.

74 Schultz, Frau
Having won permission to bring a priest to her son's burial, Frau
Gruner asks the same privilege for Frau Schultz, whose son has
also been executed.   Demassener denies the request.

75 Struber
Friend of Demassener, murdered by three men in a cafe in Trier.
His funeral procession attracted a thousand followers and enabled
Demassener to overthrow the republican government and seize
power.

76 Torner, Peter
Kapper's friend and fellow revolutionary, regarded as an "artist"
but more accurately seen as a caricaturist whose pictures ridicule
Demassener and especially Anne-Marie.

77 Trier
City on the Moselle River in the Rhineland-Palatinate, now in
western Germany. Trier was held by both France and Prussia in
the nineteenth and twentieth centuries.

78 Walpole, Sir Robert (1676-1745)
British Prime Minister (1715-17, 1721-45). When Chant, faced with
the need to bribe customs inspectors in order to get his shipment
of contraband weapons through, worries that Walpole may not
have been right, he is thinking of the prime minister's alleged
remark "All those men have their price."

79 Weber
A barge-keeper, identifiable by his blue coat, who aids the
revolutionaries by transporting the weapons purchased by Chant
from Coblenz to Trier.

80 Weber, Frau
Weber's wife, a calm, faithful woman whose happiness and
untroubled mind are attributed by Chant to her religion and her
marriage. He sees her as a foil to the anxiety, discontent, and
tired sophistication of his own class.

81 woman in *gasthaus*
The proprietress of the *gasthaus* to which Chant and Anne-Marie
go after the latter's second car crash. She panders to their mutual
but unexpressed desire by encouraging them to take food and
drink in the warmth of a private room rather than in the cold
restaurant.

RUMOUR AT NIGHTFALL (1931)

82 Alphonso
Alphonso XII, son of Isabella II; first monarch (1874-85) of the
Bourbon Restoration which followed the end of the Republic in
1874.

83 Ariel
In Shakespeare's *The Tempest*, the spirit who carries out the
schemes of the magician Prospero.

84 Balaam's ass
In Numbers 22, Balaam's ass sees an angel in the road, refuses to
pass, and is struck unjustly by his master. God then empowers the
ass to ask Balaam why he treats it thus. When Chase, on the
road to San Juan, sees a Spaniard berating an old mule, he wishes
the animal could turn "like Balaam's ass" upon its tormentor (30).

85 barber
One of Caveda's men, killed by soldiers in San Juan while he
screams out a message that Chase cannot hear distinctly. Later
it is revealed that the shooting was part of a plan by Caveda, who
did not trust the man.

86 Campion
St. Edmund Campion (1540-81), former Oxford fellow (St. John's
College) who studied at Douai and became a Jesuit priest in 1573.
He returned to England in 1580, began preaching privately there,
and was arrested, imprisoned in the Tower, and executed.

87 Cana
Town in Galilee where Jesus performed the miracle of
transforming water into wine for wedding guests (John 2: 1-11).
On the night of his own wedding to Eulelia, Crane sees the

moonlight on the street as causing the water in the drains to look like wine, as if a second miracle had been performed.

88 Carlist war
The Carlists, supporters for several decades of the claims of Don Carlos and his descendants to the Spanish throne following the death of his brother Ferdinand VII and the ascendancy of the king's daughter Isabella II in 1833, brought the country to civil war from 1833 to 1840 and again from 1873 to 1876. References in the novel to the restoration of kingship and to Alphonso, who became king in 1874, indicate that the action takes place soon after the second of these civil wars.

89 Carlos, the Pretender
Apparently Don Carlos, duque de Madrid (1848-1909), the third Don Carlos (great nephew of the first) whose Carlist followers supported his claims to the throne. His forces conquered much of the Basque territory but failed to win the civil war, which ended in 1876.

90 Caveda, Ramon
Elusive guerilla leader who carries on the war after Carlos the Pretender has surrendered. He excites both admiration as a brave hero and contempt as "thief, atheist, murderer" (44), but no one is certain whether he fights for principle, booty, or the love of adventure. Caveda never appears in the novel, yet his presence is constantly felt. As the lover of Eulelia he is the source of her guilt and Crane's jealousy; to Chase, who identifies strongly enough with him to save him by betraying Crane, Caveda embodies Liberal principles and rational, secular values--the opposites of the mysteries of Spanish Catholicism and the romanticism of Crane.

91 Chase, Francis
English newspaper correspondent who ignores his paper's cable recalling him to London and pursues the outlaw Caveda in hope of getting a major story that will make his reputation. A rationalist with thoroughly secular goals (wealth, professional success, friends), he dislikes the "barbaric" religion of Catholic Spain and feels betrayed when his friend Crane, his alter ego, is

drawn toward that faith. Chase increasingly identifies with Caveda
as a kindred spirit, and in the end he betrays Crane in order to
save Caveda's life. His subsequent guilt and remorse over the
death of Crane open him through suffering to a more complete
humanity and unite him with his friend's bride, Eulelia.

92 Cock
A tavern in Fleet Street, London, frequented by Chase, Crane,
and their fellow journalists.

93 Crane, Michael
A journalist like Chase, whom he visits in Spain in search of
adventure and an escape from or solution to his own inner
conflicts, Crane is in a sense the other half of Chase's incomplete
personality: romantic rather than realistic, cowardly and uncertain
rather than brave and confident, spiritual and intuitive rather than
secular and rational. In the love and religious faith of Eulelia
Monti he experiences briefly for the first time the peace, the
escape from fear and anxiety, which he has long sought. He
marries her but is killed by Caveda's men on the night of their
wedding.

94 Crane's mother
An inheritance from his recently-deceased mother has made
Crane's travels possible. He confesses a dislike for her: "She was
a part of England, though, insensitive, a little vulgar, grasping."
Chase, by contrast, thought her "interesting" and "reliable" (72).

95 Descartes' philosophy
In an imaginary dialogue with Eulelia Monti, Chase arrives at a
tentative understanding of how suffering gives meaning to
existence: "I suffer, therefore I am." He interprets this deduction
as a variation of "cogito ergo sum" ("I think, therefore I am"), a
central premise of the philosophy of René Descartes.

96 Diaz, General
Commandant of the army pursuing Caveda at San Juan, "a small
emaciated man with a grey moustache twisted aggressively" (249).
Aloof and haughty, he severely chastises both Riego and Chase for
the latter's involvement in the Caveda affair.

97 Dives
The name usually given to the rich man in Christ's parable (Luke
16:19-31) of Lazarus and the rich man. Having lived comfortably
and without charity in his earthly life, Dives suffered eternal
punishment in hell and was denied even a drop of water to cool
his tongue. Crane, who equates heaven with "peace," tells Chase
that we experience peace just enough to feel tormented by the
lack of it; Dives, he says, was lucky to be denied the drop of
water.

98 ecclesiastic, mind-proud
The "mind-proud ecclesiastic" who Chase thinks deserved burning
at the stake for trying to "shake mankind's faith" by turning even
the hard reality of stones into illusion is probably the idealist
philosopher Bishop George Berkeley (1785-1853).

99 Enrique
One of Caveda's men, also a pimp. When he finds Chase in the
street on the night of the fighting in San Juan, he tries first to
interest Chase in a woman and then takes him to the inn where
Chase talks to Miguel.

100 "God give me a friend like that."
This line, attributed to Eulelia by her mother, echoes Othello's
account of Desdemona's response to his stories of adventure: "she
wish'd / That heaven had made her such a man" (I,iii).

101 groom
The groom who gets Chase's horse ready for his journey to San
Juan warns Chase of the storm that will follow, but Chase ignores
the warning.

102 innkeeper
The innkeeper who hosts Chase and Crane appears to share the
confidence of Emilio, one of Caveda's men, and therefore to know
in advance of the guerillas' plans for taking San Juan.

103 Isabella
Queen Isabella of Spain (r. 1833-68).

104   Jaime
Eulelia's hairdresser, through whom Caveda tells her to send
messages.

105   Joan, St.
Crane compares Eulelia with St. Joan of Arc for the ease with
which she overthrows his mistrust and doubt by declaring her love
directly and simply.

106   Juan
Husband of the innkeeper.

107   Loyola
St. Ignatius of Loyola (1491-1556), Spanish founder of the Jesuit
order. Crane imagines that Señor Monti might be communicating
silently with Loyola and St. John of the Cross.

108   Luis
One of the two Spaniards with whom Chase and Crane share a
table at the inn. Luis wanted to marry Eulelia but refused to
accept her without a dowry.

109   Mahon
See Moltke.

110   man, old
At the inn where Chase takes shelter from the storm on his way
to San Juan, an old man warns him that by pursuing the woman
(Eulelia) in the photograph he will only bring unhappiness to
himself and her and his "friend." The man refers to the
anonymous friend (Caveda) Chase has mentioned, but Chase
thinks immediately of Crane, for whom the prophecy proves true.
The ambiguity itself is a kind of foreshadowing, since Chase will
place himself in a dilemma in which he can only save one "friend"
by betraying the other.

111   Miguel
Leader of Caveda's men in San Juan, a fat man who prides
himself in his role as "chief helper" to Caveda (272).

112 Moltke
When Riego interrupts inspection of the bags captured in the
ambush in order to attend to the dying Roca, Chase wonders
"What would have happened on the other side of the frontier a
few years ago if Mahon or Moltke had been swayed by the
thought of lost lives?" (6) Chase probably has in mind Helmuth
Von Moltke (1800-91), who as head of the Prussian and German
general staff was organizer of the victory over France in the
Franco-German war, 1870-71. Chase may also be thinking of the
French commander who was wounded and defeated at Sedan in
the key battle of that war, Marshal Marie Patrice MacMahon, who
later became president of the French Republic (1873-79).

113 Monti, Eulelia
A beautiful, proud young woman of San Juan whose photograph
and the knowledge that she is reputedly Caveda's mistress draw
the interest of Chase and, through him, Crane. Actually she gave
herself to Caveda only once, freely, not out of love but to spite
her venal mother, who has made several attempts to convert
Eulelia's beauty and chastity into material gain. She regards her
mother as the origin of everything bad in her, her father as the
source of her goodness. She will not betray Caveda to Chase, but
she forsakes him for Crane, whom she falls in love with and
secretly marries. After Crane is killed on their wedding night, she
enters mercifully into a sad union with the guilt-ridden Chase.

114 Monti, Señor
Eulelia's father, a gentle scholar who reads Campion and
Southwell. He approves and attends her marriage to Crane, and
she attributes her own best qualities to him.

115 Monti, Señora
Eulelia's mother, a venal, irrational woman whose dissatisfaction
with her husband's modest income and inability to provide a dowry
for their daughter has led to her obsession with the procuring of
a wealthy husband for Eulelia. Determined that her daughter will
marry Chase, and unaware that Eulelia has already married Crane,
she locks Crane out of the house and thereby contributes to his
death at the hands of Caveda's men. Eulelia attributes her own
worst qualities to her mother.

116 Nicodemus
A wealthy Pharisee who came to Jesus under cover of darkness
and confessed his belief (John 3:1-5). Chase, struggling to
preserve his own belief in rational truth as opposed to Crane's
acceptance of the "unseen," closes his eyes to shut out the light
through which divine revelation is often said to have been
transmitted. The darkness offers little comfort, however, for he
recalls that Nicodemus visited Jesus at night.

117 "O ye that stand"
The novel's epigraph is taken from "Shadows on the Water," by
Thomas Traherne (1637-1674).

118 officer
A guard at the gate of San Juan warns Crane that he will not be
safe on the road to Aljerema.

119 Panza, Sancho
See priest.

120 *Patria y Rey*
"Country and King," a part of the Carlist motto used as a
password by Caveda's men in San Juan.

121 Peacock
A London journalist. (See Verity.)

122 Pedro, Father
At the church where he stops to escape from the rain, Chase
hears women call the name of Father Pedro, who does not
appear.

123 priest
The priest who reluctantly marries Crane and Eulelia is a strong,
weathered man of indeterminate age and a gentle manner that
belies the coarseness of his appearance. To Crane he appears to
combine the sadness of Cervantes' Don Quixote and the humor of
his Sancho Panza.

124 Quintana, Captain
One of Riego's officers, a man whose diminutive stature corresponds, in Chase's view, to his pettiness and superficiality. Unlike Chase, he views Caveda cynically as a man interested only in a bribe.

125 Quixote
See priest.

126 Riego, Colonel
Weary veteran soldier whose determined professionalism subdues a visible melancholy owed in part to the infidelity of his wife, who ironically may have betrayed him with Caveda, the very man he pursues.

127 Roca, Luis
Spanish soldier who dies at the opening of the novel, the only casualty of the ambush of Caveda's men.

128 Rubicon
By crossing the Rubicon with his army in 49 B.C., Julius Caesar took the irrevocable step of defying the Roman senate and thus precipitated civil war. Crane feels that he has crossed a personal Rubicon by deciding to reveal to Eulelia that he and Chase are not friends but enemies of Caveda.

129 Southwell
St. Robert Southwell (1561-95), English Jesuit priest and martyr. Southwell, who was chaplain to the Countess of Arundel, was arrested in 1595, imprisoned, and executed after three years.

130 Spaniards, two
Upon arrival in San Juan, Chase shares a dinner table at the inn with two Spaniards who give him a good deal of information about Eulelia and her family.

131 Stephens
A London journalist, friend to Chase, who regards him as "too amiable, too ready to agree" (38).

132 Verity
A London journalist.   Chase recalls Peacock and Verity as
drinking companions whose enjoyment of each other's company at
the Cock Tavern centered around their exchange of dirty stories.

133 woman at the inn
At the inn where Caveda's men stay in San Juan, Chase meets the
old woman who was a wet nurse and foster mother to Caveda.

134 women, old
In the church where he takes refuge from the rain on his way to
San Juan, Chase hears three women talking animatedly about
Caveda.   They refuse to give him any information concerning
Caveda or Eulelia.

STAMBOUL TRAIN (1932)

135 Alexitch, Captain
Member of the court-martial which tries Dr. Czinner.

136 *Almanach Gaulois*
A book of dirty stories or jokes.

137 American
Pink-faced man who is rejected angrily by Mabel Warren when he
offers help after Grünlich has stolen her purse.

138 Anna
Herr Kolber's unattractive maid, who displays a "horrible
middle-aged coquetry" (95).   Grünlich fakes an attraction to her
in order to get access to Kolber's safe.

139 Anton
Grünlich's best friend, whose name he takes in his seduction of Anna.

140 Arbuckle Avenue
Mrs. Peters expresses contempt for Coral by associating her with "Arbuckle Avenue," the taxi drivers' name for the row of inexpensive, disreputable hotels in Leinster Terrace, near Paddington Station in London. (See 1134.)

141 Ayres, Ruby M. (1883-1955)
Prolific English novelist whose romantic stories, usually serialized in newspapers and magazines, were characterized by happy endings in which love triumphed over adversity. Coral reflects that although writers like Ayres might claim that chastity was more valuable than rubies, the actual price was a fur coat or something comparable.

142 Baedeker
Travel guidebook.

143 Campbell
Reporter who followed Czinner out of the courtroom at the Kamnetz trial but lost him in the crowd.

144 Carl
Waiter at the Moscowa, known by Czinner, who thinks briefly that he would risk his own safety and his friends' for news of Carl.

145 *Clarion*
The London newspaper for which Mabel Warren writes.

146 clerk
The clerk at the railway station in Subotica refuses to help Myatt when he returns to inquire about Coral.

147 Con
Mabel Warren's lesbian cousin, to whom she writes a letter on the train.

148 Coral's mother
When Coral is called a tart by Mrs. Peters, she drops her acquired
polite manners and assumes the posture and speech of her lower
class mother.

149 Cromwell and shattered statues
Thomas Cromwell (c.1485-1540), secretary to Cardinal Wolsey, was
the chief agent in the dissolution of the monasteries and the
destruction of "idolatrous" images in many churches during the
Reformation under Henry VIII.

150 Czinner, Dr. Paul
Aging physician and socialist leader who after five years of exile
in England is returning to Belgrade to join the revolution there.
His entire journey is one of suffering and defeat: in spite of his
disguise as an English schoolteacher he is identified and hounded
by the reporter Mabel Warren; he learns that the revolution has
begun prematurely; and he is arrested by soldiers at Subotica,
tried quickly and sentenced to execution, and shot to death as he
attempts to escape. He welcomes the release of death, for
although he no longer believes in the Catholic faith of his
boyhood, he feels that he has betrayed his parents, his people, and
his profession.

151 Czinner's father
Hungarian peasant who settled in Dalmatia and later moved to
Belgrade, where he became a shoemaker. His easy satisfaction in
watching more prosperous people enjoy themselves in the city
angered his son, but the younger Czinner remains grateful for the
sacrifices his father made to educate him as a doctor.

152 Delaine, Hon. Carol
Mentioned as the actress who, according to Mabel Warren's article
on Savory, will play his character Emmy Tod in a British film
production of *The Great Gay Round*.

153 Delius
Czinner knows that one of the revolutionaries killed in the fighting
loved the music of British composer Frederick Delius (1862-1934),

"the melancholy idealistic music of a man without a faith in anything but death" (81).

154 driver
A man hired to drive Myatt to Subotica and back from the village where the train is stalled. Because the extra thirty dinas he is to receive for returning before the train leaves will mean "months of comfort" to him (193), he risks his passengers' lives and his own by driving through a raging snowstorm at sixty-five miles per hour.

155 Dunn, Sidney
Director of "Dunn's Babies," the English dance company with which Coral is supposed to perform in Istanbul.

156 Eckman, Emma
Eckman's wife, a small, grey woman who dresses in fashionable clothes that seem unsuited to her. She makes clothing for the Anglican mission in Istanbul.

157 Eckman, Mr.
The head of Myatt's office in Istanbul, implicitly untrustworthy from Myatt's point of view because he is a convert from Judaism to Christianity. Myatt's concern that Eckman has been negotiating privately with Stein is proven correct, and Eckman, who has been given a month's leave, has disappeared by the time Myatt arrives.

158 Edwards
Employee of the *Clarion* in Cologne who takes Mabel Warren's telephoned reports.

159 "Everything in nature is lyrical in its ideal essence; tragic in its fate, and comic in its existence."
The novel's epigraph is from Santayana's "Carnival" in his *Soliloquies in England* (1922).

160 French letters
Slang for condoms.

161 Frenchwoman
Singer at the Petits Champs in Istanbul, seen by Myatt and Janet.

162 Garthaway, Lord
Father of actress Carol Delaine.

163 Great Birchington-on-Sea
English town where Dr. Czinner has lived for five years as Richard
John, schoolmaster. Birchington is a seaside town on the English
Channel in Kent, near Margate.

164 Grünlich, Joseph
Brutal, intensely selfish man whose pride in his long, successful
career as thief is augmented by the satisfaction he derives from
his first murder. He feigns a romantic interest in Herr Kolber's
maid in order to gain entrance to the house, kills Kolber when the
latter catches him opening the safe, and escapes on the Orient
Express only to be arrested with Czinner and Coral at Subotica.
When Czinner is shot in their attempt to escape, Coral stays with
him but Grünlich runs on; to insure his own chance of escape he
tells Myatt that Coral was not with him, thus effectively destroying
the relationship between Coral and Myatt.

165 guard, train
Trainman who tells Czinner about the time the Orient Express
was snowbound two years ago.

166 Hartep
Army officer who presides over Czinner's court martial at Subotica
and sentences him to death. Czinner had eluded arrest by Hartep
by fleeing the country during the Kamnetz trial years ago.

167 Heine
German poet and critic Heinrich Heine (1797-1856) wrote a
familiar song, "Die Lorelei," about the Lorelei rock.

168 Hobbs and Sutcliffe
Cricket players whose names, first introduced by Mr. Opie, are
repeatedly mispronounced by other passengers.

169 Isaacs
Myatt's chauffeur in London.

170 Jervis
The "affair of Jervis" in Myatt's dream is not identified.

171 John, Richard
The name taken by Czinner while he is in exile in England.

172 John, Uncle
Mabel Warren's uncle who died "almost on [her] doorstep" (83).

173 Joyce
Dependable but unintelligent employee whom Myatt puts in charge
of the office in Istanbul after giving Eckman a month's holiday.

174 Kalebdjian, Mr.
Reception clerk at Myatt's hotel in Istanbul, a man who seems
always to know what his guests are doing. His subservient manner
restores to Myatt some of the confidence Myatt had lost in his
dealings with anti-Semitic soldiers and peasants in Subotica.

175 Kamnetz, General
Five years prior to the opening of the story, General Kamnetz was
tried in Belgrade for rape. It was a foregone conclusion that the
government would not allow a conviction, but Czinner nevertheless
gave evidence as the prosecution's chief witness. To avoid arrest
and the charge of perjury he walked out of the courtroom and
fled the country.

176 Kolber, Herr
Stationmaster at Würzburg, murdered by Grünlich when he
discovers Grünlich trying to break into his safe.

177 Lukitch
Lazy clerk in the station-master's office in Subotica.

178 Moult, young
On the basis of a recent luncheon with young Moult, a business
rival, Myatt disbelieves Eckman's claim that Moult has offered to
buy Stein and Company.

179 Musker, Coral
Plucky, good-natured chorus girl enroute to Istanbul to join an
English dancing company. When Coral, who has a weak heart,
collapses from cold and weariness on the train, Myatt gives her his
sleeper and buys her food the next day; she sleeps with him out
of gratitude, wins his affection, and misses becoming his well-kept
mistress only through the coincidence of her friendship with Dr.
Czinner. Czinner gives Coral papers to mail, and the police in
Subotica arrest her as his accomplice. Later, when Czinner is
dying, she loses a chance to escape because she refuses to leave
him. After the long ordeal of hiding in the cold shed with
Czinner, she again collapses and is "rescued" by Mabel Warren, in
whose life she will now replace Janet Pardoe.

180 Myatt, Carleton
A wealthy Jewish currant merchant enroute to his company's
branch office in Istanbul. He befriends Coral and falls tentatively
in love with her, suggesting that she become his mistress. But
when he returns to Subotica with a car in hopes of rescuing her,
he is told by Grünlich that she is not there, and soon afterward he
directs his attention toward a more profitable marriage with Janet
Pardoe.

181 Myatt, Jacob
Carleton Myatt's aged father, whose control of the business is
steadily passing into the hands of his son.

182 Nikola, old
Mentioned as owner of a restaurant commandeered by soldiers
during the brief uprising.

183 Ninitch
Young frontier guard at Subotica, a man of modest but thoughtful
intelligence who has sympathy for the socialist revolutionaries and
questions why soldiers should be shooting their own people.

184 Ninitch's father
Czinner guesses, probably correctly, that Ninitch's father died of
cancer of the stomach, and he pretends to have known the father

in order to distract Ninitch while Grünlich opens the locked door, enabling them to escape.

185 Ninitch's wife
Ninitch is confident that his wife will be proud of him for surreptitiously reading several notes he delivers for Petkovich.

186 Opie, Mr.
Anglican clergyman with a great enthusiasm for cricket.

187 Page
A director of Myatt's company whose position is in fact merely honorary, an award for his two decades of dependable service as head clerk.

188 parcels clerk
The parcels clerk in the station at Subotica tells his companions that the station-master suspected by his wife of sleeping with other women actually has "other inclinations" (154).

189 Pardoe, Janet
Stein's niece, a slender, dark, beautiful woman who for three years has been the companion of Mabel Warren in a relationship which has run its course. Traveling to Istanbul to visit her uncle, she attracts the interest of Myatt and becomes a pawn in his negotiations with Stein. Myatt's view of Janet as an elegantly suitable wife for someone of his status is confirmed by the revelation that her mother was Jewish. He agrees to marry her in an arrangement whereby he will accept Eckman's purchase of Stein's company and Stein will relinquish his seat on the board of Myatt, Myatt and Page.

190 Peters, Amy
Herbert Peters' disagreeable wife, who complains everywhere about foreign beer and is hostile to Coral after the girl takes up with Myatt.

191 Peters, Herbert
English passenger who puts his hand on Coral's ankle while she tries to sleep and later resents her abandoning their seating

compartment for Myatt's sleeper. Coral's assessment of Peters and his wife--"shopkeepers on a spree, going out to Budapest on a Cook's tour" (126)--is apparently correct.

192 Petkovich, Major
A member of the court-martial which tries Czinner, Petkovich insists upon a "superficial legality" even though the outcome of the trial is predetermined.

193 Pole
Man who sold Czinner a fake passport in a Bloomsbury shop.

194 purser
As Coral leaves the cross-channel steamer, the purser advises her not to try to go all the way to Istanbul without a sleeper.

195 Savory, Quin
Popular novelist whose carefully cultivated image as the "Cockney Genius" is a sham (he was born in Balham and is not a true Cockney).   Traveling east to get material for a book about a Cockney abroad, he explains to Mabel Warren his goal of bringing "the spirit of Chaucer" to contemporary English literature (69). Modernism, he says, will not last.   Beneath his sunny, complacent exterior Savory harbors a dark side as "a man overworked, harassed by a personality which is not his own, by curiosities and lusts, a man on the edge of a nervous breakdown" (169).   (A threatened lawsuit by English novelist J.B. Priestley, who saw in Savory a portrait of himself, forced Greene to modify the character.)

196 sentries
The two sentries at the station in Subotica are hostile to Myatt because he is Jewish.

197 Spaniards Road
On his first night aboard the train Myatt dreams of picking up girls on Spaniards Road, on the north side of Hampstead Heath in north London.

198 spotted dog
A boiled pudding containing currants; also called "spotted dick."

199 station-master's wife
Jealous woman who sends her husband telegrams at night when she is away so that if he is in bed with one of the servants he will feel guilty and repent.

200 Stein, Mr.
Head of Stein and Co., a rival to Myatt's firm in the currant trade. Myatt's suspicion that Eckman is dealing secretly with Stein is proved correct when upon arriving in Istanbul he is confronted with an agreement signed by Eckman obligating Myatt to purchase Stein's business at an inflated price and to give Stein a directorship in the expanded business. The subsequent conflict between Myatt and Stein is resolved through the agreement that Myatt will marry Stein's niece, Janet Pardoe.

201 Stein's sister
Janet Pardoe's mother.

202 Stein's wife
Stein's wife's belief that they should see Janet led to his decision to bring her to Istanbul.

203 steward, Head
Wins a bet, on the steamer, that Myatt would give him a tip.

204 Subotica
City in northeast Yugoslavia, near the Hungarian border.

205 "They give up to sex what is meant for mankind."
Mabel Warren's malicious treatment of Savory falters in her report that this statement is adapted from Burke. Actually the line was written about Burke by Oliver Goldsmith, who said in "Retaliation" (1779) that Burke, "borne for the universe, narrowed his mind / And to party gave up what was meant for mankind . . . ."

206   Tod, Emmy
The "little char" (cleaning girl) in Savory's novel *The Great Gay Round*.

207   tongue of an angel
Czinner's ironic feeling that he is "alive" again now that his capture is likely, and that he will not be allowed to escape though he should speak "with the tongue of an angel" (82), echoes I Corinthians 13:1:   "Though I speak with the tongues of men and of angels, and have not charity, I am become as sounding brass, or a tinkling cymbal."

208   violinist
Musician, working on the Orient Express, who tells Myatt rather preposterously that music for Myatt's celebratory dinner will be more expensive if he wants light rather than melancholy songs.

209   Vuskovitch
Speaking in his own defense in his brief trial, Czinner accuses the soldiers there of defending "people like Vuskovitch, who steal the small savings of the poor, and live for ten years fast, stupid lives, and then shoot themselves" (198).

210   Warren, Mabel
Hard-drinking lesbian reporter who spots Dr. Czinner in the railway station at Cologne and boards the Orient Express in hope of getting an exclusive story for her London paper.   Full of self-pity over what she rightly expects to be the permanent loss of her lover Janet Pardoe, she is nevertheless untouched by the terrible events in the human interest stories in which she specializes; she is "an artist to examine critically, to watch, to listen" (37) but not to feel, and she channels her unhappiness and hatred of men into a painfully harsh treatment of the kindly Czinner. Her "rescue" of Coral at Subotica is more like a capture, since she intends for the inexperienced girl to replace Janet as her companion.

IT'S A BATTLEFIELD (1934)

211   Achilles statue
A large bronze figure by Westacott, a memorial to the Duke of Wellington and his men, erected in Hyde Park in 1822.

212   Adams
An inmate at Wandsworth Prison who quotes (roughly) parts of Longfellow's "The Day is Done."

213   Aldershot
Town in Hampshire, long associated with Britain's largest army camp.

214   American, the elderly
Recommended to Conder that he see the falls at Schaffhausen.

215   Assistant Commissioner
Dedicated Scotland Yard officer who investigates the Streatham and Paddington murder cases. After years of colonial service in the East he is troubled by the complex issues of justice surrounding the Drover case. Seeing his own job as "simply to get the right man" (2), he immerses himself in the details of investigation and leaves political and moral concerns to others, yet when tired or depressed he sometimes dreams of "an organisation which he could serve for higher reasons" (137).   Fearless, inarticulate, wearied and yellow at fifty-six from many bouts of tropical fever, he resists Lady Caroline Bury's request that he intercede in Jim Drover's behalf and survives Conrad Drover's attempt to assassinate him.

216   Barham, Mr.
Conder's friend, seen at the Fitzroy.

217   Batlow, Miss
Secretary to the manager in Conrad Drover's office.

218   Beale, old
The Minister (Home Secretary) who must decide Jim Drover's
fate.   Surrogate calls him a "temperance maniac," and Lady
Caroline regards him as a "nonentity" (92).   Concerned only about
the political consequences of Jim's case, he fears that if he
pardons Jim, as he would like to do, the action may be seen as a
sign of weakness and thus lead to more strikes.

219   Bennett, Comrade
A member of the party who distresses Surrogate by asking
questions about what practical measures are being taken to help
Drover.

220   Berkeley, the
A fashionable hotel in central London.

221   Berkhamsted
Jules and Kay spend the night together at an inn in Berkhamsted,
Graham Greene's boyhood home.   (See 2053.)

222   Bernay
A man thought by Conrad's firm to have set fire to part of his
shop in order to file an insurance claim.   But he dropped the
claim, leading them to think he may have burned stuff in order to
get rid of stolen goods.   Conrad uses this damaging knowledge to
force Bernay to sell him a revolver, but instead of live ammunition
Bernay gives him blanks.

223   Besant, Mrs. Annie (1847-1933)
Member of the Theosophical Society, active in support of liberal
causes such as self-government for India.

224   Briton, Jules
A waiter in a Soho cafe, the son of a French father who
abandoned him and an English mother whose death has left him
with the feeling that he is an alien, an Englishman only by
accident of birth. A legacy of over ten thousand francs from his

father enables him to spend a weekend in the country with Kay
Rimmer, whom he hopes to marry, but his love for her fades as
he realizes how rapidly his money is disappearing. Absorbed in
his own interest with Kay, he absent-mindedly burns the petition
he was to circulate in behalf of clemency for Jim Drover.

225 Browning, Mr.
English poet Robert Browning (1812-89).

226 Brutus
Roman senator, leader of the conspirators who assassinated Julius
Caesar. In Shakespeare's *Julius Caesar* he speaks the line quoted
by Mr. Surrogate at the party meeting: "Who here is so base that
he would be a bondman? If any, speak, for him I have offended"
(III, i).

227 Bullen
Secretary to the Assistant Commissioner.

228 Bury, Lady Caroline
A London society hostess, friend to Surrogate and the Assistant
Commissioner, who "had chosen to exercise her passion for
charity" through her interests in literature and politics (40).
Motivated by "Faith" which is not specifically religious or
ideological, she tries unsuccessfully to persuade the Assistant
Commissioner to use his influence to obtain mercy for Jim Drover.
At the end of the novel she faces a serious operation and is
troubled about the making of her will: she has no heir but does
not want to leave her wealth to the state as it is at present.

229 Bury, Justin
Deceased husband of Lady Caroline.

230 CID
Criminal Investigation Division of Scotland Yard. The Assistant
Commissioner is a CID man.

231 Cassidy, Sean
Poet who appears at Lady Caroline's luncheon. His name echoes
that of Irish poet and dramatist Sean O'Casey.

232   Cavell, Edith
An English nurse killed at Brussels in 1915. Her monument by
Frampton (1920) stands on the "island" in St. Martin's Place.

233   Cenotaph
Monument erected in Parliament Street in 1920 in memory of
those killed in the Great War.

234   Chaplain
The prison chaplain announces to the Assistant Commissioner at
the end that he is going to resign his position in protest against
the arbitrariness of human justice.

235   Chick, Mrs.
A "genteel woman in black velvet" (49), waitress at the Fitzroy,
one of Conder's acquaintances.

236   Chief
Apparently the editor of the *Evening Watch*, who is "not much
interested in Drover," according to Conder.

237   Chine
The employee whom Conrad Drover, in a promotion, is appointed
to succeed.

238   Collins
Policeman who assists in the capture of the Salvationist.

239   Collins, Lady
A woman whose wealthy husband went to prison for five years.
The secretary is reminded of her case by the prospect of
loneliness for Milly Drover.

240   Conder
Journalist for the *Evening Watch* and a member of the
Communist party who knows Kay Rimmer.   A "sad and
unsatisfied" man, Conder pretends to be a family man with six
children but is actually "an unmarried man with a collection of
foreign coins, who lived in a bed-sitting room in Little Compton
Street" (22).

241 Coney, Arthur
The policeman killed by Jim Drover.

242 Coney, Rose
Arthur Coney's wife, visited by Milly Drover, who asks her to sign a petition urging the authorities to spare Jim's life. She agrees on the condition that Milly lead the journalist Conder away from her house.

243 Coney's brother
Arthur's brother, whom the widowed Rose consults before taking any important action.

244 Crabbe
A writer, "an old man with a white moustache and red aggrieved eyes" who hasn't written a book in ten years. He appears at a luncheon hosted by Lady Caroline.

245 Crippen
Henry Harvey Crippen (1861-1910), who murdered his wife in London and tried to escape across the Atlantic to America, was captured in the first use of radio-telegraphy by police. The Assistant Commissioner remembers that Crippen shaved carefully each day of his trial, which took place in 1910.

246 Crosse, Superintendent
Policeman in charge of the arrest of the Salvationist.

247 Crowle, Janet
Murder victim in the Paddington trunk case.

248 Davis
Mr. Surrogate's manservant.

249 Drover, Conrad
Jim's brother, a shy, unconfident chief clerk for an insurance company. Named after a sailor who once lodged with his parents (an allusion to novelist Joseph Conrad), he was self-conscious about his strange name and now feels himself an outsider and a failure. While Jim is in prison Conrad begins a sad, disillusioning

affair with Jim's wife Milly, whom he has secretly loved for years.
When his brother's plight brings into focus the pent-up frustrations
of his own life, Conrad becomes obsessed with revenge, buys a
revolver, and stalks the Assistant Commissioner, whom he plans
to murder. He is struck by a car before he can shoot (the gun
has only blanks anyway) and dies in a hospital without learning
that Jim will not be executed.

250   Drover, Jim
A bus driver imprisoned for murdering a policeman in Hyde Park
during a political rally. Drover is a quiet, unobtrusive man who
is not at all violent but who acted spontaneously when he thought
the bobby was going to hit Milly.

251   Drover, Milly
Jim Drover's wife, a small, quiet woman with a face "too generous
to be beautiful" (60). Deeply pessimistic out of a fundamental
sense of injustice in the world, she fears happiness, which she
believes is the cause of Jim's misfortune: if they hadn't been so
happy together, she reasons, Jim would never have stabbed the
policeman. In spite of her love for Jim, Milly's lack of hope leads
her to betray him with his brother Conrad.

252   Eddy, Mrs.
Mary Baker Eddy (1821-1910), founder of Christian Science.

253   *Evening Watch*
Newpaper for which Conder works.

254   Fabian Society
Founded in 1894 as an organization of socialists who favored a
policy of "Fabian" (gradual) change rather than revolutionary
action.

255   Fanshawe
A clerk in a gunshop where Conrad, who has no license, tries
unsuccessfully to purchase a gun.

256 Fitzroy, the
Fitzroy Tavern in Charlotte Street, London, associated with artists
and the Bohemian life. In the novel it is frequented by Conder
and other members of the Communist party.

257 Flying Squad
A police squad.

258 girl
The shy Conder has bitter memories of the girl who laughed at
him when he made advances to her at Schaffhausen.

259 Greta
Kay Rimmer's friend and co-worker at the match factory. (See
Norma.)

260 Hardy
English novelist Thomas Hardy (1840-1928).

261 hedge schooling
Schooling conducted outdoors, as in Ireland.

262 hell in circles
A reference to Dante's *Inferno*.

263 Home Secretary
See Beale.

264 Inkerman
Russian town in the Crimea where English and French forces
defeated Russian troops on November 5, 1854.

265 Irving, Henry
English actor (1838-1905) identified with Shakespearean roles. His
memorial statue stands in Charing Cross Road, across the street
from the statue of Edith Cavell.

266 James, Henry
American-English novelist (1862-1916) whose signed photograph
hangs in Lady Caroline's house.

267 Jenks
Policeman involved in the capture of the Salvationist

268 Jules's father
M. Heysan-Bretau, whose family name was changed in England by
his English wife, who prefers *Britons*. After his death he is
revealed to have been respected and charitable, a likely mayoral
candidate for his home town of Petit Tourville--not the libertine
depicted by Jules's mother. He leaves 10,500 francs to his son.

269 Jules's mother
Jules's mother, a bitter woman of severe English uprightness
whose grudge against her husband for leaving her with a bankrupt
business to return to his native France caused her to instill in her
son the idea of that country as shameful and irresponsible but
also lively and happy.

270 Lenin
Mr. Surrogate has a plaster bust of Vladimir Lenin (1870-1924),
leader of the Russian revolution of 1917 and Soviet premier (1918-
24).

271 Lossiemuth
Fishing and resort town in northern Scotland, the home of Ramsay
MacDonald.

272 MacDonald, Mr.
Ramsay MacDonald (1866-1931), British Labour Party leader and
prime minister (1924; 1929-35).

273 manager, the
The manager of Conrad's company surprises Conrad by promoting
him because he will be "able to keep a firm hand on the clerks"
(112).

274 Marlene
Kay Rimmer's friend and co-worker at the match factory. (See
Norma.)

275   Matthews, Flossie
Victim of a rape and murder on Streatham Common.

276   Napoleon III
Nephew of Napoleon Bonaparte; Emperor of France, 1853-71.
Jules Briton fancies that he resembles Napoleon III.

277   nephew
Nephew of the managing director of Conrad's firm who is
"learning the business from the bottom" (111).   His presence in
the office is seen by Conrad as a threat.

278   Norma
Kay Rimmer's friend and co-worker at the match factory.   In this
miserable occupation Greene identifies four women whose first
names ironically recall the glamourous, romantic world of the film
stars they admire: Norma (Shearer), Greta (Garbo), Marlene
(Dietrich), and Kay (Francis).

279   Passchendaele
Belgian village near Ypres, scene of a horrible protracted battle
between British and Canadian forces and the German army, July-
November 1917.

280   Patmore
Police officer from Scotland Yard who finds Conder at the Fitzroy
and questions him about what was said at the Party meeting.

281   Persimmon
A famous thoroughbred.

282   Pierpoint
An executioner.

283   plumber
An old man with steel-rimmed glasses and a hedge-school
education, the only worker whom Mr. Surrogate has ever known
well.

284 proprietress
The owner of the cafe frequented by Conrad believes him to be
an important civil servant.

285 Rimmer, Kay
Milly Drover's sister, a factory worker who seeks in casual
promiscuity an escape from the harsh, mechanized dullness of her
life. A member of the Communist party, Kay, who "never felt
more at home than in a bed or man's arm" (57), has brief affairs
with both Mr. Surrogate and Jules Briton.

286 Rowlett
A "flushed young man" who complains to Miss Chick about being
pushed by drunks at the bar (51).

287 Russian novelist, the great
Fyodor Dostoevsky (1821-81), imprisoned in Siberia for nine years
because of his membership in a secret political society.

288 Ruttledge
Suspected of murdering Janet Crowle, but fingerprints prove that
he did not.

289 Salvationist, the
The Paddington trunk-murderer, who wears a Salvation Army
uniform and speaks of peace and forgiveness.

290 Sanatogen
A tonic wine.

291 Secretary, the private
Beale's private secretary meets the Assistant Commissioner at the
Berkeley to get information on how people in the "power points"
feel about what action should be taken in Drover's case (9). His
concern is entirely for the Minister, not for Drover; he wants a
peerage for the Minister and an undersecretaryship for himself.

292 Simpson, Mrs. Amy
The Assistant Commissioner's grumbling housekeeper.

293 Streatham Common
The Assistant Commissioner is investigating a murder and rape which occurred on the common in Streatham, an area of south London.

294 Surrogate, Margaret
Deceased wife of Mr. Surrogate, who keeps her picture in his bedroom. She was a sexually aggressive, dissatisfied artist whom Surrogate regards as "the one woman who had never failed to see through him" (57). Her "excessively phallic" paintings which decorate Lady Caroline's walls remind Surrogate of his own inadequacy, and her photograph in his bedroom satisfies his need for periodic self-abasement.

295 Surrogate, Mr. Philip
A wealthy political writer who is drawn to communism by the "lovely abstractions" of comradeship and the nobility of labor but has no interest in individuals such as Jim Drover. Under a false humility he conceals vanity, selfishness, and a tepid sensuality which leads him into a brief affair with Kay Rimmer.

296 tobacconist
A cautious man who comes to Scotland Yard to give information on the murderer of Janet Crowle.

297 Victoria Nyanza, the
Lake Victoria.

298 Walter Crane dresses
Dresses designed or inspired by Walter Crane (1845-1915), artist, illustrator, decorator, and poet influenced by William Morris, with whose socialist ideas Crane agreed.

299 warder, chief
Leads the Assistant Commissioner and the minister's secretary through the prison to see Jim Drover. Of the prisoners he remarks, "We look after 'em just like children" (14).

ENGLAND MADE ME (1935)

300 A.C.U.
The most prosperous combine of papermills in Sweden. Krogh,
the owner, is selling it to Batterson's after investing its capital in
his Amsterdam Company.

301 actress
The mysterious Hollywood actress who emerges from the
Stockholm railway station, gets into a car, and rides away leaving
expensive flowers (thrown too late) lying on the pavement strongly
suggests Greta Garbo.

302   "Aimer à loisir, / Aimer et mourir, / Au pays qui te
ressemble"
"To love without haste, / To love and die, / In the country which
resembles you." These lines from Baudelaire's "L'Invitation au
Voyage" (from *Les Fleurs du Mal*, 1857) are heard by Tony and
Kate on the radio during a break in a card game at the end of
the novel. The poem, in which the speaker addresses his lover as
both child and sister, is suffused with vague erotic and incestuous
themes.

303 Andersson
One of Krogh's workers, a socialist who is the reputed leader of
strikes in three Krogh factories. Krogh feigns friendliness toward
him but then has him framed for some misdoing at the works and
dismissed.

304 Andersson, young
Like his father, the younger Andersson is a worker in one of
Krogh's factories, but he is more conservative, trusting Krogh and
believing that his father was fired through some misunderstanding

which will be cleared up if he can talk to Krogh. He follows Krogh to Saltsjöbaden with the expectation of seeing him but is turned away by Hall, who beats Andersson brutally.

305 Annette
A young, attractive prostitute with whom Tony had an affectionate relationship in London. She disappeared one day, leaving only a note saying, "Gone out, Be back at 12:30, dear" (14). Graham Greene knew a similar girl in the early 1930's who was also named Annette, also lived in Warren Street, and disappeared leaving the same message.

306 Apslund
A director of Krogh's.

307 Aronstein
Krogh's friend who worked with him on construction jobs in Chicago and later went into the oil business.

308 Batterson's
The company to which Krogh is preparing to sell (fraudulently) the A.C.U.

309 Baxter
School friend who disappointed Minty by refusing to assist with his plans for revenge against other boys who had tormented him.

310 Bergen
A director of Krogh's.

311 Beyer
A news reporter, rival to Minty for information concerning Krogh, about whom Beyer has recently written a complimentary but inaccurate article. He is dishonest; Minty sees him at a bar "shifting the mats from under his beer-glass to his neighbour" (108).

312 *The Bride of Lammermoor* (1819)
Novel by Sir Walter Scott, source for Donizetti's opera *Lucia de Lammermoor* (1835). Loo Davidge's father is an admirer of Scott

(as were Greene's father and the father of his character Tony), and her name "Lucia" is derived from this story.

313 Calloway
Sir Ronald's English manservant.

314 *Carmen*
Opera by Bizet (1875). When Krogh tells Tony that *Tristan* is supposed to be one of the world's great love stories, Tony replies naively that Krogh must be thinking of *Carmen*.

315 Casabianca
In the Battle of the Nile (1798), French commander Louis Casabianca (1762-98) continued to fight bravely on his burning warship *Orient* in a losing cause until both he and his ten-year-old son, who refused to leave him, were killed along with most of the crew. Tony invokes Casabianca's name to make clear to Kate that he doesn't want to fight a losing battle.

316 Chantal, St. Jane Frances Fremiot de (1572-1641)
French foundress of the Order of the Visitation of Holy Mary. Minty's abdominal surgery was performed on her feast day, August 21.

317 Colbert, Claudette (1905-)
Tony's picture of American film actress Colbert "in a Roman bath" (71) is probably from her performance in the lead role in DeMille's *Cleopatra* (1934). Colbert was highly praised by Greene in his 1936 review of her performance in the light comedy *The Bride Comes Home.*

318 Collins
A history teacher at Harrow.

319 coolie
Tony tells variations of a false story in which he prevented a "coolie" from killing a "minister" with a bomb.

320 Cornell
Minty's school friend who died suddenly of scarlet fever.

321 Davidge, Lucia ("Loo")
An English girl from Coventry, on holiday in Sweden with her
parents. In dress and manner a sharp contrast to the studied
gentility of her middle-class parents, she boasts a little
unconvincingly of her liberated attitudes toward sex. Tony's
attraction to Loo derives as much from his own homesickness as
from any particular qualities she displays, but he is fond of her
nevertheless and plans to return to England to see her.

322 Davidge, Mr.
Loo Davidge's elderly father, a Coventry businessman with a great
fondness for Sir Walter Scott's works and for obscure classics such
as Lockhart's *Spanish Ballads* and Horne's epics.

323 Davidge, Mrs.
A shy, elderly woman whose delicacy of dress and manner have
not been imitated by her daughter. Loo conceals her relationship
with Tony from her mother.

324 Davidge, Roderick
Loo's brother, named after a character in Lockhart's *Scottish
Ballads*.

325—de Laszlo
Philip Alexius Laszlo de Lombos (1869-1937), Hungarian painter
who came to England in 1907 and was naturalized in 1914. He
was best known for portraits.

326 Delia
Minty's cousin. Aunt Ella's letter assumes that Minty knows about
"the affairs of Delia's twins" (81).

327 doorkeeper
The doorkeeper at Krogh's corporate headquarters annoys Krogh
by suggesting that the statue in the courtyard is odd.

328 Dowson
English poet Ernest Dowson (1867-1900), to whom one of Sir
Ronald's new poems is dedicated. The poem echoes Dowson's
most famous work, "Cynara."

329 Druid
Celtic priest, religious teacher, and sorcerer in pre-Christian Britain.

330 Du Maurier
George Du Maurier (1834-90), English novelist, illustrator, and caricaturist, best known for his novel *Trilby* and his contributions to *Punch*. Mr. Farrant's uncle had known Du Maurier.

331 Ekman
Minty's neighbor, a dustman who seems prosperous. He often comes home noisily drunk.

332 Ekman, Fru
Mrs. Ekman drinks a bit herself and does not seem to mind her husband's drunkenness.

333 Ella, Aunt
Minty's aunt, who writes to him from England for the first time in almost twenty years.

334 Elsie
Woman dreamt of by Hall when he falls asleep on the airplane.

335 Erik
Workman at the bridge-building site visited by Krogh.

336 Farrant, Anthony (Tony)
The thirty-three year old protagonist, whose boyish charm and good nature mask the petty but incurable dishonesty which cost him jobs and reputation in exotic locations (Shanghai, Bangkok, Aden) and in turn disappointed his father and his sister Kate. A drifter without real hope or ambition--"I haven't a future," he tells Kate (29)--Tony follows his sister to Stockholm, takes a job as bodyguard to her employer-lover Krogh, and seems briefly to stabilize his life before losing it when his attempt to leave Sweden in possession of secrets damaging to the company leads to his murder by Hall. Tony's love for Kate appears to lack the passionate intensity of her more obviously incestuous love for him, but the apparent difference may be a matter of his being less

willing in this situation, as in so many others, to be truthful even with himself.

337 Farrant, Kate
Anthony's twin sister, who was once so close to him that she knew when he was in pain. Her incestuous love for him leads her to conduct her life as a strategy for uniting him with her. Having left her job in a London counting house years earlier to become Krogh's secretary and eventually his mistress, she now brings Tony to Sweden, where she gets him a job as Krogh's bodyguard. Her plan fails, however, when Tony falls for an English girl traveling in Sweden; Tony and Kate grow apart and lose their ability to feel each other's pain. Although she has agreed to marry Krogh so that she cannot be forced to testify against him in court, she leaves him and Stockholm for an unspecified destination after Tony's death.

338 foreman
Enroute to Saltsjöbaden, Krogh stops to talk to the foreman of a construction crew building a bridge. Ironically, Krogh does not have a match when the man asks for one.

339 *The Four Just Men* (1905)
Thriller novel by Edgar Wallace (1875-1932). Tony carries a copy in his suitcase. (See 643.)

340 fug
A boy who does not like to play games. Minty's implication, to Tony, that at Harrow he enjoyed "kicking a fug about" is clearly the opposite of what his experience there was actually like.

341 Garbo, Greta (1905-90)
Swedish actress, popular in Hollywood films in the 1920's and '30's.

342 girl
Young Andersson is strongly attracted to the pretty daughter of the factory foreman when he sees her at the railway station.

343 girl, platinum blonde
An actress who flirts first with Hammarsten and then with Tony
at the Saltsjöbaden party. With her many accents she seems to
lack any kind of national character.

344 Gower
Professor Hammarsten's theory that "ancient Gower" in *Pericles* is
a druid absurdly contradicts the accepted view that the character
is poet John Gower, author of *Confessio Amantis* (1390).

345 guide
Shows Tony and Loo the old theatre at Drottningholm.

346 Gullie, Captain
Military attache at the British Legation in Stockholm who is proud
of his ancestry in the Scottish Cameron clan. He justifies his
collection of nudist magazines by claiming an amateur painter's
interest in the human figure.

347 Hall, Fred
Krogh's right-hand man who was once treated as an equal, on a
first-name basis, but now is deferential to Krogh. He has "no
quality but fidelity" (48) in Krogh's view and is childish or doglike
in his devotion to Krogh as well as jealous of others who have
Krogh's attention.   When Tony decides to leave Sweden in
possession of information about Krogh's fraudulent business
transactions, Hall murders him.

348 Hall's mother
Hall plans to visit his mother in Dorking, Surrey, at Christmas.

349 Hammarsten
Language teacher who works for newspapers to increase his small
income. He is bewildered when Krogh gives him 25,000 crowns
with which to produce his eccentric version of Shakespeare's
Pericles.

350 Hammond
Kate Farrant's employer in the counting-house in Leather Lane.

351 Harrow
Prestigious boys' school at Harrow-on-the-Hill in Middlesex. Tony
wears a Harrow tie to impress people but did not really attend the
school; Minty, who did attend but did not graduate, easily sees
through Tony's fakery.

352 Henriques
A teacher at Harrow, recalled by Minty.

353 Henry II
King of England (1154-89) whose knights murdered St. Thomas à
Becket in Canterbury Cathedral in 1170. The king claimed that
they had misinterpreted his orders. Hall, in his eagerness to
follow Krogh's wishes, is compared to Henry II's knights.

354 Holy Cnut
A favorite exclamation of the mild-mannered Minty. Canute, or
Cnut (994-1035) was a Danish king who ruled England from 1016
until his death.

355 Horne
Richard Henry Horne (1802-84), a poet admired by Mr. Davidge,
who likes epic poetry. Horne's most famous work is the
allegorical epic *Orion* (1843).

356 I.G.S.
One of the Krogh companies.

357 Kreuger
Ivar Kreuger (1880-1932), the Swedish "match king," whose suicide
in a Paris hotel revealed a collapsing financial empire built partly
on fraud and deception. Greene read a biography of Kreuger in
1933 and made him the primary model for Erik Krogh.

358 Krogh, Erik
Wealthy industrialist who, like the "Match King" Kreuger upon
whom his character was modeled, went from humble origins in
Sweden to America, where he worked on construction projects
until he invented a revolutionary piece of manufacturing
equipment (a cutter) which enabled him to build a vast fortune.

In spite of his spectacular success, Krogh remains essentially lonely, insecure in his tastes, isolated by the trappings of wealth and the need to present a cultured image to the public.

359 Lagerson
A young man who works in publicity at Krogh's. He envies the adventurous nature demonstrated by Tony's willingness to leave the firm.

360 landlady, Andersson's
Young Andersson is embarrassed in the presence of his pretty landlady because he hears her through the thin walls when she lies with her husband at night.

361 landlady, Minty's
Breaks Minty's tooth glass.

362 Laurie, Uncle
Minty's deceased uncle, mentioned in the letter from Aunt Ella.

363 Laurin
A director of Krogh's, regarded by Krogh himself as ineffectual.

364 Leather Lane
Street in the City of London, site of the office where Kate Farrant worked before she met Krogh.

365 Loewenstein
The Loewenstein named in Kate's stream-of-consciousness narrative early in the novel is probably Belgian financier and stockbroker Alfred Loewenstein (1877-1928), who made an enormous fortune promoting hydro-electric, chemical, and artificial silk stocks. He died under suspicious circumstances July 3, 1928, when he allegedly fell from his airplane over the English channel.

366 Mabel
Woman in London, probably a prostitute, recalled by Tony as having a "silly innocence" like Loo Davidge's, even though she was "among the toughest of them. . ." (139). Mabel may have been

Annette's friend whom Tony had gone to see when Annette answered the door instead.

367 man on the night shift
Recalled by young Anderson as a victim of poverty who went crazy and killed his wife and himself when he learned that she was pregnant again.

368 Manager (factory)
A manager of one of Krogh's factories, seen with his family at the railway station by young Andersson.

369 Manager (hotel)
Manager of the hotel in Saltsjöbaden.

370 Marina
Daughter of Pericles in Shakespeare's *Pericles*.

371 Mark, King
In Wagner's *Tristan and Isolde*, the opera attended briefly by Tony and Krogh, King Mark is the husband of Isolde and uncle of Tristan.

372 Maud
Buxom, fortyish woman with whom Tony had a relationship in London. Although he claimed to be too high-principled to accept money from her, he accepted gifts and sold them for cash.

373 Methuselah
The oldest man in the Bible, who lived 969 years (Genesis 5:27).

374 Minister
Sir Ronald.

375 Minty, Ferdinand
Lonely, isolated Englishman living a meager existence in Stockholm, where his earnings from the newspaper to which he provides news about Erik Krogh supplement his small allowance from his mother in England. As a boy at Harrow he was tormented because of his smallness and his Catholic piety; his

attempt to carry out some unspecified act of revenge (apparently
involving poison) led to his removal from the school and
eventually figured in his separation from the family he had thus
disgraced. In Stockholm he tries to create an English corner, a
"home from home," pursuing friendship with various Britishers
living abroad. A measure of Minty's loneliness is that he considers
Anthony, whom he knows only briefly, one of his best friends.

376 Minty's mother
Minty has been estranged from his mother ever since his bizarre
behavior led to his removal from Harrow. He longs to reestablish
contact with her but is afraid that any attempt to do so might
endanger his monthly allowance of fifteen pounds.

377 Mithridates
King of Pontus (120-63 B.C.), who according to legend took small
quantities of poisons until he developed immunity to them and
thereby defeated enemies who would try to poison him.

378 Mollison, Miss
Mr. Farrant did not approve of Miss Mollison's being seen at a
play with her employer.

379 Morgan
J.P. Morgan (1837-1913), wealthy and powerful American
businessman and financier. Tony claims to have met Morgan's
bodyguard in Shanghai.

380 *Mrs. Warren's Profession*
Play by Oscar Wilde (1893). Her profession is prostitution.

381 Murphy
One of Krogh's friends who worked with him on construction jobs
in Chicago.

382 *Neptune*
A ship which sank in the Indian Ocean. Tony tells a false story
in which he was injured while assisting the crew.

383 Nils
A young Swedish journalist and friend of Minty's whom Tony
meets at Krogh's.

384 O'Connor
Friend who worked with Krogh on construction jobs in Chicago.
He was killed in Panama, "buried under forty tons of mud when
a dredger broke" (126).

385 Partridge
Senior chaplain at Harrow, only recently retired. Minty knows
that Tony, if he had really attended Harrow, could not have
forgotten Partridge's name.

386 Patterson
Student at Harrow. (See Tester.)

387 *Pericles*
Play (c. 1608) by Shakespeare and, probably, George Wilkins.
The incestuous relationship between King Antiochus and his
daughter, announced in the opening lines, has an obvious parallel
in the incestuous love of Kate and Tony in Greene's novel. (See
"With whom.")

388 Pihlström
A journalist, friend of Hammarsten.

389 Prince, the
The Prince of Sweden, "an elderly man with a little pointed grey
moustache" (114), is seen with his wife at the opera in Stockholm.

390 *The Private Secretary*
School play in which Tony Farrant acted. The title reflects
ironically upon his sister's relationship with Krogh.

391 Redakteur, Herr
"Redakteur" means "editor." The editor of the newspaper for
which Minty works is ready to discharge Minty until he learns of
the reporter's friendship with Tony.

392 Ronald, Sir
Minister at the British legation.

393 Sargent
American painter John Singer Sargent (1856-1926), who lived for
many years in London.

394 Scott's Lockhart
John Gibson Lockhart (1799-1854), critic, novelist, biographer. In
1837-38 Lockhart published his *Memoirs* of Sir Walter Scott, his
father-in-law.

395 sculptor, Sweden's greatest
Karl Milles (1875-1955), whose Diana fountain stands in the center
of the courtyard in the Match Palace, Kreuger's corporate
headquarters.   The fountain described in the novel does not
resemble Milles' work, however.

396 Smith, Alexander
Poet admired by Mr. Davidge.

397 Sparrow
Student at Harrow who was Minty's friend not because they had
anything in common but "because they had no other friends" (249).

398 Stefenson
A director of Krogh's.

399 Tester
When called upon to identify himself in the photograph of his
class at Harrow, Minty (who did not stay to graduate) sometimes
points to Tester, sometimes to Patterson. Tester once received six
months for indecent assault.

400 Tony and Kate's father
Deceased father of Tony and Kate, remembered for his
old-fashioned morality and his love of Dickens, Scott, and
Shakespeare.   He was saddened by Tony's failures and long
absences from home, and he longed for Tony and Kate to be
together, with the son as the daughter's protector.

401 Tony and Kate's mother
Long-deceased mother of Tony and Kate. Tony is described as never having known her well, and presumably the same was true for Kate.

402 Travers, Puffin
Friend to Captain Gullie.

403 *Trilby*
Novel (1894) by George Du Maurier. Trilby, a Parisian model, falls under the spell of the sinister Svengali, who makes her a great singer.

404 *Troilus and Cressida*
Tragedy (1601) by Shakespeare, in which the love affair of the two title characters is aided by Pandarus, Cressida's uncle. Minty, who allows Tony and Loo to use his room and bed, is described as a "perfect Pandarus." Tony's father thought the play too cynical to have been written by Shakespeare.

405 Whitaker
Joseph Whitaker (1820-95), successful English publisher of *Gentleman's Magazine* and *Whitaker's Almanack*, may be the Whitaker mentioned in Kate's stream-of-consciousness monologue.

406 Wilber, Major
Officer who revealed to members of the English club in Shanghai that Tony's often-told story about being present at the bombing of a minister's car was a lie.

407 Williamson
Friend of Krogh's who worked with him on construction jobs in Chicago. Krogh believes that he was killed in World War I.

408 "With whom the father liking took, / And her to incest did provoke."
These lines (25-26) from Gower's speech which opens *Pericles* are quoted by Hammarsten at Saltsjöbaden.

409 woman, hawk-like
A member of the "English colony" in Stockholm whose name
Krogh cannot remember even though he has met her often at the
Legation. She tries to interest him in Sir Ronald's new poems.

410 woman on the train
On the train to Stockholm, young Andersson talks to an elderly
woman who thinks he is headed for a night on the town. She
tells him he is lucky to work for Krogh's and cautions him to stay
out of trouble in the city.

411 woman, tall handsome black-haired
Refuses to act in Hammarsten's play.

412 Yonnie
Probably "johnnie," or "fellow." The name is applied to young
Andersson by a woman at Krogh's party.

413 Zephyrinus, St.
Pope from 177 to 217. Minty, who was near death for five days
after his surgery, attributes his recovery to St. Zephyrinus.

A GUN FOR SALE (1936)

414 Acky
A defrocked clergyman with "crazy sunken flawed saint's eyes" (220), who was expelled from the church because of some unspecified sexual offense. With his evil wife Tiny he operates the bawdy house to which Davis takes Anne.

415 Aitkin
Aitkin, Mallowes, and Simmons are serious students who do not participate in the rag and are therefore accused of being "conchies" (conscientious objectors) by Buddy Fergusson.

416 *Aladdin*
A familiar English pantomime (children's play typically presented during the Christmas season) in which Anne Crowder is supposed to perform in Nottwich.

417 Alice
The humpbacked maid who looks after Raven's room in Soho. He buys her a cheap dress with money received from Davis, but she betrays him to the police.

418 Augustine, St.
Mentioned by Acky as someone who was also guilty of sins of the flesh. (See 2270.)

419 Bacon, Mr.
Plumber who repairs the toilet at St. Luke's Hall on the day of the jumble (rummage) sale.

420 Banks, Colonel
Commanding officer of the training depot ten miles from
Nottwich. Sir Marcus offers to give Calkin this post and have
Banks transferred if Calkin will see that the police kill Raven.

421 Barker
One of several underworld characters recalled disapprovingly by
Raven as having gone "soft" on a girl at some time. The others
are Jossy and Ballard, Carter, the Great Dane, Mayhew, Penrith,
and the Trooper.

422 Bleek, Alfred
Star actor in *Aladdin* (as the Widow Twankey).

423 Brewer, Mrs.
Anne's landlady in London.

424 C.B.
Calkin imagines himself the recipient of the C.B. (Commander of
the British Empire) award.

425 Caesar Augustus
Octavian, founder of the Imperial Roman government, emperor
during the life of Christ.

426 Calkin, Joseph
The Chief Constable in Nottwich, a fat, excitable man whose
prosperity in trade led to a commission and the command of the
local military tribunal, a position which gives him the sense of
pride and importance necessary to offset an unhappy home life
with a wife who despises him.

427 Callitrope
A backer of plays, of interest to Collier.

428 Carter
See Barker.

429 Charlie's
A den of gambling, drinking, and other illicit activities near Euston
Station, London. Mather goes there looking for Raven. Charlie,
the proprietor, operates a fish-and-chips shop upstairs.

430 Chief Inspector
Cusack.

431 chief reporter
Says to the crime reporter that Raven's story is no longer
important; the only news now is the impending war.

432 Chinky
Mrs. Piker's Pekinese dog.

433 Cholmondeley
An alias for Davis.

434 Cochran Stars
Charles Blake Cochran (1872-1951) was a prominent English
theatrical producer. He managed the Royal Albert Hall from
1926 to 1938.

435 Cohen
Mentioned as having quarrelled with Davis or with Davis's
nephew.

436 Collier, Mr.
Director of *Aladdin*.

437 Colson, the treasurer
University or medical school treasurer who barely escapes the
students on their rag. They let him pass, but he looks scared.

438 Connett, Miss
A secretary at Midland Steel (Davis's) who calls Davis "Willie"
until she sees that he has a client.

439   Constance
Possibly a maid; she is called once by the Vicar and once by his
wife but does not appear.

440   coroner
When the kidnapping of a surgeon by ragging students resulted in
his patient's death, the coroner concluded that "allowance" had to
be made for youth.

441   Cranbeim, Mrs.
An "intimate friend" (135) of Sir Marcus who shares with him
valuable information she gains through the confidences of an elder
British statesman with whom she has a relationship.

442   crime reporter
A sincere young man who abstains from liquor and tobacco and
is shocked when someone is sick in a telephone booth.

443   Crowder, Anne
A good-natured, resourceful chorus-girl who travels to Nottwich to
perform in a Christmas pantomime, Anne is the link between the
three other main characters. She is the fiancée of the detective
Mather; she is taken to dinner by Davis, who first tries to seduce
and then to murder her; and she is captured briefly by Raven,
who needs her ticket to avoid being identified at the railway
station.   Her genuine sympathy for Raven wins his reluctant
affection, and he rescues her from certain death in the bawdy
house where Davis has stuffed her into a chimney.   In turn she
helps him to evade police because she thinks that by carrying out
his revenge he may prevent a war.   But after learning that Raven
is the wanted political assassin and that he has just shot a
policeman in Nottwich, Anne reveals his destination to the police,
who follow Raven and kill him.   Her troubled conscience following
this betrayal is short-lived, for her action wins back the lost
confidence of Detective Mather, and the forthcoming reward will
make it possible for the pair to get married.

444   Cundifer, Lady
Donates the hat purchased by Mrs. Penny.

445 curate, the
The new curate from London displays his broad-mindedness by
getting Miss Maydew to open the jumble sale.

446 Cusack
The Chief Inspector, Mather's superior.

447 Davenant
Former backer of *Aladdin*, bought out by Davis.

448 Davis, "Willie"
A high-ranking employee in the Midland Steel offices whose work
for Sir Marcus includes the hiring and betrayal of Raven. Davis,
alias "Cholmondeley," is a fat, self-indulgent, greedy man whose
excessive love of sweets signals the moral degeneracy revealed in
his attempt first to seduce and then to murder Anne Crowder.
Before Raven kills him in revenge, Davis reveals his considerable
cowardice.

449 *Dick Whittington*
Popular pantomime based on the legend of Whittington, a poor
boy who became a wealthy merchant and mayor of London.

450 Dora
Name overheard at the jumble sale.

451 Dreid
Mentioned as being owed money by Callitrope's uncle.

452 Earl of Nottwich
Mentioned as having brought a mummy (now in the city's
museum) back from Egypt in 1843.

453 Egerton, Colonel Mark
Instigator of the inquiry which led to Acky's defrocking. In a
letter to the bishop, Acky says that the evidence against him was
"perjured and bribed" and that Egerton was his worst enemy on
the church council (220).

454 Egerton, Mrs.
Referred to in Acky's letter as a "bitch" and a "scandal-monger" whose testimony in the Church Court resulted in his condemnation and defrocking (220-21).

455 Emma
The Minister's secretary, an old, German-speaking woman who is killed by Raven.

456 Fergusson, Buddy
An immature, second-rate Nottwich medical student who takes charge of the "rag" and enjoys a brief feeling of power and importance during an air-raid drill until Raven humiliates him by stealing his clothes and leaving him half-naked in a bank clerk's garage. Part of Fergusson's bluster is the result of his own lack of confidence and his growing realization that his professional future promises to be as mediocre as his present life. (See also "Juicy Juliet.")

457 Fordhaven, Lord
Miss Maydew's father.

458 Frost
Policeman who works under Mather.

459 Galsworthy, John (1867-1933)
English novelist and dramatist, best known for the novels in *The Forsyte Saga* (1922). Raven, standing outside the theatre in Charing Cross Road, overhears a conversation about Galsworthy's gentlemanly qualities, his play *Loyalties* (1922), and his having given a Mrs. Milbanke money for the Anti-Vivisection Society.

460 Graves, Mr.
An unhappy man whose attempts to buy the "Sleepy Nuik" is thwarted when Anne pays a deposit on it.

461 Great Dane, the
See Barker.

462   Green
Real estate agent whose arrival at the Sleepy Nuik enables Anne
to escape from Raven. She pays Green a ten-pound deposit for
the house and goes with him to his office.

463   Groener, Frau
Wife of the café owner.

464   Groener, old man
Owner of the German café in Soho where Raven has a room.

465   Guy Fawkes Day
November 5. Commemorates the Gunpowder Plot by Catholics
to kill James I and the members of Parliament at the first session
of that body in 1605. Fawkes, one of the conspirators, was
apprehended before he could ignite the barrels of gunpowder
intended to blow up the House of Lords.

466   Hallows
Porter at the Metropole hotel who takes Ruby to lunch after
Davis's death. Formerly a doorman at Midland Steel, he speaks of
Sir Marcus as someone "not too bad" (209) who gave Christmas
turkeys to the employees.

467   Hanged Man, the
A card in the Tarot deck. Anne's comment to Raven that she
once knew a woman who was frighteningly good at fortune-telling
with cards is one of many echoes of T.S. Eliot's "The Waste Land"
in A Gun for Sale.

468   Harris, Henry
The vicar who presides over the jumble sale where Raven sees
Acky's wife with Anne's bag.

469   Harris, Mrs.
The vicar's wife, a "dry perky woman" (97).

470   Higginbotham
Cashier at the Westminster Bank in Nottwich. He tells the

superintendent of police about his daughter Rose's finding Buddy Fergusson in their garage.

471 Higginbotham, Rose
Found Buddy in the garage without his trousers on and gave him a "good dressing down" (217).

472 *His Chinese Concubine*
This title of one of Davis's books appears suited to his lascivious nature.

473 JK
The Minister's initials, seen on his hairbrush.

474 Joe's
A dive similar to Charlie's.

475 Jossy and Ballard
See Barker.

476 "Juicy Juliet"
Barmaid at the Metropole with whom Buddy falsely claims to have had sexual affairs.

477 Jupiter, not Venus
Davis says that he keeps a table under Venus at Metropole, where the ceiling depicts the night sky; but Anne notices that they are sitting under Jupiter instead, an indication that his identity lies with power rather than amorousness.

478 Kay
The narrator compares the emotionally cold Raven with the boy Kay in Hans Christian Andersen's fairy tale "The Snow Queen." Kay gets a piece of glass in his eye from a mirror which diminishes goodness and enlarges evil in the view of the beholder. A grain of the glass penetrates Kay's heart and turns it into a lump of ice.

479 Kite, Battling
Leader of a Brighton racecourse gang, murdered by Raven (with

the help of others) on the platform at St. Pancras station in London. Raven's account of Kite's death contradicts the one in *Brighton Rock*, where it is claimed that the gangsters meant to "carve him a little" but not to kill him. (See 603.)

480 Lance, troop leader
Leader of the St. Luke's scout troop who fails to honor the vicar's request to bring scouts to ask Mrs. Maydew to sign their autograph books.

481 landlady
Watt's landlady, who recognizes Buddy Fergusson in spite of his mask, innocently suggests that it would do Watt good to be distracted from his books for a while.

482 *Loyalties*
See Galsworthy.

483 Lucan's *Pharsalia*
Lengthy epic about civil war by the Roman poet Lucan (39-65), translated by the Vice-Chancellor into his own difficult meter.

484 Mallowes
See Aitkin.

485 Mander, Mr.
Mentioned as a worker in the jumble sale.

486 Marcus, Sir
A very old, frail, venomous man of mysterious origins, Sir Marcus is one of the wealthiest men in Europe. He seems international rather than English: "He spoke with the faintest foreign accent and it was difficult to determine whether he was Jewish or of an ancient English family. He gave the impression that very many cities had rubbed him smooth" (128). He hopes to revive the fortunes of his Midland Steel company by starting a war through the political assassination which Raven is hired to carry out. Upon discovering that Raven is loose in Nottwich, Sir Marcus tries to bribe Major Calkin to have the police shoot Raven on sight, but Raven eludes them long enough to gain entrance to

Midland's offices and kill both Davis and Sir Marcus. A model
for Sir Marcus's character was munitions manufacturer Sir Basil
Zaharoff (1850-1936).

487 Mason, Mrs.
Neighbor to Frau Groener.

488 Mather, James (Jimmy)
Reliable, methodical police detective-sergeant assigned by
Scotland Yard to pursue Raven for the theft of bank notes. He
is engaged to Anne, who loves him for his ordinariness and
predictability. Although his handling of the Raven case earns him
a promotion, Mather assumes wrongly and with characteristic
modesty that Anne, who will get a reward and publicity for her
role in the case, will no longer want to marry him.

489 Mather's brother
Recalled by Mather. Even more than Mather himself, the brother
needed to find his identity through an organization where he could
follow or give orders, but he did not do so, and "when things went
wrong" he committed suicide (103).

490 "Maud"
Poem by Tennyson (1842), heard over the radio by Raven as he
takes shelter from the cold in the garage of a large house near
the riverfront.

491 Maydew, Miss (Binns)
Stage-name of Miss Binns, the star of *Aladdin*, a well-born young
woman who entered the theatre to escape the garden parties and
other rituals of her class. She attributes her success to hard work
rather than merit. Davis asks her to dinner but is refused.

492 Mayhew
See Barker.

493 mayoress, the
Mrs. Piker.

494 Midland Steel
The large corporation headed by Sir Marcus. A decline in
Midland's fortune (the Metropole porter says it is a loss of eighty
percent of the company's employees) is behind Sir Marcus's
interest in fomenting a war.

495 Mike
Buddy's friend who proposed capturing the mummy and taking it
to the hospital for not wearing a gas-mask. He pursues Raven
with Buddy, but Raven eludes him.

496 Milbanke, Mrs.
See Galsworthy.

497 Milly
Girl with whom Buddy will have tea on the Saturday following the
rag. He dreams of seducing her but knows he will not.

498 Minister for War
The "old Czech" whom Raven is hired to kill, a humanitarian
whose opposition to war made him a target for murder. Raven
is shocked to learn that like himself the Minister was an orphan
whose father was a thief and whose mother committed suicide.
The Minister's boyhood friend in the orphanage was Sir Marcus,
who orders his murder.

499 Mollison
Sir Marcus's valet, who has hated his employer for years. He
warns Raven when Sir Marcus rings the alarm bell, and he later
tries to persuade Raven to give up, telling him that Anne is
Mather's girl and that she betrayed to the police Raven's location
at the Tower.

500 Nottwich
Nottingham, an industrial city in the Midlands. In 1925 Greene
lived for several months in Nottingham, where he worked for the
Nottingham Journal.

501 nurse
Dr. Yogel's nurse, whose unfriendly face and untidy uniform seem

appropriate to the shady office in which she works. She tries
unsuccessfully to call the police while Yogel examines Raven.

502 Old Gaunt
See "Somewhere."

503 'Opkinson, Mrs.
Name overheard at the jumble sale.

504 Oxford boys
Patrons of Charlie's.

505 Page
Girl who, Raven says, told him Dr. Yogel "did her trick fine" (29).

506 Penny, Mrs.
Worker at the jumble sale who places a very low price on a good
hat so that she can buy it herself.

507 Penrith
See Barker.

508 Phelps, Montague, M.A.
Saunders attends a meeting on "Cures for Stammerers" conducted
by Phelps.

509 Piker, Alfred
Mayor of Nottwich, called a "sport," a "dog" by Calkin, who jokes
about the air raid practice drill as affording the mayor an
opportunity to climb into a strange bed.

510 Piker, Mrs. Alfred
A rather vague woman whose company Calkin dreads. She brings
her Pekinese to the Calkinses' dinner, where Sir Marcus, who
hates all dogs, especially Pekinese, is a guest.

511 pimply youth and his sister
Operators of a sleazy magazine shop, near Charing Cross Road in
London, where Davis receives his mail.

512 Raven, James
The protagonist, a lonely, tormented young man whose emotional
coldness, alienation from society, and criminal life are attributed
primarily to his brutal childhood (his criminal father was hanged,
his mother committed suicide) and his extreme ugliness (he has a
harelip). Hired as a political assassin by Davis, he does his job
well but is paid with stolen bank notes which make him the object
of police pursuit for a crime much less serious than the one he
has committed. Determined to get revenge against his betrayers
before he is captured, he follows Davis to Nottwich on the train,
seizes Anne Crowder as a hostage, and evades the police while
attempting to discover the power behind Davis. Raven responds
warmly to Anne's sympathy and trusts her as his only friend, but
she betrays him to the police, confirming his belief that there is
no one he can trust. Although Raven carries out his revenge by
killing Davis and Sir Marcus, he is shot by Saunders and dies a
bitter, painful death.

513 Raven's father
A thief who was in jail when Raven was born; six years later the
father was hanged for another crime.

514 Raven's mother
Raven's mother did nothing to prevent her young son from
discovering the grisly scene in which she killed herself by cutting
her throat with a kitchen knife.

515 Rosen
A friend of Sir Marcus, who remembers the night when Rosen
was sick over Mrs. Ziffo's dress.

516 Ruby
Chorus-girl who has a date with Davis on the day he is killed.

517 *Saccus stercoris*
"Sack of excrement," Acky's exclamation when Raven confronts
him with a gun. What Acky means by *fauces* ("jaws" or "gullet")
is less clear.

518   St. Vitus's dance
Chorea, a disease.

519   Saunders
Stuttering police detective, companion of Mather. He kills Raven.

520   senior surgeon
A medical school doctor who fears that the ragging students will
pelt him as he crosses the courtyard on his way to surgery. Once
safely across, he reflects upon the folly of youth and the greater
folly of regarding it sentimentally.

521   Simmons
See Aitkin.

522   Sleepy Nuik
A new cottage on the edge of Nottwich. Raven hides there briefly
with Anne, who escapes when a real estate agent arrives
unexpectedly.

523   "Somewhere there's a corner of a foreign field that is forever
[England]."
Major Calkin wrongly attributes this line from Rupert Brooke's
"The Soldier" to Shakespeare's character John of Gaunt in *Richard
II.* (Actually Gaunt's speech in II,i, with its reference to England
as "this sceptered isle," "this dear, dear land . . . now leased out
. . . Like a tenement or pelting farm," is more consistent with the
themes of the novel.)

524   Soppelesa
Friend of Sir Marcus, who was often a guest on Soppelesa's "yacht
off Rhodes" (139).

525   Stephenson's rocket
In Euston Station, London, Raven sits by the model of the famous
locomotive "Rocket," designed and built by George Stephenson
(1781-1848).

526   superintendent
An efficient and humane Nottwich police officer whose manner

and performance sharply contrast with that of the blustering, drinking Calkin.

527 Tanneries, the
Area of Nottwich where the Midland Steel Tower is located.

528 Tiger Tom
A tatty stuffed tiger, mascot for the medical students in their "rags."

529 Tiny
Acky's evil, devoted wife, who admires what she believes to be the great mind of her deranged husband. Together they operate the bawdy house to which Davis brings Anne. Tiny takes Anne's purse to the jumble sale where she is seen by Raven, who recognizes it, follows her back to her house, and rescues Anne.

530 Trooper, the
See Barker.

531 "Turn as swimmers into cleanness leaping"
The surgeon recalls Rupert Brooke's "Peace" (1915).

532 tyke
A low or rough-mannered fellow.

533 Vice-Chancellor
Remembered as a classical scholar unsuited for a provincial university and unpopular even though he tried to be a sport when ragging students pelted him with flour and soot.

534 Watt
A "hound" (serious student) whose room is wrecked by Buddy and his friends. Unlike Buddy, Watt has class, intelligence, and a future that promises a practice in Harley Street and a baronetcy.

535 Weevil, the
River that flows through Nottwich.

536 *Whitaker's*
Whitaker's Almanack, a collection of information about
government, commerce, population, and the like, with emphasis on
the British Commonwealth and United States.

537 Widow Twankey
Aladdin's mother in the pantomime.

538 Winton, Druce
Heard reading a selection from Tennyson's "Maud" on the BBC.

539 woman, old
An old woman walking the streets without a gas mask is captured
by the students and taken to the hospital. She enjoys the
excitement but has no idea what is going on. She calls the boys
"Mormons"--meaning "Mohammedans"--because of their masks.

540 Yogel, Dr. Alfred
Disreputable Charlotte Street surgeon whom Raven asks to
perform surgery on his harelip. Yogel tries to give Raven gas
while his nurse telephones the police, but Raven escapes.

541 Ziffo, Mrs.
A guest aboard Soppelesa's yacht whose black satin dress was
soiled when Rosen became sick.

BRIGHTON ROCK (1938)

542 *Agnus Dei*
Pinkie frequently remembers this phrase from the confessional:
Agnus dei, qui tollis peccata mundi, dona nobis pacem. (Lamb of
God who taketh away the sins of the world, give us peace.)

543 Arnold, Ida
Ida, called "Lily" by some of her friends, is a good-natured London
barmaid in Brighton for the Whitmonday holiday. She befriends
Fred Hale shortly before his death. When the police seem
unconcerned about her belief that Hale was murdered, Ida
becomes a self-appointed detective, pursuing Pinkie and his gang
for mixed motives: concern for justice, desire for revenge, and a
bit of fun. With the aid of her winnings from Black Boy at the
racecourse Ida returns to Brighton, where she uncovers enough
information to drive Pinkie to destruction. Ida's Greek name links
her with pagan antiquity, and her function in pursuit of Pinkie
ironically resembles that of the Furies in the Oresteian tragedies
of Aeschylus. Her superstitions and her hedonistic view of life
are consistently counterpointed against the views of the Catholic
characters, Pinkie and especially Rose.

544 author, a well-known popular
The author whose plump face appears in the window of the Royal
Albion is probably J.B. Priestley.

545 Bank Holiday
In England, one of five official holidays when banks and
government offices are closed. Whitmonday is a bank holiday.

546 Barber
A bookie.

547 Baron, Peggy
A girl who, as Pinkie explains to Rose, "got mixed up with a mob"
(55) and had one of her eyes destroyed and her face severely
burned with acid.

548 Bass
A popular ale, ordered by Spicer at Snow's, where he places one
of Hale's "Kolley Kibber" cards in an attempt to establish the time
of Hale's death as later than it actually was. But Spicer makes a
serious error, since, as Ida knows, Hale did not like Bass.

549 Beale, George
A bookie.

550   Belisha beacons
Street-crossing lights.

551   Bell
Barman in the pub where Ida is first seen by Hale and Pinkie.
Ida knows him.

552   Bill
Operator of a shooting gallery. Pinkie, trying to establish an alibi,
asks him for the time.

553   Black Boy
Hale gives Ida a tip on the horse Black Boy to win the four
o'clock race on Saturday, and after Hale's disappearance she buys
a cheap watch which comes with the same free tip. Ida bets
twenty pounds at 12 to 1, Black Boy wins, and the money enables
Ida to remain in Brighton to investigate Hale's death.

554   Black Dog
When Ida places her bet on Black Boy, the bookie writes "Black
Dog" instead. The name suggests the devil: in Goethe's *Faust*
and, more importantly, in *The Witch of Edmonton*, from which
Greene took the epigraph for the novel, the devil appears as a
black dog.

555   Blue Anchor
The Nottingham pub that Spicer and a friend plan to purchase
after Spicer's retirement from Pinkie's gang.

556   bob
A shilling.

557   bogies
Policemen.

558   Boy, the
Pinkie.

559   Brewer, Bill
A bookie who has paid Pinkie for "protection." When he begins

paying Colleoni instead, Pinkie visits him late at night, slashes his face with a razor, and extracts payment.

560 Brighton
Popular resort city on the English Channel, about fifty miles south of London. Brighton attained its greatest prestige as the fashionable haunt of Prince Regent George IV, who had his seaside palace, the Royal Pavilion, remodeled into its present form. In the 1930's the Brighton racecourse was the scene of gangland wars similar to those depicted in the novel.

561 *Brighton Belle*
A pleasure boat offering cruises from Brighton.

562 Brighton rock
Stick ("rock") candy, usually pink, widely available in Brighton. The words "Brighton Rock" appear at the end of the stick no matter where it is broken.

563 Brown, Pinkie
The victim of a traumatic childhood, with bitter memories of poverty and of premature exposure to sex (the "Saturday night ritual" of his parents in the one-room flat), Pinkie is the most naturalistically conceived of Greene's protagonists. Once a choir boy who wanted to become a priest--no doubt for the celibate life more than from a sense of vocation--Pinkie combines puritanical habits (rejecting alcohol, tobacco, and sex) with enormous ambitions for control of the Brighton underworld. Following the murder of Kite, who had taken him in and become his surrogate father, Pinkie at age seventeen assumed leadership of Kite's mob. He murders Hale to avenge Kite, but finds as Macbeth did that other murders may be necessary to conceal the first. Pinkie murders Spicer, whom he no longer trusts; and he marries Rose, whom he despises, in order to prevent her from testifying against him. Determined to protect himself at all costs and to secure his "peace" on his own terms, Pinkie nevertheless continues to think of the possibility of repentance and the sacraments. Although he finally loses confidence in Rose and plans her death through a double-suicide scheme, the attrition of his hatred in response to her love suggests that he might be

capable of changing. When Ida, Dallow, and a policeman confront
the pair in Peacehaven, Pinkie pulls out his vitriol bottle only to
have it smashed in his face by the policeman's nightstick.   In
agony he runs away and leaps to his death from the cliffs.

564 buer
A woman; tramp.

565 Burgoyne, General
A horse in the four o'clock race, presumably named after the
famous British general defeated at the Battle of Saratoga in the
Revolutionary War.

566 Carter and Galloway
Estate agents in London, employers of Molly Pink.

567 Carthew, Molly
A "lovely" girl, Rose says, who "burnt" in hell because she
committed suicide, the unforgivable mortal sin of despair (139).

568 Clarence
One of Ida's friends, a "sombre thin man in black with a bowler
hat sitting beside a wine barrel" (31). He once seduced her by
pretending to be dying; she now calls him "old ghost."

569 "clouds of glory"
An allusion to Wordsworth's "Immortality Ode": "Not in entire
forgetfulness, / And not in utter nakedness, / But trailing clouds
of glory do we come / From God, who is our home: / Heaven
lies about us in our infancy."

570 Colleoni
Pinkie's powerful, successful rival in the Brighton underworld who
regards himself as "just a business man" and rules his mob from
the secure comforts of a room in the Cosmopolitan hotel.
Colleoni ordered Kite's murder and is clearly capable of destroying
Pinkie's small mob. He offers Pinkie a job but is refused. In his
introduction to the novel Greene writes that Colleoni "had his real
prototype who had retired by 1938 and lived a gracious Catholic
life in one of the Brighton crescents, although I found his name

was still law, when I demanded entrance by virtue of it, at a little London nightclub called The Nest behind Regent Street" (xi).

571 Collins, Annie
A pregnant schoolgirl who, as Pinkie explains to Dallow, committed suicide by laying her head on the railroad tracks.

572 *Corruptio optimi est pessimi.*
The old priest's words to Rose (309): "The worst is corruption of the best."

573 Cosmopolitan
Luxurious hotel (fictional) where Colleoni now inhabits the room formerly held by Napoleon III. Pinkie is refused a room there on his wedding night.

574 Crab
Once run out of Brighton by Kite's mob, Crab reappears calling himself "Colleoni's right-hand man." Crab "had been a Jew once, but a hairdresser and a surgeon had altered that" (98-99).

575 *Credo in unum Satanum*
Pinkie's ironic "creed": "I believe in one Satan."

576 Crow, Violet
A child victim of rape and murder in Brighton. Pinkie sees her face on a newspaper from 1936 at the home of Rose's parents.

577 Cubitt, John
Red-haired member of Pinkie's gang who becomes disaffected, afraid, and full of sentimental self-pity after Pinkie's murder of Spicer. Cubitt deserts the mob, tries unsuccessfully to join Colleoni's men, drinks too much and eventually reveals to Ida that Hale was murdered by Pinkie and his gang.

578 *Daily Messenger*
The newspaper for which Fred Hale works.

579 Dallow
The most loyal member of Pinkie's gang, Dallow is a simple, good-

natured, heavy-set man whose easy acceptance of life and his long-running affair with Frank's wife Judy make him a foil to the virginal, embittered Pinkie. With his doglike affection for Pinkie, he is the boy's only real friend and confidant. Even Dallow's fidelity reaches its limit, however, when he discovers Pinkie's plan for the death of Rose, and he betrays his friend to Ida and the police.

580 Deeping, Warwick
English novelist (1877-1950) whose book *Sorrell and Son* is on Ida's shelf.

581 Delia
A friend of Molly Pink, seen with her when Molly talks to Hale.

582 Digby
Recalled by Crab as exemplifying the upper-class behavior he has become accustomed to since he left Kite's mob and joined Colleoni's.

583 Eugénie
Eugénie Marie de Montijo de Gutzman (1826-1920), Empress of France (1853-1871) as wife of Napoleon III. Colleoni refers to her as a "foreign polony" who once lived in his room at the Cosmopolitan (77).

584 Feversham, Lord
Nobleman from Doncaster, where Crab has seen him. He appears briefly in the lobby of the Cosmopolitan.

585 Fields, Gracie (1898-1979)
Popular comedienne of stage and screen.

586 Frank's
Rooming house in Brighton where Pinkie and his mob live. Frank, the proprietor, is blind but is skilled at pressing suits.

587 FRESUICILLEYE
The message Ida and Old Crowe receive from the ouija board when she asks what happened to Hale. As Ida interprets it, Hale

(FRE) was driven to suicide (SUICILL) and his death demands revenge (an EYE for an eye).

588 gift of tongues
An allusion to Acts 1:4: "And they were all filled with the Holy Ghost, and began to speak with other tongues, as the Spirit gave them utterance."

589 girdle of Venus
Ida's character and her horoscope may resemble those of Chaucer's Wife of Bath, although a more immediate source for Greene's interest in her horoscope may be found in his December 1932 *Spectator* review of *Pretty Witty Nell*, Clifford Bax's horoscopic biography of Nell Gwyn.

590 *The Good Companions* (1929)
One of Ida's books, a popular novel by J.B. Priestley. (See 195; 544.)

591 Hale, Charles (Fred)
A newspaper man whose involvement with the mob leads to the murder of Kite by Colleoni's men and subsequently his own murder by Pinkie's mob in revenge. Before his death Hale is befriended by Ida Arnold, who becomes his avenger.

592 Harry
Customer at Henekey's.

593 Henekey's
Well-known pub in the Strand, London. Ida is a barmaid there.

594 Innocent, the
The feast of the Holy Innocents (December 28) commemorates Herod's massacre of the innocents, the slaughter of male children under two years old (Matthew 2:16).

595 inspector
A policeman who tries to get Pinkie to leave Brighton.

596   Irving, Henry
See 265.

597   Jefferson, Alfred
A clerk from Clapham who finds Hale's body.

598   Joe
A Negro to whom Ida speaks outside a pub in the Seven Dials
area of London.

599   Johnnie
A minor figure in Pinkie's mob, instructed by Dallow to make
certain that Prewitt safely boards the boat for France.

600   Judy
Frank's slatternly wife, who carries on a long-running affair with
Dallow.

601   Kibber, Kolley
The name by which Hale, a reporter for the *Daily Messenger*, is
to be addressed by those who recognize him and want to claim a
cash prize from the newspaper. For Greene it is a humorous play
on the name of English poet Colley Cibber (1671-1757), king of
the dunces in Pope's *Dunciad*.

602   kip
A rooming house.

603   Kite
Mob leader and father-figure to Pinkie, killed with razors at the
St. Pancras railway station in London by Colleoni's men. Cubitt's
claim to Ida that the murder was accidental ("They only meant to
carve him," 199) is contradicted by the testimony of Raven in *A
Gun for Sale*. (See 479.)

604   Langtry, Lily (1853-1929)
Beautiful English actress who was romantically involved with
Edward VII.

605   McPherson
A bookie.

606   Maisie
Rose's friend, a waitress at Snow's.

607   Memento Mori
Spicer's horse in the four o'clock race won by Black Boy.   The
ominous name means "Remember that you must die."

608   Merry Monarch
Horse in the four o'clock race.   The king who was sometimes
called the "Merry Monarch" was Charles II.

609   Moyne, Charlie
A destitute man turned out of his lodging by Carter and Galloway.
Ida gives him a quid (pound).

610   Napoleon the Third
Nephew of Napoleon Bonaparte, Emperor of France (1853-1871).
Colleoni's room at the Cosmopolitan was formerly inhabited by
Napoleon III.

611   nark
An informer.

612   Nelson Place
The Brighton slum where Rose's home is located.   Greene's
introduction (xi) emphasizes that Nelson Place was real, not
imaginary.

613   Old Crowe
Ida's friend and fellow-lodger who operates the ouija board with
her.

614   "old ghost"
Ida's friend Clarence.

615   ouija board
A device consisting of a planchette and a board bearing the

alphabet and various other symbols, used in spiritualistic seances, etc., supposedly to convey and record messages from the spirits. Ida uses a ouija board in an attempt to communicate with the spirit of the murdered Hale.

616   Palace Pier
Victorian amusement pier in Brighton, built in 1892.

617   Pankhurst, Mrs.
Emmeline Pankhurst (1858-1928), Women's Suffrage leader, founder of the Women's Social and Political Union in 1903.

618   Paradise Piece
The site of Pinkie's boyhood home, adjacent to Nelson Place.

619   Peacehaven
Coastal town a few miles east of Brighton, near Newhaven. Pinkie takes Rose to Peacehaven to carry out the double suicide scheme, and he dies there after they are discovered.

620   Piker
An unfriendly acquaintance from Pinkie's schooldays, now a waiter who serves Pinkie and Rose at the hotel in Peacehaven.

621   Pink, Molly
The London secretary whom Hale tries unsuccessfully to pick up on the Palace Pier.

622   Pinkie's parents
Pinkie confesses to Dallow that his terror of life results primarily from his exposure in childhood to the sexual activity of his parents in their impoverished one-room flat. He has no happy memories of his parents.

623   polony
A girl or young woman.

624   Prewitt
Pinkie's corrupt lawyer who assists Pinkie in arranging his marriage to Rose. Fond of literary quotations and "stranger to no wangle,

twist, contradictory clause, ambiguous word" (143), Prewitt is at Frank's when Pinkie murders Spicer. Pinkie sends Prewitt to France to escape the police and regain his nerve, but Ida's false claim to Dallow that Prewitt has been caught helps to persuade Dallow to betray Pinkie.

625 priest
The old priest who hears Rose's confession after Pinkie's death reminds her that the "appalling strangeness of the mercy of God" may extend to her and even to Pinkie.

626 "Roses, roses, all the way"
Prewitt mixes this phrase from Browning's poem "The Patriot" with the "sprig of yew" from Arnold's "Requiescat."

627 St. Pancras
Railway station in London where Kite was killed.

628 Sammy
A young man employed by the bookie Tate.

629 seven devils, the
In Luke 11:24-27, Jesus tells the parable of a man who was purged of evil spirits but remained so restless and dissatisfied that he returned to his house and took in seven spirits worse than himself.

630 Sherry's
A dance hall in Brighton, still popular in the 1930's.

631 Snow's
Restaurant where Rose works.

632 Spicer
An older member of Pinkie's mob whose fear and distress over his involvement in Hale's murder cause Pinkie to lose confidence in him. When Pinkie's attempt to have Spicer killed by Colleoni's men fails, Spicer plans to leave Brighton for a quiet life as a pub owner in Nottingham, but Pinkie murders him by pushing him from the top of a stairwell at Frank's.

633 Sylvie
Spicer's girlfriend, who professes grief over his death but readily
agrees to a tryst with Pinkie in the back seat of a car.   The
virginal Pinkie, who has murdered Spicer, fails in this attempt to
enjoy the spoils of victory.

634 Syrett, Netta (d. 1943)
Minor English novelist, author of many works including several
whose titles are suggestive of themes in *Brighton Rock*:   *The
Shutters of Eternity* (1928), *Portrait of a Rebel* and *Strange
Marriage* (1930).

635 Tate, Jim
A bookie with whom Ida places her bet on Black Boy.

636 Tavell, Bob
A bookie.

637 "This were a fine reign: to do ill and not hear of it again."
The novel's epigraph is from the Ford, Dekker, and Rowley play
The Witch of Edmonton (1623).

638 Tilley, Vesta (1864-1952)
Actress and male impersonator.

639 Tom
Ida's former husband.

640 totsies
Prostitutes or near-prostitutes.

641 Van Tromp's Victory
An engraving which hangs in Rose's room at Snow's.   Maarten
Harpertszoon Tromp (1597-1653), Dutch hero of the Anglo-Dutch
naval wars, was the subject of four paintings by J.M.W. Turner as
well as works by other maritime painters.   (Greene's perpetuation
of Turner's error in calling the admiral "Van" Tromp increases the
likelihood that the reference is to one of Turner's works.)

642 vitriol
Sulfuric acid. The bottle of vitriol Pinkie regularly carries in his
pocket is smashed in his face by a policeman's billy club when
Pinkie tries to use it to defend himself at Peacehaven.

643 Wallace, Edgar (1875-1932)
Successful and prolific writer of thrillers, including *The Four Just
Men* (1905). (See 339, 1072.)

644 Whitmonday
A bank holiday, the Monday after Pentecost. The murder of Hale
occurs on Whitmonday.

645 Whitsun
Pentecost, or "white Sunday" (after the traditional wearing of white
robes by the newly confirmed). The seventh Sunday after Easter,
Pentecost commemorates the descent of the Holy Spirit to the
Apostles, described in Acts 2:1-4.

646 Wilson, Mr.
Rose's father, a suspicious elderly man who, with his wife, enjoys
"moods" of brooding silence. He allows Pinkie to interrupt their
mood, however, so that Pinkie can give him fifteen guineas for his
permission to marry Rose.

647 Wilson, Mrs.
Rose's mother, who appears slovenly, mean-spirited, and
unintelligent. She tries to get her husband to ignore Pinkie when
he asks for permission to marry Rose.

648 Wilson, Rose
As the waitress who knows that Spicer, not Hale, left the Kolley
Kibber card at Snow's, Rose has evidence that could hang Pinkie
for the murder of Hale. Pinkie pretends to love her and marries
her to prevent her from testifying against him. Like Pinkie, Rose
is Catholic, very young (17), and the victim of an impoverished
childhood with unloving parents. Aware that he is involved in
some kind of wrongdoing, Rose nevertheless responds to his
feigned affection with profound love, but he mistrusts her and
plans her death, unsuccessfully, through a treacherous suicide pact.

At the end of the novel Rose believes herself pregnant with Pinkie's child.

THE CONFIDENTIAL AGENT (1939)

A note on names in the novel: It should be kept in mind that Greene's use of initials for the names of characters such as D., K., and L. may have been a strategy for creating mystery while avoiding the identification of the characters with a specific nationality. In any case, the use of initials is a concealment *from the reader only*, as is made clear by the narrator's comment that Rose "mispronounced" D.'s name at the embassy.

649   Alda
Sister of Oliver, betrothed to Roland, in the *Song of Roland*. She falls dead upon hearing of Roland's death. D., recalling this story, thinks of how in legends people do not have to go on living, as he does, after the death of a loved one.

650   Alexandra (1844-1925)
Queen consort of King Edward VII (m. 1863). At the customs office in Dover D. sees a picture of Edward VII naming an express train "Alexandra."

651   Bates, Joe
The local union leader at Benditch, "a youngish man with a melodramatic shock of hair and a weak mouth" (203). D. urges him to tell the miners not to return to work, but Bates says that if Lord Benditch's agent assures them that the coal is going to Holland they can work with clear consciences.

652   beggar
Lures D. into a mews where someone shoots at him.

653 Bellows, Dr.
An aging idealist who operates the Entrenationo Language Center
in London in the "timid hope" that the teaching of the
international language he invented will lead to world peace (45).

654 Benditch, Lady
Long-deceased mother of Rose Cullen, spoken of with disapproval
by Mrs. Bennett, who implies that Lady Benditch was a Socialist
sympathizer.

655 Benditch, Lord
Wealthy nobleman from whose mines D. hopes to purchase coal
for his government. Benditch's daughter Rose describes him as
"medium honest" (177), not completely trustworthy in business
affairs, unfeeling in his relations with the workmen.

656 Bennett, Mr.
Mrs. Bennett's husband lies in bed drunk and therefore poses no
threat to D., who hides in their coal shed.

657 Bennett, Mrs.
Elderly resident of Benditch, former nurse to Rose Cullen.
Although Rose sends her a note asking her to help D., she refuses
to do so when she learns that D. wants information about the
leftist union leader.

658 Berne manuscript
D.'s major scholarly achievement was the discovery of the Berne
manuscript of the *Song of Roland*, which he claims to be more
accurate and complete than the Oxford. In the Berne version,
Oliver kills Roland deliberately in retribution for the lives wasted
through Roland's pride in refusing to call for help. In fact there
are several manuscripts of *Roland*, but no Berne manuscript and
no serious rivals to the Oxford version.

659 Bloomsbury St., a
D. stays in a small hotel in Guilford St., as did Greene himself
while he wrote the novel. Bloomsbury, in central London, is the
site of the British Museum, where D. did scholarly research in
happier years.

660 Blue, Tony
A blundering cricket player recalled by Captain Currie and the
two men who capture D. at Lido.

661 Brigstock
One of Lord Benditch's business partners, the most difficult
member of the group to deal with. He insists upon payment in
gold.

662 Buzzard's
Familiar restaurant in Oxford Street.

663 Carpenter, Miss
Secretary to Dr. Bellows.

664 Chauffeur
L.'s brutish chauffeur, a large man with a cast in one eye, tries
first to rob D. and then to pick a fight with him at Captain
Currie's roadhouse. Later he beats D. severely when D. is caught
trying to escape in Rose's car.

665 child
On the steamer bound for Dover D. speaks to a child who has
bumped his head.

666 Chubby
A guest at Lido.

667 Clara
Prostitute who has befriended Else and offered to hire her as
maid and companion.

668 Constable
An elderly constable at Benditch first fails to recognize D. as the
man he is pursuing, then slips and falls, allowing D. to escape.

669 Conway
Small boy of about seven whose mother, mistaking D.'s fear of
going underground for ordinary fear of elevators, insists that the

boy hold D.'s hand as they descend in the lift at the Russell Square Underground station.

670 Crikey
A bus conductor at Benditch, member of the "gang" of anarchists who assist D.

671 Crole, Else
Fourteen-year-old maid at D.'s hotel who responds eagerly to his kindness and helps him by watching his room and hiding his papers in her stocking. He sees her as the embodiment of suffering innocence in a corrupt world, an individual whose plight calls into question the value of the civilization she inhabits. Oppressed by poverty and the cruel treatment of Marie Mendrill, Else can imagine no possible escape except a job as a prostitute's maid. D. plans to help her escape, but she is murdered by Marie for hiding his papers.

672 Crusoe
Titular hero of Daniel Defoe's *Robinson Crusoe* (1719) who is marooned on an island where he is able to find or make everything essential to his needs. D. reflects humorously that Miss Glover's apartment is not Crusoe's island.
(See 2181.)

673 Cullen, Rose
Lord Benditch's spoiled, hard-drinking daughter, who becomes involved in D.'s adventure after meeting him by chance at Dover. Her disillusionment, attributed to the world of her father's "medium honest" business (71) and Forbes's deceitfulness and casual morality, shocks D. as a kind of "savage knowledge" (72) that ought to come only at the end of life. Beneath a tough, jaded exterior, however, Rose is capable of love and sympathy, as demonstrated by her growing love for D. and her interest in his mission. At the end she leaves her luxurious life in England for a life of certain hardship with D.

674 Currie, Captain
Owner of the roadhouse where D. and Rose stop enroute from Dover to London. A military type and an acquaintance of Rose,

he appears at times to be involved with D.'s enemies, although the plot never clarifies his exact role. D. regards Currie as a fool rather than a villain.

675 D.

The confidential agent, "a forty-five-year-old man with a heavy moustache and a scarred chin and worry like a habit on his forehead" (3). A university professor of medieval French literature with a special interest in the *chanson de geste*, D. is drawn into his unlikely role in his country's civil war because he wants to live decently, yet he is devoid of illusions about his own heroism or the purity of the cause he supports. He believes that the war and the death of his wife have robbed him of the ability to feel any emotion other than fear, but events prove otherwise: he is awakened to sympathy for the innocent Else and love for Rose Cullen. Similarly, his fear of violence and his innate pacifism are overcome by his determination to punish Else's murderer. Largely a failure in his mission (he is unable to purchase the coal, although he at least prevents L. from getting it), D. is nevertheless successful on a personal level, demonstrating bravery and perseverance in the face of betrayal and hopelessness, and bringing about the emotional regeneration of both his own life and Rose's.

676 D.'s wife

D.'s wife of fifteen years was killed in the civil war three years before the narrative begins. Her death was ironic; she was shot after being taken hostage by mistake. Deeply affected by her loss, D. nevertheless finds it hard to remember her with much exactitude: "She had been a passion, and it is difficult to recall an emotion when it is dead" (9).

677 Davis

The name under which D. is registered at the Lido hotel.

678 Deslys, Mlle. Gaby (1884-1920)

French star of the Follies-Bergère and the Olympia who accumulated a large fortune and had luxurious homes in Paris and London. Mlle. Delys, who had affairs with men such as the Duc de Crussol but refused to give up her liberty by marrying, appears in one of the reproductions of famous paintings in Lord Benditch's house in Chatham Terrace.

679 Dook, a
Solecism for "Duke." Seeing the expensive car which bears L. and Lord Benditch's agent into Benditch, a child asks, "Is it a dook?" (197)

680 Eden, Mr.
Sir Anthony Eden (1895-1977), Conservative British statesman who resigned as foreign minister (the first of three terms) in 1938 in opposition to Chamberlain's appeasement of Hitler in the Munich Accord. He succeeded Churchill as prime minister (1955-57). Else reports to D. that Mr. Muckerji asks her what she thinks of Mr. Eden and writes down her answers.

681 Edward VII (1841-1910)
King of Great Britain and Ireland (1901-1910). (See 3002.)

682 Fennick, Mr.
Counsel for the police at D.'s trial, "an inferior bird-like man" (227).

683 Fetting, Lord
Somnolent senior member of the group of Benditch's business associates. He sleeps through most of the negotiations with D., then awakens and refuses to sign. His response to the group's concern over D.'s lack of credentials is that they should "sleep on it" (106).

684 Forbes (Furtstein)
Wealthy businessman whose assumed name, like his wearing of the clothing (tweeds) and manners of English country life, are attempts to escape from or conceal his Jewish ancestry: "only the shape of the skull disclosed the Furtstein past" (101). Rose describes him as honest in business dealings but not in love, since he wants to marry her but keeps a mistress. His affection for Rose leads him to assist D. by providing £2000 bail and arranging D.'s escape from England by sea.

685 Fortescue, Mr.
Emily Glover's friend who shows up at her flat just after the death
there of Mr. K. Although he tells police later about seeing a man
and a woman in the flat, he is unable to identify D. in the police
lineup.

686 Furt
Rose's nickname for Forbes (Furtstein).

687 Ganelon
In the *Song of Roland*, the jealous traitor who betrays Roland to
the Saracens. Having arranged for Roland to be given command
of the rear guard of Charlemagne's army, he reveals to the enemy
the planned route through the pass at Roncesvalles, where
Roland's men are ambushed by a much larger force.

688 Gang, the
A group of young anarchists in Benditch. Although they assist D.
by hiding him from the police and setting off an explosion at the
mine to prevent the miners from returning to work, they have no
real interest in his cause or in any causes other than their own
grudge against society.

689 German
Bald, middle-aged man seen sitting on Dr. Bellows' desk with
Winifred. He attributes his passion for English girls to their
innocence.

690 girls, two very small
Near Hyde Park Corner D. sees the royal Princesses Elizabeth and
Margaret on their way to shop at Harrod's.

691 Glover, Emily
Absent owner of the flat at 3 Chester Gardens (in Belgravia)
where D. hides after his first escape from the police and where he
later takes K. with the intention of killing him. Her library reveals
her piety.

692 Goldstein
One of Lord Benditch's business partners.

693   Goldthorb
D. asks K. if he has ever read any detective stories by Goldthorb, who he says wrote in Entrenationo.

694   Groupers
Fortescue says that he and Emily Glover are "groupers"--members of the Oxford Group, an Evangelical movement which originated in South Africa, spread to Britain, and devoted attention to social concerns.   Also called "Buchmanites," after the founder Frank Buchman (1878-1961).

695   Gwyn Cottage
Lord Benditch's house in London, named after Nell Gwyn (1650-87), actress and mistress of Charles II.   The paintings with which it is decorated supply a "vicarious sensuality" (by featuring women associated with voluptuous, immoral lives) and imply something about Lord Benditch's character as well as his taste.   Rose, his daughter, refuses to live there.

696   Hillman, Sir Terence
Barrister hired by Forbes to defend D. in court. By complaining about police methods of pressing numerous minor charges while gathering evidence for a more serious one, he is able to get D. released on bail.

697   Hogpit
A passerby in S. Audley Street who, by trying to help K., ironically seals K.'s fate.   When a policeman who thinks K. is drunk orders him to go home, Hogpit accuses the policeman of slander and offers to testify against him if K. chooses to bring suit. While the two argue, D. arrives in a taxi and takes K. away. After K.'s death, Hogpit tells police that K. had behaved strangely because someone was following him, but Hogpit cannot identify D. in the police lineup.

698   Jarvis, George
Elderly resident of Willing who rides with D. on the train to Benditch, identifying the villages they pass.   He is injured slightly in the explosion at Benditch.

699   Joe
Driver who takes D. from Lido to Southend where the ship on
which he will escape awaits.

700   Joey
A member of "the gang" in Benditch.

701   K.
One of D.'s contacts in London, a language teacher in Dr.
Bellows's school, "a little shabby and ink-stained" (47). Assigned to
watch D., K. nevertheless has not been trusted with knowledge of
D.'s mission. Observing K.'s evasive eyes, bitten nails, and signs
of poverty and insecurity, D. concludes that K. is not strong
enough to bear distrust but is instead one of those who will "live
up to the character they are allotted" (50)--a conclusion borne out
by K.'s revelation that he has sold out to L., who gives him an
appointment to the faculty of the university at home. He longs to
return there, although the doctor has told him that his severe
heart condition gives him only six months to live. When D. shoots
at him and misses, K. dies of heart failure.

702   K.C.
"King's Counsel," title of Sir Terence Hillman.

703   L.
D.'s rival, an agent for the opposition in their country's civil war,
also in London to purchase coal. D. cannot remember his name;
they have seen each other three times but have never spoken. A
titled aristocrat before the days of the republic, he has money and
influence on his side.

704   Li, Dr.
Siamese professor from Chulalankarana University, studying
Entrenationo at Dr. Bellows's school. He sternly refuses to speak
English to D.

705   Liberal, the old
One of the five Cabinet Members in D.'s country who know the
purpose of his journey. D. wonders if he is the one who betrayed

D. (since L. obviously knows what D. is after). D. recalls the old Liberal's protests against executions carried out by the government.

706 Lido
Resort hotel owned by Forbes.

707 Maintenon, Madame de
Françoise d'Aubigne (1635-1719), Protestant widow who was governess for the children of Louis XIV of France and later became the king's second wife. Her portrait appears in one of the reproductions of famous paintings in Lord Benditch's house in Chatham Terrace.

708 manservant
Steals D.'s papers prior to the business negotiations at Gwyn Cottage.

709 Mendrill, Marie
The manager of the Bloomsbury hotel where D. stays, "a dark hulking woman with spots around her mouth" (52). Her square, masculine features and the masculine furnishings of her room, including pictures of women in lingerie, suggest an aberrant sexuality. Her violent temper and her distrust of Else and D. lead her to murder the girl. Both L. and the solicitor call her mad. She confesses when Mr. Muckerji goes around asking questions of the neighbors.

710 Mersham, Lady
Heard on the radio with "Hints to the Young Housewife."

711 Minister of the Interior
One of the five Cabinet Ministers who could have betrayed D., he is especially suspect because his youth and ambition may have led him to believe that a dictatorship would offer him more opportunities than a republic would.

712 Muckerji, Mr.
Hindu lodger in the hotel where D. stays. Identifying himself as a "mass observer" who is always "on duty" (Mass Observation became a popular method of sampling public opinion in England

in the 1930's), he constantly gathers information which he sends
to the "organisers" (141-42). His inquiries following Else's murder
lead to Mrs. Mendrill's confession.

713 Oliver
Roland's closest friend among Charlemagne's knights (paladins),
Oliver dies with him at Roncevalles. To D., Oliver's restraint,
good sense, and lack of pride make him the true hero of the *Song
of Roland*. In the familiar version of the tale, Oliver accidentally
kills Roland, but in the Berne manuscript (see above) he does so
deliberately.

714 Owtram, Jack
The name Rose uses for the dead K., who she says is drunk, when
Fortescue sees him at Emily Glover's apartment.

715 Peters
One of the policemen who attempt to arrest D. in connection with
the death of Else.

716 Pig
A guest at Lido.

717 poet, English (of Italian origin)
D. remembers lines from a poem he once copied into his
notebook by an English poet of Italian origin. The few lines
recalled are so strongly reminiscent of Francis Thompson's "The
Hound of Heaven" as to suggest that Greene is inventing a poet
rather than alluding to one.

718 poetess
The "poetess" quoted by Dr. Bellows ("this is the birthday of my
life") is Christina Rossetti. The poem is "A Birthday" (1857).

719 policeman, young
Questions D. at Emily Glover's flat after seeing her message
telling the milkman not to deliver milk until Monday.

720 Pompadour, Marquise
A rose developed by Lord Benditch, named after the historical

Marquise de Pompadour (1721-64), mistress of Louis XV of France. Her picture is seen among the reproductions of famous paintings in Lord Benditch's house in Chatham Terrace. Lord Benditch's hobby also accounts for his daughter's name: Rose.

721 porter
At the railway station at Willing, the porter opens the waiting room for D. and tells him about the Benditch family and Rose Cullen's childhood.

722 Roland
The most famous of Charlemagne's paladins, a model of heroic bravery, loyalty, and self-sacrifice in service to the king. Betrayed by Ganelon, he and his men are ambushed by an overwhelming force in the pass at Roncesvalles. When Roland, in his pride and courage, waits too late to blow his horn and call for the king's help, he and all of his men are slain.

723 Rose's grandfather
A workman in the mines at Benditch.

724 Row, Mr.
Indian lodger at the Bloomsbury hotel. Else regards him as less respectable than Mr. Muckerji.

725 Sally
Forbes's mistress in Shepherd's Market.

726 Secretary, First
Staff member at D.'s embassy in London. Instead of helping D., who has been wrongly accused of several crimes, he calls the police.

727 Secretary, Second
D. says that the only person at the embassy who might perhaps be trusted to help him is the Second Secretary, who is no longer there when D. arrives.

728   solicitor
"A smart agile man with a society manner" (225), hired by Forbes
to assist D. after his arrest in Benditch.

729   Southcrawl
Seaside town where the Lido is located.

730   Spot
Bald-headed guest at the Lido.

731   Stowe, Charlie
A miner in Benditch.   The police who are pursuing D. are
convinced that he is hiding in Stowe's house, but Stowe bears
some unspecified grievance against the police--or perhaps the
government--and will not let them enter without a warrant.

732   Tearle, Conway (1878?-1938)
Well-known English film actor. The boy Conway, whom D. meets
at the Russell Square station, was named after Tearle because the
boy's parents saw a Conway Tearle film shortly before the child
was born.

733   Terry, Mrs.
Neighbor to Mrs. Bennett. When an unnamed young man from
the Royal Family offered to enter Mrs. Terry's bare house during
his visit to Benditch, his hosts told him that she was ill so that he
would go to Mrs. Bennett's instead and, presumably, form the
impression that her comfortably furnished house (made
comfortable with the help of Lord Benditch) was typical of the
miners' homes.

734   Triffen, Peter
Recalled by Mrs. Bennett as a dislikable boy who frightened the
child Rose with a mechanical mouse.

735   Turpin
Archbishop who blesses Roland and Oliver prior to their deaths
at Roncesvalles.

736 waitress
The waitress who serves D. in a café near his hotel claims
unconvincingly to have been Else's best friend and fabricates
stories about the girl's involvement with a married man in
Highbury.

737 Winifred
Angular, unattractive English girl who appears with the German
in Dr. Bellows's office.

738 "You can trust him when the wind's blowing east."
Rose says this of Forbes when revealing to D. that Forbes has
signed the contract with the others to deliver coal to L. through
Holland, thus circumventing his own country's law. The expression
may echo Isaak Walton's "Epistle to the Reader" in *The Compleat
Angler* (1653): "I shall stay with him no longer than to wish him
a rainy evening to read this following discourse; and that if he be
an honest angler, the east wind may never blow when he goes a-
fishing.")

739 Z.
A countryman of D. and L., probably an artist but possibly a
collector, whose pictures were destroyed by the people D.
represents.

THE POWER AND THE GLORY (1940)

740 Anita
Padre José happens upon the burial of Anita, a five-year-old girl
whose grandfather begs him to say a short prayer for the child,
but he refuses.

741 barkeeper
The barkeeper at the cantina in the Lehrs' village gives the priest

a glass of brandy and offers to sell him sacramental wine on credit.

742 Beckley, Henry
Director of Private Tutorials, Ltd., the London correspondence school from which Coral Fellows takes courses.

743 Brigitta (boy)
The Whisky Priest once conducted a christening ceremony while drunk, naming the boy "Brigitta" instead of the intended "Pedro."

744 Brigitta (girl)
The whisky priest's illegitimate daughter. He loves her and grieves over his conviction that she is without grace or charm and has already begun to experience worldly corruption.

745 Calles, President
Plutarcho Elias Calles (1877-1945), Mexican president (1924-28) who helped to bring about economic reform and the enforcement of anticlerical laws.

746 Calver, James
American bank robber and murderer, called the Gringo, who has escaped from Texas. When the police finally catch up with Calver and shoot him, they use the dying man to lure the priest back across the border. Calver refuses to confess but offers the priest his knife and tells him to fight his way out.

747 Cerra, Father Miguel
Former classmate of the boy Juan in the story read by Luis's mother.

748 child
A boy sent to fetch the priest for his dying mother prevents him from escaping on the riverboat.

749 Chrysogoni
The Chrysogoni, Cornelii, Cypriani, and Laurentii are Christian martyrs named in the priest's prayer for the living.

750   "Come back! Come back!"
The priest reads the ballad "Lord Ullin's Daughter," by Thomas
Campbell (1777-1844), in one of Coral's textbooks, an appropriate
choice since, unknown to him, the girl has died.

751   customs officer
Man who sees Mr. Tench at the waterfront and asks about the
teeth Tench is making for him.

752   *Domini, non sum dignus*
Lord, I am not worthy.

753   Fellows, Captain Charles
Coral's father, the manager of a banana plantation, a fairly simple
man who is complacent about the rightness of his emotions and
happy in what he considers a job suitable for a man.   After
Coral's death he leaves Mexico for England to please his wife.

754   Fellows, Coral
Precocious, brave, likable girl of about thirteen, daughter to
Captain Fellows and Trixy.   Remarkably mature, she oversees the
loading of banana boats, studies to earn a diploma from a London
correspondence school, and feeds and shelters the Whisky Priest,
to whom she explains that she lost her faith at age ten.   He
returns later to seek her help, but the family has left and Coral,
unknown to him, has died.   The cause of her death is not
specified, but the message which the mestizo brings to the priest
from Calver is written on paper which has her writing on the
other side, a strong suggestion that Calver and/or the police were
implicated in her death.

755   Fellows, Trixy
Captain Fellows' unhappy wife, a hypochondriac who seems less
mature in most respects than her young daughter.

756   "For men may come and men may go"
The priest reads from Tennyson's "The Brook" (1855) in one of
Coral's books.

757   foreman
The Lehrs' foreman finds the priest and brings him to their house.

758   girls, little
Luis's sisters, who are caught up enthusiastically in the story of Juan the martyr.

759   Governor
The Governor of Tabasco, who disbelieved the Jefe's claim that all priests in the state have been eliminated, was unhappy to learn of the Whisky Priest's attempt to escape to Vera Cruz.

760   Governor's cousin
The Governor's cousin illegally sells contraband liquor obtained from the customs office. To the priest, who wants wine for the altar and brandy for himself, he sells both but then drinks most of the wine himself.

761   guide
The muleteer hired by the priest to take him from the Lehrs' home to Las Casas receives six days' free wages when the priest decides to follow the mestizo back across the border.

762   *Hoc est enim Corpus Meum*
This is my body.

763   "I come from haunts of coot and henn"
Also from "The Brook" (See "For men may come.")

764   "Th'inclosure narrowed; the sagacious power / Of hounds and death drew nearer every hour."
The novel's epigraph is from John Dryden's poem "The Hind and the Panther" (1687).

765   Jefe
Chief of police in the capital city.

766   *Jewels Five Words Long: A Treasury of English Verse*
Coral's book which the priest finds upon his return to the plantation.

THE POWER AND THE GLORY

767 José, Padre

A fat, aging, cowardly ex-priest who saved his life by renouncing the priesthood after forty years. Taunted by children and nagged by his wife, he lives in fear and misery, believing himself in mortal sin and lacking the courage to break out of it. He refuses to hear the Whisky Priest's confession even when the lieutenant promises him that he will not come to harm by doing so.

768 José's wife

A graying woman who prides herself on being the wife of the only married priest, she keeps and feeds her husband as if he were valuable livestock. His awareness that she is calling him to bed for the 738th time implies that her sexual appetite considerably exceeds his.

769 Juan

Idealized martyr in the story read to Luis and his sisters by their mother.

770 *La Eterna Martir*

Apparent title of the book left in Mr. Tench's house by the priest. Tench hides it when he discovers that its sensational cover actually hides the priest's breviary.

771 Lehr, Miss

Mr. Lehr's kind, middle-aged sister, formerly a hotel operator, who has been living with him since the death of his wife.

772 Lehr, Mr.

German-American widower from Pennsylvania who lives comfortably with his sister across the border from Tabasco. A Lutheran who left Germany to escape military service, he disapproves of the luxuries of the Catholic church but is friendly and generous in sheltering the Whisky Priest.

773 lieutenant

A young police officer whose ascetic way of life and single-minded devotion to his ideals make him more priest-like in many respects than his antagonist, the Whisky Priest, whom he is determined to capture. The victim of an unhappy, impoverished childhood, he holds the church responsible for social evil and injustice in his country, and he is determined to destroy the church even if he must act ruthlessly to do so.   His belief that the world is meaningless and life purposeless seems ultimately contradicted by his own love of children and his determination to eradicate suffering.   The death of the humble priest, who has called the lieutenant a good man, leaves him with a sense of emptiness rather than the satisfaction he had anticipated.

774   Long, Senator Hiram
Mr. Lehr may mean Senator Huey P. Long of Louisiana (1893-1935); there was no Senator Hiram Long.

775   Lopez
Ticket agent from whom the priest expects help with passage to Vera Cruz on the *General Obregon.*   However, Lopez was executed several weeks earlier for helping undesirables escape.

776   Luis
Inquisitive fourteen-year-old boy whose interest and belief are no longer sustained by the idealized stories of the faith read to him by his mother.   He begins to admire a new ideal of heroism in the lieutenant, but after the execution of the Whisky Priest he turns bitterly against the young officer and spits at him when he passes their house.   Later that night he admits a newly-arrived priest into the house.

777   Luis's father
Better educated and more realistic than his pious wife, he speaks stoically of the need to go on living, to look beyond the ruin of the church to the prospect of life in the secular state.

778   Luis's mother
A gentle, devout woman who reads stories of the faith to her children and worries that her son's faith may have been damaged by his contact with the Whisky Priest, whom they once sheltered in their house.   She is dismayed by the boy's impatient, questioning attitude.

779 Madero
Apparently Francisco Madero (1873-1913), Mexican revolutionary
leader, a democrat and social reformer, who led the overthrow of
the Diaz regime in 1911 and served as president from 1911 to
1913. After the death of the Whisky Priest and before the arrival
of the new priest, Luis feels an enormous sadness that the last
priest and last heroes--Madero, Villa, and Zapata--have died.

780 man, old (in jail)
An old man imprisoned for possessing a crucifix calls out feebly
for "Caterina," his daughter.

781 man, old (in village)
Pleads with the weary priest to hear confessions in case the
soldiers should arrive before he can hear them the next day. The
old man has not been to confession in five years.

782 manager
The local hotel manager sends for the Governor's cousin while
allowing the priest and the beggar to wait in a hotel room to buy
wine.

783 Maria
Brigitta's mother, a peasant woman who was the priest's lover one
time, seven years ago. In their brief reunion in the novel, she
urges him to escape over the border, arguing that if he should be
captured and killed, his martyrdom would be a mockery.

784 mestizo
A miserable half-breed whose very filthiness and ugliness--
especially his fang-like teeth and yellow eyes--seem expressive of
his venality and treachery. Immediately recognizable as a Judas-
figure who wants to betray the priest for money, he misses his
first chance to do so when he falls ill with fever and is too weak
to follow his victim. Later he fails to recognize the priest in the
capital city, but he finally succeeds when the police employ him to
lure the priest back across the border to attend the dying
murderer Calver. The mestizo is pitied by the priest, who reflects
upon the terrible responsibility the man assumes. Such men, the

priest realizes, help one to understand the passion of Christ, since only a God could love, and die for, such a wretched specimen of humanity.

785 Miguel
Young man taken as hostage by the police when the people of his village refuse to identify the Whisky Priest. The priest sees him later in the yard of the jail.

786 mongrel bitch
At the plantation, in the final stages of his deprivation and humiliation, the priest is reduced to taking a bone with scraps of meat on it from a starving mongrel too weak to fight.

787 Montez, Pedro
A hostage murdered in Concepcion by police hunting the priest; later the priest gives the name "Montez" to the police who arrest him for possessing brandy.

788 Montez (Pedro's father)
Pedro's father, who sat beside the priest at the dinner given in Concepcion for the tenth anniversary of his ordination. The elder Montez spoke at length about the interests of the church, including his desire to start a Society of St. Vincent de Paul.

789 murderer (in jail)
A prisoner in the jail cell boasts of having murdered a man for insulting his mother and taunts the priest by saying that Christianity makes men cowardly.

790 Norah
Trixy Fellows' sister in England, who writes to say that Trixy and the Captain can stay with her until they find a permanent home.

791 *Ora pro nobis*
Pray for us.

792 Pacifico, Don
One of Coral's correspondence lessons concerns David Pacifico, a Portuguese consul-general in Greece, who brought claims against

the Greek government after his house was burned by a mob. Because he was a British subject, the claims were supported by Palmerston and almost led to a war.

793 Palmerston, Lord (1784-1865)
British statesman who served two terms as prime minister (1855-58; 1859-65).

794 *Pater noster qui es in coelis*
"Our Father who art in heaven" (beginning of the Lord's Prayer).

795 Pedro (boy)
A ten-year-old boy who told Brigitta that her father, because he is a priest, is not a real man and does not satisfy women.

796 Pedro (villager)
A man who bargains with the priest over the price of baptisms. He has three children.

797 priest (new)
In the night following the execution of the Whisky Priest, another unnamed priest arrives in the town and is sheltered by the boy Luis.

798 priest (the "Whisky Priest")
The unnamed protagonist is the last priest in the Mexican province of Tabasco whom the police state has not killed, driven out, or forced to abandon the priesthood. Called a "Whisky Priest" because of his heavy drinking, he is a small, lonely, frightened man who sees himself as a complete failure: he has been guilty of pride, he has fathered a child, he has brought disgrace to his office.   He feels unworthy of martyrdom and despairs of his own salvation because he loves the fruit of his sin (his daughter) and therefore cannot truly repent of that sin. Yet his very humility redeems him, and in the crucial night in a packed jail cell he experiences for the first time a generous love of humanity that is imitative of Christ's love. The event transforms him so that after escaping to safety across the border he calmly accepts the call, obviously a trap, to return to help the dying

Calver. The priest is captured executed, but his death unsettles
the lieutenant who has long pursued him and inspires the boy Luis
into a belief in heroism.

799 Quintana, Father
Mentioned by Miss Lehr as a priest who escaped into Las Casas;
he promised to return but did not.

800 Red Shirt
A teenaged soldier who discovers the priest's brandy bottle and
arrests him.

801 schoolmaster
A cynical man in the Lehrs' village who asks whether the priest's
contribution to his school is intended to relieve the priest's
conscience. The reply is yes.

802 Sergeant
Forces the priest to clean the jail cells before releasing him.

803 Society of St. Vincent de Paul
See 2907.

804 Tench, Mr.
A lonely English dentist, estranged from his wife, exiled from his
home and family. He came to Mexico intending to make good
money during a five-year stay, but the fall of the peso meant that
he could never afford to leave. Without knowing the occupation
of his guest, Tench invites the priest to his house on the day the
priest attempts to escape on the *General Obregon*. At the end of
the novel he receives a letter from his wife expressing her
forgiveness of him and asking for a divorce.

805 Tench, Sylvia
Tench's wife in Southend, England. Since the death of their son,
she and her husband have exchanged letters only once in a period
of twenty years. At the end of the novel she sends a letter saying
that she has joined the Oxford Group and that she forgives him
but wants a divorce. (See 694.)

806 Villa
Pancho Villa (c.1877-1923), Mexican bandit and revolutionary.
(See Madero.)

807 woman, Indian
An Indian woman whose three-year-old son has been shot by
police (Calver used the boy as a shield) encounters the priest after
his second visit to the banana plantation. The child dies, and the
priest travels with the mother across the mountains until they find
a Christian graveyard where she can bury him.

808 woman, peasant
An old peasant woman who has no food offers to give the priest
coffee.

809 woman, pious
A pious woman, who may have been jailed for displaying religious
pictures, begs the priest to hear her confession during his night in
the cell. Self-righteous and judgmental, she scorns her fellow-
prisoners, and when the priest confesses some of his own failings
to her, she condemns him as a bad priest who does not deserve
to live.

810 Zapata
Emiliano Zapata (c.1879-1919), Mexican Indian revolutionary who
fought against the federal Mexican governments for a decade in
an effort to repossess Indian lands. (See Madero.)

THE MINISTRY OF FEAR (1943)

811 A.B.C.
Tea shop in Clapham where Rowe has breakfast, one of a chain
operated by the Aerated Bread Company.

812 A.F.S.
Auxiliary Fire Service.

813 A.R.P.
Air Raid Precautions.

814 *The Ambassador's Diamonds*
Rowe imagines telling his mother that the history of society in his
time is contained in this and hundreds of other books, primarily
inexpensive editions, about crime, espionage, and the like. The
other titles he mentions are *Death in Piccadilly, Diplomacy, Seven
Days' Leave*, and *The Theft of Naval Papers*.

815 aunt
Rowe dreams of a small town where he used to stay with his aunt.

816 B.A.T.
Telephone exchange code for Battersea.

817 Baker
Sir Samuel White Baker (1821-93), British traveler, best known for
his exploration of the sources of the Nile and his naming of Lake
Albert. He was one of the African explorers Rowe loved to read
about in boyhood.

818 Balfour, Arthur (1848-1930)
British statesman and politician, a Conservative who held many
important positions and was prime minister (1902-05).   The
detective Prentice is described as having Balfour's "faineant"
attitude, giving the impression of idleness.

819 bank manager
A familiar face from Rowe's peaceful childhood, recalled in one
of his dreams.

820 Barnes
Major Stone's friend who was killed "on the beach," possibly by
Forester or Poole (159).

821 Battersea
Area of London south of the Thames, between Chelsea and
Clapham.

822 Beale
Policeman who takes down Rowe's statements to Graves and
Prentice at Scotland Yard.

823 Bellairs, Mrs.
A member of the spy ring, the fortune-teller at the fête in
Bloomsbury who tells Rowe the correct weight to guess for the
cake. Later he attends a seance at her house.

824 Boojie
Rowe's schoolboy nickname.

825 *Book of Golden Deeds*
Book by Charlotte M. Yonge.

826 Boyle
Mentioned as a friend of Rowe.

827 Brantôme, illustrated
A book examined by Fullove in the shop across from the Orthotex
office. Pierre de Bourdeilles, Seigneur de Brantôme (c.1530-1614),
wrote *Vies des dames galantes* and other detailed, scandalous
portraits of the courtly life of his times.

828 Bridges
Clerk in the tailoring shop where Cost works.

829 "brightness of immortality"
One of many allusions to Wordsworth's "Immortality Ode."

830 Brixton
Johns refers to Brixton Prison in south London.

831 Brothers
Young policeman who models himself after Prentice.

832   Burton
Sir Richard Francis Burton (1821-90), English traveler, author,
translator, and diplomat, one of the African explorers Rowe read
about during his boyhood.

833   Campden Hill
Area of London in Kensington, near Holland Park. Mrs. Bellairs
lives in Campden Hill.

834   Casement
Sir Roger Casement (1864-1916), Irish-born British consular
official, was executed for high treason for his attempt to lead the
Sinn Fein rebellion.   Johns tells Rowe that the present war
involves many individuals committed to ideology, whereas in the
last, "except for Irishmen like Casement--the pay was always cash"
(134).

835   Charles's Wain
A northern constellation, more often called the Great Bear. After
the bomb strikes the house where Rowe rooms, he sees Charles's
Wain, i.e., the night sky, since the roof has been destroyed.

836   chemist and his wife
See girl in dream.

837   Chief Constable
According to Prentice, the chief constable in the provincial town
where Dr. Forester's sanatorium is located served twenty years in
the Indian army and is a discriminating judge of port but is
ill-suited to pursue a group of sophisticated spies.

838   Collier
A member of the group at Mrs. Bellairs' seance, patronized yet
admired for rising from the lower classes. Formerly a head-waiter,
a tramp, and a stoker, he had written a book of "rough but
spiritual" poetry (54).

839   Comforts for Mothers of the Free Nations
Charitable organization based in London, used as a front by Willi
Hilfe and other members of a Nazi spy ring.

840 Conway
An amnesiac who committed suicide after Dr. Forester told him
about his past.

841 Cost, Mr.
"Cost" has three identities: as the "business" member of the
seance group he is Mr. Cost, who is the victim of the fake murder
that sends Rowe into hiding; as Mr. Travers he is the book buyer,
seen by Davis but not by Rowe, to whose room in the Regal
Court Hotel Rowe delivers Fullove's case; as Mr. Ford he is a
tailor in a West End shop who uses his special skill to conceal
microfilm in the shoulder pads of gentlemen's suits. He kills
himself when both Davis and Rowe arrive at his shop.

842 Cradbrooke, the Dowager Lady
A backer or sponsor of the Free Mothers organization. Her name
is used in letters of thanks to donors.

843 Cromwell, life of
See *Heroes.*

844 Crooks
Crooks, Curtis, Perry, and Vane are mentioned as Rowe's friends
who "faded away" after his arrest in the death of his wife.

845 Curtis, Tom
See Crooks.

846 Damien
One of Rowe's boyhood heroes was Father Damien (1840-89), a
Belgian priest and missionary who served many years in the leper
colony on Moloka and eventually died of leprosy there.

847 David
See Ernest.

848 *David Copperfield*
Rowe often rereads Dickens's novels *David Copperfield* and *The
Old Curiosity Shop*, not because he likes them but because he
read them in childhood and they hold "no adult memories" (15).

849   Davis (hotel clerk)
Clerk at the Regal Court Hotel who insists that Rowe remain with
the books he brought there and wait for Mr. Travers.   He
identifies Rowe at Scotland Yard and then helps to identify
Travers-Ford-Cost.

850   Davis (patient)
A patient confined to Dr. Forester's sick bay because he cried too
readily.

851   dentist
See girl in dream.

852   Dermody, Mrs.
Worker at the Free Mothers office who gets Mrs. Bellairs' address
for Rowe.

853   Digby, Richard
Name given to Rowe in Dr. Forester's sanatorium.

854   "Don't tell me the past.   Tell me the future."
The code identifying the person to whom Mrs. Bellairs is to give
the correct information for the weight of the cake containing
microfilm.

855   Dunwoody
Prentice accidentally reveals to Rowe that a man named
Dunwoody was responsible for passing secret papers from the
Ministry of Home Security into enemy hands for photographing.
The name had been kept secret because Dunwoody is the son of
a "grand old man" (207).

856   Dunwoody, Lady
Friend of Hilfe who helps to arrange his planned escape to
Ireland.

857   Ernest, David, and Minny
Rowe, trying to locate the person to whom Cost's last telephone
call was directed, is mistaken for "Ernest" by a "torrential voice"
who tells him about the death of Minny, a cat, in the air raids on

the preceding night. The voice says that "David" still hopes Minny survived (222).

858 Fishguard
Fishguard and Still, patients at Forester's sanatorium, subdue their quarrels over tennis and chess because they fear the sick bay. "They had signed away their freedom to Dr. Forester in the hope of escaping worse" (141).

859 Ford
The name used by Cost in his work as tailor.

860 Forester, Dr.
An elderly doctor whose kindly manner masks his inhumane cruelty. An idealist tinged with madness, Forester was already on the fringes of respectability before he entered the services of the Nazis, for whom he keeps the sanatorium in which Rowe and other enemies are imprisoned and, if necessary, murdered or subjected to psychological torture.

861 Fullove
Dusty, raggedy man with carious teeth who poses as a bookseller and lures Rowe into the Regal Court Hotel where the suitcase Rowe delivers for him explodes.

862 George Medal
For her heroic service as an air raid warden, Doris Wilcox was posthumously awarded the George Medal, a decoration instituted by King George VI, awarded to civilians for gallantry.

863 girl in dream
Rowe, sleeping in an air raid shelter after his escape from Mrs. Bellairs' house, has a surreal dream in which he stands in a pub yard awaiting a girl "much older than himself" who later in the dream becomes vaguely identified with his wife Alice (71). Other familiar faces in the dream include a chemist and his wife, a bank manager, a blue-chinned dentist, and a policeman who speaks in a woman's voice and tells Rowe that this is home, that there isn't anywhere else.

864 Graves
Plump police officer who first interrogates Rowe at Scotland Yard.
A specialist in "the passionate crimes of railway porters" (177), he
is distrustful of the more exotic investigations carried on by
Prentice.

865 Griggs, Mr.
"Inefficient" dentist under whom Rowe suffered in boyhood (97).
Rowe attributes his own understanding of pain to his experiences
with Griggs.

866 Guilford St.
A street in Bloomsbury, London, the site of Mrs. Purvis's house,
in which Rowe has a room.

867 "Have they brought home the haunch?"
In Yonge's *The Little Duke*, from which this epigraph is taken,
young Richard boasts to his aunt Astrida of having shot a deer on
the hunt; the question is her reply.

868 *Heroes and Hero-Worship* (1841)
Rowe finds among Poole's books this collection of Thomas
Carlyle's lectures in which history is interpreted as the
achievements of great men.   Poole, who as a Nazi would
presumably admire conquerors, also has biographies of Napoleon
and Cromwell, whom Carlyle writes about in his lecture on the
hero as king.

869 Hilfe, Anna
Willi Hilfe's sister, who has been loyal to him out of love even
though she is aware of his criminal activities. Her sympathy and
love for Rowe, however, demonstrate in her the humanity her
brother lacks; to her, death is still something that matters, and in
the end she sides with Rowe against Willi. As the only character
who understands the nature of Rowe's private suffering, she hopes
that he will not regain his memory, and to protect her he will
pretend, in their future together, that he has not regained it.

870 Hilfe, Willi
Charming, well-mannered, exceedingly handsome Austrian leader

of the Nazi spy ring operating in London. His show of willingness to help Rowe makes him seem a valuable friend, but even in his friendliness Rowe detects "an amusing nihilistic abandon" (49) which is the flip side of Hilfe's complete lack of human feeling. He orders the murders of Rowe, the detective Jones, and even his own sister, and when he is cornered with no hope of escape he takes pleasure in the destruction of Rowe's happiness by revealing that Rowe is a murderer. Hilfe takes his own life rather than risk torture and imprisonment.

871 hyoscine
Scopolamine, used by Rowe to poison his wife, and by Poole in his attempt to poison Rowe.

872 Isaacs, Mr.
Rowe asks for "Mr. Isaacs" when he dials a number in an attempt to discover where Cost's final call was directed.

873 Jack
Boy whose fortune was told by Mrs. Bellairs at the fête.

874 Jerusalem in the mind's eye of Christ when he wept
An allusion to Luke 19: 41-44, in which Jesus weeps as he foresees Jerusalem besieged by an enemy who "shall lay thee even with the ground, and thy children within thee . . . and not leave in thee one stone upon another. . . ." Rowe, whose amnesia has erased all memory of the blitz, sees the desolation of London from Prentice's car and concludes that it must have been what Jerusalem looked like in the mind's eye of Christ.

875 Johns
Idealistic young pacifist who works for Dr. Forester and admires him as a noble man persecuted by people of inferior understanding. Johns befriends Rowe and slowly begins to accept Rowe's suggestion that Forester mistreats his patients. Johns kills the doctor when he discovers that Forester has murdered Major Stone.

876 Jones, Mr.
Detective assigned by Orthotex to assist Rowe. He follows Rowe

to the office of the Free Mothers, is spotted by Willi Hilfe, and
is murdered by Nazi agents.

877 Jubilee
The Silver Jubilee (twenty-fifth anniversary) of King George V, 6
May 1935.

878 L.C.C.
London County Council.

879 lady, intense whimsical
Manager of the raffle at the fête.

880 lady, middle-aged
Offers to admit Rowe to the fête at a reduced rate if he wants to
wait another five minutes.

881 Le Queux, William (1864-1927)
Prolific English writer of thrillers. When Rowe imagines telling his
mother that the world has been remade by William LeQueux, he
is surely thinking of LeQueux's books in which England is
endangered by Germany or other hostile nations: *England's Peril*
(1899), *The Invasion of 1910, with a Full Account of the Siege of
London* (1906), *The Terror of the Air* (1920).

882 Liberty dress
A dress from Liberty's, Regent Street, well known for silks and
other fine fabrics.

883 *The Little Duke* (1854)
Juvenile novel by Charlotte M. Yonge, one of Greene's boyhood
favorites, from which the epigraphs for the novel and the chapters
are taken. (See 867.)

884 *Love in the Orient*
"Lubricious" book found beside Mrs. Bellairs' bed (203).

885 Macleod, Joseph
Heard reading a newscast on the radio.

886 maid
Mrs. Bellairs' meticulously dressed maid displays "the kind of shrewdness people learned in convents" (52).

887 man, grey-haired
An old school-mate who meets Rowe in Piccadilly Circus, invites him for a drink in a pub, tries to borrow five pounds, and sneaks away without paying the check when Rowe refuses the loan.

888 man in Homburg
Enters the W.C. where Rowe and Hilfe have their final encounter. He wears a very old Homburg pulled down over his ears and, with the noise of the bombing going on around them, understands nothing important of what Rowe and Hilfe are saying.

889 Maude, Mr.
Myopic young member of the group at Mrs. Bellairs' seance, highly attentive to Mr. Newey.

890 Mendelssohn
The music Rowe hears at the seance is probably Mendelssohn's "Fingal's Cave" overture.

891 Ministry of Fear
Johns coins the phrase "ministry of fear" to describe the Nazi spies' creation of an atmosphere of mistrust and fear. Greene's title came from Wordsworth's *Prelude* (1850).

892 Minny
See Ernest.

893 "My peace I give unto you."
Rowe, reminded by the fête of his peaceful childhood, recalls Christ's words in John 14: 27. "Peace I leave with you, my peace I give unto you: not as the world giveth, give I unto you. Let not your heart be troubled, neither let it be afraid."

894 Newey, Frederick
Gray-haired, sandal-wearing member of the group at Mrs. Bellairs' seance.

895 Newey, Mrs.
Wants her husband to return to Welwyn before the raids begin in
the evening.

896 nurse
Rowe's childhood nurse could not understand his frantic efforts to
kill a suffering rat. (See Spot.)

897 Oates
Lawrence Edward Oates (1880-1912), English explorer, a member
of Scott's ill-fated Antarctic expedition who, crippled by frostbite
on the return journey, walked out into the blizzard and sacrificed
his own life in the hope that his companions would have a chance
to survive without him.

898 *The Old Curiosity Shop*
See *David Copperfield*.

899 Orpheus
When Rowe goes to the Hilfes' flat after discovering Willi's role
in the spy ring, he finds Willi asleep with a copy of Rilke's
Sonnets to Orpheus (1922) beside him. The lines he has been
reading from the fifth sonnet assert that Orpheus undergoes many
metamorphoses, but "wherever music is, there is Orpheus."

900 Orthotex
Detective agency in Chancery Lane, advertised as the oldest in
London, hired by Rowe to investigate the attempt on his life by
Poole.

901 page
Takes Rowe to the room of "Mr. Travers" at the Regal Court,
then locks Rowe in the room.

902 Pantil, Miss
Member of the group at Mrs. Bellairs' seance, described as having
"quite extraordinary powers of painting the inner world" (53).

903 Pauling and Crosthwaite
Tailoring firm which employs Cost-Ford-Travers.

904 Perry
See Crooks.

905 police officer
Plainclothes policeman who awaits Rowe outside Rennit's office
but is too easily spotted to be effective.

906 policeman
See girl in dream.

907 Pool, the
The Pool of London, a stretch of the Thames between London
Bridge and Limehouse, used heavily by commercial ships.

908 Poole
A "dwarfish man with huge twisted shoulders and an arrogant
face" (143) who tries to poison Rowe at Mrs. Purvis's and retrieve
the microfilm from Rowe's cake. He is the photographer for the
spy ring and the keeper of the sick bay at Dr. Forester's
sanatorium.

909 Post Warden
Officer in charge of the funeral procession for Doris Wilcox.

910 Prentice
Scotland Yard detective who has been investigating the spy ring
and welcomes Rowe's evidence. Despite his calm exterior of
tweeds, a "drooping grey Edwardian moustache," and a calm
manner, he is surprisingly energetic in his pursuit and ruthless in
his treatment of the criminals.

911 *The Psycho-Analysis of Everyday Life*
One of Dr. Forester's books. (Greene may have had in mind
Freud's *The Psychopathology of Everyday Life*, 1904.)

912 Purley
Town near Croydon, just south of London.

913   Purvis, Mr.
Mrs. Purvis's late husband, whose memory is preserved in his
photograph in a World War I military uniform.

914   Purvis, Mrs.
Rowe's landlady, who after the death of her husband has been
unable to control her inordinate appetite for sweets.

915   Regal Court
The hotel where Rowe delivers Mr. Fullove's books, meets Anna
Hilfe, and is injured by the explosion.   In the autograph
manuscript this hotel is the Mount Royal, a large, well-known
hotel near Marble Arch. (See 2722, 2902.)

916   Rennit, Mr.
Head of the Orthotex detective agency, whose work chiefly
involves spying in divorce cases. He is highly suspicious of Rowe.

917   Rip Van Winkle
Character in Washington Irving's story "Rip Van Winkle" (1819)
who falls asleep for twenty years. Rowe, as his memory begins to
return, feels like Rip Van Winkle waking up.

918   Rowe, Alice
Rowe's wife, whom he killed because he could not bear to see her
suffering in a terminal illness. She was able to bear the suffering
better than he, but rather than go on living with a man she
suspected of trying to poison her, she "gave herself sadly up and
took the milk" containing hyoscine (59).

919   Rowe, Arthur
The middle-aged protagonist, a former journalist whose excess of
pity led him to the mercy-killing of his wife and consequent
destruction of his own innocence and hope.   Living alone and
essentially friendless since his release from psychiatric care, he
rereads books of his boyhood and longs for the peace and
innocence of the past.   When nostalgia draws him to a charity
bazaar, he wins a cake containing hidden microfilm on which
stolen naval plans have been photographed. The Nazi spy ring
into whose operations he has blundered tries first to kill him and

then to drive him into hiding by framing him for murder; their second attempt to murder him involves an explosive device which injures him severely enough to produce amnesia. Rowe awakens in a seemingly pleasant rural sanatorium as Digby, a happy man with no knowledge of his own past. Slowly, however, he regains memory and realizes that his caretaker is actually a member of the spy ring. He escapes, reports to Scotland Yard, and assists the police in tracking down all of the spies except Willi Hilfe, brother of the woman with whom he has fallen in love. Rowe pursues Hilfe, recovers the second microfilm copy of the government documents, and learns from Hilfe the truth of his own past, knowledge he will conceal from Anna so that in their future together she will believe him happier than he really is.

920   Rowe's mother
In imaginary conversations with his deceased mother, Rowe explains how terrifyingly different the contemporary world is from the one he knew as a child.

921   Savage, Miss
Sunday school teacher who participated in the fêtes Rowe remembers from childhood. She read books about "spies, murder, and violence" (68).

922   Scott, Captain
Robert Falcon Scott (1868-1912), British explorer of the Antarctic who perished with his men as they were returning from an expedition to the South Pole. Rowe was "brought up" on the stories of heroes like Scott, who represent to him a time when life was "simpler and grander" (187).   (See 1132.)

923   Sebastopol (Sevastopol)
Rowe reasons that Tolstoy could "preach non-resistance" because he had experienced a violent and heroic hour at Sevastopol (151). Tolstoy led a defense battery in the siege of Sevastopol (1854-55) in the Crimean War.

924   "Set a watch, O Lord, before my mouth"
Rowe, sitting in Rennit's office, remembers Psalms 141:3-4, in which the psalmist asks for protection from temptation to do evil.

925 Sinclair
Clergyman and member of the spy-ring. He tries to prevent Rowe
from leaving the fête with the cake containing microfilm. He
turns up later at Dr. Forester's institution while Prentice is
investigating the deaths of Forester and others.

926 Smythe-Philipps, Miss J.A.
Donor of tea and flour to the Free Mothers.

927 Spot
Rowe recalls a boyhood incident in which he saw a rat being
tossed by a dog named Spot; he killed the rat because he could
not bear to see it suffer.

928 Stanley
Sir Henry Morton Stanley (1841-1904), Welsh-born explorer and
journalist whose most famous adventure involved his journey, in
the employ of the *New York Herald*, to find Dr. Livingstone, who
had been in Africa for some five years when Stanley reached him
at Ujiji in 1871. Stanley was one of the African explorers Rowe
loved to read about in boyhood.

929 Steiner, Rudolf
(1861-1925) German occultist and social philosopher. Steiner
departed from his early devotion to Theosophy and established his
own system which he called "anthrosophy," which involved the
interpretation of the world through humanity's spiritual nature.

930 Still
See Fishguard.

931 Stone, Major
Patient at Forester's sanatorium, murdered by Forester after
intruding upon a secret conversation between Forester and Poole.
Although Stone's mind is not entirely clear, he rightly suspects
"treachery" when he sees men digging on the island.

932 Stone's wife
Major Stone tells Rowe he had a wife who went away because of
the treachery.

933 superintendent
According to Prentice, the superintendent of police in the small provincial town where Forester's sanatorium is located is a good man but would never have lasted with Scotland Yard and is ill-suited to deal with a group of sophisticated spies.

934 Tatham, Mr.
Provided currants for the cake won by Rowe.

935 ticket collector
The ticket collector at the station to which Rowe goes after his escape from the sanatorium recognizes him as one of Dr. Forester's patients and tries to get him to return.

936 Topling, Canon
Clergyman associated with the legitimate activities of the Free Mothers. According to Anna, he is trustworthy.

937 Travers, Mr.
See Cost.

938 Trench
Willi Hilfe cancels an appointment with Trench in order to take Rowe to see Mrs. Bellairs.

939 Troup, Mrs.
Keeper of the general store and post office, a familiar figure at the fêtes Rowe recalls from the Cambridgeshire days of his childhood.

940 Vane
See Crooks.

941 *What I Believe* (1883)
Rowe's discovery that Dr. Forester has erased his own pencil marks from this book by Tolstoy arouses Rowe's suspicion and mistrust. (Forester had erased the markings by Tolstoy's attack on patriotism.)

942   Wilcox, Doris
Athletic, domineering wife of Henry Wilcox, killed by a falling wall
while on duty as an air raid warden.

943   Wilcox, Henry
The only friend who has remained loyal to Rowe after his arrest
for the murder of Alice. Rowe visits Wilcox to ask him to cash
a check but arrives awkwardly just before the funeral of Henry's
wife Doris.

944   Wilcox, Mrs.
Henry's mother.

945   William Rufus
Rowe recalls being taught in school that William Rufus (William
II, r. 1087-1100) was a wicked king, but says that children could
not be expected to hate him.

946   Wilson
One of the people Rowe telephones in his attempt to identify the
person Cost telephoned before dying.

947   woman, old
A woman on the train in Paddington Station innocently but
effectively renders Hilfe harmless by winding her knitting wool
around his hands.

948   woman, stout
Customer at the fête who laughs at Rowe's estimate of the cake's
weight.

949   Woolton, Lord
Frederick James Marquis Woolton (1883-1964), British politician
and businessman, was in charge of the Ministry of Food from
1940, with the responsibility of overseeing the nourishment of the
country in wartime. Fullove's comment "If Lord Woolton knew"
(100) refers to his own feeding of human food (bread crumbs) to
the birds.

THE HEART OF THE MATTER (1948)

950 A.T.S.
Auxiliary Territorial Service (British Women's Service during World War II).

951 Ali
Scobie's steward who has served him for fifteen years, first as small boy and then as assistant steward. When Scobie reveals to Yusef that Ali knows of Yusef's illegal activities, Yusef has Ali murdered. Scobie's love for Ali, based upon friendship and loyalty, may be his only love that is not qualified by pity.

952 *Allan Quartermain* (1887)
Popular adventure tale by H. Rider Haggard (1856-1925).

953 Aranjunez, Senor
Friend with whom the Portuguese captain stayed one night in the port of Lobito.

954 Aristides
Athenian statesman and general (c. 530-468 B.C.), known as "the Just."

955 atabrine
Trademark for quinacrine hydrochloride, a synthetic drug used in treating malaria.

956 Bad Man
Nickname give Scobie by the natives when he stopped investigating their petty quarrels between landlords or landladies and tenants.

957 Bagster, Freddie
Flight lieutenant who befriends and attempts to seduce Helen
Rolt.

958 Bailey
A corrupt police officer who had a safety deposit box in a
different town.

959 Baker
The man announced as coming from Gambia to replace the
retiring Commissioner and thus to assume the post many believe
Scobie should have.

960 Barlows, the Tom
Friends of Louise who have left Sierra Leone. She says that since
their departure she has no friends.

961 *Bengal Lancer*
Wilson probably has in mind Henry Hathaway's 1935 film *Lives of
a Bengal Lancer.*

962 *A Bishop among the Bantus*
Asked by Mrs. Bowles to read to a small boy who is recovering
in the mission infirmary, Scobie pretends to read this missionary's
story (which Mrs. Bowles has approved) but actually makes up an
adventure story more likely to entertain the child.

963 Boling
A neighbor of Wilson and Harris who is responsible for the
sewers.

964 Bowers
Mentioned as having been sent back to England after punching
the Assistant District Commissioner at a party.

965 Bowles, Mr. and Mrs.
Missionaries at Pende. Mrs. Bowles attends patients in the rest
house; Mr. Bowles reads the funeral service for the little girl who
dies after surviving in an open boat for forty-two days.

966 Boyston
A corrupt police officer who was retired for ill health because charges against him could not be proved.

967 Brigstock
A naval officer.

968 Bromley, Teddy
Friend of Louise, pictured with his wife and Louise on a Yorkshire moor in a photo on Louise's dressing table.

969 Brown
Apparently not a character but a code name used by Yusef's small boy to gain entrance to Wilson's office. He says he has a note from "Brown."

970 Brûle, Père
Described by Scobie as "a good man" (134) who died of blackwater after twenty years in Africa without leave.

971 Bryce's *Holy Roman Empire* (1864)
A book by Oxford professor James Bryce, Viscount Bryce (1838-1922); left in Pemberton's library by Butterworth.

972 Buller, Captain
In Scobie's story, captain of Arthur Bishop's ship, which is attacked by Blackbeard.

973 Butterworth
Former D.C. at Bamba who became ill and was replaced by Pemberton.

974 Calloway
A censor who, like Mrs. Carter, reads mail.

975 Canute (c. 994-1035)
King of England (1016-1035) and of Denmark (1018-1035). In a familiar story in Holinshed's *Chronicles*, Canute sat by the shore and ordered the tide to stop rising; when it did not, he castigated

his courtiers for their flattery, telling them that although they called him king, he could not even command the water.

976 Captain, Portuguese
Portuguese captain of the *Esperanca* who conceals a letter to his daughter in the cap of the cistern in his bathroom. Against regulations, Scobie opens it, reads it, and destroys it after judging it harmless. For his kindness the Captain later gives him a medallion with the figure of a saint whose name he cannot remember.

977 Carter, Mrs.
A censor who reads mail, she is kind to Helen Rolt, to whom she gives a pouf and a bottle of gin.

978 Castel, Mrs.
Louise's friend who brings her the news of Scobie's being passed over for the Commissionership. She says that Louise could be a professional writer.

979 Clay, Father
Priest in the mission of Bamba, with short red hair and a "young, freckled Liverpool face" (94). Scobie visits him to get an account of what happened to Pemberton. Father Clay once did duty at Liverpool Gaol.

980 Clive
Employee in the Agricultural Department, a neighbor to Wilson and Harris.

981 Collinses
Friends of Louise, now living in South Africa.

982 Commissioner
The Police Commissioner, retiring after twenty-two years' service, calls Scobie to his office in order to express his regret that Scobie will not succeed him.

983 Cooper, Major
A dentist who invites Wilson to the Cape Station club.

984 Coriolanus
Scobie is compared to Shakespeare's Coriolanus in his unwillingness to appeal for sympathy by displaying his injuries.

985 Cornforth, William P.
Cornforth's motto "The best investments are honesty and enterprise" (195) appears on a commercial calendar in Wilson's U.A.C. office.

986 Couéism
Emile Coué (1856-1926) developed a system of self-healing through auto-suggestion that attained considerable popularity during the early twentieth century.

987 Crayshaw
A corrupt police officer who was caught with stolen or smuggled diamonds.

988 *cui bono*
"Who is benefited thereby?"

989 Dane, Clemence
Pseudonym of English novelist, playwright, and critic Winifred Ashton (d. 1965). One of her books arrives at the club and is noted by Mrs. Halifax as she deals out the library books.

990 Daniel
Yusef calls Scobie a Daniel among the Colonial Police because of Scobie's insistence that his men tell the truth. The Biblical Daniel was courageous in telling the prophetic truth about dreams.

991 Davis, Batty
The savage lieutenant in Scobie's version of *A Bishop.*

992 Davis, Father
A priest Louise met in Durban; unlike Father Rank, he seemed intellectual.

993 *Death Laughs at Locksmiths*
A book Pemberton had been reading just before his death.

994 Derry
Reported thefts from the mines to the new Commissioner.

995 Director of Agriculture
Wrote a letter for the Indian fortune-teller and gave the Indian a pound for reading his palm.

996 Doomsday Records of Little Withington
The *Domesday Book* recorded land ownership, area, and value in England under William the Conqueror in 1086.

997 Downham
A private boys' school attended by Harris and Wilson.

998 Druce, Captain
Police captain who leads Field Security Police in searching the *Esperanca* and other ships.

999 Dupont, Mlle.
Ill-tempered French mistress in Helen's school at Seaport.

1000 Durand
Former police chief in French Guinea, remembered by Scobie as a Norman, a "nice fellow" who is now in prison at Dakar (134).

1001 Evans
Officer in the Field Security Police.

1002 Evipan
Medication prescribed for angina, used by Scobie to commit suicide.

1003 Fellowes
Senior sanitary inspector who got Scobie's bungalow in Cape Station, the main European quarter, while Scobie was on his most recent leave. Scobie tries to like him but finds it hard. Fellowes objects to the admission of Wilson, a civilian, to the club.

1004 Ferreira, P.
A passenger aboard the ship from Lobito, possibly an agent recruited by Wilson's organization.

1005 Fisher, Jimmy
One of the injured survivors of S.S. 43. Scobie reads to him in the hospital.

1006 Forbes and Newhall
Two elderly men who survive the torpedoing of S.S. 43.

1007 Fraser
Junior officer who despises Louise for her interest in poetry.

1008 Gambia
Country on the west coast of Africa, a British colony and protectorate which gained independence in 1965.

1009 girl
A small girl who loses both of her parents in the sinking of S.S. 43 but survives forty days and nights in an open boat. After she dies with Scobie at her side, he finds her suffering difficult to reconcile with the love of God.

1010 *The Golden Treasury*
See 1873.

1011 Groener, Frau
The Captain's daughter in Friedrichstrasse, Leipzig.

1012 Gunga Din
A water carrier for a regiment of the British army in India. Harris calls the fortune-telling Indian "Gunga Din."

1013 Halifax
An officer in the Public Works Department, tiresome for his vulgar jokes and phony good will.

1014 Halifax, Mrs.
Friend of Louise who offers to share with her a two-berth cabin

en route to South Africa. She has a poor memory and reads the same novels again and again without realizing it.

1015 Harris, H.R.
A shy, insecure cable-censor who befriends Wilson and shares a small apartment with him. Harris bears, as do many of Greene's characters, unhappy memories of his days in a public (American "private") school.

1016 Horler
Sydney Horler (1888-1954), prolific English writer of mystery novels.

1017 Indian, the
Palm reader who says the Government will be pleased with Wilson because he "will capture [his] man" (68). The Indian is right in this intuition about Wilson's occupation but wrong in predicting that Wilson will win the "lady" of his heart and "sail away."

1018 Laminah, Corporal
Policeman in Sharptown, brother of Miss Wilberforce's landlady.

1019 Lancing
Public school, mentioned as a rival to Downham; attended by Fellowes.

1020 Lane, as Bunthorne
Downhamian schoolboy in the role of Bunthorne, the character in Gilbert and Sullivan's *Patience* based upon Oscar Wilde.

1021 *"Le pêcheur est au coeur même de chrétienté. . . ."*
The novel's epigraph, from the *Nouveau Théologien* XIII (1911) by French writer Charles Péguy, may be translated as follows: "The sinner is at the very heart of Christianity. . . . No one is as competent as the sinner in the matter of Christianity. No one, unless he is a saint." In this passage Péguy is discussing François Villon. (See 2030, 3038.)

1022 little flower, the
See 2906.

1023 Loder
Chief engineer on the torpedoed liner.

1024 Longfellow
Wilson reads the American poet in Palgrave. (See 2484, 2486.)

1025 Macaulay
English writer Thomas Babington Macaulay (1800-59). (See 2408.)

1026 Maine, Sir Henry (1822-88)
Cambridge scholar, author of many books on philosophy of law,
history, and politics.

1027 Maitland's *Constitutional History*
A book left in Pemberton's library by Butterworth; published in
1908 by Frederick William Maitland (1850-1906), a Cambridge
historian.

1028 Makin
Scobie, reflecting on the power of colonial African life to drive
people mad, recalls Makin, a missionary who was sent home to a
sanitarium in Chislehurst.

1029 Malcott, Miss
A survivor of S.S. 43 who was bound for Lagos to work in the
Educational Department there.

1030 Mangan
James Clarence Mangan (1803-49), Irish poet best known for
ballads and songs, including "Dark Rosaleen" and "The Nameless
One."

1031 Mark
King Mark, husband of Isolde in Wagner's *Tristan*.

1032 Maugham, Somerset (1874-1965)
Popular English novelist whose works include *Of Human Bondage*
(1915), *The Moon and Sixpence* (1919), and *Cakes and Ale*
(1930).

1033 Maybury, Ethel
Friend of Louise, now living in South Africa.

1034 Mende Sergeant
One of Scobie's policemen.

1035 navicert
Under the navicert system a country at war certifies a friendly or
neutral ship as free of contraband so that it may pass through a
naval blockade.

1036 Parkes, D.C.
Also wrote a letter of testimonial for the Indian fortune teller.

1037 *Patience*
Operetta (1881) by Gilbert and Sullivan which satirized the
Aesthetic Movement.

1038 Pemberton, "Dicky"
The young, immature District Commissioner at Bamba, who loved
drink and gambling. He committed suicide after falling into debt,
and the fact that he owed money to Yusef's store manager may
mean that Yusef is implicated in three deaths--Pemberton's as well
as Ali's and Scobie's.

1039 Pemberton's father
After Pemberton's suicide, Scobie wonders how he would feel if
he were the young man's elderly father, a retired banker whose
wife died in childbirth.

1040 Perrot
Self-important District Commissioner at Pende.

1041 Perrot, Mrs.
Tries to ignore her overbearing husband.

1042 Pimpernel
A member of the group of Englishmen in Baroness Orczy's *The
Scarlet Pimpernel* (1905) who used disguises to deceive the French
and carry out rescues during the Reign of Terror.

1043 Prog
A member of Wilson's house at Downham.

1044 Protectorate
Under British rule, Sierra Leone included both the Crown Colony,
of which Freetown was a part, and the larger Protectorate.

1045 Quartermain, Allan
Hero of the popular adventure stories *King Solomon's Mines* and
Allan Quartermain, by H. Rider Haggard (1856-1925).

1046 Rank, Father
The weary priest who left his comfortable English parish in
Northampton in an effort to discover some way of being useful to
God. A modest man without illusions about his powers of
intellect or devotion, he doubts after years of hard service that he
has accomplished much of value. When Scobie, who has earlier
been a symbolic father-confessor to him, comes to confession, he
refuses the unhappy man absolution because Scobie will not vow
to stop seeing Helen. After Scobie's death, however, he refuses
to believe that Scobie is damned, and he reminds the
unsympathetic Louise that no one can know "what goes on in a
single human heart" (320).

1047 Rees
A Naval Intelligence officer.

1048 Reith
The snobbish chief Assistant Colonial Secretary, who enjoys only
his own company and dines alone.

1049 Robinson
The bank manager, embittered by his failure to receive a post in
Nigeria, refuses to lend Scobie the 250 pounds needed to send
Louise to South Africa.

1050 Robinson, Molly
Robinson's wife.

1051   Rolt, Helen
A widow of nineteen (her husband John died in the war) and a
victim of the shipwreck, Helen is befriended by Scobie during her
recovery. The two fall in love and begin an affair during Louise's
absence, and Scobie begins to assume responsibility for Helen's
happiness as he has done for Louise's. When Helen doubts the
strength of his affection, he declares his love in a letter which
Yusef intercepts and uses to blackmail him.

1052   Scobie, Catherine
The Scobies' young daughter, who died at Bexhill in England while
Major Scobie was in Sierra Leone.

1053   Scobie, Henry
The protagonist, an assistant commissioner of police in Sierra
Leone with a distinguished record of honesty and integrity; his
record and his proud uprightness have earned enemies, however,
and he is passed over for promotion. Short of cash but concerned
to ease the disappointment and unhappiness of his neurotic wife
Louise, whom he pities but no longer loves, he borrows money
from the unscrupulous Yusef in order to send Louise on a holiday
to South Africa.   While she is away he visits survivors of a
torpedoed ship, one of whom is a suffering child who arouses such
intense pity in Scobie that he prays for God to take away his own
peace and give it to the little girl.   The prayer seems to be
answered: the child dies, and almost immediately afterward Scobie
begins an affair with a young widow, Helen Rolt, although
circumstances make it impossible for them to be happy.   Soon
Scobie realizes that the happiness of two women now depends
upon him. His situation worsens when Yusef intercepts a letter
to Helen and uses it to blackmail Scobie into assisting him in the
smuggling of diamonds; and he places his soul in torment by
receiving the Eucharist when he is not in a state of grace.
Unwilling to go on harming Helen or Louise, and unwilling to
continue to act blasphemously, he fakes an angina attack and
commits suicide.

1054   Scobie, Louise
A neurotic woman whose interests in art and literature make her
ill-suited to the colonial life in which the war has stranded her.

Looked upon contemptuously as the "city intellectual" (5) by people like Harris, Louise spends much of her time in lonely dejection.   Her husband mistakenly believes that he has successfully concealed the decline of his love for her since the death of their daughter. Louise still loves Scobie, however, and rejects the sophomoric advances of the infatuated Wilson. Louise is not deceived by Scobie's fake suicide, which leaves her with bitterness.

1055 small boy
Term applied to junior servants, young and inferior in rank.

1056 small boy, Tallit's
Secretly in the employ of Yusef, Tallit's small boy substitutes the parrot with diamonds in its crop for the one Tallit's cousin intended to take.

1057 small boy, Yusef's
Reveals to Wilson details of a visit Scobie paid to Yusef.

1058 Snakey
A squinting woman seen in one of Harris's photographs; known by both Wilson and Harris at Downham.

1059 Sykes, Dr. Jessie
During conversation over dinner at the club, she plants in Scobie the idea of faking an angina attack in order to commit suicide.

1060 Tallit
Syrian merchant, a Christian, rival to Yusef, who frames Tallit for smuggling diamonds.

1061 Tallit's cousin
Framed as a diamond smuggler by Yusef, who contrives to have his parrot switched with one that has diamonds hidden in its crop.

1062 Temne
A West African people.

1063 Thimblerigg
Junior officer, from Palestine.

1064 Ticki
Louise's nickname for Scobie.

1065 Tod
A junior officer.

1066 Travis, Dr.
A young doctor recommended to Scobie by Robinson.

1067 *Treasure Island*
Popular children's adventure story (1883) by Robert Louis Stevenson, a cousin of Greene's mother.

1068 Tristram
In the *Downhamian*, Wilson publishes a poem, dedicated to Louise Scobie, in which he identifies himself with Tristram, the ill-fated hero of the medieval romance *Tristram and Iseult* (Wagner's *Tristan and Isolde*).

1069 U.A.C.
United African Company.

1070 Undine
A sylph or water-spirit character in Fouque's fairy romance *Undine* (1811).

1071 W.A.A.F.
Women's Auxiliary Air Force.

1072 Wallace, Edgar
Wilson reads Wallace's fiction to conceal his interest in poetry. (See 643.)

1073 wharf rats
Gangs of juvenile thieves who steal from the wharf area and occasionally attack policemen.

1074 Wilberforce, Miss
Native woman who complains to Scobie in a dispute with her landlady.

1075 Wilson, E.
An M.I.5 agent sent from London to investigate diamond smuggling in Sierra Leone, Wilson poses as a clerk in a business firm. He conceals his love of poetry from his friends by feigning an interest in thrillers, but he cannot conceal his immaturity and romantic sentimentalism from Louise Scobie, with whom he falls in love. Convinced that Scobie is unworthy of Louise, he develops a hatred of the man which grows in intensity after his own rejection and humiliation by Louise.

1076 woman in Lisbon
A mistress of the captain of the *Esperanca*.

1077 Woolf, Virginia (1882-1941)
English experimental novelist, author of *Mrs. Dalloway*, *To the Lighthouse*, *The Waves*, and many other works.

1078 Wright, Colonel
Officer sent from M.I.5 in Cape Town to investigate the charges of police misconduct in the Tallit affair.

1079 Yusef
Unscrupulous Syrian merchant involved in diamond smuggling. Because he both hates and admires the upright Scobie, he longs for an opportunity to place Scobie under obligation to him; in this ambition he succeeds first by lending Scobie money for Louise's holiday, later and more dangerously by using Scobie's letter to Helen Rolt to blackmail Scobie into helping him smuggle diamonds aboard the *Esperanca*. Yusef also has Scobie's servant Ali killed to prevent Ali from discovering the illegal transaction.

THE THIRD MAN (1949)

1080 Bannock, Mrs.
Member of the literary group addressed by Martins. She objects
to Benjamin Dexter's novels because they do not tell a good story.

1081 Bates
British policeman assigned to look after Martins during the pursuit
of Lime through the Vienna sewers. He is shot and killed by
Lime.

1082 Bracer, old
School friend of Lime and Martins.

1083 Calloway, Lieutenant
The narrator, an English policeman in charge of the British zone
in post-war Vienna. He is a patient, pragmatic man who tries to
persuade Martins to leave Vienna but eventually gives credence to
Martins' doubts about the Lime case and, in the face of Martins'
persistent loyalty to his old friend, exposes Martins to the evidence
of Lime's sinister crimes. Calloway acknowledges Martins' amateur
investigation as more efficient than his own, and he volunteers in
the end to "forget" that Martins has killed Lime.

1084 Carter
Calloway's junior officer who suspects that Lime may have been
murdered and orders the body exhumed.

1085 Cooler, Colonel
Lime's American associate who brings Martins money in
accordance with the supposed dying wish of Lime. Despite his
pleasant, friendly manner he is an accomplished criminal who
progressed from comparatively harmless black market tires to
Lime's deadly penicillin racket.

1086 Crabbin
A "stout middle-aged young man" (15) who mistakes Martins
("Buck Dexter") for Benjamin Dexter, his own favorite novelist,
and arranges for Martins to speak to a local literary discussion
group on the contemporary novel in exchange for a week's room
and board.

1087 *The Curved Prow*
Crabbin's favorite among Benjamin Dexter's novels.

1088 Dexter, Benjamin
Serious novelist, a follower of Henry James but with a "wider
feminine streak" than James in both his subtle, complex style and
his personal life (30). Crabbin, an ardent admirer of Dexter,
mistakes Rollo Martins for him when Martins registers at Sacher's
Hotel as "B. Dexter."

1089 Dexter, Buck
Pseudonym of Rollo Martins, used for his paperback Western
novels.

1090 driver
The driver of the jeep that allegedly killed Harry Lime (the actual
victim was Harbin) was exonerated on the testimony of Cooler.

1091 du Maurier, Daphne (1907-89)
English novelist.

1092 Duke of Grafton
Pub in Tottenham Court Road, known by Bates and Martins.

1093 Gottman, Wolfgang
A Viennese civil servant whose bust is seen in the Central
Cemetery.

1094 Grey, Zane (1875-1939)
Popular American writer of Western novels. When asked which
writer most influenced his own work, Martins' honest reply "Grey"
is interpreted by his literary audience to mean English poet
Thomas Gray (1716-71).

1095 Hansel
Small boy who overhears the police questioning Frau Koch after
the murder of her husband; he tells his father that Martins might
be the "foreigner" who did it (63).

1096 Harbin
Lime's associate, the link between the thieves who stole penicillin
and Lime's management of the black market sales. After Harbin
became a double agent who informed the police, he was murdered
in the "accident" which supposedly killed Lime.

1097 Horseshoe
Pub in Tottenham Court Road, known by Bates and Martins.

1098 International Refugee Office
Agency in which Harry Lime held an important position.

1099 Josefstadt
Theatre where Anna Schmidt performs.

1100 journalist
A journalist recognizes Martins at the Cologne airport, flatters him
by calling him a novelist, then leaves abruptly in pursuit of the
man he was looking for, J.G. Carey.

1101 Joyce, James (1882-1941)
Irish novelist and poet.

1102 Koch, Herr
Harry Lime's former neighbor, a "little vexed man" (47) who
witnessed the accident in which Lime was supposedly killed. He
reveals to Martins what he had not revealed to the police--the
presence of a third man who carried the body to the house. He
is murdered for revealing information about the incident.

1103 Koch, Ilse
Herr Koch's enormous wife, apparently dominated by her husband.

1104 Kurtz
Lime's associate in the penicillin racket, nominally employed in

connection with the International Relief agency. He visits Martins
to express Lime's supposed dying wish that Martins be taken care
of in Vienna, but Martins instinctively distrusts him, seeing in
Kurtz's ill-fitting toupee the essence of his phoniness.

1105 Layman
A writer mentioned at the literary discussion at which Martins is
the featured guest.

1106 Lime, Harry
Long-time friend of Martins, possessed of wit and charm but
nevertheless cynical and unprincipled, possibly the "worst racketeer
who ever made a dirty living" in Vienna (24). He was trained as
a physician and had attained a distinguished post in the Relief
Organization before becoming so deeply involved in the black
market sale of adulterated penicillin that he faked his own death
and funeral to escape from police investigators. He claims to
believe in God and mercy but cares nothing for human beings.
Ironically he continues to trust Martins, who is so appalled by
Harry's crimes that he betrays his old friend to the police. Harry's
last words--"Bloody fool" (116)--may or may not express the act of
contrition Martins attributes to him.

1107 *The Lone Rider of Santa Fe*
Western by Martins.

1108 man, young
Asks for Martins' autograph at the literary discussion.

1109 Marlowe's devils
The reference is to Marlowe's *Dr. Faustus* (1604).

1110 Martins, Rollo
English writer of Westerns who goes to Vienna at the invitation
of his old friend Harry Lime to write about the Relief
Organization for which Lime works. Upon arrival he is told that
Lime has been killed in an accident, but he distrusts the police
and carries out his own investigation, eventually discovering that
Harry, now revealed as a callous racketeer, is still alive. Martins
falls in love with Anna Schmidt, Lime's girlfriend, draws Lime out

of hiding, and finally kills the badly wounded Lime himself. Calloway sees in Martins a division between "Rollo" (an impulsive, foolish lover of excitement and pleasure) and "Martins" (more thoughtful, cautious, and temperate, but also more dangerous).

1111 Milosis
Underground city in the Quartermain story. (See 1045.)

1112 O'Brien, Pat
American military policeman on the International Patrol who chivalrously protests against the Russian-directed arrest of Anna Schmidt and refuses to leave her alone with the Russian soldier while she dresses.

1113 Paine
Calloway's driver, characterized by the extreme politeness that enables him to call Martins "sir" when he has just knocked Martins down.

1114 Papa
The unnamed man who tells Martins about the death of Koch is called "Papa" by the boy Hansel.

1115 Peter Pan
Sir James Barrie's famous character, the boy who never grew up. Martins concludes that the evil Harry Lime is someone who never grew up: "evil was like Peter Pan--it carried with it the horrifying and horrible gift of eternal youth" (103).

1116 Prater
Amusement park in Vienna, site of the Great Wheel on which Martins and Lime meet.

1117 Priestley, J.B. (1894-1984)
English novelist, playwright, and critic. (See 195.)

1118 Sacher's Hotel
Famous Viennese hotel.

1119 Schmidt, Anna
Hungarian actress living in the British zone of Vienna with fake
Austrian papers provided by her lover, Harry Lime. Because of
her nationality and the fact that her father was a Nazi, she fears
that the Russians will arrest her, as they attempt to do. Martins
falls in love with her, but his revelation of Harry's criminal record
does not change her love for Lime. She leaves his funeral,
however, arm in arm with Martins.

1120 Schmidt, Mr.
Porter at Sacher's Hotel.

1121 soldier, French
Cynical member of the International Patrol who takes no serious
interest in Anna's plight but enjoys watching her as she dresses.

1122 soldier, Russian
The Russian leader of the International Patrol violates accepted
procedures by entering the British zone to arrest Anna, but he is
stopped by Calloway and Starling.

1123 Starling, Corporal
British military policeman on the International Patrol. He reports
the irregular arrest of Anna to Calloway, who arranges a
roadblock which rescues her.

1124 Susanna, St.
A portion of St. Susanna's knuckle is among Winkler's relics.

1125 von Meyersdorf, the Grafin
Member of the literary group Martins addresses.

1126 Wilbraham, Miss
Member of the literary group Martins addresses.

1127 Winkler, Dr.
Lime's medical adviser and partner, a small, stiff man of extreme
caution and exaggerated neatness. He keeps a collection of
religious relics which he regards as meaningless.

THE END OF THE AFFAIR (1951)

1128 actor, ex-
Poetry-quoting speaker who had been a familiar figure on Clapham Common before the war. Bendrix is happy to see him return in 1946.

1129 air raid warden
Apparently one of Sarah's lovers, or someone she attempted to begin an affair with. After reading her diary, Bendrix asserts that neither Dunstan nor the air raid warden mattered now.

1130 Alfred
A waiter at Rules who, by expressing his pleasure at seeing Bendrix and Sarah again after such a long absence, gives the lie to Bendrix's claim that he has been there often since Sarah ended their relationship.

1131 *The Ambitious Host*
Novel by Bendrix.

1132 "And what comes next? Is it God?"
Sarah had written this line from Browning's "In a Year" (1855) in the margin of Scott's last letter home. (See 922, 1196.)

1133 Andersen, Hans [Christian] (1895-75)
Danish writer of fairy tales. Sarah writes that the statues in churches are like the bad colored pictures in a Hans Andersen book.

1134 Arbuckle Avenue
Bendrix and Sarah go to a hotel in "Arbuckle Avenue" to make love for the first time. (See 140.)

1135 Arthur James
The name Bendrix gives to Lance Parkis when he takes the boy
with him to Smythe's flat.

1136 Ayer
Sir Alfred Jules Ayer (1910-89), Oxford professor and philosopher,
author of *Language, Truth and Logic.* (See Russell, Bertrand)

1137 Becket
St. Thomas à Becket, Archbishop of Canterbury murdered in the
cathedral by Henry II's knights in 1170.

1138 bell and candle
In the Catholic ritual of Excommunication, a candle is extinguished
as a symbol of the soul withdrawn from the sight of God; the bell
is rung to toll the symbolic death of the excommunicated soul.
Bendrix, greeted with hostility by Father Crompton, wonders if the
bell and candle will be next.

1139 Bendrix, Maurice
A moderately successful novelist who feigns an interest in Sarah,
the wife of a civil servant, in order to get material for the book
he is writing, which features a civil servant as a main character.
Unexpectedly he falls in love with her and begins a passionate
relationship which lasts five years in spite of the tension created
by his jealousies and anxieties. Accustomed only to "affairs" (he
has never known genuine love before), and unable to believe that
Sarah or anyone like her could continue to love him, Bendrix
cannot accept the fullness of Sarah's love, and makes them both
unhappy through his own jealousy and insecurity. His distrust
seems confirmed when she breaks off their relationship without
warning in 1944, leaving him desolate and more cynical than ever,
determined to substitute hatred for his failed love. His bitterness
finds an outlet when Sarah's husband Henry confesses his
suspicion that Sarah has a lover. Bendrix hires a detective to spy
on her, only to learn from her diary that the "lover" is actually
God, and that she had rejected him as part of a bargain with God
to save Bendrix's life. Understanding at last that Sarah really does
love him, he pursues her, determined to persuade her to leave her

husband, but she becomes ill and dies before he can force the issue to its final crisis.

1140 Bendrix's father
Bendrix mentions that his father, who is still living, did not call him home from school when Bendrix's mother died.

1141 Bendrix's mother
Died when Bendrix was in school.

1142 Bertram, Mr.
Sarah's father is described by her mother as a mean person who was intolerant of her practice of her Catholic faith. She defied him by having Sarah baptized secretly, and he eventually left the two of them.

1143 Bertram, Mrs.
Sarah's mother, who meets Bendrix at the cremation, goes to dinner with him, and borrows money from him as she has often done from Henry without repaying. Her sudden appearance seems an answer to Bendrix's "prayer" to Sarah to protect him from involvement with Sylvia.

1144 Besant, Sir Walter (1836-1901)
Writer, founder of the Society of Authors, and a former member of Bendrix's club, to which he presented a stag's head in 1898.

1145 Birthday Honours
Titles and other awards announced on the monarch's birthday. Henry is to be recommended for the O.B.E. (Order of the British Empire) award.

1146 Black, Sylvia
Attractive young woman whom Bendrix meets when he is interviewed by her boyfriend, the literary critic Waterbury. She takes an interest in him as a person, not just a writer, and accompanies him to Sarah's cremation in Golders Green. Bendrix likes her and realizes that he could easily win her away from Waterbury, but decides that a relationship with him would be bad

for her. The appearance of Mrs. Bertram enables him to get out of this difficult situation.

1147 Bolton case
Scandalous case of adultery, investigated successfully by Parkis, who gives Bendrix a souvenir from it--an ashtray from the Hotel Metropole, Brightlingsea.

1148 Bridges
The name Bendrix uses when he visits Smythe's flat.

1149 Brightlingsea
Coastal town in Suffolk, scene of the "Bolton case."

1150 Bristol
Hotel in "Arbuckle Avenue" where Bendrix and Sarah go. It was destroyed in the blitz.

1151 C.B.E.
Sarah's diary entry for September 12, 1944, records Henry's pleasure in being recommended, on the basis of his work in the Ministry, for the honorary title O.B.E. (Order of the British Empire); at that time he hopes to proceed eventually to C.B.E. (Commander, O.B.E.) and K.B.E. (Knight, O.B.E.). Later, Bendrix, recounting his lunch at his club with Henry on February 2, 1946, mentions that Henry has been made C.B.E. at the last Birthday Honours (presented on the monarch's birthday).

1152 Café Royal
Café in Regent St., frequented by artists and writers such as Augustus John and Aubrey Beardsley in the early twentieth century. Bendrix and Sarah meet there before going to Rules for the last time.

1153 Carter, Nick
Detective hero of American popular dime novels by John R. Coryell, Thomas C. Harbaugh, and Frederick Van Rensselaer Dey. Parkis fears that his son, by reading Nick Carter stories, will develop expectations about detectives that Parkis will be unable to satisfy.

1154   Cedar Road
Street in Clapham, south London. Smythe lives at number 16.

1155   Chief Warden
Man who kissed Sarah while Henry and the mayor were inspecting
the deep shelter at Bigwell. She returned the kiss, but nothing
further developed between the two.

1156   *The Children of the New Forest* (1847)
One of Sarah's books, a children's story by Captain Frederick
Marryat (1792-1848).

1157   Collins, Beatrice
One of Sarah's schoolmates, whose name Bendrix finds, along with
those of Miss Duncan and Mary Pippit, among the performers in
the program for a school awards ceremony.

1158   Common
Clapham Common, in south London, is a grassy expanse of about
220 acres. Bendrix inhabits a bed-sitting room on the South Side.
Henry and Sarah live at number 14 on the more fashionable
North Side, which was Graham Greene's address from 1935 until
the war made it necessary for his family to leave London.

1159   Cophetua
Legendary African king who fell in love with and married a
humble girl. Bendrix coins the phrase "Cophetua complex" to
describe his difficulty in feeling sexual desire unaccompanied by a
sense of his own mental or physical superiority. Because Sarah is
beautiful, he did not expect to fall in love with her.

1160   Crompton, Father
The priest whom Sarah had been seeing prior to her death.
Knowing of her wish to become Catholic, he tries to persuade
Henry to give her a Catholic burial, but Bendrix persuades Henry
to proceed with the plans for cremation.

1161   *The Crowned Image*
Novel by Bendrix.

1162 Discus Thrower
Henry has on his desk a copy of "The Discus Thrower," probably
the bronze statue (c. 450 B.C.) attributed to Myron.

1163 doctor (Parkis's)
After Parkis's doctor says that the ill Lance must be kept quiet,
Parkis returns Sarah's book to Henry because it excites the boy
too much.

1164 doctor (Sarah's)
Sarah's doctor says that he could have saved her life if he had
been called a few days earlier.

1165 doorkeeper, stage
Parkis strikes up a conversation with the stage doorkeeper of the
Vaudeville Theatre in order to continue his surveillance of Rules,
where Bendrix and Sarah are eating.

1166 Doyle, Conan
Sir Arthur Conan Doyle (1859-1930), creator of Sherlock Holmes,
was a member of Bendrix's club.

1167 Duncan, Miss, R.C.M.
See Collins, Beatrice.

1168 Dunstan
Henry's chief, with whom Sarah attempts unsuccessfully to begin
an affair in order to forget Bendrix.

1169 engineer
Visits the deep shelter in Bigwell-on-Sea with Henry and Sarah.

1170 "eye of newt"
Henry quotes this line from Shakespeare's witches in *Macbeth* (IV,
i) to compare Christian belief with superstition.

1171 Fauntleroy, Little Lord
Bendrix compares Lance Parkis, dressed in his best clothes to
accompany Bendrix to Cedar Road, to the protagonist of Frances

Hodgson Burnett's popular *Little Lord Fauntleroy* (1886), whose velvet suit started a fashion.

1172 Forster, E.M.(1879-1970)
English novelist.   Waterbury asks Bendrix what he thinks of Forster.

1173 Foyles
Famous large bookstore in Charing Cross Road in central London.

1174 Garvice, Charles
Member of Bendrix's club.

1175 Gibbon
Henry Miles' study has a complete set of Edward Gibbon (1737-94), best known for *The Decline and Fall of the Roman Empire*.   Bendrix doubts whether these books have been opened.

1176 girl (prostitute)
Bendrix, angry at Sarah after a quarrel, picks up a prostitute in Soho and buys her a drink but then decides he does not want her. He also picks up a girl after Sarah's death, when Henry is away at a conference, but again he is unable to feel any desire for her.

1177 Golders Green
Village in north London, site of the crematorium where Sarah's funeral is conducted. (Greene's first residence after his marriage in 1926 was at no. 8 Heathcroft, Hampstead Way, in Golders Green.)

1178 *The Golliwog at the North Pole*
One of Sarah's childhood books.   The Golliwog is a black rag-doll character in numerous stories by Florence and Bertha Upton.

1179 Gordon, General
Charles George Gordon (1833-85), British soldier and colonial administrator, killed during the siege of Khartoum by the followers of the Mahdi.   At the end of his narrative Bendrix is at work on a commissioned biography of Gordon.

1180   Gould, Nat
One of the authors for whom Bendrix's club was founded.

1181   *The Grave on the Waterfront*
Novel by Bendrix.

1182   Great Missenden
Current residence of Mrs. Bertram; a town in Buckinghamshire,
near Berkhamsted, Greene's boyhood home.

1183   Henry's father
In Henry's photograph of his father Bendrix sees a "Victorian look
of confidence, of being at home in the world" (10) which makes
Bendrix aware of how much more he has in common with the
insecure son.

1184   Henrys, one of the
Sarah is thinking of Henry II, who vowed that since God had
robbed him of the town he loved, he would rob God of what God
loved most in him.   Sarah plans to complete a similar act of
revenge by committing adultery in a hotel room in Bigwell Regis,
but finds herself unable to do so.

1185   I.L.P.
Independent Labour Party.

1186   Indian
Studies the complete works of George Eliot in the Reading Room
of the British Museum.   Bendrix cannot imagine him involved in
sexual jealousy.

1187   Isola Bella
Restaurant where Bendrix takes Mrs. Bertram for dinner; he
avoids taking her to a place where he has taken Sarah.

1188   James, Henry (1843-1916)
American-born novelist, resident in England for the most
productive period of his life.   Greene, an avid reader and admirer
of James, published essays on James in 1933 and 1936.

1189 Januarius, St. (272?-305?)
A Christian martyr, patron saint of Naples, where his head and
some of his blood are kept in the cathedral. Bendrix mentions St.
Januarius to Father Crompton as an example of the church's
dependence upon superstition.

1190 Jew
After the end of her marriage to Sarah's father, Mrs. Bertram
married a Jewish man whom she expected to be generous but
found to be mean.

1191 Jones
The prostitute Bendrix picks up in Sackville St. has a canary
named "Jones" after the client who gave it to her.

1192 Judas, jealous
Bendrix writes that if we judged them on the basis of actions
alone, rather than what we have been taught, it would be hard to
determine who loved Christ, "the jealous Judas or the cowardly
Peter" (29) (who denied Christ three times; see Matthew 26:39-75).

1193 landlady (Bendrix's)
Bendrix's landlady moves to her basement out of fear of air raids,
thus leaving Bendrix and Sarah more privacy than they had
enjoyed previously. Bendrix is injured when a bomb strikes the
house as he goes to the basement to see about her.

1194 landlady (pub)
A buxom young woman who looks at her customers with contempt
and is the object of the obscene scrawl Bendrix sees in the men's
room.

1195 Lang, Andrew (1844-1912)
English writer of considerable achievement in poetry, biography,
history, essays, and more, probably best known for his fairy tales,
including *The Blue Fairy Book* (1889). Parkis borrows one of
Sarah's childhood books by Lang for his son Lance when the boy
is ill; the child thinks the words Sarah wrote in it were especially
for him.

1196 *The Last Expedition*
One of Sarah's books, *Scott's Last Expedition* (1913), Robert
Falcon Scott's account of his fatal second Antarctic expedition.

1197 *The Last Siren*
Bendrix's jealousy and hatred are aroused when he opens the
Tatler at his club and sees a picture of Sarah and Henry attending
the gala night of this film.

1198 Lazarus
Raised from the dead by Jesus (John 11).

1199 Lewis
A Welsh liberal M.P. who, by planning to ask a question about
widows in the House of Commons, forces Henry to stay at home
evenings and allows Bendrix and Sarah to be alone together. As
Bendrix says, Lewis "made our bed for us that first night" (49).

1200 Macbeth, Lady
Bendrix alludes to Shakespeare's *Macbeth*, V, i, where Lady
Macbeth complains that "all the perfumes of Arabia" will not
remove the smell of blood from her hands.

1201 Mallock, Sir William
Old, important dinner guest at the Mileses'. He was an adviser
to Lloyd George on National Insurance.

1202 man driving tractor
When Bendrix and Sarah make love in a field, a man drives a
tractor past them without turning his head.

1203 "Man has places in his heart which do not yet exist, and
into them enters suffering, in order that they may have existence."
The novel's epigraph is from Léon Bloy's letter to Georges
Landry, 25 April 1873, published in Bloy's *Lettres de jeunesse*
(1920).

1204 Maud
Sarah's maid, who helps Parkis by appearing outside Smythe's flat
when Sarah goes there.

1205 Maugham
English writer William Somerset Maugham (1874-1965), best
known for his semi-autobiographical novel *Of Human Bondage*
(1915). Bendrix speculates that the critic Waterbury will place him
a little above Maugham, not because he is a better writer but
because, unlike Maugham, he is not popular.

1206 mayor
The mayor of Bigwell-by-Sea leads Henry through the town's civil
defense shelters.

1207 Miles, Henry
A mild-mannered civil servant in the Ministry of Home Security
whose acquaintance Bendrix cultivates in order to gather material
for a novel. As a husband Henry is loyal and affectionate but
passionless and naive, becoming suspicious of his wife's infidelities
only long after they have occurred. Out of characteristic
generosity as well as loneliness he offers to share his house with
Bendrix after Sarah's death, and his sincere grief and loneliness
transform Bendrix's former contempt for him into sympathy and
ultimately respect and friendship.

1208 Miles, Sarah
The adulterous wife of a passionless civil servant, Sarah progresses
in her relationship with Bendrix from simple lust to genuine
human love--the first she has ever known--to the experience of
divine love. Already questioning her own life and curious about
the possibilities of belief, she makes the leap of faith when she
believes Bendrix to have been killed in an air raid. She prays for
Bendrix's life, offering to give up her own relationship with him if
God will let him live. Bendrix survives, and Sarah undergoes
profound suffering and loneliness as she is drawn toward God and
ultimately away from human concerns. Her diary records her
spiritual progress and her fundamental goodness and generosity.
After her death from pneumonia, Sarah's saintly presence is felt
in the healing of Smythe, whose disfigured face she kissed, and
Lance Parkis, who borrows her book and says that she visited him
during the night. After her cremation it is revealed that she had
been baptized into the church when she was a child.

1209 mouse's nest
At the end of his narrative Bendrix declares his hatred for the
God who has ruined his happiness "as a harvester ruins a mouse's
nest" (239)--an allusion to Robert Burns's poem "To a Mouse"
(1785).

1210 *noche oscura*
The dark night of the soul. (See 1581.)

1211 nurse
The nurse attending Sarah failed to call Henry in time for him to
be with Sarah at her death.

1212 Parkis, Alfred
The humble, gentle detective hired by Bendrix to discover Sarah's
intrigue, a task he performs very well in spite of some comic
blunders. He provides a useful record of Sarah's activities and
secures the diary which reveals the truth about her alleged
betrayal of Bendrix. Parkis's honesty and devotion to his son are
complemented by his intuitive recognition of Sarah's goodness, the
very quality to which Bendrix is blind.

1213 Parkis, Lance
Parkis's son, erroneously named after the knight Parkis believed
to have found the Holy Grail.   Lance assists Bendrix by
accompanying him to Smythe's flat, and he is strongly attracted to
Sarah, whom he associates with his mother. When he becomes
seriously ill he talks to Sarah, dreams that she has promised him
a present, and appears to be miraculously cured when his father
brings him one of her childhood books.

1214 Parkis's wife
Parkis's deceased wife was so distressed by affairs such as the
Bolton case that he often withheld the details from her.

1215 *peine forte et dure*
Intense and severe punishment.

1216 Peter, cowardly
See Judas.

1217 Peter Jones
Large department store at Sloane Square, Chelsea. Sarah has lunch there and buys a lamp for Henry's study.

1218 Pippit, Mary
See Collins, Beatrice.

1219 *Poems* of Thomas Hood
One of Sarah's books. Thomas Hood (1799-1845) was a minor English poet.

1220 Pontefract Arms
Pub in Clapham where Bendrix and Henry drink together on the night Henry confesses his mistrust of Sarah.

1221 Potter, Beatrix
Sarah's childhood books included many by Beatrix Potter (1866-1943), English writer of *Peter Rabbit* and other popular children's stories.

1222 Prentice
Savage's assistant, a severe man who criticizes Parkis, in front of Parkis's son, for blunders ("floaters").

1223 Redemptorists
At first sight Bendrix thinks that Father Crompton may be a Redemptorist, a member of the Roman Catholic Congregation of the Most Holy Redeemer. Redemptorists have largely devoted themselves to work among the poor.

1224 Rules
A long-established traditional English restaurant in Maiden Lane, near the Strand. It is the favorite haunt of Bendrix and Sarah.

1225 Russell
Bertrand Russell (1872-1970), Cambridge professor and philosopher, author of *The Principles of Mathematics* (1903) and many other works. Bendrix says that Ayer and Russell are now in fashion, but he doubts that Smythe's library contains any of the logical positivists.

1226 Russell case
The case Parkis is working on after completing his work for
Bendrix.

1227 Savage, Mr.
Head of the detective agency for which Parkis works.

1228 Schwenigen
Cited by Smythe as having refuted the argument from design (one
of the familiar "proofs" of the existence of God) twenty-five years
ago.

1229 Scott
The works of novelist Sir Walter Scott (1771-1832) in Henry's
study probably belonged to his father.

1230 secretary (club)
The secretary of Bendrix's club is a grey-bearded man who writes
reminiscences (such as *Forever Fido*) of dogs he has known. On
the night when Bendrix has tormented Henry to the point where
Henry seems ready to hit him, the secretary's entrance into the
room distracts them.

1231 Smythe, Miss
Richard Smythe's sister, "a middle-aged woman with the grey tired
hair of charity bazaars" (91).

1232 Smythe, Richard
Rationalist-atheist "preacher" whom Sarah sees on Clapham
Common and later visits in the vain hope that he will be able to
convince her not to believe in God. But Smythe's atheism seems
less a matter of disbelief than of anger toward God. Smythe's
face, disfigured by a large, ugly strawberry birthmark, is healed
after Sarah's death. His fear that it may have been healed by her,
or perhaps through his possession of a lock of her hair,
undermines his confidence in his own disbelief.

1233 stream of consciousness
Bendrix is annoyed when Waterbury asks why he abandoned the
stream of consciousness method after using it in one book.

Greene himself largely abandoned the method after using it in
The Man Within (1929), *England Made Me* (1935), and "The
Bear Fell Free" (1935).

1234 *Tatler*
Bendrix sees Henry's photograph in this magazine at his club. It
changes his attitude just when he might have been ready to tear
up Parkis's report and leave Sarah alone.

1235 Torquemada
With characteristically caustic irony, Bendrix describes Father
Crompton as having a "Torquemada nose" (218).   Tomás de
Torquemada (1420-1498), grand inquisitor general of Spain, was
a religious fanatic whose intolerance and cruelty were responsible
for thousands of executions and expulsions.   He had a large,
flattened nose.

1236 Troilus
Hero of Chaucer's *Troilus and Criseyde* (c.1385) and
Shakespeare's *Troilus and Cressida* (1602), cited by Bendrix to
illustrate his claim that betrayed lovers are tragic rather than
comic.

1237 Universal certificate
The rating of a film as suitable for all audiences.

1238 V-E Day
May 8, 1945, the date of Germany's surrender and the official end
of the war in Europe.

1239 V1's
Robot-bombs, similar to jet-propelled pilotless aircraft, used by
Germany against England late in World War II.

1240 veganin
An analgesic.

1241 Victoria Gardens
Park on the Thames embankment, near the Strand.

1242 Waterbury
A critic writing an article on the work of Bendrix, whom he
interviews on the day of Sarah's cremation.

1243 Weyman, Stanley (1855-1928)
Author of historical romances, including *A Gentleman of France*
(1893). He was a member of Bendrix's club. (Weyman belonged
to the Athenaeum, a club popular with writers.)

1244 Whitehall
Street extending from Trafalgar Square to the Houses of
Parliament; the center of national government in London.

1245 Wilcox
Bendrix pretends to be looking for "Mr. Wilcox" when he goes to
Smythe's flat.

1246 Wilson
Having told Miss Smythe that he was looking for "Mr. Wilcox,"
Bendrix later slips and says it was "Wilson."

1247 woman, stout
Delivers Sarah's book and a message from Parkis to Henry.

1248 X
Bendrix's code for the unknown lover for whom Sarah has
abandoned him. X turns out to be God.

THE QUIET AMERICAN (1955)

1249 *The Advance of Red China*
Book by York Harding.

1250 Annamite
A native of Annam, a French administrative area of east-central
Vietnam. Phuong is an Annamite.

1251 Anne
The only woman for whom Fowler experienced a consuming
passion. He left her because he was afraid that she was changing
and that he would lose her.

1252 *Aphrodite*
Novel by Pierre Louys (1870-1925) in the library of the planter
whose flat Fowler considers buying.

1253 Berkeleian
Adherent to the idealist philosophy of Bishop George Berkeley
(1685-1753). Fowler says he is not a Berkeleian. (See 1625.)

1254 Bin Xuyen
One of the "private armies who sold their services for money or
revenge" (18).

1255 Bishop of Phat Diem
Local Catholic leader who retains political influence even though
the army he once commanded has been disbanded by the French,
leaving him with only a brass band. On his travels in Europe he
became devoted to Our Lady of Fatima, in whose honor he built
a shrine and established an annual procession on her feast day.

1256 bren
English-made .303 calibre submachine gun.

1257 Cabot
Pyle tells Fowler that living in Boston can be "cramping" even for those who are not Cabots or Lowells, prestigious Boston families.

1258 Caodaism
A religion, invented by a Cochin civil servant, which contains elements of Catholicism (including a Pope and female cardinals), Buddhism, and Confucianism.

1259 Caodaists
Depicted by Fowler as primarily a political group which uses an invented religion to unify its followers and controls "a private army of twenty-five thousand men, armed with mortars made out of the exhaust-pipes of old cars, allies of the French who turned neutral at the moment of danger" (85).

1260 Cholon
Chinese suburb of Saigon, where Mr. Chou lives.

1261 Chou, Mr.
Ancient, emaciated Chinese gentleman to whom Fowler is sent by Dominguez for information about Pyle's attempts to establish a Third Force. Mr. Chou, who smokes 150 pipes of opium per day, is not very helpful, but his associate Heng is.

1262 colonel
The French colonel at Phat Diem says that the drink of whisky given him by Fowler is the first he has had since leaving Paris.

1263 colonel, young French
Handsome officer who presides over a press conference in which probing questions by Granger, Fowler, and others lead him to an angry revelation of the very circumstances he had intended to conceal: the deteriorating French military position.

1264 commandant
Caodaist in Tanyin who sends for a mechanic to repair Pyle's car.

1265 Connolly
Granger's assistant who is unavailable for helping Granger when
the latter, whose son is ill, most needs help. Because Connolly is
pretending to be ill but is actually pursuing a woman in Singapore,
Granger must cover for him to prevent him from being sacked.

1266 Continental
Restaurant or hotel in Saigon.

1267 Crane
American writer Stephen Crane (1876-1900), author of the
distinguished Civil War novel *The Red Badge of Courage*.
Granger justifies his own faking of news articles about battles he
has not seen by saying that Crane wrote about war without seeing
one.

1268 Dante
Dante Alighieri (1265-1321), Italian poet, author of *Divine
Comedy*. Fowler, upon receiving the telegram of promotion that
will necessitate his return to London and, consequently, his
abandonment of Phuong to Pyle, says that "Dante never thought
up that turn of the screw for his condemned lovers. Paolo was
never promoted to Purgatory" (69).

1269 DeLattre
General de Lattre de Tassigny, French commander who
successfully defended Hanoi for several years but was eventually
defeated. He died of cancer in Paris prior to the end of the war.

1270 deputy, Pope's
Caodaist priest whom Fowler interviews in an unsuccessful attempt
to get information about General Thé.

1271 Dominguez
Fowler's intelligent and reliable assistant, an Indian who attends
minor press conferences, carries Fowler's messages, and reports
significant local gossip and rumor. Dominguez alerts Fowler to
Heng's discovery of the connection between Pyle and General Thé.

1272 Dubois
Mentioned by Trouin as a friend of his father. Trouin sometimes
imagines that the Vietnamese villages he bombs with napalm are
the French village in which he grew up, and that the dying people
are M. Dubois and the baker.

1273 Duke
Pyle's dog, a black chow with a black tongue. The wet cement
found between Duke's toes convinces Vigot that on the night of
his murder Pyle visited Fowler.

1274 Duparc, Captain
Member of the Press Liaison Service, one of the guests Granger
is entertaining at the Vieux Moulin on the night Pyle is killed.

1275 Duprez, Madame
Wife of a public relations officer, at the Vieux Moulin table with
Granger and Duparc.

1276 elevenses
Midmorning snack with a beverage.

1277 First Secretary
Official who threatened to prohibit all imports in diplomatic
parcels after the accidental opening of one revealed that it
contained plastic.

1278 Flynn, Errol
Fowler cannot recall whether Errol Flynn or Tyrone Power starred
in *Scaramouche* (1952), the film he saw on the night of Pyle's
murder. (Actually it was Stewart Granger.)

1279 Foreign Legion
A former French military unit made up of volunteers of various
nationalities.

1280 Fowler, Helen
Fowler's estranged wife in England, a devout Catholic who has
long refused on religious and personal grounds to give him a
divorce but relents at the very end.

1281   Fowler, Thomas
An English newspaper correspondent covering the French
Indo-China war for a London paper, Fowler is a middle-aged,
atheistic, somewhat cynical man. His relationship with Phuong, his
Vietnamese mistress for whom he has genuine affection if not
passion, is threatened by the refusal of his estranged Catholic wife
to divorce him. His desire to remain strictly an objective "reporter"
who does not take sides in the conflict cannot withstand the
complicated emotions arising from his friendship with Pyle, the
"quiet American" whose courage and good nature he admires but
whose destructive "innocence" he fears. By betraying Pyle to the
Communists--primarily because Pyle's attempt to create a "Third
Force" has led to the indiscriminate murder of innocent
civilians--Fowler enacts the truth of Heng's comment that sooner
or later one must take sides in order to remain human. But
Fowler must live on with the knowledge that his own action
cannot be separated from his jealousy of Pyle, who had taken
Phuong from him; or from the guilt of betrayal, since Pyle was a
friend who had saved Fowler's own life.

1282   Frogs
Slang for "French."

1283   Gaboriau
Emile Gaboriau (1835-73), creator of the fictional detective Lecoq
and a pioneer writer of detective stories in France. Vigot says a
love of Gaboriau was one of the factors that made him become
a policeman.

1284   girls, American
Shortly before the explosion in the square in Saigon, Fowler
overhears two young American girls say that they had better be
going just to be on the safe side. Someone named Warren has
told them not to stay at the Pavilion past 11:25 a.m.

1285   Grande Monde
Dance hall in Saigon where Fowler first met Phuong, who was a
hostess there.

1286 Granger, Bill
Loud, vulgar American reporter whose rude behavior sharply
contrasts with that of Pyle, the "quiet" American. Granger, whose
news reports are often phoney, shares a strong mutual dislike with
the more conscientious journalist Fowler, but Granger's suffering
after he receives news that his son has polio moves Fowler to
sympathy for him.

1287 Granger's son
Suffers from polio but is reported at the end to be out of danger.

1288 *The Great Train Robbery*
Classic silent American film (1903) by Edwin S. Porter, seen by
Fowler in Saigon.

1289 Harding, York
Pyle's hero and mentor, a Harvard professor who visited the Far
East briefly and wrote numerous books about Asian military and
political affairs. Pyle's uncritical acceptance of Harding's theories,
especially his idea of the desirability of creating a "Third Force,"
leads to Pyle's fatal involvement with General Thé; thus, Fowler
remarks that Harding killed Pyle from a great distance.

1290 Hei, Miss
Phuong's older sister who is determined to see that Phuong makes
an expedient marriage. She is opposed to Fowler, who is neither
single nor wealthy.

1291 Heng
Chou's Communist manager who reveals to Fowler Pyle's
involvement in making plastic explosives available to General Thé.
Heng, who tells Fowler that "Sooner or later one must take sides
if one is to remain human" (194), arranges the murder of Pyle.

1292 Hoa-Haos
Another of the "private armies" that flourish around Saigon.

1293 "I do not like being moved. . . ."
The epigraph is from Arthur Hugh Clough's "Amours de Voyage"
(1858).

1294 Joe
Pyle's friend, the Economic Attaché who gets Phuong's sister an
American job.

1295 joss sticks
Sticks of incense, normally burned before a joss, or Chinese idol.
Fowler says he burns them to keep down bad smells.

· 1296 juju
An object believed to have supernatural power, used as a fetish,
charm, or amulet in West Africa. Fowler calls the holy medal
around a dead child's neck a juju that was no good.

1297 knacker's yard
A knacker buys dead or worthless livestock and sells the hides or
meat. Fowler recalls how in childhood he feared the knacker's
yard in his home town.

1298 *La Garçonne*
One of the planter's books; possibly the novel *La Garçonne* (1866)
by French writer Victor Margueritte (1867-1942).

1299 "The lamps shone o'er fair women and brave men."
Wilkins quotes from Byron's "Childe Harold's Pilgrimage," Canto
III, st. 21 (1816).

1300 Le Club
The Saigon restaurant preferred by French officers.

1301 Lecoq
Famous detective hero of fiction by Emile Gaboriau (1835-73).
Vigot says modestly that he is not Lecoq or Maigret, the detective
created by Georges Simenon (1903-89).

1302 lieutenant
A French lieutenant allows Fowler to accompany his men as they
search for the enemy at Phat Diem.

1303 Lowell
See Cabot.

1304 Maigret
See Lecoq.

1305 Majestic
Luxury hotel in Saigon.

1306 manager, Muoi's
Came to Chou's in hopes of retrieving the mould and the drums
marked "Diolacton."

1307 Managing Editor
The managing editor of Fowler's paper wants to make Fowler the
foreign editor, with a London office, and replace him with a new
correspondent in Saigon.

1308 men in hut
Two Vietnamese soldiers guard the watch tower in which Fowler
and Pyle hide after running out of gasoline on the road from
Tanyin to Saigon. One of them is apparently killed when the
Communists discover the car and attack the tower. Fowler, who
has escaped along with Pyle, hears the other crying in the dark
and feels responsible for the fates of both.

1309 Merchant Limited
The *Merchants Limited*, a New York-Boston express train.

1310 *métisse*
A woman of mixed French-Canadian and Indian ancestry. The
métisse Fowler and Trouin see at the opium den is a prostitute;
Fowler takes her to bed, but his unhappiness over the loss of
Phuong makes him impotent.

1311 Mick
The name Granger gives to the anonymous drunken Frenchman
he brings to the Continental restaurant.

1312 *Nana* (1880)
Novel by Emile Zola (1840-1902); the protagonist is a prostitute.

1313   Pascal
The detective Vigot is an admirer of French philosopher, mathematician, and scientist Blaise Pascal (1623-62), whose *Pensées* he is reading when he first interrogates Fowler. Later he quotes to Fowler Pascal's comment on wagering that God exists: "If you gain, you gain all; if you lose you lose nothing" (153).

1314   Peraud, Lt.
A serious young man who describes to Fowler the Vietminh attack on Phat Diem, an action which to Peraud is "like a judgement on the superstitions of his fellows" (44).

1315   Perrin, Lt.
In recommending to Fowler the services of the métisse at the opium house, Trouin says that both he and Perrin have slept with her.

1316   Pham-Van-Tu
Accountant at the Bank of Indo-China who studies Wordsworth and writes nature poetry; an acquaintance of Fowler.

1317   Phan-Van-Muoi, Mr.
As the husband of a relative of General Thé, Muoi provides evidence of the link between Pyle, Thé, and the bicycle bombs in Saigon.   After discovering that used Diolacton drums and a mould in his possession were carelessly thrown away, he calls at the American Legation and asks for Pyle.

1318   Phat Diem
Catholic town which, under the protection of the Prince-Bishop, had been in Fowler's estimate the liveliest in the country. Upon returning there, however, he finds it severely damaged and devitalized by Communist attacks.

1319   Phuong
Fowler's mistress, whose beauty and childlike simplicity make her immediately attractive to Pyle, who falls in love with her and adopts a protective attitude that underestimates her strength and resiliency (her name means "Phoenix"). Phuong follows the English Royal Family in *Paris-Match* and longs to see the

West--America or England--but her naive enthusiasm does not extend to romantic infatuation. Desiring security and affection, she accepts Pyle's offer of marriage when she learns that Fowler, who is married, has been called back to England; yet she quietly accepts Fowler again after Pyle's death and is happy to marry him when his wife consents to a divorce.

1320 Pietre
A Sureté officer, a Corsican with a pretty Tonkinese wife. Like Fowler, he does not want to return home.

1321 planter
A rubber planter who is returning to Paris and offers to sell Fowler his flat complete with his collection of art and fiction, both of which heavily emphasize the erotic.

1322 Power, Tyrone
See Flynn.

1323 priest
The priest Fowler meets at Phat Diem ("European" but not French, since the Bishop would not tolerate a French priest) does double duty as a surgeon at the hospital there.

1324 Prince
Pyle named one of his dogs "Prince" after the Black Prince, unaware that the Black Prince was responsible for the massacre of women and children at Limoges.

1325 Pyle, Alden
The "quiet American," a good-natured young man whose innocent idealism makes him dangerous. Ostensibly in Viet Nam to work for the Economic Aid Mission, he tries to apply the theories of Professor York Harding by discovering a "Third Force" which American strategists can use to gain ascendancy in the conflict there. Fowler at first believes Pyle harmless, although Pyle falls in love with Fowler's mistress Phuong and pursues her openly, winning her affection and trying simultaneously to preserve his friendship with Fowler. Pyle proves his honor in the affair by saving Fowler's life when the two are stranded on the road from

Tanyin to Saigon. But when Pyle supplies explosives for the activities of General Thé, whose terrorist bombings kill innocent civilians, Fowler decides that Pyle must be stopped. He betrays his friendly rival to the Communists, who murder Pyle.

1326 Pyle, Mrs.
Pyle's mother, mentioned by the Economic Attaché.

1327 Pyle, Professor Harold C.
Alden Pyle's father, the world's foremost authority on underwater erosion. His picture was once on the cover of *Time*.

1328 *Quatre Cent Vingt-et-un*
A game played with three dice; the numbers 4-2-1 (quatre cent vingt-et-un) are a winning combination.

1329 *"qu'est-ce que c'est la liberté?"*
Fowler, skeptical of Pyle's claim that the liberty of the Vietnamese must be fought for or is even something that the people could understand in Western terms, asks, "What is liberty?" (103)

1330 Reuter's
British news agency.

1331 *The Rôle of the West*
Book by York Harding. Fowler takes it as a memento from among Pyle's things.

1332 Rops
Félicien Rops (1833-98), Belgian painter, etcher, and printmaker, did illustrations for Péladan's *Le Vice sûpreme* and other works with erotic subjects. The planter has a reproduction of Rops in his bathroom.

1333 Russell and the old *Times*
Sir William Howard Russell (1820-1907) was a distinguished war-correspondent for *The Times*, best known for his writings on the Crimean War.

1334 St. Cyr
The French national military academy.

1335 Salisbury, Lord
The plaque of Salisbury (Robert Cecil, 1830-1903) mentioned by
Fowler is in Printing House Square, where *The Times* was
formerly printed.

1336 "So pleasant it is to have money."
A line from Clough's "Dipsychus" (1865).

1337 Sorel, Captain
Plays Quatre Cent Vingt-et-un with Fowler at Phat Diem.

1338 Squadron Gascogne
French military flying unit at Haiphong. Fowler has friends in the
squadron who allow him to accompany the squadron on a
dive-bombing mission.

1339 sten guns
British-made rapid-fire light submachine guns.

1340 Sun Yat Sen (1866-1925)
Revolutionary Chinese leader whose image appears near that of
"St. Victor Hugo" in the Caodaist Cathedral.

1341 *Sureté*
The police.

1342 Tanyin
Town forty-eight miles n.w. of Saigon; center of the Caodaist
religion and site of its Holy See.

1343 Thé, General
Former Caodaist Chief of Staff, now a renegade who holds out
with his army in the mountains near Tanyin and declares his
opposition to both the French and the Communists. Pyle sees in
Thé a likely "Third Force" that would correspond to York
Harding's theories, but Thé uses the explosives given him by Pyle

for indiscriminate terrorist bombings in which innocent civilians are killed.

1344   Third Force
York Harding theorized that what was needed to bring about freedom in Vietnam was a "Third Force" free of both Communism and the taint of colonialism.

1345   "This is the patent age of new inventions. . . ."
The epigraph is from Canto I, cxxxii, of Lord Byron's *Don Juan* (1819-24).

1346   trachoma team
Trachoma is a viral disease which affects the conjunctiva of the eye.   Pyle's interest in the American "trachoma team" is a front for his more serious involvement in political and military intrigue.

1347   Trouin
A flyer in the Squadron Gascogne and friend to Fowler, whom he takes along on a dive bombing raid. Trouin hates war and knows, as he explains to Fowler, that the French cannot win and that the eventual peace settlement will probably be no better than the one they could have had years ago, so that conflict of the past several years is likely to prove meaningless.

1348   Victor Hugo, St.
The Caodaists venerate French novelist Victor Hugo (1802-85) as a saint.

1349   Vietminh
Originally a coalition of nationalist and Communist groups opposed to the Japanese in World War II, the Vietminh eventually became dominated by the Communists and identified specifically with the Communists of North Vietnam.

1350   Vieux Moulin
Saigon restaurant where Fowler offered to meet Pyle on the night of Pyle's murder.

1351   Vigot
French police detective who diligently but unsuccessfully pursues
his just suspicion that Fowler was somehow involved in the death
of Pyle. A modest man who reads Pascal, Vigot projects through
his interrogation of Fowler a philosophical view of life and a sense
of weariness with the human condition.

1352   Vigot's wife
The detective's blonde wife, said to have betrayed him with junior
officers.

1353   Warren
Unidentified character who warned the American girls not to stay
at the Pavilion past 11:25 on the morning of the explosion.

1354   Wilkins
Reporter for Associated News, seen by Fowler at the Majestic
Hotel on the night Pyle is murdered. Wilkins laments the passing
of an older style of journalism that allowed more "fancy writing"
(202).

1355   woman and child
The most troubling and haunting image of the war for Fowler is
that of a woman he sees near the canal at Phat Diem, holding in
her lap her dead child whose body she covers with her hat.

LOSER TAKES ALL (1955)

1356   Arnold, Mr.
Chief accountant in Bertram's firm, whose position Bertram will
assume after his promotion.

1357 Bertram
The narrator and protagonist, a middle-aged accountant who
accepts an invitation to spend his honeymoon in Monte Carlo and
aboard a yacht as the guest of his employer, Dreuther. When
Dreuther fails to show up as planned, Bertram uses his skill at
mathematics to invent a system of winning at roulette in order to
pay his expenses. He wins a fortune and, briefly, crucial shares of
stock in Dreuther's company, but his obsession with gambling and
wealth so alienates his bride that he must choose between his
system and her. With advice from Dreuther, who finally arrives,
he deliberately loses his money in order to regain his love--and is
rewarded with a promotion in the firm.

1358 Bird's Nest
Middle-aged woman with two gold teeth and a frightful blonde wig
who begs tokens from men who win at the gaming tables.
Bertram, desperate to live up to his boast to Cary that he also has
a dinner date, takes Bird's Nest to an expensive restaurant. (See
Devereux.)

1359 Blister
Employees' name for Blixon.

1360 Blixon, Sir Walter
Self-important executive and stockholder who shares power but not
popularity with Dreuther. Blixon, a churchwarden without friends
or admirers among his employees, is consumed by jealousy over
what he feels is the greater deference paid to Dreuther.

1361 Bowles, A.N.
Minor but important stockholder whose shares control the balance
of power between Dreuther and Blixon. A gambler obsessed with
the desire to prove that his own system works, he risks his shares
in a wager with Bertram.

1362 boy, small
A member of the wedding party seen briefly by Bertram and Cary,
he discharges a handful of rice in the groom's face.

1363   Bullen, Miss
Dreuther's secretary in London.

1364   C.H.
Companion of Honour.

1365   Cary
Bertram's bride and second wife, a twenty-year-old woman whose
appeal lies especially in her innocent, childlike response to
experience. Cary cheerfully endures embarrassment and hunger
when Bertram runs out of money at their expensive hotel, but her
affection wanes when his success at gambling makes him greedy
as well as wealthy. She flirts briefly with an unsuccessful young
gambler but returns to Bertram when he chooses her love over his
system. Her name may be a pun on "carré," a bet (in European
Roulette) on numbers that form a square on the layout (for
example, 1,2,4, and 5).

1366   Chantier, Philippe
The "hungry young man" (165) who becomes romantically
interested in Cary but proves himself more interested in money
and gambling than in love.

1367   Charteris, Celia
Mentioned by Dreuther as a guest who will board his yacht at
Portofino.

1368   Clemenceau
Georges Clemenceau (1841-1929), twice premier of France (1906-
09, 1917-20). The mayor resembles Clemenceau.

1369   *Code Napoléon*
The code of French civil law, created in 1804.

1370   Devereux, Robert
The name used by Bertram in signing the guest register at the
expensive restaurant to which he takes Bird's Nest. The name
humorously recalls Robert Devereux, Earl of Essex, and his
romance with Queen Elizabeth I, who, like Bird's Nest, wore a
wig.

1371 Dirty
Cary's name for Bertram's first wife, whom he recalls as "dark and
plump and sexy with pekingese eyes" (171).   Bertram tells
Dreuther that his first wife was a bad woman.

1372 Dreuther, Herbert
The "GOM," Bertram's wise and wealthy employer who invites
Bertram and Cary to honeymoon as his guests but then forgets
about it.   He shows up just in time to give Bertram essential
advice on the value of a good marriage (he has had four
unsuccessful ones himself) and on a strategy for renouncing wealth
and regaining his bride.

1373 Dupont, Madame
Bertram, angry and jealous over Cary's dinner date with Philippe,
says that he also has an engagement--with "Madame Dupont," an
imaginary character.

1374 GOM, the
Acronym for "Grand Old Man," the name given Dreuther by those
employees who either dislike him or are too distant to have any
feelings toward him at all.

1375 Haroun
According to Bertram, the GOM saw himself as a "haroun," one
"who could raise a man from obscurity and make him ruler over
provinces" (141).   The name probably derives from Haroun-al-
Raschid (764?-809), caliph of Baghdad.

1376 *impair*
An odd number. (See *manqué.*)

1377 liftman
Expresses surprise that Bertram does not know who resides in
room 10 in his office building.

1378 *"Luxe, calme et volupte"*
"Luxury, calm, and voluptuousness."   Dreuther quotes from
Baudelaire's "Invitation au Voyage," a poem in *Les Fleurs du Mal*
(1857). (See 302.)

1379 *Mairie*
Town hall.

1380 man, furniture
Gives Bertram and Cary a lift in his van when they are about to
be late for their own wedding.

1381 manager
The manager of the hotel at Monte Carlo knows that Bertram is
short of money and surprises him by lending him 250,000 francs
just when Bertram expects to be ejected from the hotel.

1382 *manqué*
In European Roulette, a bet on the lower numbers, from one to
eighteen. *Passe* is a bet on the higher (19-36), *rouge* a bet on
red, and *noir* a bet on black. *Pair* is an even number, *impair* an
odd.

1383 Marion, Aunt
Cary's aunt, with whom she has lived since the death of her
parents in the blitz.

1384 matron, somber
Member of the wedding party seen briefly by Bertram and Cary.

1385 mayor
An old man who resembled Clemenceau; a witness to the
marriage of Bertram and Cary.

1386 Naismith
A man who is in Dreuther's office when Bertram first goes there.

1387 *noir*
See *manqué*.

1388 O.M.
Order of Merit.

1389 *pair*
See *manqué*.

1390 Pascal
See 1313.

1391 Racine
Bertram says he prefers Racine to Baudelaire, but Dreuther cautions him that there are "moments in Racine when--the abyss opens" (138).

1392 *rouge*
See *manqué.*

1393 Rousseau
Bertram's narrative comment that Rousseau "might have written that man was born rich and is everywhere impoverished" (175) is a humorous variation on that Frenchman's famous words in "The Social Contract" (1762): "Man is born free, and everywhere he is in chains."

1394 *Seagull*
Dreuther's yacht.

1395 Sitra
Dreuther's company.

1396 squinting man
Cary, who fears the working of fate, tells Bertram as they ride toward their wedding that they will see a "squinting man" next. When the driver of their carriage turns around almost immediately, she sees that he has a squint. "Squinting" is slang for "being without something necessary," such as food--the condition Cary and Bertram will find themselves in shortly after their marriage.

1397 Tissand, M.
One of Dreuther's employees in Nice.

1398 "Trollope, not Dickens; Stevenson, not Scott"
Bertram is pleased to see that Dreuther's collection of English classics includes "Trollope, not Dickens; Stevenson, not Scott." The choices indicate that he has bought books he really wants

(and presumably reads), not just obvious choices intended to impress visitors.

1399   Vicar
Cary fears that the Vicar of St. Luke's, Maida Hill, will have hurt feelings if they do not carry out their plan to be married in his church.

1400   *"Vois sur ses canaux / Dormir ces vaisseaux. . . ."*
Lines from Baudelaire's "Invitation au Voyage," quoted to Cary by Dreuther: "See, on these canals, / The sleeping ships; / It is to satisfy your least desire / That they have come from around the world." (See 302.)

1401   Widow, the
Champagne.

OUR MAN IN HAVANA (1958)

1402   A.O.
Accounting Office.

1403   Agnes, Sister
A sad, pretty nun who teaches in Milly's school, believed to have had an unhappy experience of love when she was young.

1404   Albany
The Chief lives in Albany, a prestigious block of flats adjacent to the Burlington Arcade in Piccadilly.

1405   Alice, Aunt
In the letter to his sister Wormold asks about Aunt Alice with "the famous wax in her ears" (66).

1406 Ambassador
The British Ambassador upon learning of Wormold's difficulties with both the Foreign Office and the Cuban police, persuades Wormold to leave for England immediately.

1407 "And the sad man is cock of all his jests."
The novel's epigraph is from "The Church Porch," the poem introductory to George Herbert's *The Temple* (1633).

1408 Angelica
A secretary in the Secret Service pool.

1409 Arviragus
One of the lost sons of Cymbeline in Shakespeare's *Cymbeline*.

1410 Ashworth, Mrs.
See Henry.

1411 Belsen
A Nazi concentration camp near Hanover, Germany.

1412 boy, small
A small boy with a damp towel is recalled by Wormold as exemplifying schoolboy cruelty.

1413 Braun, Dr.
President of the European Traders' Association who invites Wormold to address the group at its annual banquet.

1414 Brewer
The Chief's valet.

1415 C.T.S.
Catholic Truth Societies.

1416 Cadwal
The name used by Arviragus during his childhood in Wales.

1417 Caesar, the King's friend
King Edward VII's dog.

1418 cardinal
Maria Sanchez's cousin, mentioned as having intervened in some
unspecified way in her husband's adulterous affair.

1419 Carter, William
An enemy agent who poses as a vacuum cleaner salesman and
tries to murder Wormold at the Traders' banquet. He wears
tweeds and conveys the attitude of snobbery and security Wormold
associates with the English midlands.   Carter murders
Hasselbacher in the Wonder Bar and attempts to kill Wormold
before the latter kills him with Segura's gun.

1420 Catholic Action
An organization dedicated to promoting the practice of Catholic
beliefs in everyday life.

1421 Cetewayo (c. 1836-1884)
Zulu king who led brave resistance to European colonizers but
was defeated by British soldiers in 1879.

1422 chap in Denmark
A British agent in Denmark saw the German fleet sailing the
Kattegat and realized that a Nazi takeover of Denmark was
imminent. He burned his papers and flushed them down the
toilet, but the pipes were frozen and the ashes floated up into a
bathtub in the flat below.

1423 Chief
The head of the secret service in London is so fond of his own
literary idea of Wormold as an old fashioned Englishman
belonging to the "Kipling age" that he pays inadequate attention
to details of Wormold's activities.

1424 Chief Engineer
Wormold sees this officer of the *Juan Belmonte* drinking in
Cienfuegos and makes him a fictional agent.

1425   Christ the King
A feast which asserts Christ's authority to reign over whole nations as well as the hearts and minds of individuals.

1426   Christmas Island
Site of Britain's H-bomb tests in 1957.

1427   Cifuentes
An engineer whose name Wormold gets from the membership list of the Country Club. He makes Cifuentes a supplier of technical intelligence.

1428   Cleon
Cleon and Dionyza, characters in Shakespeare's *Pericles*, are used in a coded message from Hawthorne to Wormold.

1429   clown
Wormold recalls having seen a circus clown who represented something permanent, a way to live "unaffected by the vagaries of public men and the enormous discoveries of the great" (30). Clowns, he thinks, do not destroy their peace by learning from experience.

1430   Consul-General
American diplomat who speaks vaguely at the Traders' Association banquet about the relationship between spiritual and commercial ties between countries.

1431   Cooper
A friend of Wormold and Hasselbacher, mentioned as having left Havana for home.

1432   *coup de foudre*
Love at first sight.

1433   Creole smuggler
A narcotics smuggler practiced in bribing customs officers is also a British agent who brings Rudy's radio and photographic equipment into Cuba.

1434 Davis
Mentioned by Carter as his roommate at Nottwich.

1435 Deuxième Bureau
The French Intelligence organization.

1436 Dominguez, Raul
An imaginary alcoholic pilot named Raul Dominguez, invented by
Wormold as a fictional agent, turns out to have a real-life
counterpart who is killed by enemy agents as a result of the claims
made for him in Wormold's reports.

1437 Dreyfus
See 2102.

1438 duenna
Wormold feels that Milly sometimes carries with her an "invisible"
duenna, an elderly woman employed by a Spanish or Portuguese
family as governess and companion or chaperon for their daughter.

1439 Edward, Uncle
In his letter to his sister, Wormold asks whether his Uncle Edward
is still living.

1440 Ethel
Miss Jenkinson's secretary in London.

1441 F.O.
Foreign Office.

1442 Frazer, Sir James [George] (1854-1941)
Cambridge anthropologist whose major work *The Golden Bough*
(12 vols., 1890-1915), a study of ancient myth, religion, and ritual,
increased the popularity of anthropology and had a considerable
influence upon a number of modern writers, including T.S. Eliot
and D.H. Lawrence.

1443 Fuchs case
Klaus Emil Fuchs (1911-88), German-born British physicist, was a
Communist spy who gave secret information on the U.S. atomic

bomb project and British atomic research at Harwell to the
Soviets. He was convicted of spying and imprisoned from 1950 to
1959. The Permanent Under-Secretary points out to the Chief
that since the Fuchs case the Americans and the British have not
shared information with each other as freely as before.

1444 Gilbert, Sir Humphrey (c.1539-1583)
English explorer and soldier whose expeditions included an
attempt to discover the Northwest Passage. In 1583 Gilbert
claimed Newfoundland for England and tried to establish a colony
there, but he perished soon afterward when his ship sank off the
coast of Nova Scotia.

1445 "Go, bid the soldiers shoot."
The last line of Shakespeare's *Hamlet*, quoted by Milly in a note
to her father.

1446 Guiderius
One of the two sons of Cymbeline in Shakespeare's play.

1447 Hasselbacher, Dr.
Wormold's closest friend, an eccentric man who pursues "research"
into the blueness of cheese and other esoteric phenomena in order
to escape the reality of his time, which he says is too horrible to
be faced. Staunchly independent, he resists allegiance to East or
West and urges Wormold not to cooperate with either. An expert
cryptographer who was once a German cavalry officer, he betrays
Wormold by cracking his friend's code after Segura's men have
destroyed his own experiments and therefore his will to live. But
he warns Wormold that an attempt on his life will be made at the
Traders' banquet, and for this kindness he is murdered by Carter.

1448 Hasselbacher, Emma
An imaginary woman with a Ph.D., invented by Wormold as his
mistress to explain his actions to the police in Santiago.

1449 Hawthorne, Henry
British intelligence agent who recruits Wormold as "our man in
Havana." He is easily fooled by Wormold's fakery, and his own
work reflects poorly on his chief, who in hiring Hawthorne refused

to believe his own subordinates who said that Hawthorne was not
a good judge of men.

1450 head-waiter
Wormold assumes that the head-waiter at the Nacional is agent
stroke-7, who has been assigned to kill him.

1451 Henry
Wormold has to wait in line at the bank while the teller talks on
the phone, first to a wealthy customer named Henry, then to a
Mrs. Ashworth.

1452 Humpelnicker
A friend mentioned by Hasselbacher.

1453 "I have come back victorious. The dog it was that died."
Following the attempt to poison him, which resulted in the
accidental poisoning of a dog, Wormold quotes from Oliver
Goldsmith's "Elegy on the Death of a Mad Dog" (1766).

1454 Jefatura
Havana police headquarters, a place where "unpleasant doings"
regularly go on out of sight (22).

1455 Jenkinson, Miss
Head of the secretaries' pool in the British intelligence
headquarters in London, the only person in the building who does
not go by a Christian name. She exerts her authority somewhat
capriciously, assigning Beatrice, whose French is excellent, to work
for Wormold, who needs a Spanish-speaking assistant.

1456 Joe
A Negro who walks the Havana streets slowly, counting his steps
and occasionally selling pornographic postcards.

1457 Jude, St.
When Milly talks of how she will help pay for the stabling of her
horse, Wormold suggests woefully that she pray to St. Jude, the
Apostle whose aid is often sought in times of unusual hardship.

1458 KLM pilots
Three KLM (Royal Dutch Airlines) pilots and an air hostess appear with Beatrice at the Tropicana on the night of Milly's party.

1459 Kate
Wormold's great-aunt in Oxford.

1460 Lamb's *Tales from Shakespeare* (1807)
A prose version of Shakespeare for young readers, written by Charles Lamb and his sister Mary. Wormold and Hawthorne use it for their book code.

1461 Leadbetter, Henry
One of the names by which coded messages for Wormold are addressed.

1462 Lopez
Wormold's shop assistant who has never learned to pronounce Wormold's name. He is annoyed by customers because they distract his attention from *Confidential* magazine.

1463 lovely woman
Suspecting that Wormold is meeting a woman in the Seville-Biltmore, Hasselbacher echoes the familiar "Song" ("When lovely woman stoops to folly") from Oliver Goldsmith's *The Vicar of Wakefield* (1766).

1464 MacDougall
A friendly Scotsman who offers Wormold a drink at the Traders' Banquet and is wrongly suspected of trying to poison him.

1465 man with screwdriver
A pimp at the Shanghai Theatre who tries to interest Wormold in Maria.

1466 Maria
A fat prostitute who is also a performer at the Shanghai Theatre. Her services are offered to Wormold when he goes there in search of Teresa.

1467   Marie
A French girl at Milly's convent school who says that "all true love is a *coup de foudre*" (99).

1468   Mark
Wormold's nephew, whose age Wormold invariably forgets. He sends the boy stamps and notes appropriate for someone much younger.

1469   Marlowe
A friend of Wormold and Hasselbacher, mentioned as being in the hospital.

1470   Mary (Wormold's ex-wife)
Wormold's ex-wife, who left him after a quarrel in which she accused him of never doing anything or acting "any way at all" (27). Milly prays that Mary will become a good Catholic again.

1471   Mary (Wormold's sister)
Wormold's younger sister in Northampton, to whom he writes annually while on his business tour.

1472   Mendez, Father
Priest whom Wormold recently heard preaching about the effects of the hydrogen bomb, warning that "Those who believe in creating a heaven on earth . . . are creating a hell" (4).

1473   Miguel
A black man who bribes the police with Wormold's money to allow Wormold, Beatrice, and Teresa's sister to escape from the Shanghai Theatre.

1474   Miguel
The name Wormold uses for a blind beggar who, he tells Beatrice, is one of his spies and is not really blind.

1475   Minister
A dark, squinting man addressed briefly by Dr. Braun in his introduction of Wormold at the Traders' Association Banquet.

1476 Morgan, Harry
A patron of the Seville-Biltmore bar whose existence is teasingly
denied by Hasselbacher.

1477 Muller, Captain
Apparently Muller, the name by which the Kaiser once spoke to
Hasselbacher, is the doctor's real name.

1478 music in Alexandria
In act four of Shakespeare's *Antony and Cleopatra*, supernatural
music reveals to Antony's soldiers that his guardian spirit Hercules
has left him.

1479 negress
A woman who sees Beatrice arrive outside Wormold's business,
praises her for squirting Segura with soda water, and helps her
carry Rudy's enormous suitcase.

1480 Ossian
Ossian, or Oisin, was a warrior and bard of Gaelic legend, best
known to English readers through the forgeries of James
MacPherson, a Scotsman who published as the works of Ossian
two volumes of his own poetry (1761, 1763).

1481 Our Lady of Guadalupe
In her room, Milly keeps a light burning before this image of the
Virgin.

1482 P.M.
The Permanent Under-Secretary tells the Chief that the P.M.
(prime minister) is urging them to inform the Americans of the
military installations discovered by Wormold.

1483 Parkman, Thomas Earl
A small boy at the convent school who was set on fire by Milly
after he pulled her hair. Vincent Parkman may be his father.

1484 Parkman, Vincent C.
A member of the Country Club whom Wormold proposes to

recruit as a supplier of political information, only to learn that Parkman is already an American agent.

1485 Paul, St.
Hawthorne refers to St. Paul's words in I Corinthians 9:22:   "I have become all things to all men, that I might by all means save some."

1486 Pedro
The pimp for whom Teresa's sister works.

1487 Pendennis
Inexpensive hotel near Gower St. where Wormold and Beatrice are reunited after their return to London.

1488 Penny, Lake
One of the names by which coded messages for Wormold are addressed.

1489 Perez, Senor
Mentioned by Milly as someone who would hire her as a governess, a possibility that distresses Wormold because Perez is now living with his fourth wife.

1490 Permanent Under-Secretary
British government official who discusses Wormold's findings over dinner at the Chief's flat.

1491 Pfunk, Miss
Approximate name of air-hostess who tells the KLM pilots at the Tropicana that they cannot drink Bols before they return to Amsterdam.

1492 Poe's Raven
Milly's repetition of "never" when she vows never to trust novenas again (because they did not help her to get a horse) reminds her father of the "nevermore" of Poe's Raven.

1493 Polydore
The name used by Guiderius in the Welsh forest in *Cymbeline*.

1494 President
The Cuban president whose regime is described as nearing an end
is Juan Battista.

1495 Red Vulture
Segura.

1496 Reverend Mother
Head of the convent school attended by Milly.   She shocks
Wormold by telling him of Milly's behavior.

1497 Rodriguez
One of Wormold's fictional agents, called "a night-club king" (98).

1498 Rudy
An agent who arrives with Beatrice to carry out radio
communications and other tasks while serving ostensibly as
Wormold's assistant accountant.

1499 Rutherford, Lord
Ernest Rutherford (1871-1937), British physicist, distinguished for
atomic research; winner of the Nobel Prize in 1908.

1500 Sanchez, Maria
Professor Sanchez's jealous wife, mentioned as the cause of great
anxiety for her husband's mistress.

1501 Sanchez, Professor
Listed by Wormold as a sub-agent who provides economic
intelligence. When Wormold goes to Sanchez's house to warn him
that his life may be in danger, he is suspected by Sanchez and
his mistress of being in the employ of Sanchez's jealous wife
Maria.

1502 Savage
A member of the Secret Service in London who noticed that
Wormold's sketches looked suspiciously like parts of a vacuum
cleaner.

1503   Segura, Captain
Head police officer in the Havana suburb of Vedado, called the
"Red Vulture" because he "specializes in torture and mutilation"
(36).   He is in love with Milly.

1504   Seraphina
(1) Milly's given name, which in Cuba means "a double of the
second class" (11); (2) Milly's horse.

1505   Severn, Beatrice
Agreeable, spirited, half-French secretary sent from London to
serve as Wormold's assistant.   Her French is excellent, but what
he really needs is a Spanish speaker.   On her first appearance
Beatrice squirts Segura with a soda water siphon at the Tropicana.
She falls in love with Wormold and is reunited with him in
London.

1506   Severn, Peter
Beatrice's husband, described as a humorless, sensitive, intellectual
type who "sort of faded away" (100).   His infidelities (apparently)
were easy to see through.

1507   Someone who wore green orchids
Probably Oscar Wilde, who wore green cornflowers.

1508   Stein, Gertrude (1874-1946)
The repetitive speech of a drunk man in a Santiago bar reminds
Wormold of modernist American writer Gertrude Stein.   Wormold
is probably comparing the man's "Cuba is Cuba is Cuba" with
Stein's well-known line "A rose is a rose is a rose" (67).

1509   Svenson
Gloomy Swedish businessman at the Traders' Association banquet.

1510   Tattersall's
Upon arrival in London, Milly wants to buy a horse at this long-
established auction-house for bloodstock.

1511   Teresa
Invented by Wormold as his Mata Hari, a subagent who dances

at the Shanghai Theatre and is mistress to two high-ranking members of the Cuban government. Ironically, a dancer and part-time prostitute named Teresa does work at the Shanghai.

1512 Teresa's sister
A Shanghai Theatre dancer who responds to Wormold's half-hearted call for Teresa. He takes her with him for the purpose of warning her sister, but they are stopped by the police and she is eventually released.

1513 Therese, St.
Milly points out that St. Therese was younger than Milly when she entered the convent. (See 2906.)

1514 tourist
The recent shooting of a tourist who was photographing a beggar near the palace in Havana signifies the decline of the Battista regime.

1515 *Tristan*
Hasselbacher plays a recording of Wagner's *Tristan* when Wormold and Beatrice visit him.

1516 UNO
United Nations Organization.

1517 Uhlan
Hasselbacher was once an officer in the Uhlan, or German cavalry.

1518 woman, young
Professor Sanchez's mistress.

1519 Wonder Bar
The usual drinking place for Wormold and his friend Hasselbacher, who is murdered there by Carter.

1520 Wormold, James
The protagonist, a middle-aged Englishman who sells vacuum cleaners in Havana, where he lives alone with his lively and costly

daughter Milly. Hard-pressed for money to support Milly's tastes and habits, he allows himself to be pressed into service as agent for the British Secret Service, a line of work for which he has little interest or qualification. To satisfy his new employers he prepares reports adapted loosely from *Time* magazine and the Cuban newspapers, and he invents imaginary agents drawn from the membership list of the Country Club and other sources. The grandest of his fabrications is a secret military installation which he derives from expanded diagrams of his vacuum cleaners. Some of his imaginary agents have real-life counterparts, however, and when their lives are endangered Wormold is drawn into the world of real espionage and danger. By the time his supposed facts are revealed as fictions, he has avenged the murder of his friend Hasselbacher and won the love of his assistant Beatrice; and he has received so much money and involved so many people that the service, because it cannot afford to punish him, rewards him with a medal and a teaching job.

1521 Wormold, Milly
Wormold's beautiful seventeen-year-old daughter, whose combination of precocity and piety gives her the upper hand over her hapless and devoted father most of the time. Her purchase of a horse and her other extravagances lead Wormold to accept and then exploit his post with the Secret Service in order to pay the bills.

A BURNT-OUT CASE (1961)

1522 "A man who starts looking for God has already found him."
The novel's epigraph is from Pascal's *Pensées* (1670).

1523 administrator
A young man who spends one night in the leproserie and departs

abruptly, leaving behind a copy of the English journal *Architectural Review.*

1524 Agnes, Mother
Mother Superior to the colony of nuns adjoining the leproserie. She believes Marie's accusations against Querry and insists that he stay away from their house.

1525 Akimbu, Marie
African woman who teaches the catechism to boys in the village. Father Thomas disapproves of her because she becomes pregnant every year by a different man.

1526 Algiers
See Hola Camp.

1527 "Aren't I the end of every man's desire?"
Parkinson quotes from Swinburne's "L'Envoy" to *A Ballad of Burdens*: "For life is sweet, but after life is death, / This is the end of every man's desire."

1528 Aretine
Pietro Aretino (1492-1556), Italian writer with a reputation for ribaldry and licentiousness. According to Querry, Aretino determined that there are only thirty-two positions for sexual intercourse.

1529 Attention
A leper who becomes dangerously violent in reaction to the drug D.D.S. and is afraid he will kill his son.

1530 Bardot, Brigitte (1934-)
French actress who became an international sex symbol in the 1950's and 1960's; mentioned by Father Jean.

1531 Bernhardt's Marguerite Gauthier
The role of Marguerite, the courtesan in Dumas' *La Dame aux Camellias,* was central to the repertoire of the great French actress Sarah Bernhardt. The narrator compares Marie Rycker's

enactment of a grand passion before Father Thomas and Mother Agnes to Bernhardt's Marguerite.

1532 Bishop
A tall, rakish man who has a roving eye and flirts briefly with Marie Rycker at the Governor's cocktail party.

1533 Braun, Eva
Hitler's companion, whom he married a few days before their deaths in 1945. (See also Fair Rosamund.)

1534 *cafard*
A mood of boredom or the blues.

1535 captain
The captain of the Bishop's boat which brings Querry to the leproserie is a priest who does not care for river life. He later becomes a teacher of moral theology at Wakanga.

1536 captain, new
The new captain, also a priest, recognizes Querry and offers him beer but shows little curiosity toward him.

1537 Cassin, Mme.
Wife of the Director of Public Works. She attends the Governor's party.

1538 Chartres
The identity of the architect of the great Gothic cathedral at Chartres is unknown. Querry contrasts himself with that architect who worked out of love rather than vanity.

1539 Clare, Sister
A nun who serves as a nurse in the leproserie.

1540 Colin, Dr.
Physician whose life and work are in many respects foils to Querry's: Colin has no vanity, does not desire fame, and works entirely out of humane love; and he has had the experience of a genuine love in a happy marriage which left him, after his wife's

death, without the need for affairs with other women. Colin's loss of faith occurred long ago, and unlike Querry he is not distressed by his atheism. On the contrary, he regards his work as a "gamble" on the belief that life is worthwhile and human goodness possible.

1541 Colin's mother
Mentioned as currently enjoying a holiday in the Swiss Alps.

1542 Colin's wife
Deceased wife of Dr. Colin, by his own account the only woman he ever needed. She lies buried only a hundred yards from the leproserie.

1543 controller
The controller of customs for Otraco is an elderly Flemish man who speaks little French. When Querry visits him to ask for help in locating a parcel containing Colin's medical equipment, the man is cordial until he learns that Querry is from the leproserie; then he is uneasy for fear of infection.

1544 D.D.S.   ,
Dianinodiphenyl sulfone, also called Dapsone, a drug used in the treatment of leprosy.

1545 de Rubempré, Lucien
A young poet, a central character in Balzac's *Illusions Perdues* (1837-43).

1546 Deo Gratias
A fingerless, toeless victim of leprosy, a "burnt-out case" in whom the disease has run its course, Deo Gratias is given a job as Querry's servant because he wants to remain in the village. His disappearance in search of Pendélé and his subsequent rescue by Querry enable the protagonist to demonstrate, in spite of his protests to the contrary, that he does care about something or someone and does desire happiness.

1547 *Exegi monumentum*
Parkinson incorrectly attributes to Virgil the line from Horace.
(See 1673.)

1548 Fair Rosamund
Rosamund Clifford, whose name Parkinson invokes along with that
of Eva Braun to argue that history is the product of gossip writers,
was believed to have been the mistress of Henry II. According to
some stories she was killed by Queen Eleanor.

1549 Fatima
Parkinson wants to know whether Querry visited the shrine at
Fatima, the Portuguese town where the Virgin is said to have
appeared in a vision to three illiterate children on May 13, 1917,
asking that a shrine be built in her honor.

1550 Francis, St.
Parkinson intends somewhat cynically to depict Querry as a saintly
person who, like St. Francis of Assisi, turned away from worldly
life to pursue a spiritual calling.

1551 Garrigou-Lagrange, Father
After his imprisonment for the murder of Querry, Rycker reads
Garrigou-Lagrange, who is said to have written about
predestination.

1552 Grison
Senior employee in the Post Office who challenged Querry to a
duel after Querry left Grison's wife.

1553 Gropius
Walter Gropius (1883-1944), German/American architect, founder
of the Bauhaus (1919) and a major influence on the theory and
design of twentieth-century architecture.

1554 Guelle, Mme.
The governor's wife, who upon hearing about Querry's covering
Deo Gratias with his own body on the night of the rescue wonders
whether Querry might be homosexual.

1555 Helene, Sister
Telephones Father Thomas to report the news of Querry's alleged
involvement with Marie Rycker.

1556 Henri
A young African employed in Colin's dispensary.

1557 Hoghe
The name, as Querry can best recall, of the young architectural
student loved by Marie Morel before she fell in love with Querry.

1558 Hola Camp
Dr. Colin reflects that "Hola Camp, Sharpeville, and Algiers had
justified all possible belief in European cruelty" (44). In Hola
Camp, Kenya, in 1959, eleven Mau-Mau prisoners were beaten to
death by British soldiers. In Sharpeville, in the Transvaal, police
in March 1960 fired into a crowd of 10,000 protesting the pass
laws; 67 people were killed, 181 injured. In Algiers in 1954-55,
French paratroopers used torture to obtain information to help
them fight the terrorist F.L.N. (Front of National Liberation).

1559 "I did not die, yet nothing of life remained."
The epigraph is from Dante's *Inferno*, Canto XXXIV. (See 1268.)

1560 *The Imitation of Christ*
Marie Rycker reads this highly influential mystical work attributed
to Thomas à Kempis (1380-1471). It traces the upward path of
the Christian soul from renunciation of the world toward union
with God.

1561 Irish singer
Rycker refers to John McCormack (1884-1945), who was made a
count in the Papal peerage in 1928.

1562 Jean, Father
A tall, thin man whose hearty appetite belies his "cadaverous"
appearance (93).   For unspecified reasons he submerges his
background as a superb moral theologian under the guise of a film
fan.

1563 Jeweller
In the parable Querry tells to Marie, the King is a figure of God, and the jeweller who earns fame and wealth but cannot love is Querry himself.

1564 Joseph, Father
A priest whose long service in Africa has given him some of the inflection and manner of the Africans. He works alongside the men on the construction work he supervises.

1565 Lejeune, André
See *Manon Lescaut.*

1566 leper
The leper who finds Deo Gratias' staff is afraid to search for him in the night, even with Querry along.

1567 "Let me have men about me that are fat."
Parkinson quotes from Shakespeare's *Julius Caesar* (I,ii).

1568 Loretto, Holy House of
A community of Catholic women founded in 1609 by Mary Ward. The "house" of Loretto, which is devoted to the instruction of young women in preparation for work as lay apostles, has no enclosure.

1569 Luc
Regional capital.

1570 man, old
A very old man dying of high blood pressure accepts his fate graciously, inquires after Colin's mother, and says he will die tomorrow. He believes in both Christ and the native god Nzambi.

1571 man with elephantiasis
One of the lepers also suffers from elephantiasis and has testicles so large that he must support them with his hands when he walks.

1572 *Manon Lescaut*
The girls in Marie's convent all enjoyed this novel, which Marie

concealed from the nuns by pasting the cover of Lejeune's *History of the Wars of Religion* over it. (See 1721.)

1573   *Marie-Chantal*
Marie Rycker reads serial fiction in this magazine, which always arrives two months late.

1574   Marie's father
Marie's father, who worked for the company that employs Rycker, sent his wife back to Europe for the birth of their child.

1575   Marie's mother
Wrote to tell Marie that their dog Maxime had five puppies.

1576   Matisse
Querry calls the French painter Henri Matisse an amateur when Parkinson talks about his designing of a Dominican chapel on the Cote d'Azur.

1577   mistress, Querry's
See Toute à toi.

1578   Morel, Anne/Marie
Reminded by Rycker of the story of Anne Morel, the girl of eighteen who was said to have killed herself for love of him, Querry replies that the woman's name was Marie, that she was twenty-five at the time, and that she took her own life to escape Querry.

1579   "My name is writ in water."
This line, which Parkinson attributes to Shelley, approximates the epitaph Keats wrote for himself: "Here lies one whose name is writ in water."

1580   "Nature I loved and next to Nature Art."
Parkinson adds this line to Querry's funeral wreath and attributes the words to Browning. Actually it comes from Walter Savage Landor's "I Strove with None" (1853).

1581 *noche oscura*
Father Thomas sees Querry as experiencing the *noche oscura* (dark night of the soul) described in the spiritual writings of St. John of the Cross (1542-91), Spanish Carmelite friar and mystic.

1582 Nzambi
A god whose worship the natives often combine with Christian worship.

1583 O.T.R.A.C.O.
Office de l'Exploitation de Transports Coloniaux (Congolese railway and river transportation administration).

1584 Okapa, Henry
A native of the village where the leproserie is located.

1585 Olo, Thomas
A native of the village where the leproserie is located.

1586 Parkinson, Montagu
Enormously fat journalist who pursues Querry in order to exploit his life for newspaper copy. Parkinson has little respect for either the truth or the private suffering of an individual like Querry. His frequent errors in quoting famous writers may be taken as symptomatic of the distortion of fact in his own writing.

1587 Parkinson's father
The doctors were not honest with Parkinson's father, who died believing that he had nothing but a duodenal ulcer.

1588 Pascal
Dr. Colin says that one must, like Pascal, "gamble on his superstition" (144). (See 1313.)

1589 Paul, Father
With Brother Philippe, in charge of the dynamo which supplies electricity to the Mission and the leper village.

1590 Pendélé
The village of Deo Gratias' boyhood, associated with dancing and

happiness beside a waterfall. To Querry it becomes symbolic of
his own desire for a simple, peaceful, happy life.

1591   Perrins, the
Operators of a local plantation.

1592   Philippe, Brother
A quiet man whose chief responsibility is the overseeing of the
mission's dynamo and electrical system. He speaks only Flemish
and is deferential to the fathers even though he is older than any
of them.

1593   Querry
A world-famous church architect who has become, in his mid-
fifties, figuratively a "burnt-out case," having reached the condition
of spiritual dryness in which he has lost all desire, feeling, and
ambition. Convinced that his works and his many love affairs
have expressed nothing more that his own pride and self-love, he
journeys to the remote interior of the African Congo with the
intention of leaving his entire world behind and living in solitude
where he can harm no one and carry out no more spiritless work.
Nevertheless, his experience there offers the hope of spiritual
regeneration: he displays Christian love for his servant Deo
Gratias, forms valuable friendships with the priests and especially
with Dr. Colin, and progresses in good works from doing minor
errands for the doctor to designing a new hospital for the
leproserie. He even begins to laugh. In the end, however, the
world in the form of the vulgar journalist Parkinson seeks him out,
and his friendship with Marie Rycker--for once an innocent and
selfless relationship with a woman--leads to his murder by her
jealous husband when she claims that he is the father of her
unborn child.

1594   Querry's mother
Querry's mother was English, his father French.

1595   "Quoth the raven never more."
Parkinson quotes the famous line but cannot remember that Poe
wrote it.

1596 Rycker
The middle-aged manager of a palm oil factory who, as a young man, wanted to be a priest and spent six years in a Jesuit seminary. The failure of his vocation makes him perpetually dissatisfied, yet he relishes his enduring trials of the soul as evidence of his spiritual superiority. His marriage to the much younger Marie provides him a housekeeper and companion and protects him from sexual temptation; his self-righteous domination of her life destroys the fragile basis of her affection and thereby exacerbates his secret fear that he cannot satisfy her physically. When Marie tells him that she has had an affair with Querry, whom Rycker has wanted to see as a heroic, saintly character, he shoots Querry in a fit of jealous rage.

1597 Rycker, Marie
Rycker's wife of two years, an inexperienced and unhappy young woman whose convent schooling and her imagination fed by romantic fiction have left her ill-prepared for life with a domineering, sanctimonious husband old enough to be her father. Drawn to Querry partly because he is a sympathetic stranger and partly because of his reputation with women, she uses him to gain revenge against her husband by claiming falsely that Querry is the father of her unborn child.

1598 Salvation Army leader
Wanted by police for defrauding the Africans of blankets and money.

1599 Sharpeville
See Hola Camp.

1600 Simon
Some of the villagers worship a man called Simon who died in jail twenty years ago and is expected to rise again.

1601 storekeeper, Greek
An old man who, having been cuckolded by a young clerk in his employ, ran over the man with a car and then killed himself.

1602   Suetonius (c.70-40 A.D.)
Roman historian, author of *Lives of the Caesars*, invoked by
Parkinson as justification for embellishing fact with imagined
details in order to make a story more interesting.

1603   Superior
Confident, cheroot-smoking director of the Mission, an older priest
who has reached that point of experience where he no longer
finds it desirable to pry too deeply into the motives behind even
the noblest actions of individuals. He is called away to Luc by his
bishop and is replaced by Father Thomas.

1604   Therese of Lisieux, St.
See 2322.

1605   Thérèse, Sister
A nun in Marie's convent school, remembered for breaking her
ankle.

1606   "This too solid flesh is surely melting"
Parkinson paraphrases Hamlet's speech: "O! that this too solid
flesh would melt. . ." (*Hamlet* I,ii).

1607   Thomas, Father
Superintendent of the missionary schools, a young, relatively
inexperienced priest who attempts to overcome his own doubts
and uneasiness in his missionary role by seeing Querry as a saintly
hero.

1608   "To think I am further off from heaven"
Parkinson attributes to Poe a line from Thomas Hood's "I
Remember, I Remember" (1827):   "Now 'tis little joy / To know
I'm farther off from heaven / Than when I was a boy."

1609   *Toute à toi*
The mistress whom Querry left three months ago sends him a
letter signed "toute à toi" ("yours ever"), as he always signed letters
to her. After receiving the letter he refers to her as "toute à toi."

1610 "When we are a child"
The Father Superior paraphrases I Corinthians 13:11:   "When I
was a child, I spake as a child, I thought as a child; but when I
became a man, I put away childish things." The basis for Querry's
reply can be found in Matthew 18:4:   "Whoever humbles himself
like this child, he is the greatest in the kingdom of heaven."

1611 woman, African
Querry suspects that the woman who opens the door at the
Controller's office has been sleeping with the Controller.

1612 woman in market
A colonial woman trying to buy potatoes in the market is told that
none are available, but after saying that she is entertaining the
Governor she is allowed to buy.

1613 woman with palsied fingers
A leper treated by Dr. Colin.

THE COMEDIANS (1966)

1614 Addams, Charles (1912-88)
American cartoonist, best known for his macabre cartoons in the
New Yorker.

1615 *Almanac de Gotha*
Brown's mother says she did not check the *Almanac,* a record of
the European aristocracy, to see whether the count's title was
authentic.

1616 André
Pineda's excellent cook at the embassy, distinguished for his
souffles. To help Brown, Martha stages a quarrel with André and
has him sacked so that Brown can hire him for the Trianon.

1617   Anti-Blood Sports League
American organization whose members voted for Smith.

1618   Asprey's
A prestigious store in New Bond Street, London, long a supplier of jewelry, silver, and ornate objets d'art to the Royal Family.

1619   Barbot
A defector, executed with his companions in Port-au-Prince a month before Brown left for New York.

1620   Baron Samedi
Name used by some Haitians for Papa Doc. In voodoo mythology Baron Samedi "haunts the cemeteries in his top-hat and tails, smoking his big cigar" (30).

1621   Barrymore, John (1882-1942)
American actor for whom the Trianon suite in which the Smiths stay is named, an ironic situation in that Barrymore was a notorious alcoholic, and the Smiths pointedly abstain from alcohol as well as meat.

1622   Baxter, Mr.
Passenger aboard the *Medea,* a pharmaceutical salesman who was an air raid warden in London during the blitz. At the farewell party he wears a steel helmet and recites his dramatic monologue called "The Warden's Patrol." Brown's suspicion that Baxter has a weak heart proves correct: he dies of a heart attack later and is buried in Santo Domingo.

1623   beggar
Legless man in Duvalierville who tries to sell a cheap statuette to Mr. Smith. When the Secretary of Social Welfare calls the man an "artist" who is cared for by the government, Smith pays him anyway, but the beggar's money is immediately stolen.

1624   Benoit
Haitian artist whose pictures have been purchased for the Museum of Modern Art.

1625 Berkeleyan
Martha calls Brown a Berkeleyan, meaning a follower of the
idealistic philosophy of Bishop George Berkeley (1685-1753), who
insisted that reality is created by the mind. (See 1253.)

1626 Boadicea (d. A.D. 61)
Ancient British queen who led her people, the Iceni, in a failed
rebellion against the Romans.   Jones claims to have played
Boadicea once before an audience that included Lord
Mountbatten.

1627 Bormann, Martin (1900?-1945)
Nazi leader and close adviser to Hitler.   Pineda, whose wife
Martha is the daughter of a Nazi war criminal, says to Brown that
children are innocent, that Bormann's son became a priest in the
Congo.

1628 Bourbon
A European family from which descended rulers of France, Spain,
Sicily, and Parma.

1629 bren
English-made .303 calibre submachine gun.

1630 Brown
The protagonist and narrator, a middle-aged proprietor of a
Haitian resort hotel. Left as a child to the care and tutelage of
Jesuits, he once believed himself to have a vocation but eventually
drifted away from the church and belief.   Having left Haiti
because the oppressive political climate has destroyed the tourist
trade on which his business depends, he returns because of his
attachment to his mistress Martha Pineda and because his hotel
affords the only sense of home he has known.   Determinedly
uncommitted to any faith or ideology, he is nevertheless drawn
into the political conflict against his will as he aids the Smiths in
their dealings with the local authorities, befriends the widow
Philipot and her nephew, and helps Jones first to escape from the
Tontons and later to join the rebel forces in the hills. Because
this last action makes it impossible for him to return to his hotel,

he takes a job in Mr. Fernandez's funeral parlor in Santo Domingo.

1631 Brown, Maggie
Name taken by Brown's mother when the hiring of Englishwomen was fashionable in Port au Prince.

1632 Brown's father
Brown has never known his father, whom his mother describes as "a bit of a swine" (81). She believes him to be dead but is not certain.

1633 Brutus
The Roman names of Brutus (owner of a Haitian boulangerie) and Cato (owner of a garage) make Brown aware of how "the stubborn memories of this black people preserved the memories of a better republic" (319).

1634 call-girl
Because Brown used the services of a call-girl in New York, he assumes that Martha was similarly unfaithful in his absence.

1635 Capone, Al (1899-1947)
Notorious gangster, head of a Chicago-based crime syndicate.

1636 *capote anglaise*
Condom.

1637 Capriole, Father Thomas
A Jesuit priest Brown promised his teachers he would get in touch with after leaving school.

1638 captain
The captain of the *Medea* is a well-scrubbed, rather distant Dutchman who is unwilling to smuggle Jones out of Haiti on his ship but courageously refuses to let the Tontons search it while Jones hides on board.

1639 captain's wife
The captain of the *Medea* has a photograph of his wife, whose
hair seems to Brown to be set in concrete.

1640 cashier
The cashier at the casino in Port-au-Prince identified the Pinedas
for Brown before he met them.

1641 Catherine, Mère
Operator of a well-known brothel in Port-au-Prince.

1642 Cato
See Brutus.

1643 *"ce ci gros neg"*
"This big black man," as Dr. Magiot refers to himself in his
farewell letter to Brown.

1644 chargé, British
Friendly, hollow-chested man whose "amused air of defeat" and
"sensitive features" remind Brown of R.L. Stevenson (122). He
defies the Tontons by putting on black glasses whenever he sees
them.

1645 Charters
Acquaintance of Jones in Imphal who actually could smell water,
as Jones claims to have done.

1646 chef
The chef on the *Medea* performs for the passengers at the
farewell party, singing solos and leading an "orchestra" of his
assistants who play on kitchen utensils.

1647 Chiang Kai-Shek (1887-1975)
Chinese Nationalist leader, president of Taiwan from 1950 until his
death in 1975; mentioned by Magiot as one who fed communists
"into the boilers of railway engines" (353).

1648 Christophe, Emperor
Henri Christophe (1767-1820), a freed black slave who helped

Toussaint L'Ouverture in the liberation of Haiti and later became a tyrannical king, ruling in North Haiti as King Henri I from 1806 until his suicide in 1820.

1649   Colonel of the palace guard
The third "devil" for whom Henri Philipot plans to fashion a silver bullet; the other two are Papa Doc and Fat Gracia.

1650   Comtesse, la
See Lascot-Villiers.

1651   Concasseur
Malevolent officer of the Tontons Macoute who menaces Brown, whom he dislikes, and exposes the fraudulence of Jones. He is killed by Philipot's men.

1652   cook
The cook at the Trianon when Brown first arrived there was so bad that Brown ate grapefruit most of the time. This cook was replaced by a later one, the specialist in souffles, who had been in Pineda's employ but was fired after Martha staged an altercation with him in order to make him available to Brown.

1653   corridors of power
The novel about "corridors of power" which Brown finds so boring that he does not bother to pick it up after dropping it from his deck chair on the *Medea* is probably C.P. Snow's *Corridors of Power* (1963), published three years before *The Comedians*. (See 2444.)

1654   *Corruptio optimi*
See 572.

1655   Coward, Noel (1899-1973)
English actor, composer, playwright, and director. Coward performed for the troops at Imphal when Jones was in charge of entertainment there, but Jones did not meet him.

1656   *crise de foie*
A liver attack.

1657 Croupier
A scowling man whose darkening face seems to reflect
unhappiness over the government-run casino in Port-au-Prince.

1658 Dahomey
Formerly part of West Africa, since 1975 called Benin.
Voodooists, as Magiot explains, believe in both the Christian god
and the gods of Dahomey.

1659 *Das Kapital*
This principal work (1867-1894) of Karl Marx is among the books
in Dr. Magiot's library.

1660 Dechaux, M.
Former owner of the Trianon, who tried to evade taxes by putting
the hotel in the name of his secretary, Brown's mother. She
agreed to leave it to Dechaux in her will, but he died at thirty-
five in an automobile accident.

1661 Dechaux's wife
A fat Haitian woman who, according to Brown's mother, was
detested by her husband and could never have run the Trianon.

1662 *Dégoutant*
Disgusting.

1663 "The devil is like a roaring lion seeking whom he may
devour."
Dr. Magiot quotes loosely from I Peter 5.

1664 Dewey
Thomas E. Dewey, Truman's opponent in the 1948 presidential
campaign.

1665 "Distance lends enchantment to the view."
Petit-Pierre inaccurately attributes to Wordsworth this line from
Thomas Campbell's "The Pleasures of Hope" (1799).

1666 Don Juan
Pineda's dog.

1667 Dubois, Alexandre
Brown's mother's lawyer, a nominal shareholder in the Trianon.

1668 Dupont, Monsieur Clement
Funeral director in charge, with his brother, of services for Philipot.

1669 Dupont, Monsieur Hercule
Twin brother and partner of Clement Dupont.

1670 Duvalierville
Uncompleted, corruption-ridden project intended to become Haiti's model city along the lines of Brasilia. Mr. Smith wants to open a vegetarian center there until his visit to the site reveals the hopelessness of his plan.

1671 E.N.S.A.
Entertainments National Service Association, the organization in which Jones, who was rejected by the army, actually served.

1672 Emil
One of Philipot's men, wounded in the foot in the fighting.

1673 *Exegi monumentum aere perenius*
"I have executed a memorial longer lasting than bronze" (from Horace's *Epistles* xxx.1). Brown, who has forgotten most of his Latin, recalls this passage on the day when his mother dies and he suddenly realizes that he wants to make the Trianon the premier Caribbean tourist hotel.

1674 Fernandez, Mr.
A passenger on the *Medea* whose unexplained weeping on the last night aboard is later attributed to his mother's illness. An undertaker in Santo Domingo, he hires Brown after the latter's escape from Haiti.

1675 Fernandez's mother
Believed by her son to have been seriously ill, she is later reported to have only a benign tumor and to have been converted to vegetarianism by Mrs. Smith.

1676 Ferry, Madame
Magiot's cook and housekeeper.

1677 French letters
Slang for condoms.

1678 Frère Laurent
Friar Lawrence in Shakespeare's *Romeo and Juliet*, played by
Brown in a school performance.

1679 "From whence cometh our help."
Jones quotes loosely from Psalm 121: "I lift up mine eyes unto
the hills, from whence cometh my help."

1680 gardener
Mentioned as having left the Trianon in fear when M. Philipot
came.

1681 George, Henry (1839-97)
American economist who advocated a single tax on land to pay
the costs of government.   Smith recalls that another minor
candidate in the 1948 presidential race was a disciple of George.

1682 Gracia, Fat
Head of the Tontons Macoute.

1683 *The Great Good Place* (1900)
Brown reads this tale by Henry James in which a man oppressed
by the weight of his work as a writer and his social obligations
dreams of life in a hotel-like establishment where all is peaceful
and someone else attends to his work.

1684 Greco, Juliette
Petit Pierre has ordered recordings by popular singers Juliette
Greco, Johnny Halliday, and Françoise Hardy for his new stereo.

1685 grippe
In Brown's sense, affliction.

1686　Halliday, Johnny
See Greco.

1687　Hamit
Syrian storekeeper who rents a room to Brown and Martha.
Later he is revealed to be an agent for the revolutionary forces,
an ally of Henri Philipot.

1688　hanged man
A card in the Tarot pack of fortune-telling cards.　　Brown
associates it with Martha's father, who was hanged.

1689　Hardy, Francoise
See Greco.

1690　Hochstrudel, Wilbur K.
Mentioned as an expected guest at the Ambassador Hotel in
Santo Domingo.

1691　Holyrood
The Royal Scottish palace in Edinburgh.

1692　houngan
Voodoo priest.

1693　Hugo
Mrs. Smith diligently studies *Hugo's French Simplified* or one of
the similar publications of Hugo's Language Institute, London.

1694　Hyppolite
Haitian artist whose paintings have been purchased by both Pineda
and the Comtesse.

1695　Imphal
City in Manchipur, India.

1696　"Je suis le Drapeau Haitien, Uni et Indivisible."
Duvalier's motto:　"I am the Haitian flag, united and indivisible."

1697   Jones, H.J.
A likable con-artist who arrives with Brown and the Smiths on the *Medea* for the purpose of stealing money from the Haitian government through a fraudulent arms sale. When his scheme is exposed he escapes, with Brown's help, to Pineda's embassy, where his growing friendship with Martha arouses the jealousy of Brown. Brown uses Jones's boasting about his heroic military exploits to trick him into agreeing to lead the Haitian rebels; Jones confesses that he was never in the army but is nevertheless happy to have a chance to end his life with a heroic gesture. He dies in combat and is celebrated as a hero by his comrades.

1698   Joseph
Brown's bartender and man of all work at the Trianon, best known for his rum punches. Counting himself among the ignorant people who believe in voodoo, he participates in the ritual in which young Philipot prepares for revolutionary battle, and he too joins the campaign. Prior to the opening of the novel he was made impotent by a severe beating from the Tontons Macoute.

1699   justice of the peace
An old man who is one of the only two inhabitants seen in Duvalierville during Mr. Smith's visit. He steals the money Smith gives to the other resident, a legless beggar.

1700   Kenyatta, Mr.
James Kenyatta (1893?-1978), well-known leader of pan-African nationalist movements, first president of Kenya.

1701   Kerouac
Jack Kerouac (1922-69), American "Beat" writer. A young man in Philipot's former group of artists and writers wanted to become the Kerouac of Haiti.

1702   King Charles's head
In Dickens's *David Copperfield* the lovable lunatic Mr. Dick cannot complete his memoirs because the head of King Charles keeps appearing in the writing. Mr. Smith is aware that some people at home think the vegetarian center is his King Charles's head.

1703 *lacrimae rerum*
Tears for the world's suffering.

1704 Lascot-Villiers, Comtesse de
Brown's mother, an adventuress whose remarkable life has
demonstrated a zest for love and living and, in her involvement in
the French underground, the kind of involvement her son's life
lacks.

1705 Leger
Fernand Leger (1910-55), French painter.

1706 *Les Fleurs du Mal*
Philipot acknowledges that his poetry was strongly imitative of
Baudelaire's volume *Les Fleurs du Mal.* (See 1760.)

1707 *Les Miserables* (1862)
Novel by Victor Hugo, in Magiot's library.

1708 *Les Mystères de Paris* (1843)
Novel by Eugene Sue, in Magiot's library.

1709 lieutenant, Dominican
Dominican officer in charge of the border guard at Pedro Santana
near the Haitian border. He recognizes Brown and is hospitable
to the wounded rebels who cross into his country.

1710 lieutenant, police
A gold-toothed officer, noted for his powerful punch, who tries
unsuccessfully to get the captain of the *Medea* to allow him to
search the ship for Jones.

1711 Louise
One of Mère Catherine's girls, a favorite of Concasseur, who
offers her to Brown to show his own freedom from jealousy.

1712 Lucy, St.
Patron saint of those afflicted in the eyes. Her banner is carried
in the voodoo ritual witnessed by Brown.

1713 Luigi
Italian engineer known by Brown.

1714 Lumumba
Patrice Lumumba (1925-61), first prime minister of the Congo
Republic (now Zaire). Jones claims to have been in Leopoldville
during Lumumba's time.

1715 Macmillan
Harold Macmillan (1894-1986), Conservative British statesman,
prime minster from 1957 to 1963.

1716 Magiot, Dr.
A distinguished heart specialist who is a Marxist supporter of the
rebel faction in Haiti. He was a friend and admirer of Brown's
mother and is a friend and counselor to Brown himself, whom he
advises to find a new faith to replace the one he has lost. Magiot
is murdered by the Tontons.

1717 Maigret
Famous detective created by Georges Simenon (1903-89).

1718 *mal de mer*
Seasickness.

1719 Man Friday
The British chargé refers to Jones's driver as his Man Friday
(after Robinson Crusoe's Friday).

1720 Manichean
A follower of the religion or ideas of the prophet Mani, who
believed in the dualism of good and evil. Brown refers to himself
as a Manichean.

1721 Manon
The amoral young girl in Abbe Prevost's novel *Manon Lescaut*
(1731) who resists attempts to make her a nun and becomes
instead the unfaithful mistress of Des Grieux, who loves her
ardently. Brown decides that his initial misinterpreting of the

signature on his mother's postcard as "Manon" rather than "Maman" (mama) was appropriate. (See 1572.)

1722 maquis
Underground forces.

1723 Marcel
The black lover of la Comtesse, who leaves him a share in the hotel which he promptly sells to Brown before committing suicide in despair over her death.

1724 marksman
Haiti's best sharpshooter, whose house was burned down after he was suspected (without evidence) of participating in a plot to kidnap Duvalier's children.

1725 Martha's father
A Nazi, hanged in the American zone during the occupation of Germany.

1726 *Medea*
The Dutch cargo ship on which Brown, Smith, and Jones arrive in Haiti.

1727 "Men have died and worms have eaten them, but not for love"
Brown quotes from Shakespeare's *As You Like It* (IV,i,110).

1728 Midge
Jones's name for the Pineda's dog, to which the dog answers.

1729 militia man
See woman, peasant.

1730 Mindszenty
Josef Mindszenty (1892-1975), Roman Catholic cardinal who was sentenced to life imprisonment by the Hungarian government for his anti-Communist sympathies. During the rebellion of 1956 he escaped to the U.S. legation, where he remained for several years.

1731 Minister for Social Welfare
See Secretary for Social Welfare.

1732 Mountbatten, Lord (1900-79)
British admiral, supreme commander of the allied forces in Southeast Asia (1943-46), Viceroy of India (1948). Jones claims to have performed before him.

1733 Msloz
Name used by Brown to sell mass-produced paintings. When people would not buy the works of Msloz, he changed the signature to "Weill."

1734 N.A.A.F.I.
Navy, Army, and Air Force Institutes, an organization which oversees canteens, clubs, and certain provisions for the British armed forces.

1735 Nelson, Mr. Chick
American customer during happier days at the Trianon.

1736 Ochs's, the Henry S.
Friends who entertained the Smiths in Philadelphia prior to their departure on the *Medea.*

1737 Ogoun Ferraille
A voodoo god, the patron of warriors.

1738 Othello and Desdemona
Brown suspects Jones of winning Martha's love through his tales of adventure, as Othello won Desdemona's in Shakespeare's *Othello.* (See 100.)

1739 painter, aging
Member of young Philipot's group who drove a camion by day and painted at the American art center at night.

1740 *Panem nostrum quotidianum da nobis hodie.*
"Give us this day our daily bread." Fragments of the Lord's

Prayer and other familiar prayers are heard in the voodoo ritual witnessed by Brown.

1741 Papa Doc
Nickname of Francois Duvalier (1907-71), a physician who served in the government of Haiti, rose to power and ruled the country as president in a brutal, oppressive dictatorship from 1957 to 1971.

1742 patois
Provincial dialect.

1743 peasant
A man sent by the Tontons to lure Dr. Magiot out of his house by asking him to help a sick child. He is killed, probably accidentally, when they shoot Magiot.

1744 Pétionville
The location of Brown's Trianon hotel.

1745 Petit Pierre
Haitian journalist, a small energetic man whose constant laughter seems at odds with the grimness of current conditions. Rumored to have connections with the Tontons, he nevertheless risks occasional satire in his gossip column.

1746 Philipot, Dr.
Haitian Secretary for Social Welfare, "not bad as government officials go" (58), who commits suicide in the swimming pool at the Trianon after getting in trouble with the Duvalier regime.

1747 Philipot, Henri
The late Monsieur Philipot's nephew, a poet turned revolutionary who enlists Brown's aid in the recruitment of Jones for the rebel cause.

1748 Philipot, Mrs.
Beautiful widow who bravely defies the police and the Tontons in a hopeless attempt to give her husband a proper burial.

1749 Philipot's son
The young son of Secretary Philipot asks for ice cream during the
interruptions of his father's funeral procession.

1750 Piaf, Edith (1915-63)
Popular French nightclub singer.

1751 Pineda, Angel
Martha's plump young son, inordinately fond of sweets and
demanding of his mother's attention. Brown dislikes the child,
recognizing him as the chief rival for Martha's affection.

1752 Pineda, Luis
Stout, middle-aged ambassador from a small, unnamed South
American country. He maintains an air of superiority and, toward
his wife Martha, possessiveness even though he almost certainly
suspects her affair with Brown.

1753 Pineda, Martha
Brown's mistress, the discontented wife of a South American
diplomat and daughter of a Nazi war criminal. Although she loves
Brown, her unwillingness to jeopardize her son's happiness by
leaving her family makes it impossible for her to gain Brown's
trust. Her innocent friendship with Jones sparks an irrational
jealousy in Brown that destroys their relationship.

1754 *pompes funebres*
Brown refers to his later work as that of an *entrepreneur de
pompes funebres,* or undertaker.

1755 *pretre manqué*
A failed priest.

1756 priest at police station
Brown recalls having seen a priest wait all day to see someone at
the police station only to be turned away when the station closed.

1757 priest in Santo Domingo
At the Mass for Joseph and his three dead companions in Santo

Domingo, the priest advocates going up to Jerusalem to die with
St. Thomas.

1758 purser
Convivial officer on the *Medea*, good-humored and fond of drink.
Unable to find balloons for decorations at the ship's concert, he
inflates condoms and paints faces on them.

1759 *putain*
Whore.

1760 *"Quelle est cette ile triste et noire?"*
Philipot quotes from Baudelaire's "A Voyage to Cythera" lines
which may be translated as follows: "What is that sad, dark
island? / 'Cythera' someone says--'a country famous in song, /
Eldorado of old men. / Look, it is only a poor country after all.'"

1761 Renan's *Vie de Jesus*
Dr. Magiot's library includes this best-known volume from the part
of the study of Christianity from a historical perspective by Ernest
Renan (1823-92).

1762 *Revenge*
In heroic defense of one of her girls, Mère Catherine reminds
Brown of "a little *Revenge*, prepared to take on a fleet" (174).
The *Revenge*, flagship of Sir Francis Drake in his campaign
against the Spanish Armada, fought a famous last battle under the
command of Sir Richard Grenville in 1591, holding out for over
half a day against fifteen Spanish warships.

1763 Rizzio
Italian secretary and favorite of Mary, Queen of Scots, murdered
in Holyrood Palace in 1566 by conspirators supported by her
husband Darnley and other Scots noblemen.

1764 "rolled round earth's diurnal course"
Brown quotes Wordsworth's "A Slumber did my Spirit Seal"
(1800).

1765   Sans Souci
Luxurious palace built by Christophe.

1766   Secretary for Social Welfare
Haitian official who shows Mr. Smith Duvalierville and tries to
lure him into a scheme for defrauding the Haitian government as
well as the American contributors.

1767   Secretary of State
Accepts a bribe from Smith to help get Jones out of the Haitian
jail.

1768   Smith, Mrs.
The loyal and affectionate wife who has shared her husband's
vegetarian ideals and his various campaigns, including the freedom-
bus rides in Nashville.   In spite of her pacifism she has a fiery
temper and great courage which enable her to drive Concasseur
and his men out of the Trianon, saving Brown from serious injury
and probably from death.

1769   Smith, William Abel
Eccentric but courageous and high-minded American who comes
to Haiti to arrange for the creation of a vegetarian center. Called
"the Presidential Candidate" because he ran in the 1948 race, he
also participated in campaigns against racism in the South.
Because his dedication to the welfare of blacks blinds him at first
to the nature of the government in Haiti, he maintains an
idealistic hopefulness in the face of mounting evidence of the
corruption and brutality of the Duvalier regime, but eventually he
is forced to give up and leave. Brown regards Smith at first as a
comic figure but later sees him as heroic.

1770   *Sortes Virgilianae*
The technique of looking at random into the works of the poet
Virgil to divine the future or otherwise obtain wisdom.   (See
1902.)

1771   Sotheby's
Famous auction house in London.

1772 statue of St. Clare
In the church in Santo Domingo where they meet for the last
time, Brown and Martha stand by a "hideous statue" of St. Clare
(351) as she tells him of Pineda's transfer to Lima. St. Clare was
the first abbess of the Order of St. Clare, a religious order for
women founded by St. Francis in 1212.

1773 "That aspects are within us. . . ."
The novel's epigraph is from the final stanza of Thomas Hardy's
"A Young Man's Exhortation" (1867): "If I have seen one thing
/ It is the passing preciousness of dreams; / That aspects are
within us; and who seems / Most kingly is the king." (See 2591.)

1774 Tin-Tin
One of Mère Catherine's prostitutes, a favorite of Brown.
Concasseur hires her for Jones.

1775 toff
A stylishly-dressed person; a "swell" or a snob.

1776 Tontons Macoute
The "bogey-men," Duvalier's special police who wear dark glasses
to heighten the terror they instill in their victims.

1777 Tooting Bec
Area of south London, near Clapham.

1778 Trianon
Brown's hotel, inherited from his mother. (It may be more than
coincidence that Graham Greene lived for several years in Albany,
Piccadilly, a couple of blocks from one of London's best-known
and most prestigious hostelries, Brown's Hotel.)

1779 Truman's daughter
Margaret Truman Daniel, daughter of the American president.

1780 Tshombe
Henri Philipot says the Haitian rebels need mercenary soldiers
such as those who served Moise Tshombe (1919-69), leader of the

attempt of the Katanga province to secede from the newly independent Congo state, which he later served as premier.

1781 Vendeuse
Shopgirl or saleswoman.

1782 "the wild waters of our horrible times"
Reading this line in *The Great Good Place*, Brown puzzles over what might have disturbed Henry James in that era which seems so confident and stable in contrast to Brown's own. (See 1683.)

1783 Wilson, Schuyler
American who declines to hire Brown as catering manager for his firm, which operates a bauxite mine near Santo Domingo.

1784 Wingate
Orde Charles Wingate (1903-44), British army officer whose guerilla force, known as "Wingate's Raiders" or the "Chindits," campaigned effectively against the Japanese forces in the Burmese jungles in World War II. Brown asks Jones whether he was one of Wingate's men in Burma and is told that Jones served in a similar outfit.

1785 woman in Monte Carlo
A woman fifteen years Brown's senior, who meets him in the casino, invites him to her room, and provides his first experience of sex.

1786 woman, peasant
Forced by a militia man to give sexual favors before she is allowed to pass a roadblock on her way to Kinscoff, she goes with him into a deserted garden where she discovers the body of Mr. Philipot.

TRAVELS WITH MY AUNT (1969)

1787 A.D.
These initials on his aunt's postcard are almost certainly, as Henry
suspects, those of her former lover Achille Dambreuse.

1788 *A chacun son goût*
Each to his own taste.

1789 Abdul, General
The old friend whom Augusta travels to Istanbul to see, bearing
with her a gold ingot which she intends to invest in some
speculative scheme he has proposed. Upon arrival she learns that
he has been arrested and then shot by the police in an attempted
escape.

1790 Ada
A middle-aged woman whom Wordsworth was forced to accept in
a date-swapping party for Heathrow employees.

1791 Alexander VI (1431-1503)
The "Borgia Pope," whose fathering of Caesare and Lucretia
Borgia was one measure of his worldliness.

1792 Alma Tadema, Sir
Sir Lawrence Alma-Tadema (1836-1912), Dutch-English painter
best known for his studies of Greek and Roman life.

1793 American boy and girl
A young couple on the train, bound for Istanbul and the Gulhane,
who are joined briefly by Tooley.

1794 Aretino
See 1528.

1795 Atwell, Mabel Lucy
Painter mentioned by the vicar of St. John's, who recently purchased one of her drawings.

1796 Bertram, Aunt Augusta
Henry Pulling's 75-year-old aunt, who shows up at his mother's cremation and draws him into a series of adventures which alter his life and outlook forever. With flaming red hair and wide-spaced teeth which, like the Wife of Bath's, suggest a strong sensual life, she is in every respect the opposite of Henry--extravagant, energetic, pleasure-seeking, and romantic in the sense that she believes in abandonment to love. She takes Henry on literal journeys to Brighton, Paris, Boulogne, Istanbul, and Paraguay, while her wonderful stories of past lovers and adventures are travels of the mind which create in him an enthusiasm for the kind of life he has never known. Augusta is finally reunited with her true love, Mr. Visconti, and decides to settle down to a life centered around his smuggling racket in Paraguay. Henry remains with her, having realized at last that she is his mother.

1797 Blennerhasset, Mrs.
A former customer at Henry's bank who read lips and thus thought that Henry, who habitually moves his lips when he is thinking, was talking to her when he said to himself that she was lovely.

1798 Brighton Belle
A fashionable Pullman train which ran between London and Brighton for many years until the 1970's.

1799 Butlin's Camp
A type of English holiday camp for families, consisting of cottages surrounding a center where entertainment (films, dancing, card-playing, and the like) is available.

1800 Callot, Anne-Marie
Augusta's friend, a young woman who was murdered and
dismembered on the train between Paris and Calais by the
Monster of the Chemins de Fer.

1801 Camilla
Beautiful daughter of the Chief of Police in Asunción. Henry
dances with her at Visconti's party.

1802 Carpenter, Edward (1844-1929)
English writer and social reformer. (See Ellis.)

1803 Charge, Major
Henry's brusque neighbor, who agrees to care for Henry's dahlias
in his absence, almost destroys them by withholding water in order
to teach them discipline.

1804 Chicken
London restaurant or caterer which often delivers Henry's meals
to his home.

1805 chief customs officer
Enormously fat guest at the party given by Visconti and Aunt
Augusta. He advises everyone to eat meat and complains that his
daughter Maria does not eat enough. He introduces Maria to
Henry and approves later of their engagement.

1806 chief of Police
A guest at Visconti's party.

1807 Collins, Wilkie
Henry says that if he could have been a writer he would have
styled himself after one of the minor Victorians--Wilkie Collins,
Robert Louis Stevenson, or Charles Reade.

1808 Comfort
One of Augusta's stories concerns a girl named "Comfort" who fell
in love with a man named "Courage" who was afraid of mice. She
eventually married a man called Payne and became sufficiently
unhappy to commit suicide in a "comfort station."

1809   Crawford, Marion
Henry's father had a complete set of the works of Francis Marion
Crawford (1854-1909), an Italian-born American romantic novelist.

1810   Crowder, Harvey
Crowder (a Chicago meatpacker) and Weissman (a German), are
the friends to whom General Abdul appealed for money to
advance his unspecified schemes in Istanbul. Hakim says that both
have been arrested and have talked.

1811   Crown and Anchor
Pub over which Augusta's London flat is located.

1812   Curlew, Melany
William Curlew's near-perfect wife, whose only flaw, a considerable
demand for sex, would only have added to her perfection in the
mind of a more virile husband.

1813   Curlew, William
Henry's father's partner, regarded as weak by Augusta,
experienced a failure of passion and tried to protect his vanity by
convincing his wife that he had been unfaithful. Unfortunately she
did not leave him as he expected but remained loving and
forgiving and eager for sex.

1814   Curran, Mr.
An animal trainer whose career in the circus ended after an
elephant stepped on his toe, the Rev. (for "Revered") Curran had
a romantic affair with Augusta, with whom he founded a profitable
church for dogs in Brighton. He married and baptized dogs but
refused to divorce them. Unable to find legal basis for closing the
church, the police finally drove Curran away by arresting him for
speaking to girls on the waterfront.

1815   Czech
A passenger on the boat to Asunción who explains that he once
made two million straws, expecting to sell them in Argentina, but
was able to sell only a hundred. He adds, perhaps ominously, that
he now manufactures "plastic material" (237). Later he offers to
sell the straws at half cost to Mr. Visconti.

1816 Dakota
A Douglas DC-3 airplane.

1817 Dambreuse, Monsieur Achille
One of Augusta's lovers, a lecherous married man of over fifty
who had retired from business because of ill health. He kept two
mistresses, Augusta and Louise, in separate parts of a Parisian
hotel. Even after discovering that she shared his affection with
another woman in addition to Dambreuse's wife, Augusta did not
reject him.

1818 de Gaulle, Madame
General de Gaulle's wife is credited--or blamed--by Augusta for
having rid Paris of a great deal of vice.

1819 "Death is the end of life; ah, why should life all labour be?"
From Tennyson's "The Lotos-Eaters" (1832).

1820 drawing, Leonardo da Vinci
A valuable Leonardo drawing of a dredge, stolen from an Italian
prince by the Nazis, is the object of O'Toole's pursuit of Visconti.
After he purchases it for ten thousand dollars and an agreement
that Interpol investigations of Visconti will end, he leaves and
Visconti explains to Henry that the picture is only a copy; the real
one was destroyed in the war.

1821 DuPont, Louise
The woman with whom M. Dambreuse spent several afternoons
every week when Augusta thought he was at work.

1822 Ellis, Dr. Havelock (1859-1939)
British psychologist, author of several important works on the
psychology of sex; mentioned by Aunt Augusta as having attended
the cremation at which she accidentally sent the casket into the
flames before the service began. The list of people in attendance,
an indication of the prominent circles in which she moved in the
early post-World War I years, also included Mr. and Mrs. Bernard
Shaw, H.G. Wells, Edith Nesbit, Edward Carpenter, and Ramsay
MacDonald.

1823 Emperor Jones
Brutus Jones, a black American who was formerly a Pullman
porter, establishes himself as emperor of a West Indian island in
Eugene O'Neill's play *The Emperor Jones* (1920). Upon first
meeting Wordsworth, Augusta asked him if he was the Emperor
Jones.

1824 *Esmond*
Pulling attributes his preference among Thackeray's novels for
Henry Esmond (1852) over *The Newcomes* (1853-55) to his
"romantic side" (198), but other factors may also be involved.
The protagonist of *Esmond* not only has the same Christian name
but, like Pulling, discovers a new identity when it is revealed that
one of his parents (Pulling's mother, Esmond's father) is not the
person he thought.

1825 Fernandez, Mr.
Cattle farmer who attended the Shanghai Theatre with Augusta.

1826 Francis de Sales, St. (1567-1622)
Italian-born priest and scholar, Bishop of Geneva from 1622.
With St. Jane Francis de Chantal he founded the Order of the
Visitation, an order of nuns dedicated to humility and acts of
mercy.   Among his best-known writings is the influential
Introduction to the Devout Life (1609), a book designed to
instruct the faithful in the preservation of devoted Christian life
amid the distractions and temptations of the secular world.

1827 Frau General
A German general's wife preparing to leave Rome to escape the
Allied invasion confesses her three adulteries to Visconti, who is
disguised as a monsignor. He refuses to give absolution and
thereby forces her to take him in her car so that she can continue
the confession. She does do, leaving her cuckolded husband
behind to face the enemy.

1828 General, the
Alfredo Stroessner (1912-), who became president of Paraguay
after leading a military coup in 1954. He was overthrown in 1989.

1829 gentleman, old
See woman in Maxim's.

1830 girl in jodhpurs
An obscene reference by a girl in jodhpurs at the Crown and
Anchor reminds Henry that he has left his mother's ashes at his
aunt's flat.

1831 girl in Rome
When Visconti was disguised as a monsignor in his effort to
escape from Rome, a promiscuous young woman in a hotel bar
implored him to hear her confession, which he did in a lavatory,
with some difficulty because the extensive intimate confession
excited his own lecherous impulses.

1832 "God's in his Heaven-- / All's right with the world!"
From "Pippa's Song" in Browning's "Pippa Passes" (1841). Henry
and his child bride-to-be read Browning together in the evenings.

1833 Golden Arrow
An all-Pullman train which for decades was the most stylish mode
of travel between London and Paris.

1834 Grenada Palace
Cinema where Wordsworth worked as doorman before Augusta
found him.

1835 *Guy Mannering* (1815)
See Scott.

1836 Hakim, Colonel
Asthmatic, partially deaf Turkish policeman who comes to
Augusta's hotel room in Istanbul to question her about General
Abdul and Mr. Visconti.

1837 Hannibal
The elephant that stepped on Mr. Curran's toe would appear to
be named humorously after the Carthaginian general who crossed
the Alps with elephants to attack Rome (217 B.C.).

1838 Hatty
Augusta's friend who worked with her and Curran in the doggie church; now a fortune-teller in Brighton, where Augusta and Henry visit her.

1839 "He lies where he longed to be . . . home from the hill."
Henry and his aunt quote from Robert Louis Stevenson's "Requiem" (1887).

1840 Hughes, Mr.
South African land surveyor who has proposed to Miss Keene. Her letter asking Henry's advice in the matter clearly expresses a last shy hope that Henry will ask her to return to England and marry him instead.

1841 "If I ask Her to receive me, / Will she say me nay?"
Pulling imagines Wordsworth, on his fatal attempt to see Augusta, "reciting a hymn to keep his courage up" (317). The lines quoted are from John Mason Neale's translation of St. Stephen the Sabaite's "Art thou weary, art thou languid?" Pulling substitutes "Her" (meaning Augusta) for "Him" (meaning Christ).

1842 Indian Queen
A racehorse.

1843 Izquierdo, Mr.
The name on Mr. Visconti's Argentine passport.

1844 Julian
Tooley's boyfriend, a hippie artist who wants to imitate Andy Warhol's work.

1845 Keene, Sir Alfred
An important depositor in Henry's bank who threatened to withdraw his accounts unless the bank made Henry a permanent rather than acting manager. That Sir Alfred often asked Henry's advice about investments but never took it reflects ironically upon Henry's judgment in such matters.

1846   Keene, Barbara
Sir Alfred's daughter, a shy spinster who does tatting and preserves a long friendship with Henry Pulling even after she has moved to South Africa. Her hope that he might ask her to return to England and marry him might have had at least a faint chance had he not met his adventurous aunt.

1847   "Let the dead bury their dead."
Mr. Visconti's favorite biblical quotation is from Matthew 8:22.

1848   Little Flower
See 2906.

1849   MacDonald, Mr. Ramsay
See Ellis.

1850   Mahony
Francis Sylvester Mahony (1804-66), an Irish priest who left the church to become a journalist and poet. Henry says that if he had been a poet he would have been happy to be known as an English Mahony, celebrating his own Southwood as Mahony celebrated the village of Shandon.

1851   man in street
Hits Henry for blowing his nose into a red scarf. (Red is the color of the ruling Colorado party.)

1852   man, little old
The murderer of Wordsworth, whom Visconti fired at Henry's insistence.

1853   man, old
A very old man who speaks no English buys Henry drinks on the steamer for the privilege of reading his hand.

1854   Maria
The chief customs officer's young daughter, whom Henry meets at Visconti's party. She loves English poetry, they are attracted to each other, and they become engaged to be married after her sixteenth birthday.

1855 maté
Paraguayan tea.

1856 "Maud"
Henry's quotations from Tennyson's "Maud" (1855) lead into his
relationship with Maria.

1857 men in *The Merchant of Venice*
The "poor men" Augusta recalls from Shakespeare's play are the
Prince of Morocco and the Prince of Arragon, suitors who fail the
test of the three caskets in their attempt to win Portia's hand in
marriage.

1858 Mengeles, Dr.
Probably Josef Mengele (1921?-1979?), a scholarly Nazi doctor
responsible for many deaths at Auschwitz.   Menegele died in
South America.

1859 merchant
A grey-faced import-export merchant with a twitching nose shares
a table on the river steamer with Henry and O'Toole. Later he
appears at Visconti's party.

1860 Monster of the Chemins de Fer
Notorious murderer who traveled the French railroads with a case
full of brassieres which he persuaded young women to try on; he
murdered those who liked the wrong ones.

1861 Nancy
Miss Truman's shy, quiet partner in the Abbey Restaurant.

1862 Nesbit, Miss E.
Edith Nesbit (1858-1924), English writer best known for children's
books, especially her stories about the "Bastables." (See Ellis.)

1863 *The Newcomes*
See *Esmond.*

1864 Newman, Sir Oswald
See Urquhart, Rose.

1865 Nkrumah, Ex-President
Kwame Nkrumah (1909-), leader of African independence and
pan-African movements; he became the first prime minister of the
Commonwealth state of Ghana in 1957.

1866 nurse
The nurse who attended the eccentric Jo Pulling followed him
through the house, sleeping one week behind him as he
progressed on his "travels" from room to room.

1867 O'Toole, James
Tooley's father, a CIA agent who pursues Mr. Visconti to
Paraguay to recover a stolen da Vinci drawing. Henry meets him
on the river journey to Asunción.

1868 O'Toole, Lucinda ("Tooley")
Tooley, a lively American girl whom Henry meets enroute to
Istanbul, is disarmingly frank, affectionate, and unconventional.
She gives the staid Henry a marijuana cigarette, calls him
"Smudge," and makes him a confidant who shares her unhappiness
over her parents' divorce and her fear (a false alarm) that she is
pregnant. When last heard of she is in Katmandu.

1869 O'Toole's wife
O'Toole divorced his wife because she began bringing her
boyfriend home and was corrupting their daughter.

1870 officer, young
Policeman who knocks Henry down when he carelessly blows his
nose on the red scarf a second time.

1871 Old Steine
Henry is correct is thinking that this Brighton street was not
named for the wicked Lord Steyne in Thackeray's *Vanity Fair*.

1872 Pakistani
One of Augusta's friends who stole a packet of notes worth £1000
in Karachi but could not find anyone to exchange them for him.

1873 Palgrave's *Golden Treasury*
A familiar anthology of songs and poems in English compiled by
Francis Turner Palgrave (1824-97). Henry's love of poetry,
especially Wordsworth, Tennyson, and Browning, is heavily
influenced by the copy of Palgrave he inherited from his father.

1874 Paterson, Miss Dorothy ("Dolly")
Richard Pulling's mistress, whom Henry meets when he and Aunt
Augusta visit his father's grave in Boulogne. The elder Pulling
first took Miss Paterson to Boulogne to give her a holiday because
he was worried about her health. He died in her arms there in
1923.

1875 Player King
In Tunis Augusta saw a performance of *Hamlet* in which the
Player King was severely injured when molten lead was poured
into his ear. The police, who knew the play, arrested Hamlet's
uncle.

1876 pleasant land of Blake
Henry alludes to familiar lines from the prefatory poem to Blake's
Milton (1804-08): "Till we have built the new Jerusalem / In
England's green and pleasant land."

1877 Pottifer, Charles
A former tax collector for the Inland Revenue, Pottifer so hated
that agency that he became a tax counsellor with inventive
schemes for avoiding taxes. He created a fictional company called
Meerkat Products, Ltd., in which Augusta Bertram and several
other women became "directors" and their incomes "directors'
fees."

1878 Poupée
Miss Paterson's alias during the war.

1879 preacher, Dominican
Mentioned as having believed that the alleged proclamation of the
Virgin ("The crooked ways shall be made straight," 106) regarding
the railway "monster" was actually a disparaging comment on the
murderer's Jesuit education.

1880   priest, fat
A priest who resembles Winston Churchill shares a dinner table
with Henry and O'Toole on the steamer.

1881   Pucelle, La
Augusta's repeated insistence that her sister Angelica was "pucelle"
(virginal) and should have had a white funeral is an early
indication that Angelica was not Henry's mother. Joan of Arc was
called "La Pucelle."

1882   Pulling, Angelica
Energetic, austere wife of Richard Pulling. She wore padding to
simulate pregnancy and thus make credible the claim that Henry,
her younger sister's child, was her own child. Angelica preserved
her virginity throughout her marriage to Richard Pulling.

1883   Pulling, Henry
The narrator and protagonist, a quiet, cautious man who has
recently retired from his life's work as a bank manager in order
to settle into a life of bachelorhood centered around dull routines
and the care of his dahlias. At his mother's funeral he meets his
Aunt Augusta, who invites him to join her in travels to Brighton,
Istanbul, Paris, and various other places; by doing so he becomes
awakened to the fuller experience of life she embodies.   In
awakening to the pleasure and excitement of her adventures and
her advocacy of love, he gains literally a new identity, discovering
not only that he has a greater capacity for the enjoyment of life
than he had realized, but that he is Augusta's son.

1884   Pulling, Honest Jo
Henry's uncle, a bookmaker, a fat man who loved to travel but
was unable to do so after having a stroke. He therefore asked
Augusta to find him a house with a different room for every day
of the year so that he could spend a night in each. With her help
he purchased a run-down Italian mansion with fifty-two rooms, but
he got only as far as the fifty-first before his death one night on
the way to the lavatory. Even then, as Augusta remarks, he died
traveling.

1885 Pulling, Richard
Henry Pulling's father, who died forty years before the opening of
the novel, was a building contractor of lethargic disposition and
eccentric habits.   Married to a perpetually virginal wife, he
consoled himself with a love of Victorian writers, especially Scott,
and an affectionate mistress in Miss Paterson.

1886 *quindicina*
La quindicina was the traveling "business" (apparently prostitution)
Aunt Augusta was in briefly in her youth. The term may suggest
young girls--about age fifteen.

1887 Quixote
See Sancho.

1888 Reade, Charles (1814-84)
English novelist. (See Collins, Wilkie.)

1889 rear-admiral
One of Henry's bank customers was a rear-admiral who treated
Henry like a sub-lieutenant.

1890 Rita
A prostitute in Paris, introduced by Wordsworth to Henry, who
does not want her.

1891 *Rob Roy* (1817)
It was in *Rob Roy*, Richard Pulling's favorite among Scott's novels,
that he placed the photograph of Augusta which Henry finds. The
elder Pulling had tried unsuccessfully to get her to read the novel.

1892 Rodriguez
Visconti knows a Dr. Rodriguez who would help him create a
medical hoax to promote the sale of drinking straws.

1893 Rose
The first girl Henry's father ever slept with had an appropriate
name, since she worked in a flower shop.

1894 San Martin, General
José de San Martin (1778-1850), Argentine military leader in the South American struggles for independence from Spain.

1895 Sancho
Henry feels as if he is a Sancho being "dragged along" by a Quixote--his aunt--who pursues fun instead of chivalry.

1896 Scott, Sir Walter
Henry Pulling inherited a complete set of Scott's works from his father, "a great reader but not an adventurous one" (37). By the time the father had read all of Scott, he had forgotten the earlier works and so began once more with *Guy Mannering.*

1897 *The Second Mrs. Tanqueray*
Augusta's weeping account of an old love in the Albany Hotel in Paris makes Henry feel as if he is onstage in a revival of this 1893 play by Arthur Wing Pinero. *Tanqueray* concerns a man's attempt to overcome his moral revulsion against his wife's past, and is set in another "Albany" in London.

1898 "Sell all you have and give it to the poor."
Julian's contemptuous advice to Tooley echoes Matthew 19:21.

1899 Shaw, Mr. and Mrs. Bernard
See Ellis. ——

1900 "She only said, 'The night is dreary, / He cometh not,' she said."
Aunt Augusta quotes from Tennyson's "Mariana" (1830), which she learned from Henry's father.

1901 Smudge
Tooley's dog, which she talked to during the traumatic period of her parents' divorce. Because Henry is a sympathetic listener, she affectionately calls him Smudge.

1902 *Sortes Virgilianae*
Henry plays the *Sortes* with his father's favorite novel, *Rob Roy,* and reflects upon how his mother considered the activity

blasphemous when performed with any book other than the Bible. (See 1770.)

1903 Sparrow, John
Scotland Yard detective who questions Henry about the urn and ashes and, later, about Augusta's involvement with Mr. Visconti.

1904 Stevenson, R.L.
See Collins.

1905 Superman
A professional sex performer in the lowlife entertainment world of Havana. Augusta mentions having seen him.

1906 taxi driver
When Henry, wanting a quiet place to drink, asks a taxi driver in Istanbul to take him to a "safe" place, the driver takes him to a bordello.

1907 "Then take the broidery frame"
From Tennyson's "Day-Dream" (1842).

1908 Thomas of Hereford, St. (c.1218-1282)
English priest, educated in Oxford and Paris; became chancellor of Oxford and in 1275, Bishop of Hereford.

1909 "thou child of joy"
In this passage Augusta quotes loosely from Wordsworth's "Intimations Ode" (1802-4).

1910 "To hear each other's whispered speech"
From Tennyson's "The Lotos-Eaters" (1832).

1911 Tobias
In the apocryphal book of Tobit, Tobias is Tobit's son who, guided by the angel Raphael, heals his father's blindness and drives a demon out of Sarah.

1912 Truman, Miss
Proprietress of the Abbey Restaurant where Henry eats Christmas

dinner. She served in the women's navy and prefers to be called Peter.

1913   Trumbull, Councillor
In St. John's Church, Henry always sits beneath the stained glass window dedicated to Trumbull, a Victorian philanthropist who built an orphanage.

1914   Urquhart, Rose
Maiden name of the widow of Sir Oswald Newman, whose obituary Henry reads in the *Telegraph*, wondering whether Rose loved her husband as much as Miss Paterson loved Henry's father.

1915   Urquiza
Justo José de Urquiza (1801-70), Argentine general who successfully led the revolt against the Rosas dictatorship and became president of the Argentine Confederation (1854-60).

1916   Vernon, Die
Scott's heroine in *Rob Roy*. Henry discovers a photograph of Aunt Augusta which his father had concealed in this favorite novel, on the page containing words of Die Vernon which suggest that he identified the real woman with the fictional: "Be patient and quiet, and let me take my own way; for when I take the bit between my teeth, there is no bridle will stop me" (171).

1917   Vicar of St. John's
A garrulous clergyman who tries to sell Sparrow and Woodrow subscriptions to his parish magazine.

1918   Vietnamese boy and girl
Passengers on the train to Istanbul, brief acquaintances of Tooley.

1919   Visconti Mario
Mr. Visconti's son, a handsome author of verse plays, meets Augusta at the station in Milan. He prefers to think of her as his mother, since he detests his own mother.

1920   Visconti, Mr.
An Italian rogue whose long career on the shady side of the law

includes theft, smuggling, impersonation of a priest, and collaboration with the Nazis (to serve his own ends), Mr. Visconti has spent much of his life in hiding and disguise, surviving on his wit and skill in the art of deception. Because he has never made demands upon her loyalty or freedom (although he has taken her money), Visconti remains the greatest love in Augusta's life in spite of their long absences from each other. United with her permanently at the end of the novel, he has settled down to a relatively sedate life of smuggling in Paraguay. The police detective's reference to him as a "viper" is a private joke based upon Greene's often-quoted statement that early in life he discovered the embodiment of evil in a character named Visconti in Marjorie Bowen's *The Viper of Milan* (1906).

1921 Warhol, Andy (1927-87)
American pop artist whose familiar works include large paintings of Campbell's soup cans. Tooley's friend, the not very original artist Julian, wants to do large paintings of Heinz soup cans.

1922 Weissman
See Crowder.

1923 Wells, Mr. H.G.
See Ellis.

1924 "Where shall the traitor rest . . ."
A song from Scott's *Marmion* (1808), Canto Third, xi.

1925 woman in Maxim's
Augusta tells the story of how an old gentleman in a famous Paris restaurant was embarrassed by a woman who was accidentally a ventriloquist; she caused other patrons to think her comic expressions were his.

1926 woman, young
A young woman who prayed for the railway monster was said to have had a vision of the Virgin.

1927 Woodrow, Detective-Inspector
An officer from the Special Branch who attends the Christmas

service at St. John's in order to discuss with Henry an Interpol
inquiry about Aunt Augusta's involvement with Mr. Visconti.

1928 Wordsworth, Zachary
Aunt Augusta's black lover, whose other activities include
trafficking in marijuana. He is jealous of Augusta and in effect
dies for love of her, since he follows her to the house where she
lives with Mr. Visconti and is killed by a guard on the night of
their party. Henry considers Wordsworth a genuine romantic who
died for love.

1929 Wordsworth's great Ode
William Wordsworth's "Ode: Intimations of Immortality" (1802-4).
Henry had known the great Ode so well from his father's copy of
Palgrave that when he first entered the bank as junior clerk he
thought of it as his "prison-house." The novel contains many
allusions to the poem.

1930 Wright, Wilbur (1867-1912)
Augusta says that she knew the older Wright brother well and flew
with him several times.

THE HONORARY CONSUL (1973)

1931 abogado
Lawyer.

1932 Ana
Plarr's pretty secretary, whose starchy dignity and piety prevent her
from being sexually attractive to him.

1933 Arden
Headmaster of the English school in Buenos Aires attended by
Fortnum; called "Smells" by the boys.

1934   Avila, Saint of
St. Teresa de Jésus (1515-82), a Spanish Carmelite nun, author of
several mystical works. In the face of opposition by both civil and
ecclesiastical authorities, she sought to reform the Carmelite order
and traveled extensively in Spain to promote reform.   She
established the first reformed convent in 1562.

1935   Bagno Regio
Character in one of Borge's stories read by Plarr.

1936   Belfrage, Sir Henry
The cautious, good-willed British Ambassador to whom Plarr
appeals for help with Fortnum's case. Sir Henry's response is to
suggest the formation of an English club for the purpose of
publicizing Fortnum's plight in the London *Times* and the *Daily
Telegraph.*

1937   Belfrage, Lady
The British Ambassador's wife, who calls Charley "Mr. Mason."

1938   Benevento, Dr.
Local physician who looks after the girls in Señora Sanchez's
brothel.

1939   Borges, Jorge Luis (1899-1986)
Argentine writer admired by Plarr.   Borges shares the tastes of
Plarr's father for English writers Conan Doyle, Stevenson, and
Chesterton, and represents to Plarr a welcome change from the
machismo and heroics of Saveedra's world.

1940   Borgia, Caesar
Author of an article on calcium deficiency Plarr reads in the
British Medical Journal.

1941   Bradshaw
A British railway guide (see 2513).   León, reading a detective
mystery, comically interprets "Bradshaw" as a character with
fabulous powers of memory.

1942 Bruce, Robert (1274-1329)
Robert the Bruce, King of Scotland from 1306 to 1329, was excommunicated by the Pope and declared an outlaw by King Edward of England. He went into hiding and solitude on Rathlin Island near the Irish coast, where according to legend he learned the value of unyielding perseverance by watching a spider continue to work at spinning her web in spite of repeated failures.

1943 Buller
A bank manager, a guest at Ambassador Belfrage's cocktail party.

1944 Burton, Richard
Clara's enthusiasm for Hollywood stars Burton and Elizabeth Taylor may involve a private joke by the author, since they were the principal players in the 1967 film version of his novel *The Comedians.*

1945 CC
Consular Corps.

1946 CD
Corps Diplomatique.

1947 Callow
Belfrage's predecessor as British Ambassador to Argentina.

1948 Capablanca
Cuban chess master José Raoul Capablanca (1888-1942), world champion from 1921 to 1927.

1949 Capone, Al
Plarr says that Colonel Perez sounds like American gangster Al Capone, who believed in shooting first and sending wreaths later.

1950 Carlota
One-eyed daughter of Castillo in a story by Saveedra.

1951 Castillo
One of Saveedra's characters, somewhat reminiscent of the

protagonist of Hemingway's *The Old Man and the Sea.* He is shot defending his daughter from rape.

1952 Caterina
A character in Saveedra's most recent novel, drawn from his cleaning woman.

1953 Chateaubriand
René François, vicomte de Chateaubriand (1768-1848), French romantic writer. Plarr, reading from one of Saveedra's books, reflects on how Chateaubriand, Rousseau, and Constant have been more influential in South America than the writings of Freud.

1954 Che
Ernesto "Che" Guevara (1928-1967), Argentine-born leader of guerilla warfare in the Cuban revolution. After serving as Castro's Minister of Industry, he left Cuba in 1965 to promote revolutions in Latin America. In 1967 he was captured in Bolivia and executed.

1955 Chipas
A cake or loaf made from cassava or maize.

1956 Clara's father
A cane cutter who is growing too old to work. Clara says that her parents would starve without the money she sends them.

1957 Clara's sister
Clara's sister died after bearing a child in the fields and strangling it.

1958 Consul, American
The American consul from whom Charley receives the necessary papers concerning the death of his first wife is cordial and pleasant; he invites Charley and Clara for champagne after their wedding.

1959 Crichton
Press Attaché at the British Embassy who complains to Sir Henry

Belfrage about the flood of telephone inquiries concerning Fortnum's kidnapping.

1960 Cyclops
Saveedra explains that his one-eyed character Carlota is a "cyclops symbol" (64) which represents the novelist's art. A "two-eyed" novelist lacks sufficient concentration and, like cinema, includes too much.

1961 Della
Della Street, secretary to the fictional lawyer Perry Mason, was by Plarr's testimony the woman who first awakened his sexual appetite.

1962 Diego, Corredo
Driver for the kidnappers, killed by the police when he resists arrest.

1963 Duran, Señor
A friend, probably a current lover, who accompanies Señora Vallejo to Plarr's funeral.

1964 El Tigre
The supreme leader of the guerrillas, El Tigre is often mentioned but never appears. Aquino complains that El Tigre lives in comfort and safety and never seems to risk his life as Aquino and his comrades are risking theirs.

1965 Escobar, Gustavo
Margarita's husband, who she says is passionately jealous. In fact he has many women and may not have cared much about her affair with Plarr; his claim that he has missed seeing Plarr seems sincere.

1966 Escobar, Señora Margarita
A married woman with whom Plarr once had an affair, as did Perez and Vallejo.

1967 F.O.
Foreign Office.

1968 Final Solution
Nazi euphemism for the extermination of the Jews.

1969 Fisher
Secretary of the Anglo-Argentinian Society, a guest at Ambassador
Belfrage's cocktail party.

1970 Forage
An old gentleman usually to be found at the Hurlingham Club; he
is a guest at Ambassador Belfrage's cocktail party.

1971 Fortnum, Charley
The amiable, alcoholic honorary consul of the title, a man in his
sixties who marries a young prostitute from a local brothel and
lives with her in complaisant ignorance of her affair with his friend
Plarr.   When Fortnum is accidentally kidnapped by guerilla
revolutionaries who mistake him for an American Ambassador, no
one but Plarr takes a serious interest in his case; he is not
important enough to bring about a serious international incident.
Charley is little concerned about his own fate but deeply worried
about his wife and their unborn child; the strength of his love for
Clara earns the respect of Plarr, who realizes that love makes
Charley the winner after all. The kidnappers plan to kill Charley
if their demands are not met, but they delay long enough to allow
the police to catch them. He survives, and he finds the generosity
of heart to forgive both Plarr, who is killed, and Clara, and to
love the coming child even though it is Plarr's and not his own.

1972 Fortnum, Clara
A young prostitute of Indian descent working at Señora Sanchez's
brothel, where she first attracts the attention of Plarr and
Fortnum. Fortnum marries her, but she begins an affair with
Plarr after he buys her a pair of sunglasses. Clara loves Plarr, but
she recognizes in the strength of Charley's affection something of
value which Plarr cannot match, so that in spite of her genuine
grief over Plarr's death she is not altogether unhappy to return to
Charley.

1973   Fortnum, Evelyn
Charley's coldly intellectual first wife, who died in Idaho years ago.
She was a Christian Scientist who refused a Catholic marriage.

1974   Fortnum's father
Charley's father, a heavy drinker who died of a stroke, loved to
ride horses, which his son feared. The father insisted that Charley
try to conquer fear to avoid being conquered by it.

1975   Fortnum's mother
Fortnum's mother died when he was born.

1976   Fortnum's Pride
Charley's Land Rover.

1977   Galvao, Father
A Portuguese Jesuit priest who attracts the confidences of women,
Father Galvao advised Plarr's mother to give up her vain hope for
her husband in order to preserve her own health.

1978   General in Asunción
Stroessner.

1979   Governor
Hosts a diplomatic dinner after which Charley Fortnum, whom he
invites only because Fortnum speaks English and can talk to the
American Ambassador, is kidnapped by mistake.

1980   Gruber
One of Plarr's best friends, an optician and photographic dealer.
When Gruber was a boy in Germany during the height of Nazi
persecution of the Jews in 1936, his parents sent him away with
a cake in which their only treasures, their rings, were concealed.
He never heard from them again.

1981   Guarani
A group of South American Indian tribes who originally were
located chiefly in Paraguay. The Guarani language, spoken by
their racially mixed descendants, is still the principal language of
rural Paraguay.

1982   headmaster
The current headmaster of Charley's English school in Buenos
Aires sent him a letter of congratulations after his appointment as
Honorary Consul.

1983   Humphries, Dr.
An old Englishman, friend of Plarr. Fortnum sees in the
moralizing Humphries "the soul of a pedagogue" (153), and
Humphries disapproves so strongly of Fortnum's behavior that he
refuses absolutely to participate in efforts to save him.

1984   Izquierdo, Captain
Charley never fulfills his intention to tell Plarr a story about
"Captain Izquierdo."

1985   John
León, who has lost faith in the church, explains that he was
ordained during the reign of Pope John XXIII (1958-63), a pontiff
much loved for his concern for social welfare and world peace.
León says he is not patient enough to wait for another John, and
he dislikes what has been made of the church since Pope John's
death.

1986   José
An old, blind villager whose wife dies during the night. He comes
to Pablo's hut to ask for the priest, village gossip having told him
that Pablo's friend is a very good priest. The kidnappers are
afraid he may have been sent as a spy, and in any case his arrival
indicates how widely known their presence is.

1987   journalist
One of the two journalists who visit Clara while Plarr is asleep is
a former client of the brothel; because he had believed that Clara
preferred him to other men, his *machismo* is hurt by the discovery
of her pregnancy.

1988   Juventud Febrerista
The "young Febreristas," an ineffectual guerilla organization to
which Plarr and Rivas once belonged. The Febrerista party, an
important force in Paraguayan politics, took its name from the

February 1936 revolution in which army officers overthrew the
liberal government and placed Col. Rafael Franco in power.

1989 Lopez
The Lopez for whom Saveedra's ancestors gave their hearts was
either Carlos Antonio Lopez (1790-1862), dictatorial president of
Paraguay from 1844 until his death; or his warlike son and
successor Francisco Lopez (1826?-70), who led the country into
war with Brazil, Uruguay, and Argentina.

1990 Madonna of Pompeii
See waiter.

1991 man in Buenos Aires
Plarr knew a man of illegitimate birth who searched for years to
learn the identity of his father, only to discover at last that his
father was an international banker who had been dead for years.

1992 manager
The manager of the Hotel Bolivar, where Humphries lives, stays
cooler by sitting with his fly open.

1993 mandioca
Cassava, a tropical plant with edible starchy roots.

1994 Maria
A prostitute at Señora Sanchez's, singled out by Fortnum as a girl
of good family who seems virginal. Plarr later learns from Clara
that Maria was really bad--so much so that she was murdered.

1995 Martin
The British Ambassador's consul, who does not earn enough to
purchase cars for import and resale, as Fortnum does.

1996 *Martin Fierro*
Saveedra's epic poem, said by many to have had a significant
effect on the Argentine novel. But Saveedra himself says that his
poem *is* Argentina.

1997 Mason, Perry
Fictional lawyer in popular American mysteries by Erle Stanley
Gardner (1889-1970). In school, León Rivas was a great reader
and collector of Perry Mason stories; he saw Gardner's character
as a heroic defender of the poor and innocent.

1998 Miguel
One of the kidnappers, an Indian unable to speak Spanish or
English; once it is discovered that Fortnum is not the U.S.
Ambassador, Miguel wants the group to kill Fortnum.

1999 Montez
Successful young novelist once highly praised by Saveedra, who
took a fatherly interest in him. Now he has wounded Saveedra
deeply by publishing an article which calls Saveedra mediocre and
makes fun of his work.

2000 Moreno, Julio
Heroic character in Saveedra's novel *The Taciturn Heart.* Some
readers feel that Moreno may represent what Saveedra would like
to have been.

2001 murderer/assassin
Plarr recalls going with Perez to inspect the body of a murder
victim brought in by the murderer for Christian burial.

2002 Pablo
A black kidnapper whose hut is used as the group's hideaway.

2003 Paul, St.
To explain his own difficult position León loosely quotes Romans
7:15: "I do not understand my own actions. For I do not what I
want, but I do the very thing I hate."

2004 Perez, Colonel
Tough, intelligent Chief of Police who easily sees through Plarr's
lies and quickly intuits that the kidnappers wanted someone other
than Fortnum.

2005 Plarr, Dr. Eduardo
An Argentine doctor in his mid-thirties, Plarr regards himself as
an outsider (his father was English, his mother Paraguayan) with
no commitments to individuals or causes and no religious beliefs.
Generous in his care of poor patients, he is nevertheless cold in
his human relations and has had a series of meaningless affairs
with married women. Attracted by the possibility of gaining his
father's release from political prison, Plarr is drawn into the
kidnapping scheme by his school friend León Rivas, whom he
helps by providing information about the schedule of the American
Ambassador. When the guerrillas capture Fortnum by mistake
and believe him seriously ill, Plarr visits him and is recognized by
Fortnum, a dangerous circumstance made even more difficult by
the fact that Plarr is Fortnum's friend who has been having an
affair with Fortnum's wife. He does everything he can to secure
Fortnum's release and pleads with the kidnappers not to kill
Fortnum as they have threatened, but nothing seems to work.
Plarr himself is puzzled over his own motives: he has long felt
himself unable to love, yet he clearly has a strong feeling for
Clara, and he admires Fortnum for his possession of the greatest
of virtues, the ability to love deeply and unselfishly. Plarr is killed
by the soldiers who rescue Fortnum.

2006 Plarr, Henry
Eduardo's English father, an opponent of the Stroessner regime
in Paraguay who sent his family across the border to safety and
remained to face the danger alone. He was captured, imprisoned
for fifteen years, and finally killed during an attempted escape.
Plarr remembers him for his characteristically English show of
courage as a stiff upper lip and for his love of Victorian and
Edwardian writers.

2007 Plarr, Mrs. (Eduardo's mother)
Henry Plarr's once-pretty wife whose affection and grief for her
husband are transmuted into self-indulgence (the eating of sweets)
and buried under increasing layers of fat so that her son
eventually doubts whether she ever really loved his father.
Eduardo visits his mother dutifully, but their relationship is
emotionally cold.

2008 poet
A man with a high-pitched voice who appears at the British
Ambassador's cocktail party.

2009 Representative of British Council
A regular guest at Ambassador Belfrage's cocktail parties, a
scared, slight, balding man whose name Plarr always forgets "for
some Freudian reason" (75).

2010 Ribera, Aquino
One of the guerrillas, a young man who once wanted to be a
poet. Encouraged by his friend León Rivas, he made a promising
start as a writer but made a fatal mistake in sending a letter
critical of America to a newspaper in Asunción; afterward he
could get nothing published, although he continued to write poems
about death. Accused of being a "politico," he became one and
eventually ended up in the Paraguayan prison where Plarr's father
was held; and he escaped in the incident in which the elder Plarr
was killed.

2011 Rivas, León
A school friend of Plarr, Rivas surprised and disappointed his old
friend by becoming a priest Now having renounced the priesthood
in favor of political activism, he has taken a wife and has
embraced political violence as a means of obtaining the social
justice from which the church, in his view, seems to have turned
away. He does not believe that God becomes involved in human
wars and political struggles. Nevertheless, he has not completely
lost faith; he retains belief in an evolutionary God whose goodness
or "day side" grows with good human actions just as his "night
side" grows with human evil. In this way León preserves a belief
in God and in the meaning of human action. He is killed by the
soldiers who rescue Fortnum.

2012 Rockefeller
Nelson A. Rockefeller (1908-1979), whose visit in Paraguay is cited
by Wilbur as proof that the U.S. is regarded favorably there.

2013 Rosas
Saveedra plans a new novel to be set in the time of Argentine

dictator Juan Manuel de Rosas (1793-1877), who ruled from 1835 to 1852.

2014 Rousseau
See Chateaubriand.

2015 Russell
British film director Ken Russell (1927-).

2016 Sanchez, Señora
Operator of the bordello where Clara worked; said to be the town's richest woman.

2017 Saveedra, Jorge Julio
Plarr's patient and friend, an aging novelist whose somewhat old-fashioned works celebrate the quality of *machismo* in the Argentine character. Saveedra, whose reputation is in decline, lives modestly and continues to work diligently, visiting Sanchez's brothel every week to prevent fleshly desires from interfering with his work. Asked to sign Plarr's urgent letter from the "Anglo-Argentine Society" to the British newspapers, he refuses to do so because he finds the style inferior and will not undergo the humiliation of having it published. Yet he demonstrates courage and a romantic spirit by offering to take Fortnum's place as hostage.

2018 "Shoot if you must this old grey head."
When the soldiers have surrounded the kidnappers' hut, Plarr remembers stories his father used to read to him about heroic individuals under fire. The quoted line is from one of Plarr's favorite poems, John Greenleaf Whittier's "Barbara Frietchie" (1894), which continues, "But spare your country's flag."

2019 Stroessner, General
See 1828.

2020 Struwwelpeter
From *Struwwelpeter* (1845), a German book of cautionary tales in verse by Heinrich Hoffman (1809-94), Fortnum recalls a nursery-story character who had his thumbs cut off.

2021 "Suffer little children."
León alludes to the words of Jesus in Matthew 19:14. In this
paragraph he also alludes to Matthew 19:21 ("Sell all you have")
and 18:5-6 ("It were better that a millstone").

2022 Taylor, Elizabeth
See Burton.

2023 Teresa
A prostitute at Sanchez's brothel, Teresa is a favorite of Saveedra.
Plarr visits her once.

2024 Tiberius
Saveedra says that a contemporary novelist who wants to write
about tyranny would do better to write about the Roman emperor
Tiberius (ruled A.D. 14-37) rather than Paraguayan dictator
Stroessner.

2025 Torres, Father
Francisco Torres (1504-1584), Catholic priest and scholar whose
theological writings were prolific and controversial.

2026 Trotsky
Leon Trotsky (1879-1940), Bolshevik leader second in power to
Lenin. A victim of Stalin's ascendancy after Lenin's death, Trotsky
was expelled from the party and exiled from Russia. He was
assassinated in Mexico in 1940. Aquino says that Trotsky, upon
being shown his Mexican house which had supposedly been made
secure against assassins, said that it reminded him of his first
prison.

2027 Vallejo, Gaspar
Margarita Escobar's current lover.

2028 Vega, Señora
A woman with whom Plarr had an affair.

2029 Velardo, Captain
Colonel Perez's colleague whom Plarr meets on the plane from
Buenos Aires.

2030 Villon
Aquino says León compared his work with that of French poet
François Villon (1431?-65), who was also a criminal.

2031 waiter, Italian
A waiter at the Italian club believes Humphries to have the "evil
eye" because Humphries said something disrespectful about the
Madonna of Pompeii.

2032 wife of finance secretary
One of Plarr's patients, who has a slight fever.

2033 Wilbur
Chummy, Coca-Cola drinking American Ambassador who insists
on being called "Wilbur." He refuses to believe that he was the
intended victim of the kidnapping in which Fortnum was taken by
mistake.

2034 woman, dark
Fortnum's unfriendly housekeeper.

THE HUMAN FACTOR (1978)

2035 aflatoxin
Poison with which Percival murders Daintry.   It produces
symptoms similar to those of cirrhosis of the liver.

2036 Agbo
Employee of Radio Zaire whom the MI6 agent there wants to
recruit as a subagent.

2037 Albany
Dr. Percival lives in Albany, a prestigious group of flats adjacent

to Burlington House in Piccadilly. Once exclusively a bachelors' residence, Albany has been home to many writers, including Byron, Macaulay, and for several years Graham Greene.

2038 Aldermaston
A Berkshire village, site of the Atomic Weapons Research Establishment. Davis, who completed some of his military service at Aldermaston, remarks to Castle that everyone knows the place is closed down.

2039 Amin Dada, Field Marshal
Idi Amin Dada (c.1925-), president of Uganda, notorious for his brutal regime from its inception in 1971 until his overthrow in 1979.

2040 Anna
Daily maid in Moscow who helps Castle learn Russian.

2041 Anna Karenina
Heroine of Tolstoy's *Anna Karenina* (1873-77) whose passionate affair with Vronsky leads to her ruin. Castle believes that deep love such as his love for Sarah always involves danger and risk, as affirmed by literature: Anna, Tristan (hero of Wagner's *Tristan and Isolde*), and Lovelace (in Richardson's *Clarissa*) all demonstrate that danger.

2042 Archangel
Port city on the White Sea in northwest Russia.

2043 *aspergillus flavus*
Bacterium which causes a mould which grows on peanuts; the mould produces the deadly poison aflatoxin.

2044 assistant porter
Purchases Maltesers for Colonel Daintry to give to Mrs. Hargreaves.

2045 BOSS
Bureau of State Security (later Department of National Security) in South Africa.

2046   Baines, Mrs.
One of the Reverend Daintry's parishioners whose confidences to Mrs. Daintry became "second-hand" confessions because Mrs. Daintry dutifully repeated them to her husband.

2047   Bantu
A member of one of several central or Southern African tribes. In South African usage, as when Muller speaks of Sarah as a Bantu woman, the term commonly applies to native blacks.

2048   Barker, Dr.
Sam's doctor.

2049   Barker, Mr.
Barman at the King's Arms, where Daintry stops after visiting Castle in Berkhamsted.

2050   Bates
English defector, living in Moscow at the expense of the Soviet government.

2051   Battle of Jutland
Daintry's father was a naval chaplain in the Battle of Jutland, May 31, 1916, the only major battle between the British and German fleets in World War I.

2052   Bellamy
Homosexual English defector whom Castle meets in Moscow; formerly in the British Council in West Berlin.

2053 Berkhamsted
A small town in the Chiltern hills, about twenty miles northwest of London. Berkhamsted is the birthplace and home of the protagonist Castle, whose name may be derived from the Castle which is the most important historical feature of the town. The town was the birthplace and boyhood home of Graham Greene; one of the main streets, Castle Street, runs past the Berkhamsted School where Greene's father was headmaster.

2054 Blake
George Blake, former Royal Navy lieutenant who became a double agent. He was recalled to London in 1961, tried and convicted of treason, and given a forty-two-year prison sentence. Daintry remarks to Percival that vetting (screening) "has been done very efficiently since the Blake case broke. . ." (17).

2055 Blit
Castle's former contact in the American embassy, later transferred to Mexico "perhaps because he couldn't speak Spanish" (284). He meets Castle by chance at the hotel near Heathrow on the night Castle escapes to Moscow.

2056 Bond, James
Hero of popular spy novels by Ian Fleming.

2057 Bonne Chance
See Taylor.

2058 Boris
Castle's former Soviet contact who is sent back to England after Castle's report on Muller arrives in Moscow.

2059 Bottomley, Ezra
Friend of Mrs. Castle's, returned recently from the mission field in Rhodesia.

2060 Browne
Economic adviser to the prime minister, seen in Pall Mall by Percival and Hargreaves.

2061 Brummell, George Bryan
"Beau" Brummell (1778-1840), Regency man of fashion and friend to Prince Regent George IV.

2062 Buffy
A guest at Hargreaves' shooting weekend who later sees Daintry in London and invites him to White's for a drink.

2063   Buller
Castle's boxer dog, purchased as a watchdog to protect Sam and
Sarah, but hopelessly fond of strangers.

2064   Burgess
Guy Burgess (1911-63), a British diplomat who had served as a
BBC correspondent and as a member of MI6 intelligence, was a
high-ranking member of the Foreign Office who defected to the
Soviet Union and was subsequently revealed to have been a Soviet
spy for many years.

2065   Bury, Mr.
Mrs. Castle's lawyer.

2066   Butler, Inspector
Policeman who questions Sarah at Mrs. Castle's after neighbors in
Berkhamsted discover the dying Buller.

2067   C.
The chief of Military Intelligence, Sir John Hargreaves.

2068   Carbury, Lady
An authoress in Trollope's *The Way We Live Now*.

2069   Carson
Communist agent in South Africa who helped Sarah escape from
the authorities after her violation of the race laws (through her
relationship with Maurice) had been discovered. Castle attributes
his half-belief in Communism to Carson, who gave Communism a
human face; his gratitude to Carson is a major factor in his
decision to become a double agent. According to Muller, Carson
died of pneumonia in prison, but Castle believes that he was killed
by BOSS.

2070   Castle, Maurice
The protagonist, a thirty-year veteran of the British Secret Service
(MI6) who for several years has been a double agent, passing
secret information concerning South Africa to the Soviets. Castle
is no more a Communist, however, than he is an English patriot;
he holds no religious or ideological faith but acts out of both

gratitude to the Communist agent who helped his black wife Sarah escape the South African police (her relationship with Castle violated the laws of apartheid) and love for Sarah and her people. When a security leak in his section is discovered, Castle's seeming dullness, quiet domestic life, and long service shield him from suspicion, which falls instead upon his innocent assistant Davis. The murder of Davis by the overzealous Dr. Percival reveals to Castle that he cannot continue his own work safely. At sixty-two he longs to retire anyway, to escape from the loneliness and secrecy of his work into the only country he cherishes, the one called "Peace of Mind." Yet he risks that hope in order to transmit information about the pernicious "Uncle Remus" plan; he is detected and is forced to escape from England to Moscow, where he faces a lonely future with virtually no hope of reunion with his family. In Moscow he discovers that the information for which he sacrificed his and Sarah's happiness was of no importance to the Soviets but was merely used to lead the British to believe they had a Soviet defector working for them.

2071 Castle, Mrs.
Castle's eighty-five-year-old mother, with whom he has a dutiful but strained relationship. A patriot who attends Conservative rallies and who once received the George Medal for her service as head warden in the blitz, she remains tall, trim, and mistrustful of emotions. Her claim to Sarah that she would have turned Maurice over to the police if she had known of his treason is convincing.

2072 Castle, Roger
Maurice Castle's cousin in the Treasury, known by Daintry at Oxford.

2073 Castle, Sam
The child of Sarah and an African father, Sam is deeply loved by his adoptive father Castle, who regrets his inability to develop a closer relationship with the boy.

2074 Castle, Sarah MaNkoski
Castle's young African wife, formerly an MI6 agent, who was forced to flee South Africa to escape prosecution under the

apartheid laws. Her deep love for her husband and her son make possible a genuine happiness in the alien environment of English suburban life, but Castle's sudden departure leaves her in miserable isolation. Prevented by Percival and Castle's mother from taking her son out of the country, she is forced to choose between loyalties and must give up her husband in order to care for the boy.

2075 Castle's father
Maurice Castle's deceased father, an old fashioned general practitioner and member of the Liberal party who "looked after his patients for a lifetime and forgot to send in bills" (100).

2076 Chaka, Emperor
Zulu chief (1787?-1828), mentioned by Hargreaves as representing the "old Africa" and being much better than Idi Amin.

2077 "Change and decay in all around I see"
Castle quotes from "Abide With Me," a hymn he used to sing in school.

2078 Chilton
The oldest agent in MI6, currently dealing with Ethiopia.

2079 *Clarissa Harlowe*
Novel (1747-48) by English writer Samuel Richardson; used by Castle for his book code.

2080 Clough, Colin
Elizabeth Daintry's new husband, an advertising man who promotes Jameson's Baby Powder.

2081 Connolly (or O'Connell)
Priest who worked in the Soweto slums. His example made Castle a half-believer in his faith, just as Castle had been a half-believer in Carson's.

2082 Corpus
Corpus Christi College, Oxford, where Daintry and Castle's cousin were acquaintances.

2083 cousin
Davis's only living relative, a cousin who is a dentist in Droitwich.

2084 Cruickshank
English defector, living in Moscow at the expense of the Soviet government.

2085 customer
Convivial patron of the King's Arms who is determined to guess Daintry's occupation.

2086 Cynthia
Secretary in MI6 with whom Davis is in love. The daughter of a major-general, she is "dashing as a young commando" and appears to be looking for "a [Philip] Sidney" rather than someone like Davis (53).

2087 DI
Defence Intelligence.

2088 *dacha*
Russian country house.

2089 Daintry, Elizabeth
Daintry's beautiful daughter, with whom he has an unhappily distant relationship. She will not visit him in his flat because she thinks that would be disloyal to her mother.

2090 Daintry, Colonel John
The new "broom" in charge of security in MI6, a quiet, serious, hatchet-faced man who appears to belong to both elegant rooms and hunting parties. Estranged from his wife, distant from his daughter, and generally without friends or relationships outside his profession, Daintry feels detached from life as if it were "a secret code for which he did not have the book" (41). Nevertheless, he is high-principled, as revealed in his outrage at the murder of Davis, and he has a genuine impulse of friendliness toward Castle, whom he likes. Forced by duty to investigate when Castle falls under suspicion, he seriously considers allowing Castle to escape, and vows that he will resign after turning Castle in.

2091 Daintry, Sylvia
Colonel Daintry's estranged wife, whose main concern in life is her
collection of china owls.

2092 Daintry's father
Colonel Daintry's father, a clergyman, was a chaplain in the Royal
Navy at the Battle of Jutland.

2093 Dar-es-Salaam
Tanzanian port city on the Indian Ocean.

2094 Davis, Arthur
Castle's assistant, a good-natured young man who has already
grown weary of his job and his bachelor life. He dreams
hopelessly of marriage to Cynthia and reassignment to an exotic
post in Lourenço Marques, but his inexperience, careless work
habits, and reputation as a heavy drinker make him the prime
suspect when a security leak is discovered. Davis is poisoned by
Percival and dies without being given a chance to prove his
innocence.

2095 Davis, William
Arthur Davis's father, who gave his son his own copy of selections
from Browning.

2096 DeBeers
Long-established South African mining company with a near
monopoly on the diamond market in that country. In 1959
DeBeers assumed control of the marketing of Russian diamonds
outside the Soviet bloc.

2097 deed poll
Davis says he may change his name by "deed poll," a one-party
deed (originally written on "polled" or straight-edged parchment).

2098 defector, Soviet
The defector who remains in the Soviet Union and supplies
information to British intelligence either does not exist at all or is
not a defector. The ruse is employed by the Russians to make
the British believe they have a reliable agent in Moscow.

2099 Dibba, Philip
MI6 agent in Kinshasa, rumored to have been forced to resign as Director of the Post Office there because he had stamps misprinted for his private collection.

2100 Dicky
Guest at Hargreaves' shooting weekend who sees Daintry again at White's in London. He has the unfriendly manner of an interrogator, perhaps because he was in MI5 during the Second World War.

2101 Dodo
Unidentified guest at Hargreaves'.

2102 Dreyfus case
Alfred Dreyfus, a Jewish officer in the French army, was convicted of treason in 1895 in a case that attracted international attention. After serving time in prison he was retried four years later and, in 1906, acquitted and reinstated into the army. Castle's recollection that "The Dreyfus case had exposed the perils of a wastepaper basket nearly a century ago" (12) refers to the fact that the incriminating document allegedly bearing Dreyfus' handwriting was said to have been discovered in a wastebasket in the German embassy.

2103 Dubcek
Alexander Dubcek (1921-), liberal Communist leader of Czechoslovakia whose efforts to bring about democratization led to the Soviet invasion and takeover in 1968. Old Halliday sums up Dubcek's career by calling him a "dangerous driver" (281).

2104 Enigma
Enigma was a mechanical device used by the Germans for encrypting coded messages in World War II.

2105 Estoril
Resort city on the Portuguese Atlantic coast, near Lisbon.

2106 "Everything seemed at sixes and sevens."
Everything seemed confused or disorderly.

2107 Fortnum's
Fortnum and Mason's, an elegant department store in Piccadilly.

2108 girl
Unattractive woman of thirty-five chosen by a computer as Buffy's
date even though the two have almost nothing in common.

2109 girl and tree trunk hiding place
A shy, ugly seven-year-old girl for whom Castle, at age ten, once
left a gift of candy and a love note in the hollow of the tree trunk
where he now leaves "drops" of secret information.

2110 Halliday
Kindly older man, a romantic Marxist who runs the book shop in
Old Compton Street used by Castle to convey information to
Soviet agents. Castle assumes that old Halliday is an innocent link
between Castle and the actual agent, Halliday's son, but Halliday
himself is revealed to be the one when he arrives to help Castle
escape from England.

2111 Halliday, younger
The operator of a pornographic bookshop across the street from
his father's more respectable shop. Castle's mistaken belief that
young Halliday is the Soviet agent he is dealing with has dire
consequences when the young man is arrested for dealing in
pornography. Assuming that young Halliday has identified or will
identify him, Castle confesses to Daintry his own role as double
agent.

2112 Hargreaves, Sir John
A former District Commissioner on the Gold Coast, now head of
Military Intelligence in London, Hargreaves remembers
nostalgically the simplicity of colonial Africa. He makes clear his
desire that the security leak in MI6 be found and "eliminated"
without being brought before the public eye, yet he is shocked by
the precipitous action of Percival in the murder of Davis. Like
Percival, however, he finds it easy enough to plot the fates of
others from the serene, elegant world of gentlemen's clubs in
London and shooting weekends at his country estate. Regretful
over the turn of events in the cases of Davis and Castle, he

identifies at the end with the isolated character Melmotte in Trollope's *The Way We Live Now*.

2113 Hargreaves, Lady Mary
"Impeccably American" wife of Sir John.

2114 Harry
Unidentified guest at Hargreaves'.

2115 Hatchard, William
The question "Aren't you William Hatchard?" is part of the code of identification used to lead Castle to Boris, his contact in Watford.   The name is appropriate to the spy who conveys information through book codes, since Hatchard's is a well-known bookstore in Piccadilly.

2116 "hell in heaven's despite"
In thinking that men like Captain Van Donck "made a hell in heaven's despite" (124) Castle inverts lines from Blake's "The Clod and the Pebble" (1794): "Love seeketh not itself to please, / Nor for itself hath any case, / But for another gives its ease, / And builds a Heaven in Hell's despair."

2117 Hertzog Prize
Awarded annually by the South African Academy of Arts and Sciences to the writer of the best work of literature or belles lettres in the Afrikaans language.

2118 Heyer, Georgette (1902-74)
Popular English novelist of detective stories and historical romances. Mrs. Castle reads Heyer.

2119 Hiss case
Alger Hiss (1904-   ), a foreign policy coordinator in the U.S. Department of State, was accused of transmitting secret documents to the Russians. He was convicted of perjury in 1950. Castle, making a copy of Muller's notes for transmission to the Russians, recalls that "the anonymity of a typewriter was only partial" (222), as the Hiss case proved, and does not bother to type the notes.

The tracing of certain documents to Hiss's Woodstock typewriter led to his conviction.

2120 "I only know that he who forms a tie is lost."
The novel's epigraph is from Joseph Conrad's *Victory* (1915).

2121 Ian
Ian Fleming (1908-64), English writer best known for his "James Bond" thrillers.

2122 *in camera*
Private hearing of a court case, often in the judge's chambers.

2123 Inns of Court OTC
Officers' Training Corps for young lawyers (members of the four Inns of Court in London).

2124 Ivan
The man who replaced Boris as Castle's Soviet contact in England. Ivan is less friendly than Boris and less trusting of Castle. In Moscow he seems to blame Castle for his own recall from England.

2125 Jellicoe, Admiral
John Rushworth Jellicoe (1859-1935), commander of the British fleet in the Battle of Jutland, widely criticized for his strategy in that encounter and relieved of his command the following year.

2126 John Thomas
Davis, following the example of D.H. Lawrence's character Mellors (in *Lady Chatterley's Lover*), refers to his penis as "John Thomas."

2127 Joiner, Edward
Sylvia Daintry's companion, a guest at Elizabeth's wedding party.

2128 KGB
Soviet State Security Committee (Secret Police).

2129 Kalamazoo
See Taylor.

2130 Krus
An African tribe Hargreaves associates with bravery.

2131 Laker
MI6 agent in charge of North African Arab republics.

2132 "The Laughing Cavalier"
Familiar portrait (1624) by the Dutch painter Frans Hals. Castle
has kept the stained glass "Laughing Cavalier" over the front door
at his home even though it reminds him unpleasantly of dentists'
offices.

2133 Lord's
Cricket ground in St. John's Wood, London.

2134 Lourenço Marques
Capital city of Mozambique, now called Maputo. Sarah escaped
from South Africa to join Castle in Lourenço Marques, and Davis
dreams of being transferred there.

2135 Lovelace
See Anna Karenina.

2136 MI5, MI6
MI5 is the British Security Service, the intelligence agency
responsible for internal security and counterespionage. MI5 works
cooperatively with the Special Branch of Scotland Yard. MI6 is
the British Secret Intelligence Service, responsible for collecting,
analyzing, and disseminating foreign intelligence. The names MI5
and MI6 derive from the agencies' earlier designations as sections
five and six of Military Intelligence.

2137 Maclean
Donald Maclean (1913-83), member of the British Foreign Office
who defected to Russia and was revealed to have been a spy for
the Soviets. He had held important positions in the British
Embassy in Washington, D.C., and was secretary to the Combined
Policy Committee on Atomic Development.

2138 Maltesers
Chocolate-coated malted milk candy.

2139 man with black moustache
Brings Castle's plane ticket and instructions to the airport hotel in
London.

2140 Mary
Castle's first wife, killed in the blitz while he was safe in Lisbon.
Although they had no children (Castle was sterile), they were very
happy.

2141 Maude, Aylmer
Castle uses Maude's translation of Tolstoy's *War and Peace* for his
book code.

2142 Melmotte, old
Augustus Melmotte, corrupt financier in Trollope's *The Way We
Live Now*. Hargreaves, feeling lonely and isolated in his regret
over the murder of the innocent Davis, identifies with Melmotte,
whose guilt leaves him in wretched isolation.

2143 Meredith
Daintry's predecessor, in charge of security in MI6.

2144 Miró room
The colorful abstract paintings of Spanish surrealist Joan Miró
(1893-1983) often have an underlying suggestion of horror, a
quality appropriate to the character of Dr. Percival, who is given
the Miró bedroom on the shooting weekend at Sir John's.

2145 morgen
Two and one-fourth acres (Dutch measurement).

2146 Muller, Cornelius
A high-ranking South African agent in BOSS who comes to
London to discuss details of the "Uncle Remus" project with
British Intelligence officials. Years earlier, Muller had used
blackmail in an attempt to force Castle to work for him,
threatening to ruin Castle's career by exposing his relationship with

Sarah. Muller gives Castle notes which Castle passes on to Soviet agents even though it is inevitable that he will be discovered and forced to leave the country.

2147 Muller's grandfather
An "ostrich millionaire" whose business in ostrich feathers was destroyed by World War I.

2148 Naomi
A film star's wife who, in a magazine interview read by Castle, discusses her marital sex life.

2149 Ngambo, Mark
Black nationalist in South Africa. The information Castle gives Muller on Ngambo is nothing Muller does not already have.

2150 Nicholson, Ben
English painter (1894-1962) best known for abstract geometric renderings of landscape and still life. Daintry, who stays in the Nicholson room at Sir John's, is advised by Percival to worry only about the yellow square, not about the blue and red.

2151 O'Connell
See Connolly.

2152 officer
Muller tells Hargreaves about one of their agents who viewed intelligence work as a game of chess. When the game became too easy, he began to play against his own side. Muller adds that the officer is dead now.

2153 Official Secrets Act
A law passed by Parliament in 1911, establishing penalties for the publication of cabinet documents.

2154 Old Contemptibles
Members of the large British Expeditionary Force that joined the French and Belgians against Germany in 1914.

2155 Oppenheimer
Sir Ernest Oppenheimer (1880-1957), wealthy industrialist, financier, and philanthropist. Oppenheimer gained control of the DeBeers diamond mining company and was a leader in that industry in South Africa and Rhodesia.

2156 "Over the borders a sin without pardon"
Castle reads from R.L. Stevenson's *A Child's Garden of Verses.* (See 2211.)

2157 Overton's
Restaurant in St. James's Street, below Daintry's flat.

2158 pantechnicon
See porter.

2159 Parish pump
Limited in scope, outlook, or knowledge; of local importance only.

2160 Partridge
The name used by Castle as he escapes England.

2161 Patricia
Tomlinson's niece, in the secretarial pool.

2162 Penelope
Secretary who takes Cynthia's place when she is upset over the death of Davis.

2163 Penkovsky
Percival cites the trial of Penkovsky for treason as contrary to the usual Soviet practice of simply eliminating such offenders.

2164 Percival, Dr. Emmanuel
Formerly a practicing physician, now a liaison between Sir John Hargreaves' MI6 and the biological warfare group, Dr. Percival preserves a coldly logical, merciless mind behind his plump, rosy-cheeked exterior. He takes great delight in good food and wine, fishing, and the pleasures of espionage which he likens to those of chess; but he has no human passions at all, and he

distrusts people who believe in something outside themselves. On the basis of slight circumstantial evidence he condemns and murders the innocent Davis, and he experiences no remorse at the discovery of his error. His name, like his profession as healer, is ironic: "Emmanuel" means bearer of good news, and Percival was a noble knight in quest of the Holy Grail.

2165 Philby
Harold "Kim" Philby (1912-88), British intelligence officer and Soviet spy. Philby became a Communist at Cambridge and in 1933 joined the British Secret Service, rising to important positions including, in 1949, that of first secretary of the British Embassy in Washington, D.C. In 1963 he escaped to Moscow, from where he eventually published a book about his exploits, *My Secret War* (1968). Greene's introduction to the novel denies that his character Maurice Castle was drawn from Philby (4).

2166 Piper
MI6 officer who works with Taylor on the security check in Davis's flat. He becomes suspicious of a copy of Browning in which Davis had recently marked passages that he connected with Cynthia.

2167 porter
Told to send three pounds of Maltesers from Daintry to Lady Hargreaves, the amused porter at MI6 headquarters asks if he can hire a pantechnicon (a large truck or van).

2168 Portland affair
A 1961 espionage case in which several people (Gee, Houghton, Lonsdale, and the Krogers) were tried for espionage carried out at the Underwater Weapons Establishment in Portland, site of the development of equipment for the nuclear-powered submarine *Dreadnought*.

2169 Porton
Center of research for bacteriological warfare. Percival, the liaison between MI6 and this research group, has "a fellow at Porton" prepare the aflatoxin with which he poisons Davis (103). Porton is a town in Wiltshire, a few miles northeast of Salisbury.

2170 priest
Desperate in his need to unburden himself to another person,
Castle, an atheist, tries to talk to a priest in the confessional box
in a Watford church but is turned away by the priest, who suggests
he see a doctor.

2171 Proudie, Mrs.
Wife of the Bishop of Barchester in Trollope's Barsetshire novels,
a fervent Evangelical. She reminds Sir John of the Governor's
wife in West Africa.

2172 Pullen
MI5 man who attends a conference in MI6 to help distinguish
between the duties of the two branches.

2173 Q.E.D.
"Quod erat demonstrandum" (which was to be demonstrated).

2174 Raymond's Revuebar
Castle, Davis, and Percival go to this popular London nightclub,
which features striptease.

2175 Rector
The rector who presides over Davis's funeral did not know Davis
and does not know anyone who attends.

2176 Reform Club
A club in Pall Mall. Percival, who keeps a membership because
he thinks the food there the best in London, says that he could
not belong if he had a conscience (the club was founded for
Radicals in 1852). It is next door to the Travellers Club, to which
Hargreaves belongs.

2177 registrar
Marries Elizabeth Daintry and Colin Clough at the registry office
in Victoria Street, London.

2178 Restif de la Bretonne, Nicolas (1734-1806)
French author of licentious novels, including *Monsieur Nicolas*, a
title used in Castle's book code.

2179 Robbins
American novelist Harold Robbins (1912-), the favorite of the
younger Halliday, who likes trashy literature.

2180 Robins, Denise
Novelist read by an anonymous woman Castle sees on a train.

2181 *Robinson Crusoe*
Castle reads this book in Moscow, an appropriate choice since he
is figuratively a Crusoe-like figure himself. (The other books he
provides for his library are Shakespeare's plays, Dickens's *Hard
Times* and *Oliver Twist*, and Fielding's *Tom Jones*.) (See 672.)

2182 Rolls, Rita
Striptease dancer at Raymond's Revuebar.

2183 Rougemont
Farmer in the Free State whom Castle liked almost as much as he
liked Carson. Castle dreams of Rougemont after the death of
Davis.

2184 Ruth
Sarah's remark to Castle that he is her people reminds him of the
words of Ruth in Ruth 1:16: "Whither thou goest, I will go . . .
thy people shall be my people, and thy God my God."

2185 Saladin
Sultan of Egypt and Syria (1138?-1193) who held Jerusalem in
captivity until driven out by the Crusaders under Richard I of
England and Philip II of France. Percival invokes Saladin's name
to contrast the current struggle, which he sees as a game, with the
holy wars of the past.

2186 Sam's father
Sam's natural father is believed by Sarah to have been killed in a
riot; he was called an Uncle Tom by people at the university and
is remembered by Sarah as tepid; she hopes Sam will be different.
After Castle's escape to Moscow, Dr. Percival tells Sarah of
Muller's claim that Sam's father is alive and prepared to claim
patrimony.

2187 Scott's
Scott's Restaurant in Mount Street, in London's Mayfair district.

2188 "She should never have looked at me"
Davis quotes from Robert Browning's "Christina" (1842).

2189 Simpson's
Simpson's-in-the-Strand, a familiar London restaurant. Elizabeth
Daintry considers Simpson's atmosphere excessively masculine and
refuses to go there with her father.

2190 Slope
A clergyman in Trollope's *Barchester Towers* who reminded
Hargreaves of a type of self-righteous District Commissioner in
Africa.

2191 Smarties
Chocolate candy, similar to M&M's.

2192 Sorge
Mentioned by Halliday as a hero whose image was put on a
Russian postage stamp--an honor he thinks may be in store for
Castle.

2193 Special Branch
A division of Scotland Yard which works in cooperation with MI5
to investigate treason, sabotage, and subversive activities. The
Special Branch also guards visiting dignitaries and investigates
aliens in Britain.

2194 Stone's
Chop house in Panton Street where Daintry takes his daughter
Elizabeth to dinner.

2195 Swinburne
English poet Algernon Charles Swinburne (1837-1909). Bellamy,
who formerly lectured on Swinburne, invokes the line "the foreign
faces, the tongueless vigil and all the pain" from Swinburne's
"Atalanta in Calydon" (1865) to describe his feelings when he first
arrived in Moscow.

2196 Taylor
MI officer who carries out the security check in Davis's flat after
Davis dies. He thinks the horses' names--Widow Twanky, Bonne
Chance, and Kalamazoo--may be part of a code.

2197 "Those that are in Judea must take refuge in the
mountains."
Castle associates this passage from Matthew 24:16 with his own
sense of imminent danger.

2198 *The Three Sisters* (1901)
Halliday quotes from Irina's lines in Act One of Chekhov's play.

2199 Tinker Bell
Mrs. Castle's Siamese cat, presumably named for the fairy in Sir
James Barrie's *Peter Pan* (1904).

2200 Tomlinson, Brigadier
High-ranking officer in MI6.

2201 Topsy
A little slave girl in Harriet Beecher Stowe's novel *Uncle Tom's
Cabin* (1852). A golfer calls Sarah "Topsy" and orders her off the
fairway when she walks on the course near Mrs. Castle's.

2202 Trappist
Cistercian monastic order noted for austerity and discipline
requiring silence. Castle, weary of the secrecy and loneliness
imposed by his work, regretfully feels that like the Trappists he
has chosen "the profession of silence" (332).

2203 Tristan
See Anna Karenina.

2204 Trollope
Anthony Trollope (1815-82), English novelist whose works include
the "Barsetshire" and "Palliser" series. Hargreaves is an admirer
of Trollope.

2205   Uncle Remus
An American plan, in which the British and South African governments are partners, for the use of tactical nuclear weapons against the native population in the event of racial conflict that threatens to disrupt the supplies of gold and uranium to the West. The plan is named after the kind-hearted old black storyteller in Joel Chandler Harris's *Tales of Uncle Remus*.

2206   Van Donck, Captain
An officer in the South African Security Police, a "brutal and simple man" (124) who interrogated Castle regarding his violation of the Race-Relations Act through his involvement with Sarah. Muller had Van Donck demoted after Sarah's escape.

2207   Vassall
John Vassall, sentenced in 1962 to an eighteen-year prison term for giving secret information to the Soviet Union.

2208   ward in chancery
To prevent Sarah from taking Sam to Moscow, Mrs. Castle threatens to have him made a ward in chancery, i.e., placed under the legal guardianship of the Court of Chancery.

2209   Watson
Castle's chief, in charge of MI6.

2210   *The Way We Live Now* (1875)
Novel by Anthony Trollope usually regarded as his most serious indictment of capitalism; it is read by both Hargreaves, after the death of Davis, and Castle, to whom old Halliday gives the book as a farewell gift.

2211   "Whenever the moon and stars are set"
Castle reads to Sam the boy's favorite poem, Robert Louis Stevenson's "Windy Nights" (from *A Child's Garden of Verses*, 1885).

2212   Whitehouse, Mrs.
Interviewed on the news as she welcomes a campaign against pornography.

2213 White's
White's, at 37-38 St. James's St., is the oldest and probably the most prestigious of London's gentlemen's clubs.

2214 Widow Twanky
See Taylor.

2215 Wilkins
Mentioned by Watson as a new employee in Section 6C who requires attention.

2216 Willie
Buffy's morose friend who recalls having talked about Smarties as his marriage was breaking up. He is a guest at the shooting weekend at Hargreaves' and is present at White's.

2217 "Worth how well, those dark grey eyes"
Davis has marked with a "C." (for Cynthia) these passages from Browning's "By the Fireside" (1855).

2218 "Yet I will but say what mere friends say"
See 2217.

2219 "You say I am not free"
This passage from Tolstoy's *War and Peace*, chosen by Castle for this final coded message, is appropriate because it represents his own attempt to carry out a free act.

DOCTOR FISCHER OF GENEVA
OR THE BOMB PARTY (1980)

2220 Albert
Dr. Fischer's haughty secretary.

2221 *The Beaches of Dunkirk*
One of Richard Deane's films.

2222 Belmont, Monsieur
One of the "toads," a tax adviser who according to Anna-Luise has
not had enough of a private life to enable him to develop a soul.
He appears mysteriously at the wedding of Jones and Anna-Luise,
and at the Mass on Christmas Eve, when he brings the invitation
to Jones from Dr. Fischer.

2223 chief
Alfred Jones's chief is frightened by the discovery that Jones is
married to Dr. Fischer's daughter.

2224 Chin Shengt'an's "33 Happy Moments"
Jones reads this selection from *The Knapsack* as he awaits
Anna-Luise's return from the slopes. (See also Pascal.)

2225 Christmas cracker
A Christmas novelty package that pops loudly when opened.

2226 confectioner, Spanish
Jones has a business lunch in Geneva with a Spanish confectioner
who talks of nothing but chocolate.

2227 Cork, mayor of
Terence MacSwiney, who died in Brixton prison, London, after a
seventy-five day hunger strike in 1920. Jones thinks of the mayor
when he considers starving himself to death after his wife dies.

2228 Darling, Mr.
The father in *Peter Pan*.

2229 Deane, Richard
One of the "toads," a declining, alcoholic film star whose former
popularity depended on sex appeal rather than acting ability. Vain
and self-satisfied, he owns and regularly watches copies of his own
films. At the bomb party he passes out drunk after pulling his
cracker.

2230 doctor, young
Attends Anna-Luise after her injury; he seems shy and embarrassed when he must tell Jones of her death.

2231 Ekland, Britt
Swedish actress (1942-).

2232 Englishman
Garrulous man who is present when the injured Anna-Luise is brought down from the mountain. Unaware that she is Jones's wife, he tells Jones to stand back.

2233 Excoffier, Monsieur
Official witness at the wedding of Jones and Anna-Luise.

2234 Falstaff
Dr. Fischer's taunting remark that Deane is no actor and could never play Shakespeare's Falstaff may be taken as a slur upon Deane's sexual prowess as well as his acting skills.

2235 Faverjohn, Madame
Considered the greediest of all the toads by Dr. Fischer, she committed suicide, probably in self-hatred, two years prior to the first party Jones attends, at which she is toasted.

2236 Fischer, Dr.
Wealthy, mysterious, powerful businessman, the inventor of Dentophil toothpaste, whose life is shaped by "pride, contempt of all the world, cruelty" (16). The terrible parties at which he alternately humiliates and rewards his guests in order to prove that they will debase themselves for material gifts are conceived in mocking imitation of a god whose "dark side" is revealed through his punishing of the creatures who love him for his occasional gifts. The worst of these events is the climactic "bomb party" where the guests play a form of Russian roulette by pulling Christmas crackers, all but one of which contain checks for two million francs; the other is said to contain a bomb. Dr. Fischer's extraordinary misanthropy seems to stem partly from his natural pride and partly from his desire for vengeance against the world after his wife betrayed him. When his pleasure in the humiliation

of others is finally thwarted by the resistance of his son-in-law Jones, he kills himself.

2237 Fischer, Mrs.
Dr. Fischer's unhappy wife was a victim of her husband's pride: he could not tolerate her love of music because he did not understand music himself. When she found a friend in Steiner who loved music and shared it with her, Fischer had him fired and thus destroyed their friendship. Anna-Luise believes that her mother willed herself to die.

2238 Groseli, Monsieur
A former toad who attended only two dinners before dying of cancer.

2239 Heifetz
Jascha Heifetz (1901-87), renowned Russian-American violinist. Anna-Luise's mother and Mr. Steiner listened together to recordings of Heifetz.

2240 ICFC, Inc.
Mentioned as an American firm which purchased weapons from Czechoslovakia for eventual shipment to the Middle East. The resemblance in name to the British Industrial and Commercial Finance Corporation is probably coincidental.

2241 Jones, Alfred
Protagonist and narrator, a middle-aged translator and letter writer for a Swiss chocolate factory, handicapped by the loss of his left hand in the fire of London in the 1940 blitz. As a lonely widower he marries the much younger Anna-Luise, Dr. Fischer's daughter, whose love for him he accepts as wonderful mystery. At her urging he accepts his first invitation to one of her father's parties in order to prove his own ability to resist the evil doctor's gifts and therefore his control; in doing so he humiliates the other guests far more than Fischer himself had been able to do. After Anna-Luise dies in a skiing accident he accepts a second invitation in order to escape thought. At this event, the bomb party, he buys the Divisionnaire's cracker for two million francs, hoping for death, only to find that the bomb is a hoax. By proving that the loss of

love cannot be supplanted by material possessions, his resistance destroys Dr. Fischer's malicious pleasure in contempt of others and precipitates Fischer's suicide.

2242   Jones, Anna-Luise
Dr. Fischer's pretty, intelligent daughter who marries Jones, more than thirty years her senior, and brings him intense happiness for the brief period before her death in a skiing accident. She hates her father for his mistreatment of her mother, and her marriage to an older man may owe something to her desire for a loving father. Jones attributes to her an unusual wisdom and implicitly accepts her theory of the soullessness of the "toads."

2243   Jones, Sir Frederick
The narrator's father, a minor diplomat whose penchant for Anglo-Saxon history led him to name his son Alfred. He was killed in the blitz on the night Alfred lost his hand.

2244   Jones, Mary
Jones's first wife, who died in childbirth twenty years prior to the events of the story. The baby, who also died, was a girl.

2245   Jones, Mrs. (Alfred's mother)
Died with her husband when their West Kensington house was destroyed in the blitz.

2246   Kips
Dr. Fischer's lawyer and one of the "toads," a thin, aging man whose deformed spine gives him such a bent posture that he resembles the number seven. Dr. Fischer, who feels compelled to humiliate Kips because Kips knows that the doctor was betrayed by his wife, ridicules him through the publication of a cartoon book called *Adventures of Mr. Kips*. The large retaining fee paid to Kips prevents him from protesting although he regains a small measure of dignity by refusing to gamble at the bomb party.

2247   *The Knapsack* (1939)
A pocket-sized anthology of English poetry, edited by Herbert Read, popular with British soldiers in World War II.

2248 Krueger, "General"
One of the "toads," actually a Divisionnaire (high-ranking officer)
rather than a general, who usually chooses the wine for Fischer's
parties. Anna-Luise sees in him an unhappiness that may indicate
his possession of a soul. He weeps at the final party when he
cannot summon the courage to open his cracker.

2249 Krupp, Herr
Gustav Krupp von Bohlen und Halbach (1870-1950) and his son
Alfred (1907-67) were heads of Germany's huge Krupp armament
works, which became the principal manufacturer of arms for the
Nazis. Alfred was tried and convicted as a war criminal in 1948.

2250 landlord
The Swiss landlord of the Winston Churchill pub in Geneva resists
Jones's attempts to draw him into conversation.

2251 "The Last Days of Dr. Donne" (1670)
Izaak Walton's account of Donne's passing; in *The Knapsack*.

2252 Montgomery, Mr.
Deceased husband of Mrs. Montgomery, whose love for him
during their twenty-five year marriage is attributed by Dr. Fischer
to Mr. Montgomery's sizable bank account.

2253 Montgomery, Mrs.
A blue-haired American widow who, as the only woman among
the "toads," acts as hostess at Dr. Fischer's parties. She is the first
to open a Christmas cracker at the bomb party.

2254 "Ode on a Grecian Urn" (1819)
Jones was reading Keats's famous ode on the night he lost his
hand in a bomb explosion.

2255 Pascal
French philosopher, mathematician, and scientist Blaise Pascal
(1623-62). Although not a believer himself, Jones prefers the

Christian philosopher Pascal to the "horrible complacency" of Oriental wisdom.

2256 Read, [Sir] Herbert (1893-1968)
Distinguished poet, critic (of art and literature), novelist, and editor; a friend of Graham Greene.

2257 *Retreat from St. Quentin*
When Anna-Luise is brought from the ski slopes on a stretcher, Jones is by his own account like the soldier in Herbert Read's *Retreat from St. Quentin* (in *The Knapsack*) who does not realize at first that he has been wounded.

2258 "The Seafarer"
Poem by Ezra Pound, read by Jones while he waits for the return of Anna-Luise from the ski slopes.

2259 Secretary of Embassy, young
Pushed Jones, then a child, into the deep end of a *piscine.* Since that time Jones has feared drowning.

2260 Skoda
Emil von Skoda (1839-1900), Czech industrialist who founded the massive Skoda Armament Works at Pilsen.

2261 Steiner, Mr.
Gentle music-store clerk who collapses at the sight of Anna-Luise because she so strongly resembles her mother Anna, whom he loved. Steiner says that Anna never loved him, that their relationship was innocent, and that Anna died because she did not want to live without love. Dr. Fischer discovered the friendship between Steiner and his wife and paid Kips, who owned Steiner's company, to have him sacked without references. Steiner later comes to Fischer's to "spit in God Almighty's face" (148).

2262 Taxi-man
Warns Jones about Fischer as being "un peu farfelu" (33) (bizarre, extravagant, crazy).

2263 "To him that hath shall be given"
Dr. Fischer quotes Christ's answer, in Matthew 13:11-12, to the
question why He teaches in parables: "Because it is given unto
you to know the mysteries of the kingdom of heaven, but to them,
it is not given. For Whosover hath, to him shall be given, and he
shall have more abundance: but whosoever hath not, from him
shall be taken away even that he hath." Dr. Fischer's view that
these words of Christ are cynical (68) would appear to be a willful
misinterpretation, since Fischer confuses material gifts such as he
provides with gifts of the spirit.

2264 Toads
Anna-Luise's name for Dr. Fischer's greedy "friends" who submit
to his outrageous treatment of them in order to receive his gifts,
which in fact they could purchase for themselves.

2265 waiter
Surly man who is impatient with Jones for ordering only coffee in
the hotel where he awaits Anna-Luise. Returning to pay the
check after discovering that his wife is seriously injured, Jones
throws the waiter's tip on the floor to humiliate him, thus gaining
a brief taste of what it is like to treat others contemptuously as
Dr. Fischer does.

2266 "Who has but once dined his friends has tasted whatever it
is to be Caesar."
The novel's epigraph is taken from chapter 34 of Melville's *Moby
Dick.*

MONSIGNOR QUIXOTE (1982)

2267 Abraham
The Mayor thinks the biblical Abraham a scoundrel for his
willingness to kill his own son.

2268 *Amadis of Gaul*
Sixteenth-century Spanish chivalric romance by Garcia de Montalvo. (See *Palmerin.*)

2269 assistant
The assistant in the ecclesiastical tailoring shop where Father Quixote buys his purple socks is suspicious of Father Quixote and the Mayor; he reports the priest's license number to the police.

2270 Augustine, St.
As his *Confessions* reveal, St. Augustine of Hippo (354-430), who was converted to Christianity at the age of thirty-two, lived a sinful life as a young man and was especially vulnerable to sexual temptation. Father Quixote, discussing lust with the Mayor, recalls phrases from St. Augustine's *The City of God* and reflects that Augustine's writings about sex were at least informed by actual experience. Later, having left his copy of St. Francis de Sales in Rocinante, he chooses St. Augustine's *Confessions* and Caussade's *Spiritual Letters* to read during his captivity by the bishop.

2271 Bishop of Motopo
An Italian bishop who recommends the promotion of Father Quixote after the latter provides him generous assistance and hospitality when he runs out of gas near Quixote's home.

2272 bishop, Quixote's
Father Quixote's bishop dislikes him, regards him as little better than a peasant, and is distressed when Quixote is made a Monsignor. After receiving reports of Quixote's erratic behavior he quickly pronounces him Suspensio a Divinis--forbidden to say Mass.

2273 Botin's
The mayor takes Father Quixote to lunch at Botin's, a restaurant in Madrid with Fascist associations.

2274 butcher
The butcher of El Toboso is "a bit of a scoundrel" (167), but probably a believer, according to Father Quixote.

2275 Cana
The Bishop of Motopo says that no wine since the marriage at
Cana is unimportant. (See 87.)

2276 Caussade, Father
Jean Pierre de Caussade (1675-1751), Jesuit teacher in whose
Spiritual Letters Father Quixote found consolation when he was
a young seminarian.

2277 Cervantes
Held captive in his own house by Dr. Galván and Father Herrera,
Father Quixote compares himself with Cervantes, who spent five
years as a captive of pirates and was twice imprisoned for debt.

2278 Claret, Antonio
Claret, author of the *Catecismo de la Doctrina Cristiana* read by
Quixote as a child, was a 19th-century missionary who became
confessor to Isabella II and archbishop of Santiago de Cuba. He
founded the Clarentian order.

2279 *Communist Manifesto*
Upon reading Marx and Engels' *Manifesto* (1848), Father Quixote
determines that Marx was a good man.

2280 *Corpus Domini nostri*
The body of our Lord.

2281 Curia
The Mayor says that the Curia Romana, the Papal Court, has
killed the church.

2282 de León, Fray Luis (1527-91)
Poet, linguist, and biblical scholar who taught at the University of
Salamanca. The Mayor mentions that St. John of the Cross was
one of de León's students.

2283 Descartes
Led Father Leopoldo out of skepticism and into the church. (See
95.)

2284 Diego
Former fellow student of the Mayor, and an acquaintance of
Marquez.

2285 Diego, Señor
Gentleman farmer and vineyard keeper who refuses to sell wine
to the wealthy Mexicans who he believes have corrupted the local
priests. He gives wine generously to Father Quixote and the
Mayor, however, and sends a gift of wine to the monastery of
Osera.

2286 Dulcinea
In *Don Quixote*, the peasant girl Alonza Lorenzo is chosen by the
hero as his sweetheart, Dulcinea al Toboso.

2287 ETA
The motto "Euskadi Ta Azkatasuna" (Basque nation and liberty).

2288 El Toboso
Father Quixote's parish.

2289 *Esto mihi in Deum protectorum et in locum refugii.*
Father Quixote's words to the Guardia are perhaps deliberately
not in good Latin but may be translated loosely, "God be to me
a protector and place of refuge."

2290 *Et introibo ad altare Dei, qui laeatificat juventutum meam.*
I will go up to the altar of God, the giver of youth and happiness.

2291 Fascist, black
Sancho's successor as Mayor.

2292 Felipe, Father
An old priest who acts as guest master at the Osera monastery.

2293 Francis de Sales, St.
The favorite religious writer of Father Quixote, who points out
that in St. Francis's eight hundred pages on *The Love of God*
there is no reference to mortal sin. (See 1826.)

2294 Francisco, Father
A Trappist monk at Osera who telephones for a doctor after
Father Quixote's accident.

2295 fugitive
Father Quixote gets in trouble with the Guardia by hiding a
comically inept fugitive in the trunk of Rocinante. The man wears
the wrong shoes by mistake, uses a fake moustache that will not
stay in place, and runs out of gas because he forgot to fill his tank
before setting out to commit robbery. He forces Father Quixote
at gunpoint to drive him to León.

2296 Galicians
Inhabitants of Galicia, a region of northwest Spain, north of
Portugal, bordering the Atlantic.

2297 Galván, Dr.
Physician who injects the sleeping Father Quixote with a powerful
sedative so that he and Father Herrera can take the priest to El
Toboso against his will.

2298 Galván's cousin
Dr. Galván's cousin in the Ministry of the Interior is influential in
securing the cooperation of the police in the capture of Father
Quixote.

2299 garagist
Local mechanic who earns Father Quixote's affection by taking
excellent care of Rocinante.

2300 Generalissimo
Francisco Franco (1892-1975), Fascist ruler of Spain from 1939
until his death.

2301 girl, American
See Ronald.

2302 "Had I but served my God with half the zeal. . . ."
Father Quixote quotes from Shakespeare's *Henry VIII* (III,ii,456).

2303 "He was in the world. . . ."
The Mayor quotes John 1:10.

2304 Herrera, Father
The young priest sent by the bishop to look after the parish of El Toboso in Father Quixote's absence. His exceptional cleanliness makes Father Quixote feel like a rough countryman. He is ambitious, cautious, eager to curry favor with the bishop, and highly suspicious of Father Quixote.

2305 *Hic est enim calix sanguinus mei.*
For this is the chalice of my blood.

2306 His Excellency at Avila
The Bishop of Avila intercedes, at the request of Father Quixote's bishop, to persuade the Guardia not to arrest the priest.

2307 *Hoc est enim corpus meum*
For this my body.

2308 Ignatius, St.
The Bishop of Motopo points out that like the fictional Don Quixote, St. Ignatius of Loyola was believed by many to be a madman. As a Jesuit, St. Ignatius is an unsympathetic subject to Father Leopoldo. (See also 107.)

2309 *In partibus infidelium*
"In the lands of unbelievers." The term denotes areas where the church once prospered but has given way to unchristian elements; the memory of the sees in such areas is preserved through the assigning of their names to auxiliary bishops in missionary work.

2310 In Vinculis
Political organization to which Father Quixote has contributed, much to the displeasure of his bishop.

2311 jester
A skeptical man in the crowd in Galicia loudly ridicules the local practice of selling the right to carry the image of the Virgin.

2312 John of the Cross, Saint
Quixote keeps a copy of St. John's writings in the trunk of
Rocinante. (See 2894.)

2313 Jone, Father Heribert
A German moral theologian, highly regarded by Father Herrera;
but his writings on the subject are seen by Father Quixote as "like
a book of military regulations" (82). Jone's *Moral Theology* was
reprinted in English several times in the 1940's and '50's. A letter
from Greene to David Low, reprinted in *Dear David, Dear
Graham* (Oxford: Alembic Press, 1989), mentions his amusement
with Jone's writing and his intention of using it in *Monsignor
Quixote.*

2314 José, Father
Señor Diego's grandson, a priest driven out of his parish by other
priests who would not tolerate his unwillingness to follow their
greedy practices.

2315 landlord
The landlord of a restaurant in El Toboso is suspected by the
Mayor of accepting a bribe (a new deep freeze from a mysterious
stranger) for his vote and political influence.

2316 *Laquesus contritus est et nos liberati sumus.*
Spoken by Father Quixote to confuse the Guardia, the phrase is
not in good Latin, but may be translated loosely as "Our fetters
("laqueus," not "laquesus") have been worn away and we have
been liberated."

2317 Leopoldo, Father
A priest in the Trappist monastery at Osera, Father Leopoldo is
a poor cook but an earnest scholar and a courageous man who
refuses to let the Guardia take the injured Father Quixote away.
A follower of Descartes, Father Leopoldo is convinced that in the
end one cannot distinguish between fact and fiction but must
simply choose one or the other; thus, he has no difficulty
accepting the claim that Father Quixote is a descendant of the
fictional hero.

2318 "Let's go up to Jerusalem and die with Him."
John 11 records the story of Jesus's decision to go to Judea to attend Lazarus, who was ill. When the other disciples warned him that the Jews might stone him to death, Thomas alone said, "Let us go, that we may die with him."

2319 Lope de Vega (1562-1635)
Poet and dramatist of the Spanish "golden age."

2320 Mambrino's helmet
Cervantes' hero uses as his helmet a barber's brass bowl which he believes to be the magic helmet from *Orlando Furioso*.

2321 Marquez
A wealthy, pious businessman who, after reading in Heribert Jone that *coitus interruptus* was permissible in the case of the arrival of a third person, hired a butler and established an elaborate code of signals whereby the butler could interrupt him and his wife in the act of sex and thereby provide birth control. He was disappointed to be reminded by Diego that the behavior was allowable only in the case of unforeseen necessity.

2322 Martin of Lisieux, Señorita
The girl who was Father Quixote's Dulcinea, his true love, even though she died many years before he knew her. She is generally known as Saint Thérèse. (See 2906.)

2323 Mayor
The ex-mayor of El Toboso, an educated Marxist who once wanted to be a priest himself, invites Father Quixote to travel with him and becomes a worthy Sancho Panza to the idealistic priest. More worldly and practical than his friend, he delights in their friendly disagreements over the relative merits of Marxism and Catholicism and in their sharing of wine, food, and fellowship. When Father Quixote is imprisoned by the bishop and Father Herrera, the Mayor rescues him and attempts to take him to sanctuary at the Osera monastery, but they are prevented by the police. After Father Quixote's death, the Mayor is profoundly affected by the lingering power of his love for the priest.

2324 Mexican
Father Quixote and the Mayor encounter a Mexican who has been
refused the wine he wants to purchase from Señor Diego for use
in bribing a priest. Later, when Father Quixote interrupts the
procession, the Mexican calls him an atheist and urges the priest
leading it to call the Guardia.

2325 Naaman, the Syrian
The curing of Naaman's leprosy by bathing in the Jordan is
recorded in II Kings 5: 9-14.

2326 *Nihil Obstat*
A Roman Catholic censor's pronunciation that a book under
examination does not contradict the faith or morality taught by the
church.

2327 Opus Dei
The bishop objects to Father Quixote's contributions of money to
Opus Dei, a Roman Catholic organization (originally for lay
persons only) founded in Madrid in 1828 for the purpose of
promoting the conduct of daily life according to Christian tenets.

2328 *Palmerin of England*
Sixteenth-century chivalric romance, believed the work of the
Portuguese Francisco do Moraes. In *Don Quixote*, the curate and
the barber who are destroying such romances made special
exceptions for *Amadis de Gaul* and *Palmerin*.

2329 Panza, Sancho
The faithful squire of Cervantes' Don Quixote, a portly peasant
whose common-sense grasp of reality is a foil to the idealism of
his master.

2330 "Patience and shuffle the cards."
Father Quixote quotes from Cervantes' *Don Quixote*, III, 23.

2331 *pechera*
A stomacher or shirt-frill worn by a monsignor.

2332 Pilbeam, Professor
American scholar from Notre Dame who is visiting the Osera
monastery. He is said to be the greatest living authority on St.
Ignatius.

2333 prayer of the Roman centurion
Found in Matthew 8:8-9; Luke 7:6-8: "Lord, I am not worthy that
thou shouldest come under my roof; but speak the word only, and
my servant shall be healed."

2334 priest in processional
The mercenary priest who has sold places in the procession and
has allowed the figure of the Virgin to be covered with money is
intimidated when Father Quixote introduces himself as a
monsignor, accuses the priest of blasphemy, and orders the
procession stopped.

2335 priest, young
Diego's grandson, who has been driven away from his own parish
by mercenary priests because he refused to accept money for
saying responses when someone died.

2336 Prodigal Son
In Sancho's Marxist version of the biblical story, the prodigal son
rebels against the wealth and luxury of his father's estate; after
losing his fortune and returning home, he understands the nature
of class struggle, returns to the peasant whom he now recognizes
as his spiritual father, and begs forgiveness.

2337 Queen of Sweden
The queen "led into the church by Descartes" (204) was Christina,
who abdicated in 1654, joined the Catholic church, and moved to
Rome.

2338 Quixote, Don
Father Quixote's illustrious "ancestor," the eponymous hero of
Cervantes' *Don Quixote de la Mancha* (1605, 1615).   Don
Quixote, a good-hearted old country gentleman, is so affected by
his reading of chivalric romance that he sets out to do battle
against the evils of the world. In the company of his rustic squire

Sancho Panza and his horse Rocinante, he becomes involved in many comic adventures which eventually defeat his idealism and lead him, near the end of his life, to renounce his role as knight-errant.

2339 Quixote, Father
A gentle, modest village priest who believes himself a descendant of Cervantes' famous hero, Father Quixote is elevated suddenly to the rank of Monsignor as a result of his chance encounter with the Bishop of Motopo. Given a period of repose before assuming new duties, he is enticed by the invitation of his friend Zancas, the ex-mayor (called the Mayor) to travel. In the comic journey that follows, Father Quixote stays overnight in a brothel, views a pornographic film, hears confession in a toilet stall, and helps a thief escape from the police. In spite of his innocence in all of these matters, his behavior is considered scandalous by his bishop, who together with Father Herrera succeeds in having Father Quixote captured and brought back to El Toboso. Suspected of madness and made a prisoner in his own home, he escapes with the aid of the Mayor and journeys to Galicia, where he interrupts a village procession in which a figure of the Virgin is draped with money. The police pursue Father Quixote and the Mayor, shoot their tires as they approach the monastery of Osera, and thereby cause a wreck in which the priest is fatally injured.

2340 "Religion is the opium of the people."
A statement by Marx in the introduction to *Critique of the Hegelian Philosophy of Right* (1844).

2341 Rocinante
Father Quixote's car, an aging Seat 600, which he has named after Don Quixote's horse.

2342 Roland
See 722.

2343 Ronald
An American stopped by the roadside for lunch with his girlfriend is asked by the Mayor about Father Quixote, who has disappeared.

2344 saint, popular
Father Quixote tells of a popular saint in La Mancha who
submitted to rape rather than kill her attacker with her knife and
risk destroying his chance of salvation.

2345 *Scio cui credidi*
"I know in whom I have believed."

2346 Teresa
Father Quixote's housekeeper, "a square woman with protruding
teeth and an embryo moustache" who "trusted no one living" (19)
but maintained a strong loyalty to, and brusque affection for, the
priest himself.

2347 Teresa, Saint
St. Teresa (also Theresa) of Avila (1515-82), a Spanish nun and
mystic, a reformer of the Carmelite order whose path toward
sainthood began at age seven when she sought martyrdom by
preaching to the Moors. Her spiritual autobiography, letters, and
mystical writings, including *The Interior Castle* (1583), have been
widely read. This latter book may be the one Father Quixote
carries in the trunk of Rocinante.

2348 "There is nothing either good or bad but thinking makes it
so."
The novel's epigraph is from *Hamlet* II, ii.

2349 Thérèse, Saint
See Martin, Señorita.

2350 Unamuno
Miguel de Unamuno (1864-1936), Spanish writer, philosopher, and
scholar, who joined the University of Salamanca as Professor of
Greek in 1891 and later served as Rector there until he was
removed in 1914 for his vocal attacks on the national government,
only one of many incidents in which his political beliefs placed
him in difficulty. The Mayor remembers Unamuno for his "half
belief" and for being the one professor he could listen to.

2351 Undertaker
The man who follows Father Quixote and the Mayor in Valladolid
looks suspiciously like a secret policeman, but he turns out to be
an undertaker who implores the priest to hear his confession, since
he has just buried his own priest. In the confession, which Father
Quixote hears in a toilet stall, he admits to having stolen the brass
handles from his priest's coffin.

2352 Zancas, Enriques
The Mayor. Zancas was also the name of Cervantes' Sancho
Panza.

THE TENTH MAN (1985)

2353 barber
One of the prisoners.

2354 Carosse, M.
An actor whom Chavel meets by chance on a dark Parisian street
and who mistakes Chavel for someone named Pidot. He gives
Chavel 300 francs to take a message to his wife. Later Carosse,
who is a fugitive (he is a murderer and was a collaborationist),
turns up at Brinac, impersonating Chavel and telling Thérèse that
"Charlot's" stories about her brother have been lies. He murders
Chavel when the latter exposes him.

2355 Charlot, Jean-Louis
Name used by Chavel after his release from the prison camp.

2356 Chavel, Jean-Louis
Chavel, the protagonist, is a guilt-ridden man, formerly a
prosperous Parisian lawyer, who gives all of his considerable
wealth and property to Janvier (Michel Mangeot), who in turn dies
in Chavel's place in a German prison. After the war Chavel takes

the name Charlot and attempts to start a new life but is unable
to find work. Without friends or money, he is drawn irresistibly
back to Brinac, his country home, now in the possession of
Michel's mother and his sister Thérèse. Thérèse hires him to do
odd jobs and confides in him her hatred for Chavel; and Chavel
falls in love with her and yearns to lift the burden of hatred from
her heart. When the murderer Carosse enters the scene
pretending to be Chavel and intending to exploit the girl, Chavel
reveals his identity and sacrifices his life to protect Thérèse. This
concluding action offers him a kind of personal redemption and
enables the girl to put aside her corrosive hatred.

2357 Chavel's father
Chavel recalls his father's dislike of electricity and his preference
for oil lamps and mechanical doorbells.

2358 Chavel's grandfather
Mentioned as having watched for visitors, as Chavel's mother did.

2359 Chavel's mother
Used to keep lookout for visitors she didn't want to meet.

2360 clerks
Three clerks are among the prisoners. One of these, a thin,
elderly man, suggests that the prisoners draw lots to determine
which of them will lose their lives.

2361 cook
An old woman who loved the boy Chavel and gave him merry-
thoughts (wishbones), toys made of potatoes, and the like.

2362 employer
Interviews Chavel for an unspecified job but refuses to accept
Chavel's prison dossier as proper identification.

2363 greengrocer
One of the prisoners.

2364 housekeeper
Recalled by Chavel as having always been satisfied with the kitchen.

2365 Janvier
Name by which Michel Mangeot was known in the prison camp.

2366 Jules
Headwaiter in Chavel's accustomed café in Paris who at first ignores Chavel, upon the latter's return, in favor of an American soldier with a wad of money. But after recognizing his former customer the waiter offers him a place to stay and gives him food and drink for the evening. He says he has tried to remain "correct," serving Frenchmen first even before German generals, but he is insensitive to Chavel's unhappiness over the loss of Brinac.

2367 Krogh
One of the prisoners, an Alsatian who asks whether they need to volunteer.

2368 Lenôtre
One of the prisoners, an elderly clerk who prepares the slips for the lottery. He is the eighth man to draw, and he draws the second marked slip.

2369 Louchard, Pierre
Mentioned by Carosse as a "grand part" he once played (124), a character who was a roué, a seducer, yet was loved by women.

2370 man, dapper thin
Turns down Chavel's application to teach in a language institute, saying that Chavel's accent is not good enough.

2371 man, old
Interviews Chavel for a job in an apparently moribund company which would require the investment of his savings as a condition of employment. Chavel declines.

2372 man, old (gardener)
Chavel's gardener, whom he told to keep the garden stocked and to sell vegetables for what he could get. Chavel wonders whether the man is still living.

2373 Mangeot, Madame
Aging mother of Thérèse and Michel, a huge woman who was formerly a modest shopkeeper and seems unable to adapt herself to the life of a wealthy woman. Believing that her son still lives and has made a fortune in England or a faraway country, she suspects Chavel of having been the young man's servant and thus resents his presence at their table. She dies after the arrival of Carosse.

2374 Mangeot, Michel
The prisoner who sells his life to Chavel in exchange for Chavel's wealth and property, which Michel then leaves to his mother and his sister.

2375 Mangeot, Thérèse
A young, thin, attractive woman who resembles her brother in both her appearance and her recklessness and unpredictability. Hurt and angry that her brother thought she would rather have a house and money than him, she thinks at times of burning the house and concentrates her unhappiness in a hatred of Chavel. She is capable of gentleness and affection, however, and is redeemed by a self-consciousness of the intensity of her hatred, which is finally laid to rest by Chavel's self-revelation and sacrifice at the end of the novel.

2376 Mayor of Bourge
One of the prisoners. His pride in his large silver watch leads him to constant quarreling with Pierre, who has an alarm clock.

2377 officer
A young officer who tries awkwardly to be authoritative announces that because of murders in the town, one of every ten prisoners will be executed.

2378 Pidot
Carosse's friend for whom he mistakes Chavel.

2379 Pierre
One of the prisoners, an engine-driver who owns an alarm clock
and disputes the time with the Mayor.

2380 priest
The priest who attends Madame Mangeot at her death insists that
unless Thérèse finds a female companion to live with her, Chavel
will have to leave.

2381 Richard III
Carosse, revealing to Chavel his plan to marry Thérèse, compares
himself to the eponymous hero of Shakespeare's play, whom he
quotes: "Was ever woman in this humour wooed?" (I,ii) The
answer, he says, is yes.

2382 Roche
Farmer near Brinac, head of the local resistance during the war,
who almost recognizes Chavel when he gives Chavel and Thérèse
a ride in his wagon. Formerly a friend of Chavel, he turned
against him in envy and pride after losing his arm in a tractor
accident.

2383 Russe, Father
Priest at St. Jean, now deceased; recalled by Chavel.

2384 Thérèse's father
Thérèse's father had been ambitious for his children, sending her
to secretarial school and Michel to a technical college.

2385 tobacconist
One of the prisoners.

2386 Toupard
A man murdered and robbed by Carosse.

2387 Voisin
The prisoner who draws first and gets one of three marked pieces.

2388   Warnier, Madame
An old family servant whom the boy Chavel spied upon one night
and saw her removing her hair, an event which led him to believe
for a time that all hair was detachable.

THE CAPTAIN AND THE ENEMY (1988)

2389   Alma Terrace
Street in Camden Town, London, where Liza lives with Jim.

2390   Amalekites
Ancient nomadic people, treated in the Old Testament as enemies
of God's people (see, e.g., Exodus 17:8-16; I Samuel 30:1-20). Jim
calls himself an Amalekite and uses the term to describe other
"outcasts" at the school.

2391   "And the Babylonians came to her in the bed of love. . . ."
This passage (from Ezekiel 23:17-19) is an allegory in which
Israel's pursuit of heathen cults is depicted as the moral decline
of the sisters Aholah and Aholibah. After Jim reads it to Liza,
she never again asks him to read aloud to her.

2392   "And you, O son of man, take a sharp sword. . . ."
Jim reads Ezekiel 5:1-3.

2393   Bates
Headmaster who writes to his father after the boy's disappearance
from school.

2394   Baxter, Mr. ("Devil")
A hard, unemotional man disliked by everyone who knows him,
referred to as "the devil" by his son Jim, his wife, the Captain, and
Liza. Since his wife's death, Baxter has been a stranger to Jim,
keeping the boy at a boarding school or, during the holidays, at

his aunt's. He fathers Liza's aborted child and loses his own son
in a backgammon game with the Captain. Nevertheless, Jim has
doubts whether his father was really as bad as he believed.

2395 Baxter, Victor ("Jim")
The narrator and protagonist, who recounts his history with the
Captain and Liza in an attempt to make those characters clear to
himself and thereby to understand their love. On his twelfth
birthday he is removed from his boarding school and taken to
London by the Captain, who has won Jim from the boy's father
in a backgammon game. Jim accepts his new life in Camden
Town, with the Captain's long absences and mysterious activities,
and his own role as surrogate son to the Captain's mistress Liza,
but he remains emotionally distant from the pair. Eventually Jim
grows tired of what he sees as the comedy of Liza's life and leaves
her to become a second-rate journalist working for a paper he
despises.   Upon Liza's death he goes to Panama to see the
Captain, but the two quarrel and Jim inadvertently betrays the
Captain to political enemies who have him killed. Jim puts aside
his manuscript and leaves to pursue his own destiny by journeying
to the Valparaiso he dreamt of as a boy. An epilogue reveals
that he is killed in a suspicious accident enroute to the airport.

2396 Brown
The Captain says that "Brown" was his name at birth, but Jim
doubts that he is telling the truth.

2397 Browne
When the Captain demands that Jim send a cable to someone in
London to inquire about Liza's condition, Jim invents a friend
named "Browne" for the purpose.

2398 Captain
The mysterious man who becomes a kind of tutor and foster
father to Jim after winning the boy from his father at
backgammon. A man of many aliases and roles (thief, adventurer,
smuggler, sentimental lover), the Captain began his life of
adventure to escape from boredom, and in his living of it he
becomes a citizen of the Valparaiso of Jim's adolescent
imaginations. Only his first name, Roger, is known for certain,

and it is richly suggestive of his role as modern-day pirate who longs to emulate such buccaneers as Morgan and Drake. As a fugitive he cannot remain by the side of Liza, whom he loves and provides for, but his loving her from afar is also a consequence of his lack of confidence that she returns his love. After her death he no longer wishes to live, and he dies in a futile, suicidal attempt to help his friends by killing Somoza, leader of the Sandinistas in Nicaragua.

2399 Cardigan
An alias used by the Captain.

2400 Carver
An alias used by the Captain.

2401 Clara
A girl Jim once believed he loved. His discovery of the draft of a letter to her makes him aware that their relationship was only a physical one.

2402 Claridge, Colonel
The alias used by the Captain at the time he first met Liza.

2403 *The Daughter of Tarzan*
The film (apparently invented by Greene) playing at the local theatre on the day Jim leaves his school with the Captain. The landlord at the Swan says that it involves a love scene between a girl and an ape, suggesting a parallel with *King Kong*, which is mentioned frequently in the novel.

2404 Drake
Sir Francis Drake (1540-96), hero in the defeat of the Spanish Armada (1588); in earlier years a raider of the American coasts. The Captain admires Sir Francis Drake and Welsh buccaneer Sir Henry Morgan as "Pirates sailing the Seven Seas in search of gold" (64). But he prefers Drake, he says, because Drake captured the gold without destroying a city.

2405 editor
The editor of the local paper for which Jim writes first hired him on the basis of a sensational story he made up.

2406 "God bless the something [thoughtful] islands"
To illustrate his idea of good poetry, the Captain quotes approximately from Kipling's "The Broken Men" (1902).

2407 Harding, Mr.
Jim's housemaster at school, who always paid allowances on Sunday so that the boys could not spend all their money immediately.

2408 "Horatius"
A poem from *Lays of Ancient Rome*, by Thomas Babington Macaulay (1800-59), quoted by Jim when he is asked by the Captain whether he has been taught poetry. The Captain prefers King Kong to Macaulay's hero.

2409 jeweller
The Captain participates in the robbery of a London jeweller to provide money for the care of Liza and Jim.

2410 Jim's mother
Jim's mother, whom he remembers on her deathbed a few years earlier. She told him his father was a "devil."

2411 *King Kong* (1933)
Many years after taking the boy to see this classic horror film, the Captain reveals to Jim that he identifies in a curious way with the great ape-protagonist of the film because Kong is bound by love to carry others (a girl, at least) as a burden when the whole world is against him. After both the Captain and Jim are dead, Colonel Martinez suspects that "King Kong" is some code used by the two.

2412 *King Solomon's Mines* (1886)
Jim has read this novel by H. Rider Haggard four times. It was one of Greene's boyhood favorites.

2413 Kipling
Rudyard Kipling (1865-1936), the Captain's favorite poet.

2414 landlord
The landlord of The Swan hotel, easily deceived by the Captain's
lies about his attempt to be a good father to Jim, allows the two
to steal a dinner.

2415 Liza
The Captain's mistress whom he loves devotedly but chiefly from
afar. As a young woman she became pregnant through an affair
with Jim's father, who arranged the abortion which made her
unable to bear children. The Captain wins Jim in order to
provide Liza with a child, and she cares for the boy affectionately
until he leaves her. After being hit by a car, Liza dies in a
hospital, leaving a letter for the Captain which reveals that in spite
of his doubts she really did love him, although she prefers
kindness to love.

2416 Lowndes
A nosy neighbor whom Liza suspects of reporting Jim to the
authorities as a boy who should be in school.

2417 Lunardi, Mr.
On the wall in Jim's room at Alma Terrace is a picture of a Mr.
Lunardi leaving Richmond Park (where Jim formerly lived) in a
balloon.

2418 Martinez, Colonel
Officer in the Panamanian National Guard who has kept a close
watch on the activities of the Captain, Quigly, and Jim. His chief
concern is to prevent any kind of incident that might jeopardize
the signing of the Canal Treaty with the U.S.

2419 Morgan, Sir Henry (1635?-88)
See Drake.

2420 Muriel, Aunt
Jim's maternal aunt who keeps him after his mother's death. An
unmarried, boring woman whose speech frequently resembles the

Book of Common Prayer, she is a good woman but is readily abandoned by Jim when he has a chance to go away with the Captain. She hires a detective to find him after he disappears.

2421 Pablo
The agreeable bodyguard provided for Jim in Panama by the Captain.

2422 policeman
Officer who comes to Alma Terrace in search of "Colonel Claridge."

2423 Quigly
A very tall, thin man, known as "Fred" to his friends, who claims to work for an American newspaper as a financial consultant. Quigly deals in information but does not use all of it for his paper. He is a mysterious man: he was born in Brighton but sounds American; he is named Cyril but called Fred; he gathers information for American papers but admits that some of it has other uses. Martinez suspects that Quigly informed the Somoza government of the Captain's flight and therefore contributed to his death.

2424 "The sins of the fathers are visited upon the children."
The phrase which Quigly attributes to the "unholy Bible" (123) approximates Exodus 20:5.

2425 Smith, Mr.
An alias used by the Captain in Panama.

2426 *Toad of Toad Hall*
Popular pantomime in which Jim once performed a very minor part.

2427 tuckshop
A sweet shop or pastry shop.

2428 Twining
A schoolboy who made Jim miserable as an Amalekite and was therefore the only person Jim can remember wanting to hurt.

CHAPTER THREE: COLLECTED STORIES (1972)
and "THE BEAR FELL FREE" (1935)

Part One: MAY WE BORROW YOUR HUSBAND?
AND OTHER COMEDIES OF THE SEXUAL LIFE

"May We Borrow Your Husband?" [1962]

2429 Alec
Stephen's associate who painted Mrs. Clarenty's mural.

2430 Algerian
A man who appears regularly on the ramparts by the sea, as if
looking for something--perhaps safety.

2431 Barry, Mrs.
Actress with whom the poet Rochester had a relationship.

2432 boy
Harris sees Stephen and Tony entertaining a boy of about
eighteen in a sailors' bar.

2433 Clarenty, Mrs.
A customer who writes to Stephen to object to the mural with
which her bedroom was decorated.

2434 duchess
Stephen and Tony decorated a house in Kensington for a duchess
with a strong interest in the Napoleonic wars.

2435 Feucard's, Mrs.
Baths in Leather Lane, London, where Rochester stayed.

2436 Harris, William
The narrator, a writer whose age, residence in Antibes, and work
on a book about the Earl of Rochester bear an obvious likeness
to Greene himself. As a man of the world drawn unwillingly into
the sordid plot by which two homosexuals seduce a young man on
his honeymoon, he is not quite a detached observer of the sordid
plot that unfolds before him: he is a little in love with the young
wife himself and wants to warn her away from the situation she
is in, yet he is uncertain about how to tell her, doubtful that she
would believe him, and unsure that her error is retrievable.

2437 "hypocrite lecteur"
Hypocrite reader.   Greene's narrator echoes Baudelaire's "Au
Lecteur" in *Les Fleurs du Mal*, as Eliot does at the end of Part
I of "The Waste Land."

2438 Loo of Lucullus
Name given by Stephen and Tony to the "obscene vegetable
forms" with which Mrs. Clarenty's bedroom was decorated.
Lucullus (110-57 B.C.), a wealthy Roman whose name is associated
with gluttony, was a military leader who devoted his late years to
high living and good food. "Loo" is British slang for "toilet."

2439 Lou-Lou
Proprietress of the restaurant where Harris and Poopy dine
together.

2440 Mansfield, Jayne
Poopy regrets that she does not have the ample proportions of the
buxom American actress Jayne Mansfield (1932-67).

2441 "Passing Away"
Poem (1862) by Christina Rossetti.

2442 Rochester
John Wilmot, second Earl of Rochester (1647-80), Restoration lyric
poet and satirist.   Greene's biography of Rochester, *Lord
Rochester's Monkey*, was published in 1974.

2443 Rossetti, Christina (1830-94)
English poet.   Poopy thinks she might die "like someone in
Christina Rossetti" if she lost Peter (28).

2444 Snow, Sir Charles
One of the writers Poopy likes. (See 1653.)

2445 Stephen
Stephen and Tony, both interior decorators, are homosexual lovers
who delay their departure from a hotel in Antibes in order to
undertake the seduction of the newly arrived Peter Travis. Stephen
is regarded by the narrator as stupid; Tony is more intelligent and
has a streak of cruelty.   Their efforts succeed, and they plan to
continue a relationship with Travis that will destroy his marriage.

2446 "Then talk not of inconstancy"
From Rochester's "Song" ("All my past life is mine no more,"
1680).

2447 Tony
See Stephen.

2448 Travis, Peter
The young husband, an agent for his father's large estate in
Hampshire. Clearly loved by his wife Poopy, although his attitude
toward her is less clear, Peter is seduced by Stephen and Tony
with an ease that leads the narrator to speculate that the marriage
may have been either a last desperate attempt by Peter to prove

himself heterosexual, or a cover for his true nature, or a response to his father's expectation of heirs.

2449 Travis, Poopy
Slender, attractive, innocent young bride who does not recognize the substantial evidence of her husband's homosexuality and thus blames herself for his lack of interest in her. She naively approves of his friendship with Stephen and Tony and expects it to have a salubrious effect on her married life.

2450 Walpole, Sir Hugh (1884-1941)
Popular English novelist, a favorite of Poopy.

2451 Winstanley, Colin
A friend of Peter and a customer of Stephen, apparently homosexual.

2452 Yates, Dornford
Pseudonym of Cecil William Mercer (1885-1960), popular English novelist, whose books Poopy recalls with nostalgia.

"Beauty" [1963]

2453 Beauty
A beautiful, pampered Pekinese dog that receives lavish care and attention from his owner, an aging American woman who gives Beauty bottled water to drink rather than trust the taps in Antibes. The dog escapes from his owner and is seen in dirty streets, pulling the intestine of some unknown animal out of a trash can to chew on while wallowing in ordure.

2454 man
English friend of Beauty's owner.

2455 narrator
A resident of Antibes who, after seeing Beauty disgracing himself
by rolling in filth and offal, cannot resist walking past the house
of the dog's owner. Seeing her call her pet, he almost feels pity
for the "old sterile thing, calling for lost Beauty," but is prevented
from pity by the sight of her "hideous" hat (47).

2456 woman, American
Beauty's owner, an old woman who wears a horrible orange toque,
calls British M.P.'s "Congressmen," and refuses an invitation to
London because she is unwilling to put Beauty in quarantine.

2457 woman, English
A friend of Beauty's owner.

"Chagrin in Three Parts" [1966]

2458 Crawley, Mr.
The narrator juxtaposes Victorian and contemporary morality as
he observes the lesbian seduction while he reads about Trollope's
admirable character, the Reverend Josiah Crawley in *The Last
Chronicle of Barset* (1867). (See 2204.)

2459 Dejoie, Jacques
Madame Dejoie's late husband, who early in their marriage was
able to satisfy her sexually but failed to do so later because he
lacked "fantaisie."

2460 Dejoie, Madame ("Emmy")
A forceful woman who meets the unhappy Madame Volet in a
café, encourages her to drink excessively, and entices her into a
sexual relationship.

2461 Felix, Monsieur
A writer.

2462 narrator
A writer living in Antibes (as his creator did) who, in a manner
he regards as typical of his profession, takes a voyeuristic pleasure
in observing the skillful seduction of Madame Volet by Madame
Dejoie. Even so, his narrative is tinged with faint sadness as he
compares contemporary mores with those of the Victorian age
seen in Trollope's writing, and although he is glad to see Madame
Volet happy again he feels chagrin at the thought of his own
missed opportunities.

2463 Pauline
The woman who Madame Dejoie says enabled her to discover her
"capacity for love" (54).

2464 Trollope
English novelist Anthony Trollope (1815-82). (See Crawley, Mr.)

2465 Volet, Madame
A "young and extravagantly pretty" woman (49), unhappy because
her husband has abandoned her, yet also unsatisfied because his
lovemaking lacked variety.   She is consoled and seduced by
Madame Dejoie.

2466 Volet, Paul
Madame Volet's husband who left her for another woman.

"The Over-night Bag" [1965]

2467 Bertha
"Your cuddly Bertha" (58), as she signs her letter to Tiny, is the
friend for whom Tiny carries presents on the plane.

2468 Bosch, Hieronymus (1450-1516)
Henry's favorite picture, hanging in his living room, is a reproduction of a painting by the Flemish painter Bosch which he clipped from *Life* magazine.

2469 *The Cases of Sir Bernard Spilsburg*
A book in which the taxi driver read something about how bodies cannot bruise after death.

2470 Cooper, Henry
A small, graying, shadowy man who tells a fellow passenger on the Nice-London flight and a cab driver in London that the overnight bag he is carrying contains his wife's dead baby. This unlikely story, together with his comment to his mother about finding a toe in some marmalade, suggests that he enjoys a macabre fantasy life. (Greene may have intended a humorous irony in giving this character the name of Henry Cooper, the British heavyweight champion boxer at the time of this story's appearance in 1965.)

2471 Cooper's mother
A woman whose brief appearance is enough to suggest that she dominates her son.

2472 Cooper's wife
Cooper's wife, who may be entirely fictional, is described by him as a "conventional woman" (59) who mistrusted foreign coffins and therefore wanted her baby (not Henry's child) carried in the over-night bag.

2473 driver
The cab driver from Heathrow airport is enormously happy, having just won fifty pounds in the pools. He is neither surprised nor affected by Henry's claim to be carrying a dead baby.

2474 House of Stare
The building in London containing Henry's flat.

2475 Tiny
Very large woman who sits next to Cooper on the plane.

"Mortmain" [1963]

2476 Carter, Julia
Attractive, generous, sexy wife of Carter, sympathetic to Josephine
(because they both have loved the same man) and increasingly
disapproving of her husband's uncharitable attitude toward
Josephine. As Julia begins to feel that Carter justly feels guilty for
mistreating his former mistress, her persistent defense of
Josephine's motives leads to a serious quarrel.

2477 Carter, Philip
A writer who at the age of forty-two has married for the first time
and is eager to enjoy the peace and security that marriage should
bring. His happiness is constantly interrupted, however, by the
intrusion into his married life by his former mistress of ten years
Josephine, who showers the couple with notes, letters, gifts, and
other acts of apparent kindness. Carter's interpretation of her
messages as attempts at revenge eventually leads to a quarrel
between the newlyweds, who then for the first time spend a night
at home without making love.

2478 Heckstall-Jones, Josephine
Carter's mistress of ten years, a successful fashion designer who
brushes away a tear at his wedding and then overwhelms the
married couple with seeming kindness, doing favors, leaving gifts,
sending affectionate notes and letters. Her motives are never
revealed, but Carter's belief that she is determined to destroy his
happiness accurately describes the effect if not the intention of her
actions.

2479 "port after stormie seas"
The line Carter tries to recall is from the counsel of despair

in Edmund Spenser's *The Faerie Queen,* I, ix, 40: "Is not short paine well borne, that brings long ease, / And layes the soule to sleepe in quiet grave? / Sleepe after toyle, port after stormie seas, / Ease after warre, death after life does greatly please."

"Cheap in August" [1964]

2480 Hickslaughter, Henry
A fat, aging, unattractive American who becomes Mary Watson's lover on the final night of her Jamaican holiday. He confesses to having been some kind of pirate in the past, and he is currently blackmailing his own brother, yet his loneliness and fear of dying draw Mary to him.

2481 Joe
Hickslaughter's letter to his brother Joe, read by Mary, reveals his intention of blackmailing Joe for small amounts of money.

2482 Margaret
Fictional companion of Mary's holiday, invented by Mary to deceive Charlie when she travels alone.

2483 nancies
Hickslaughter's term for the young homosexuals he and Mary see in the hotel bar.

2484 "Spanish sailors with bearded lips"
Hickslaughter quotes from Longfellow's "My Lost Youth" (1855).

2485 Thomas, Lowell (1892-1981)
Radio and television news commentator, travel writer. In the 1950's Thomas narrated several popular travelogues filmed in the wide-screen Cinerama process.

2486 Thomson, James (1700-48)
Scottish-born pre-Romantic poet, best known for *The Castle of Indolence* and *The Seasons.*

2487 "The thoughts of youth are long, long thoughts."
Mary completes Hickslaughter's quotation from Longfellow.

2488 Trollope, Mrs.
Frances Trollope (1780-1863), prolific English writer, mother of Anthony Trollope.

2489 Twist, Oliver
Hickslaughter, eagerly holding out a plate when Mary offers him her tomatoes, resembles Dickens' famous character who asked for "More."

2490 Watson, Charlie
Mary's husband, a dutiful but unexciting man whose real passions are literary; he works on a study of Thomson's *The Seasons* while Mary takes a solitary vacation. A slender man who hates anything gross and has never been seen by his wife to weep over anything except a publisher's rejection of his book, he is a foil to Hickslaughter, who cries in fear and loneliness.

2491 Watson, Mary
An Englishwoman of thirty-nine who takes a solitary vacation in Jamaica, where it is "cheap in August," with the intention of having a romantic affair before settling down into middle age in her complacent marriage to an American husband. After three unsuccessful weeks she is drawn through curiosity and pity into a one-night stand with Hickslaughter, an unlikely lover who provides neither excitement nor romance but, through his articulation of the fear of failure, loneliness, and death, alters her view of Americans and her own self-understanding. Mary therefore gains an ironic measure of the deeper knowledge of life she had hoped to attain.

2492 wife of Professor of Romance Languages
Mary's friend who confessed having had a brief affair in Antibes.

2493 Wilkinsons, the Harry
In a letter to Mary, Charlie mentions having dinner with these friends.

2494 Williams, Tennessee (1911-83)
The "nancies" are overheard talking about the American playwright.

2495 woman from St. Louis
A hotel guest who invites Mary to join her group's visit to the botanic gardens but is refused.

"A Shocking Accident" [1957]

2496 Jemmy
Sally's nickname for Jerome.

2497 Jerome
An accountant, now engaged to be married, still haunted by the memory of his father's "shocking accident" that occurred when Jerome was a boy in prep school.

2498 Jerome's aunt
A humorless woman who tells everyone the story of her brother's death.

2499 Jerome's father
A roaming writer of travel books, believed by his worshipful son to have been a gun-runner or a secret service agent. The absurd manner of his death--he was killed by a pig that fell from a balcony in Naples--haunts Jerome's adult memory.

2500 Sally
The attractive fiancée whom Jerome fears he will be unable to go
on loving if she laughs when his aunt tells her the story of the
shocking accident.   But Sally, as Jerome himself had done on
hearing of the event, simply asks what happened to the pig; the
result is that his love for her increases.

2501 Wordsworth, Mr.
Headmaster at Jerome's public school.

"The Invisible Japanese Gentlemen" [1965]

2502 *The Azure Blue*
Redundant title the girl proposes for her next novel.

2503 *The Chelsea Set*
Title chosen by the publisher for the girl's first novel, which she
had called *The Ever-Rolling Stream.*

2504 Dwight
The publisher who praises the young authoress as a keen observer
and predicts a bright future for her.

2505 fiancé
A young man who shows "weakness and sensitivity" and seems
"doomed to defeat" (119), a defeat that seems all too apparent
since the girl he plans to marry has suddenly outstripped him with
the success of her novel and already speaks to him in a
patronizing way, suggesting that a job with her publisher would be
better than the one he had planned on with his uncle.

2506 girl
Attractive young woman who buys her fiancé dinner at Bentley's
to celebrate her receipt of an advance for the publication of her

first novel. Puffed up by her publisher's praise for her "powers of observation," she sits throughout the evening by a table of eight Japanese gentlemen whom she never once notices.

2507 Japanese gentlemen
Eight Japanese men eat a fish dinner next to the young writer who fails completely to notice them.

2508 narrator
An experienced writer who listens to the conversation of the young author and her fiancé and concludes that her publisher probably has overestimated her and certainly has not prepared her adequately for the expectations of a writer's difficult career.

2509 Nelson
Lord Nelson, commander of the English naval forces in the Napoleonic Wars, hero of the Battle of Trafalgar.

2510 Ward, Mrs. Humphry (1851-1920)
Popular 19th century English novelist.

"Awful When You Think of It" [1957]

2511 narrator
The unnamed narrator, left briefly to watch a stranger's baby in a railway carriage, exercises his habit of seeing in the infant's face the adult the child will become. He carries on an imaginary conversation with the baby about drinks and the stockmarket.

"Dr. Crombie" [1965]

2512 Bankstead
Town where Dr. Crombie practiced and the narrator grew up. It
has obvious resemblances to the Berkhamsted of Greene's
boyhood.

2513 *Bradshaw*
Dr. Crombie read *Bradshaw's Guide*, a famous railway guide
published from 1841 to 1961, on the train-spotting outings with the
narrator. (See 1941.)

2514 Crombie, Dr.
Eccentric doctor who served as physician for the boys at
Bankstead School until the community became aware of his odd
but tenaciously held theory that sexual activity is the "most
frequent" cause of cancer (134). After the revelation of that belief
ruined his practice, he survived a few years on private income,
devoting most of his time to the writing of unpublished articles for
medical journals.

2515 Fred's father
Fred's notably virile father who, unknown to the boy, was already
suffering from cancer.

2516 girl in Castle St.
A girl with bobbed hair who was the object of the narrator's
youthful love.

2517 Israelite, a British
See Turner.

2518 narrator
A man in his sixties who in his youth was a friend of Dr.

Crombie, with whom he used to go train-spotting. He had forgotten about the doctor and his strange ideas until his present physician diagnosed his illness as lung cancer, attributed to years of heavy smoking. Having been married four times, the narrator is amused to believe with Dr. Crombie that his illness "has been caused by excesses of a more agreeable nature" (135).

2519 narrator's father
After hearing his son's report that Dr. Crombie had warned the schoolboys that "playing with oneself" (129) caused cancer, the narrator's father reassured his son that playing alone with trains--his son's understanding of that phrase--was a harmless activity.

2520 narrator's mother
The narrator's mother left the room when her son asked his parents what Dr. Crombie meant by "playing with oneself" (129).

2521 Parker, Colonel
See Turner.

2522 Turner, Horace
Turner, who devised a system for converting the national debt into a credit, was one of the few patients to stay with Dr. Crombie after the doctor's eccentric theories were revealed. The others were Colonel Parker, Miss Warrender, and the British Israelite.

2523 Warrender, Miss
A woman who kept twenty-five cats. (See Turner.)

2524 Wright, Fred
A schoolboy who precipitated Dr. Crombie's decline when, fearing a "social disease" as the consequence of visiting a brothel in London, he visited Crombie and was warned that cancer resulted from "prolonged sexual relations" (132).

"The Root of all Evil" [1964]

2525 Anna
Name used by Puckler in his disguise as a female cook.

2526 Braun, Herr
Owner of the house with the large cellar where the wine-drinkers
meet. The only member of the group who does not know Herr
Puckler directly, he does not see through Puckler's disguise and
hires him as cook for the group.

2527 Dobel, Herr
One of the wine drinkers.

2528 Freemason
Member of the secret society of the Masons.

2529 Grand Duke
During an anarchist uprising in a nearby town, there had been
rumors of an attempt to assassinate the Grand Duke.

2530 Hackenworth, Frau
A woman who had kept her wig a secret even from her husband
until Herr Puckler pulled it off in the street one night.

2531 Kalnitz, Mayor
Mentioned as having died in 1887 or 1888.

2532 Kastner, Herr
Member of the wine-drinking group.

2533 Muller, Frau
Forceful woman who organizes the several lonely wives like herself
into a group that meets regularly for sewing, coffee, and talk.
Soon afterward she suggests that their husbands get together to
drink wine in the evening, which they do.

2534 Muller, Herr
Member of the wine-drinking group.

2535 narrator's father
"A man of absolute rectitude" (136), born a German Protestant,
who told the story to the narrator with the intention that it
illustrate the sin of secrecy as the root of all evil. In spite of his
strenuous objection to secrecy, however, he would not reveal to his
young son the meaning of "the terrible sin of Sodom" (151).

2536 policeman
The policeman who investigates the alleged anarchist plot sees
through Schmidt's female disguise and reports that members of the
secret society dress as women and go to bawdy houses. An
excellent maker of pasties, he is forced by duty to disguise himself
as a woman in order to serve as "Anna's" assistant cook.

2537 Puckler, Frau
A member of the women's group who has no curiosity at all and
therefore has no idea of either the dislike the other men have for
her husband or the wild suspicions he holds about them.

2538 Puckler, Herr
A "little vinegary man" who "could empty any bar" by entering it
(139). The other men dislike his company so much that they go
to enormous lengths to conceal their small drinking circle from
him, with the result that Puckler, unable to find anyone around on
nights when the men are together, suspects them of an anarchist
conspiracy and reports them to the police. To gain evidence
against them he disguises as a woman, poses as a cook, and is
hired by the drinkers himself. When the men suspect him of
trying to poison them in revenge for being left out of their society,
a fight breaks out and Puckler dies after being hit with a chamber
pot.

2539 Schmidt, Frau
A woman in her sixties, a non-drinker who longs for women's
company in the evenings instead of that of her solitary
wine-drinking husband. Her unhappiness leads her to confide in
Frau Muller and ultimately to the formation of the separate men's
and women's groups.

2540 Schmidt, Herr
Heavy-drinking man in his seventies who, fearing that drinking
alone in the evenings will hasten his death, proposes to several
friends that they get together secretly and avoid the company of
Puckler. In his attempt to serve his turn as decoy to lead the
suspicious Puckler off the trail of the group, he goes inadvertently
into a brothel from which he escapes disguised as a woman, thus
adding "unnatural orgies" to the crimes of which the men are
suspected by Puckler and the police.

2541 Superintendent of police
Is sufficiently alarmed by Puckler's allegations of an anarchist
conspiracy to assign an officer to investigate.

"Two Gentle People" [1967]

2542 Duval, Marie Claire
Attractive, modest woman who meets Henry Greaves in a park,
has dinner with him and briefly glimpses the kind of happiness
that they might have shared together, then returns to her unhappy
marriage to a homosexual husband.

2543 François
A painter, one of M. Duval's male lovers.

2544 Greaves, Henry C.
Modest, sensitive, middle-aged American whose Edwardian

moustache seems appropriate to his old-fashioned manners. He
lives abroad because he is disillusioned with life in his own
country. His merciful killing of an injured pigeon leads to a brief
encounter with a French woman, Marie Duval, and to their mutual
discovery that had they met fifteen years earlier they might have
brought each other the happiness both have missed.

2545 louts, teen-age
Teenagers who walk through the park playing a loud radio and
kicking pigeons draw Greaves and Marie into conversation.

2546 "Lut-lut-lut"
Greaves attempts to recall the name of Sir Edward Lutyens
(1869-1944), architect of the new Delhi, which Greaves dislikes.

2547 Marie's husband
Marie Duval's husband is at home with one of his homosexual
lovers on the night Marie has dinner with Henry.

2548 Parc Monceau
Park in Antibes where Greaves and Marie meet.

2549 Patience
Greaves's jealous, shrewish wife, who correctly suspects him of
having been with a woman but wrongly assumes that it was a
prostitute.

2550 Pierre
M. Duval's current homosexual companion.

2551 Toni
One of M. Duval's male lovers, a ballet dancer who claims to
have modeled for the stone phallus that is an objet d'art in the
Duval living room.

2552 Yvonne, Tante
General De Gaulle's wife, seen by Marie in a cheese shop.

Part Two: A SENSE OF REALITY

"Under the Garden" [1963]

2553 Agincourt
Henry V, English king, defeated the French at Agincourt in 1415.

2554 "And what good came of it at last?/ Said little Peterkin."
Wilditch, looking at one of his mother's old books, finds these
lines from Robert Southey's poem "After Blenheim" (1798)
"pencilled furiously" beside an enthusiastic account of the battle of
Agincourt (181). In the poem, little Peterkin asks his grandfather
this question with regard to the Battle of Blenheim.

2555 Black Mamba
Venomous African snake.

2556 brother, elder
In Wilditch's story, the elder brother wants to go to Oxford, but
lacks money and must go to sea instead.

2557 Burke
Robert O'Hara Burke (1821-61), the first white man to cross the
Australian continent, was not killed by aborigines, as Wilditch
believes, but starved to death in the wilderness in June, 1861, on
his return journey from the Gulf of Carpenteria to Melbourne.

2558 Cave, Dr.
Wilditch's doctor who shows him x-rays of his lungs and recommends more extensive examination.

2559 Civil War leader
Probably John Hampden (1594-1643), who was mortally wounded in battle at Chalgrove Field near Oxford.

2560 Dark Walk
A laurel-lined path at Winton which leads to a gate opening onto the green. (See 2924.)

2561 dauphin
Louis XVII of France (1785-95?), the "lost dauphin."

2562 Dean
The Dean of Warbury wrote a defensive letter to Mrs. Wilditch protesting that the school had not subjected young Wilditch to religious instruction but did attempt to foster the development of the imagination in students.

2563 Dedham, Sir Silas
In the story Wilditch wrote for the school magazine, Dedham is a man in the City who holds a mortgage to Tom's mother's house.

2564 dugong
A large aquatic mammal (sea cow) native to the Indian seas.

2565 Epstein's virgin
Possibly the "Virgin and Child" (1950), a dark bronze sculpture by Sir Jacob Epstein (1880-1959) at the Convent of the Holy Child Jesus in Cavendish Square, London.

2566 Ernest
Gardener at Winton.

2567 George's children
George's children are mentioned as having no interest in Winton Hall.

2568   *The Golden Age (1895)*
At thirteen Wilditch read these tales of a family of five orphans, written by Kenneth Graham (1859-1932), who became Secretary of the Bank of England in 1898.

2569   Grey, [Sir] George (1812-98)
Another of Wilditch's heroes, an English explorer of Australia who later became governor of South Australia.

2570   Haidee
The name Wilditch finds inscribed in rubies may be an allusion to Byron's character Haidée, who falls in love with the hero in Canto Two of *Don Juan*.

2571   Harrod's
Because Mary went to this most famous of London department stores with him only days before her death, George no longer goes there.

2572   Javitt
In the fantasy recalled by Wilditch, a tall, one-legged old man whom Wilditch finds seated upon a lavatory seat in the fabulous world under the garden. Javitt's manner is gruff, his expression coarse, but in their lengthy conversation he voices ideas that appeal to Wilditch on a deep level of thought: he teaches the boy the virtue of disloyalty as necessary for survival of the species, and of extensive travel as necessary for the discovery of beauty and love. His claim that his excretions enter the earth to reemerge as some form of life may perhaps be taken as a bizarre metaphor for the process whereby experience is converted through imagination into vital expressions of art.

2573   Joe
A dog Wilditch had at the time of his underground adventure.

2574   Jung
Carl Gustave Jung (1875-1961), Swiss psychologist whose theories stressed the contributions of racial and cultural inheritance to the psychology of an individual.

2575 Iuba
Black African people inhabiting the southeastern Congo.

2576 Mafeking
The most recent events Wilditch reads about in the old
newspapers are the celebrations following the relief of Mafeking,
a South African town where a British garrison held off a Boer
siege for 217 days in the South African War (1899-1902).

2577 Maria
Javitt's woman, whose real name is not Maria. She is old, dirty,
and balding, with brown-spotted hands curved like a bird's claw.
Because her mouth has no roof, she cannot speak but can only
squawk.

2578 Mary
George's wife, deceased.

2579 Montgomery, Lady Isabel
Opened the fête which Wilditch reads about in the 1885
newspaper.

2580 *My Apprenticeship*
See Webb, Beatrice.

2581 Ramsgate, Miss
Javitt says that the beautiful Miss Ramsgate Wilditch sees in
cheesecake pictures is his daughter. The boy resolves to pursue
her.

2582 *Romance of Australian Exploration*
George had been reading this book aloud to Wilditch a month
before his adventure under the garden took place.

2583 Sampson, Sir Nigel
Specialist who examines Wilditch and recommends surgery for lung
cancer.

2584   Silver, Long John
One-legged buccaneer who plots to steal the treasure in
Stevenson's *Treasure Island*.

2585   Sturt
Charles Sturt (1795-1869), English explorer who led two
expeditions into the interior of Australia in search of an inland
sea.

2586   Three Keys
A pub near Winton, sadly modernized almost beyond recognition.

2587   Tom
Protagonist of Wilditch's boyhood story.

2588   *Treasure Island* (1883)
Romantic adventure story by R.L. Stevenson.

2589   *The Warburian*
School magazine in which Wilditch's story was printed.

2590   Webb, Beatrice   (1858-1943)
Social reformer and theorist, a leading member of the Fabian
Society.   Mrs. Wilditch's copy of Webb's autobiographical *My
Apprenticeship* (1926) was one of the books George was unable
to sell to the booksellers.

2591   "Who seems most kingly is the king."
From Thomas Hardy's "A Young Man's Exhortation" (1867). (See
1773.)

2592   Wilditch, George
William's brother, an unsentimental man who believes himself
sentimental for not throwing away a book of his mother's that he
was unable to sell. He has remodeled Winton Hall and sold off
most of the land.

2593   Wilditch One
George, as referred to by his mother in marginal notes in *The
Warburian*.

2594 Wilditch, William
The protagonist and narrator, a middle-aged man who upon
learning that he may be terminally ill returns to the house that
was the scene of his most important childhood memories. After
somewhat distant conversation with the brother who stayed in
place while Wilditch traveled the world, he rereads a story he
wrote as a boy, then recalls the childhood dream or fantasy that
inspired it--a dream of discovering a strange old man and woman
living beneath tree roots under the garden. Drawn to the site as
a way of seeking his former self, Wilditch discovers an old tin pot
that may have been the source of the "golden po" (chamber pot)
on which he sat in the dream--or is it the golden po itself? Less
certain than before of the boundaries between reality and
imagination, Wilditch contemplates with renewed curiosity the
prospects of life and death.

2595 Wilditch's father
George thinks his mother blamed their father "in her heart" for
"dying when he did without providing for holidays at the sea"
(178).

2596 Wilditch's mother
A Fabian socialist who cared little for Winton Hall, quarreled with
the gardener, disliked the mystery of the Dark Walk, and opposed
anything in her son's education which could be identified with
religion or the mysterious. She tolerated detective stories because
they were less like mysteries than like puzzles which always
promised a rational solution. She objected to her son's receiving
any religious instruction at Warbury, and she was displeased with
the publication of his fantasy story which betrayed traces of
religion. She saw it as a kind of religious allegory.

2597 Winterbottom, Lady Caroline
Javitt and Maria laugh at her obituary in an old newspaper.

2598 Winton Hall
House in East Anglia which belonged to Wilditch's bachelor uncle,
who lent it to his mother in the summer. It was left to George
Wilditch, although for a time it had been "virtually" Wilditch's.

"A Visit to Morin" [1957]

2599 Augustinian
Morin says that he has been called an Augustinian, or one who
follows the teachings of St. Augustine (354-430), who saw
humankind as afflicted by original sin and undeserving of salvation,
grace as God's gift independent of human merit, belief as the
necessary precondition of understanding, and the conflict between
love of self and love of God as a cause of self-division in the
individual.

2600 chaplain
An army chaplain who, asked by Dunlop why he believed in the
Catholic faith, responded by lending him books.

2601 Chesterton
G.K. Chesterton (1874-1936), Catholic writer of fiction, biography,
criticism, and essays.

2602 Cie, M.
Morin says he has not yet been "mummified" by Cie and Hachette,
French publishers of literary classics.

2603 Collingworth
School attended by Dunlop.

2604 Corneille
Mr. Strangeways probably expected Dunlop to become a literary
scholar, writing a biography of French dramatist Pierre Corneille
(1606-84) or some similar work.

2605 Dunlop
The narrator, who as a boy developed a strong interest in the
writings of Morin when that writer's work was thought

revolutionary. Many years later he is drawn by business to the French town of Colmar, near Morin's residence. He speaks to the writer at midnight Mass, is invited to his house, and spends an agreeable time with Morin, discussing problems of belief and other matters set forth in the narrative, which he intends to publish after Morin's death.

2606 Durobier
A fictional character whose unusual stretching of the limits of orthodox Catholic belief may reflect the attitudes of his creator Morin.

2607 Hachette, M.
See Cie, M.

2608 Jansenism
The belief, after Cornelis Jansen (1585-1638), that only individuals chosen by God for conversion away from corrupt human nature can love God, and that the individual soul can experience a relationship with God only through the Catholic church. Morin has sometimes been accused of Jansenism.

2609 Lamartine
Alphonse Marie Louis de Lamartine (1790-1869), French romantic writer who served briefly as head of the provisional government after the February Revolution of 1848.

2610 *Le Diable au Ciel*
"The Devil in Heaven," a novel by Morin.

2611 man, hungry
Because a hungry man once died nearby in a snowstorm when no one would open a door to him, Morin always leaves his door unlocked when he is away.

2612 Morin, Pierre
An aging Catholic novelist whose works were once read and interpreted eagerly by readers and critics who sought in him a basis for or confirmation of their own beliefs. His popularity has long since declined, but a number of devoted readers remain. To

Dunlop he confesses the paradox of his religion: because he chose to cut himself off from the church for twenty years while he was involved in an adulterous relationship he did not want to relinquish, he lost his belief just as the church taught that one who turned away from it would do; now, five years after the death of the woman he loved, he is unwilling to return to the church for fear that belief might not return. In that way he gives up belief in order to retain faith.

2613 Porlock, caller from
Dunlop has in mind Coleridge's story of how his composition of "Kubla Khan" was interrupted by the arrival of a man from Porlock; after the visitor left, Coleridge was unable to recall the rest of his dream-vision and finish the poem.

2614 Rasputin
Grigori Yefimovich Rasputin (1872-1916), Russian peasant who rose to power and influence over the royal family and the government through his ability to stop the bleeding of the hemophiliac Czarevich. He combined sexual license with religious fanaticism and was considered so dangerous that the Russian nobles had him assassinated. Morin claims to have once led a life like Rasputin's, giving belief to women he slept with even after he had lost his own belief.

2615 Sagrin
One of Morin's characters; he does not believe in the literal assumption of the Virgin.

2616 shop assistant
A woman in the bookshop at Colmar expresses pride in Morin's residence in the area and insists that Catholics still maintain an interest in his works.

2617 Strangeways, Mr.
French teacher who helped the young Dunlop to develop an interest in the novels of Morin.

"The Blessing" (1956)

2618 Archbishop
Blesses the tanks and weapons about to be sent to war.

2619 Caper
Hughes' boss, apparently an editor.

2620 Collins
A United Press reporter.

2621 Crowe
Chief sub-editor in the foreign room of a newspaper.

2622 Hughes
An Associated Press reporter who asks Weld to telephone him if
something unusual occurs at the ceremonial blessing.

2623 man, old
Stands next to Weld, weeping as the Archbishop completes the
blessing. He calls the Archbishop a "saint" even though he himself
opposes war, saying that blessing is what you do "when you want
to love and can't manage it" (262).

2624 Martha
A loose woman whose favors are shared by many men; because
her husband is suspected of being a Nazi sympathizer, the men
enjoy betraying him.

2625 native
Interrogated by Tumbril about how weapons can be blessed if they
are about to be used in an unjust war.

2626 Smiley
Weld's chief, who may have sent Weld on this assignment to
"blacken [Weld's] reputation in London" (257).

2627 Tumbril
A Reuters reporter who asks a native how they can bless weapons
in an unjustified war.

2628 Weld
A reporter with pacifist sympathies sent to an unnamed southern
port to do a minor news story on the blessing of weapons.
Having written his story already, he goes to the event on the
chance that something interesting might turn up. At the ceremony
he meets an old man who talks about the need to bless those
things we cannot love. Weld, unable to explain this encounter to
his colleagues, follows the old man's example in his own way,
blessing the cigarettes he believes will someday be the instruments
of his own death.

"Church Militant" (1956)

2629 Archbishop
A genial man whose good-natured optimism, which reminds the
narrator of the attitude of a cheerleader, may arise from a kind
of blindness or even callousness, since in offering to secure native
land for the French women he shows little concern for the
dangerous political situation or the safety of the women
themselves.

2630 Donnell, Father
Missionary priest whose love of practical jokes may indicate a lack
of complete maturity. His attempt to persuade the Archbishop
that the taking of additional land from the Kikuyu is ill-advised
reveals a measure of practical wisdom, yet he foolishly believes

that Mau Mau terrorism is being perpetrated by simple, ignorant people who have been misled but would act differently if they knew better.

2631 Kikuyu
A large African tribe living primarily in the highlands of northeastern Kenya.

2632 Kimathi, General
Kenyan nationalist leader Dedan Kimathi, commander of Mau-Mau forces in the Aberares forests. Kimathi was captured in 1956 and executed.

2633 Little Sisters of Charles de Foucault
A group of French women from this society have come to the region to live and work like African women; they do not want to serve in conventional roles as nurses or teachers. They have asked for a small piece (one-half hectare) of land which the Archbishop grants in spite of the misgivings of the other priests.

2634 Mau-Mau
A Kenyanese terrorist group which drew most of its members from Kikuyu tribesmen. The Mau Mau carried out bloody attacks on Europeans in a rebellion against British rule from 1952 until 1956.

2635 narrator
One of the missionaries, a detached observer until, at the end of the story, he places empty bottles in the back of Father Donnell's jeep in order to frighten the Archbishop with the noise and thus to cheer up Father Schmidt. No one pays attention to his joke, however, and he is left with the fear that the clanking bottles will attract the attention of the Mau Mau.

2636 Patsy One-Eye
Mentioned by Father Donnell; apparently a servant.

2637 Schmidt, Father
A very old, white-haired missionary priest who lives with nuns in the relatively prosperous and carefully guarded Niguru mission.

He is alarmed by the Archbishop's gift of land to the French women in a place where Schmidt is certain they will be murdered.

"Dear Dr. Falkenheim" [1963]

2638 Browne's
Department store that hires the helicopter.

2639 Doppeldorf, Dr.
Author of a book recommended by Dr. Falkenheim and read by the narrator.

2640 Drew, Jeff
The old man who, dressed as Father Christmas, was killed by the helicopter.

2641 Elias
The prophet Elijah, in II Kings 2:11.

2642 Falkenheim, Dr.
Apparently an analyst to whom the story-as-letter is addressed.

2643 Father Christmas
Santa Claus.

2644 narrator
Writes to Dr. Falkenheim for advice about how to treat his son, who saw "Father Christmas" killed by a helicopter blade and therefore cannot give up his childhood belief in the reality of the myth.

2645 O'Connor, Father
Attends the arrival of Father Christmas in the department store.

2646 Perkins
A rival store.

2647 son
An English boy living with his parents in Western Canada. He is ridiculed and even beaten by his schoolmates because, at age twelve, he retains his belief in Father Christmas, a belief seemingly made permanent by the trauma of seeing a Father Christmas killed by a helicopter.

"Dream of a Strange Land" [1963]

2648 Bovary, Madame
The protagonist of Flaubert's *Madame Bovary* (1856), who poisons herself with arsenic. The professor confesses never having heard of the book.

2649 Colonel, Herr
Vigorous, tweed-wearing officer who sees his body as a machine that will never wear out. He asks the Professor to violate the law against gambling by allowing his house to be used as a casino for the celebration of the general's birthday.

2650 Commissioner
In remarking that his men had fought the only wars their country had ever engaged in, the police commissioner shows the jealousy of the army that exists among higher police officials.

2651 *Faites vos jeux*
"Place your bets."

2652 General, Herr
Well-preserved officer with a passion for gambling. Because he

is ill, his friends want to bring the gaming tables, with a croupier
and two assistants from Cannes, to him.

2653   General Director of the National Bank, Herr
Telephones the Colonel with news of the quarantine.

2654   *Ghosts* (1881)
The professor is unfamiliar with this play by Henrik Ibsen in which
a young man has discovered that he has hereditary syphilis.

2655   girl
The house where the General's party was originally to take place
is quarantined because a girl living there has scarlatina.

2656   patient, poorer
A lifetime bank clerk who never rose above the position of second
cashier.   When he is diagnosed as having leprosy, he begs the
professor not to report the disease because then the bank will not
take him back and he will have a very small pension. Leprosy, he
says, is not a disease but a word that cannot be cured.   When he
goes to make a final appeal to be spared hospitalization with the
disease, he becomes convinced that he has come to the wrong
house. He sees the Professor looking forlorn and concludes there
is no way the two of them could meet in this place. He finds a
gun and commits suicide.

2657   Professor, Herr
A retired doctor of sixty-seven who lives on a plantation that
seems secluded even though it is only twenty minutes from the
capital. He works only for a few favored patients and reads only
medical books.   Asked to violate the law concerning medical
reports to preserve the job of a poor bank clerk whose need is
genuine, he refuses; yet under pressure from the Colonel he
violates laws against gambling by allowing his house to be
transformed into the "strange land" of a casino where he is forced
to act as host.

2658   Prometheus
In Greek mythology, Prometheus gave fire to men and was
punished by being chained to a rock; a vulture ate his liver every

day, and every night it grew back, so that his suffering was perpetual. With more humor than compassion, the doctor has sometimes referred to his massive bronze paperweight of Prometheus when revealing to patients that they suffer from cirrhosis of the liver.

2659 Schopenhauer
The professor's reading of philosopher Arthur Schopenhauer (1788-1860) "to soothe himself" (291) while his house is being transformed against his will may be ironically appropriate, since Schopenhauer wrote of the necessity of moderating desire and subordinating the will to the intellect.

"A Discovery in the Woods" [1963]

2660 Bottom
The fishing village, so called because it lies at the foot of the rocks.

2661 Foxes
One of only two families in the village with more than one child.

2662 Liz
A bandy-legged seven-year-old girl whom the boys allowed into the gang because she can tie a knot the others cannot tie. The discovery of the skeleton of a man who was tall and straight rather than dwarfed and crooked like her own people moves her to genuine grief which in turn arouses Pete's affection for her.

2663 Liz's father
Liz says that her pa will "bash" a girl.

2664 Moon
Mentioned as the tallest man the people of Bottom have ever

known, Moon is still a foot shorter than the skeleton the children discover.

2665 Noh
According to Pete's mother, Noh (like the biblical Noah) was involved in some disaster that befell their ancestors long ago.

2666 Number One
A gang member, a cautious child with sparse hair who resembles an old man. He does not want to join the adventure which will take them into new territory in search of fruit, and he refuses to take an oath promising not to reveal what they have done.

2667 Number Three
A gang member who volunteers to go on the adventure and wants to punish Number One for refusing to vow silence.

2668 Number Two
A gang member who is willing to risk a new adventure once he is assured that it is worthwhile.

2669 Pete
A fisherman's son of either seven years (his mother's estimate) or nine (his father's). In what will probably be his final summer on land before joining the fishermen in boats, he is the leader of a gang of four other children who go into unexplored territory in search of fruit and discover the ruins of the vessel *France*, which has come to rest like Noah's ark on a hilltop.

2670 Pete's father
A fisherman.

2671 Pete's mother
Believed the wisest of women in the village, Pete's mother is clumsy in movement and speech, but her voice seems musical to him, and she has retained the capability of generalizing, something Pete and his father cannot do.

2672 Torts
A village family with triplets.

Part Three: TWENTY-ONE STORIES

"The Destructors" (1954)

2673 Bank Holiday
Any of several official British holidays when banks and most businesses are closed.

2674 Blackie
Former leader of the Wormsley Common Gang who loses his position of leadership when the gang accepts Trevor's plan. He considers dropping out of the group, but the prospect of fame leads him to cooperate. Later he comes to Trevor's aid by agreeing to guard the back of the house when no one else will do it, thus saving Trevor's position of leadership.

2675 Joe
A fat boy, member of the gang.

2676 lorry driver
Innocent agent of the final destruction of the house: the boys tie his truck to the last supports holding up the building, so that when he drives away the next morning, the house collapses.

2677 Mike
Member of the gang, still young enough at age nine to be "surprised by everything" (327). When he sees Mr. Thomas returning home early, he runs all the way to the house to warn the other boys and save the project from discovery.

2678 Old Misery
The gang's name for Mr. Thomas.

2679 Summers
Member of the gang, a "thin yellow boy" (329) who distrusts Mr.
Thomas's gift of candy and is quick to turn against Trevor when
Trevor is at a momentary disadvantage.

2680 Thomas, Mr.
An old man, formerly a builder and decorator, who survived the
blitz along with his beautiful Wren house in which he now lives
alone. Although the boys suspect him of miserliness and fail to
see the friendliness behind the grumpy manner in which he gives
them chocolates, Trevor insists that the destruction of the house
is not directed against Mr. Thomas himself. Thomas's concern
about his horoscope ("Danger of serious crash," 343) proves
justified when he emerges from capture in his own outhouse to
find his house completely destroyed.

2681 Trevor
Quiet, brooding new member of the gang, called "T." by the others
because they cannot use the upper class "Trevor" without laughing.
He risks ridicule by calling the Wren house beautiful, then gains
the position of gang leader by proposing to destroy it. Because
he understands the construction of the house, apparently having
learned from his architect-father, he is able to organize a highly
efficient and successful method of destruction. Ultimately nihilistic
in his attitude, he insists that the destruction is impersonal, that
ideas like love and hate are meaningless, and that only things
matter.

2682 Trevor's father
A former architect, now a clerk, who explains to Trevor the
importance of Mr. Thomas's house as a Wren house.

2683 Trevor's mother
Mentioned as a woman who "considered herself better than her
neighbours" (327).

2684 Wormsley Common Gang
A group of boys living in a London neighborhood heavily damaged by the blitz. Normally they spend their free time in relatively harmless pranks such as stealing rides on buses, but the newcomer Trevor entices them into a highly organized plan for destroying a Wren house that survived the bombing.

2685 Wren
Sir Christopher Wren (1631-1723), chief architect of the rebuilding of London after the great fire. His best known building is St. Paul's Cathedral.

"Special Duties" [1954]

2686 Christie's
Famous auction house in London.

2687 Corpus Christi
A festival day of the church, celebrated on the first Thursday after Trinity Sunday.

2688 Dewes, Father
The latest of the priests--Jesuit or Dominican--who for the past ten years have lived in Mrs. Ferraro's wing of the house and served as her companion and spiritual adviser. He has "a taste for good wine and whisky and an emergency bell in his room" (347).

2689 Etheldreda, St. (d. 679)
Anglo-Saxon woman who founded the double monastery at Ely in about 673 and served as its abbess until her death.

2690 Ferraro, Mrs.
William Ferraro's wife, who believes herself an invalid and attempts to live every day as if it were her last.

2691 Ferraro, William
A wealthy businessman and art collector whose busy, highly
organized life leaves no time for the personal pursuit of the
salvation he desires. Instead of seeking spiritual perfection
through charitable acts and the lessening of material instincts, he
attempts to purchase his release from purgatory in a businesslike
manner, hiring an "assistant confidential secretary" to secure
indulgences for him by performing the necessary rituals at various
churches and shrines. When he discovers that his secretary has
deceived him for three years and that he has acquired no
indulgences for his expense, he still fails to see the need for
spiritual reform but instead contemplates the hiring of a new
secretary.

2692 Ferraro's grandfather
Mr. Ferraro's grandfather, a "fellow exile with Mazzini" (347), was
a firmly practical man who founded the business of Ferraro and
Smith.

2693 Hopkinson
Ferraro's confidential secretary.

2694 Maverick
Agent who purchases pictures for Ferraro.

2695 Montagu Square
Mr. Ferraro's address, an elegant square in Mayfair in the West
End of London.

2696 North, Lord
Frederick North (1732-92), prime minister during the American
Revolution.

2697 plenary indulgences
In Roman Catholic doctrine, a plenary indulgence cancels the
sinner's full temporal punishment.

2698 Saunders, Miss
Mr. Ferraro's assistant confidential secretary, a woman of about
thirty whose remarkably clear blue eyes make her resemble a holy

statue.   For three years her "special duties" have supposedly involved the obtaining of indulgences for her employer, but in fact she has merely deceived him.

"The Blue Film"   (1954)

2699   Carter
A middle-aged businessman travelling in the Far East who has brought his wife along to assuage his feelings of guilt at having left her behind so often.   His lack of desire makes her an unhappy companion, however.   To stop her complaints that they never go to exciting night spots, he takes her to see blue films.   When one of the films turns out to be one he made over a quarter of a century ago and had forgotten about--made to help a girl he loved who needed money--he endures his wife's nagging criticism, inspects his aging body in the mirror in their hotel bathroom, and prays for his wife's death. Instead she is alive with passion. After they make love, Carter feels lonely and guilty, as if he has betrayed the woman he really loved.

2700   Carter, Mrs.
Carter's bored wife who craves the excitement of "Spots"--daring places where she believes her husband would go if she were not with him.   She wants to smoke opium, but he tells her it isn't done here--in Saigon, yes, but not here.   When she sees her husband in the blue film she is outraged and says she never would have married him if she had known.   But she watches nevertheless, and the experience arouses her desire so strongly that in their lovemaking later that night she experiences her first orgasm in years.

2701   Girl
The girl in the film, who earned fifty pounds for her part, was

someone Carter had known for about twelve months.   He
remembers wistfully that she disappeared.

2702 Guide
Boy who first offers Carter young female or male prostitutes, then
"French films." He guides the Carters to the latter.

"The Hint of an Explanation" (1948)

2703 Blacker
The free-thinking baker, an ugly, wall-eyed man who attempts to
avenge himself against God and the world by corrupting young
David Martin's belief in the sacraments and tempting the boy to
steal a communion wafer for him.

2704 Carey, Father
The priest in David's chapel.

2705 Gisors
Town in Normandy where the narrator recalls having seen once
before the face of a completely happy man.

2706 Lucy, Aunt
Martin's aunt.

2707 Martin, David (Popey)
The Catholic "companion" the narrator meets on the train. He
tells the story of how Blacker's attempt to get him to steal the
Host caused him to believe for the first time in the power of what
had formerly been for him only a lifeless ritual. He later became
a priest who sees the incident as one of many examples of how
the "Thing's" (Satan's) weapons are turned against the Thing itself.

2708 narrator
An agnostic who, although occasionally moved to belief by
extraordinary coincidences, finds revolting the idea of a God who
allows His creatures to suffer free will.

"When Greek Meets Greek" (1941)

2709 audit-ale
Several colleges of Oxford and Cambridge brewed a strong ale
which was first drunk on the day student accounts had to be paid.

2710 Bellen, Lord
Former employer from whom Driver learned petty theft.

2711 Borstal
Reformatory.

2712 Brown, Tom
Hero of Thomas Hughes' popular *Tom Brown's Schooldays* (1857).
In a less successful sequel, *Tom Brown at Oxford* (1861), he
attends Oxford.

2713 chokey
Jail or prison.

2714 Cross, Elisabeth
Fennick's young, pretty niece whom he plans to train as bursar.
Upset at first by the discovery that St. Ambrose's is a swindle, she
nevertheless accepts it as the least harmful of wartime rackets.
Elisabeth is no more deceived by Frederick's pose as a lord's son
than he by hers as a college president's niece, but they fall in love
anyway.   Together they plan to expand the business of St.
Ambrose's, after first collecting all the money they can from his

father and her uncle while those two frauds are still deceiving each other.

2715 Debrett
A standard reference work on the English peerage. Fennick says he learned from Debrett that the Drivers have always been a military family.

2716 Driver, Frederick
Driver enrolls his son Frederick in St. Ambrose's in order to give the boy a college degree as a gift upon Frederick's return from Borstal. After Milan does the examinations for him, Frederick is judged the only student of St. Ambrose's to show intelligence. He meets and falls in love with Elisabeth, and the two plan to marry.

2717 Driver, Mr. ("Lord")
A former manservant and butler who has served several prison terms for unspecified offenses. Posing as "Lord" Driver in order to obtain credit, he enrolls his son in St. Ambrose's college with the intention of purchasing, but not actually paying for, an Oxford degree for his son.

2718 Fennick, Nicholas, B.A.
An amiable con-man who serves as President and Bursar of the sham "Oxford" correspondence school, St. Ambrose's.

2719 landlady
Driver's landlady in London is suspicious when she sees mail addressed to him as "Lord."

2720 Manville, Lord Charles
Former employer from whom Driver learned the arched eyebrow.

2721 Milan, Reverend Simon
A clergyman of aristocratic bearing, one of Driver's fellow inmates at Wormwood Scrubs, where he sometimes spoke Latin to the wardens. Willing to do almost anything for a few drinks, he is hired by Driver to write Frederick's examinations.

2722   Mount Royal
West End London hotel where Frederick Driver is awarded his
degree in a private room. (See 915, 2902.)

2723   Priskett
Middle-aged Oxford chemist who first suggested to Fennick the
idea of starting a correspondence school while the military is
taking over colleges and tutors are unemployed. He becomes the
science tutor for St. Ambrose's.

2724   quod
Jail or prison.

2725   St. Ambrose's College, Oxford
A fraudulent correspondence school through which Fennick,
Priskett, and Elisabeth sell "Oxford" degrees to unwary pupils who
assume that the school is affiliated with Oxford University.

2726   Scrubs
Wormwood Scrubs, a prison in south London where Lord Driver
has stayed more than once.

2727   Swinburne
Fennick's account of Swinburne's expulsion is not quite correct.
(See 3075.)

2728   "We are such stuff as dreams are made of."
Fennick's quotations in this passsage are all from Shakespeare's
The Tempest (IV,i).

2729   "When Greek Meets Greek"
Greene's title echoes Nathaniel Lee's *The Rival Queens*, IV,ii
(1677):   "When Greek joined Greeks, then was the tug of war."

"Men at Work" (1940)

2730 Bone
Author of a pamphlet on the British Empire which is intended to
be circulated in fifty thousand copies but actually gets nowhere
because several commonwealth nations and the U.S. object to
parts of it. Later Bone himself objects to it as "unrecognizable"
after the many modifications it has undergone.

2731 Graves, H.
Member of the junior staff.

2732 Hill
Member of the Book Committee, "the voice of reason" (398).

2733 King
Once an advertising man, he tries to "sell" the war as he had once
sold products and schemes. He lost his job when an unpopular
slogan he promoted in support of the meat ration cost the
government (Ministry of Information) twenty thousand pounds.
Subsequently he was given a higher salary as head of the Books
Division of the Ministry, where he would be harmless.

2734 Lawrence
Mentioned as a writer who might be able to help the Book
Committee with a pamphlet on "The Problem of India"; he is
author of the "naughty novel" *Parson's Pleasure* and is called a
"good chap" by Lowndes (401).

2735 Lewis
A veteran of Gallipoli in World War I who works in the Empire
Division; he dozes during discussion of Wilkinson's case.

2736 Lowndes
Committee member who returns from lunch smelling of wine and
bearing news of increasing losses of aircraft in the Battle of
Britain.

2737 Manners, Miss
Skate's buxom assistant, who mothers him.

2738 Priestley
See 195.

2739 Savage, Mr.
Miss Manners reports that Savage, who according to Skate "always
was a bit wild" (395), telephoned Skate to say he had joined the
Air Force and wanted to show Skate his uniform.

2740 Skate, Richard
Middle-aged civil servant in the Establishments branch of the vast
Ministry of Information. Formerly an English master in small
public schools and a lecturer in night schools, he had always
struggled to get by, but now his wartime job makes him feel
permanent and happy. Skate sees his work in Propaganda not as
something useful but as just a way of passing time; he is the only
member of the committee who is aware of the slowness and
meaninglessness of most of the bureaucratic activity these "men at
work" are involved in--how trivial it is beside the "work" of those
in battle.

2741 Wilkinson
A popular novelist who had wanted to do a study of the A.T.S.
but for unknown reasons was denied permission by the military
authorities. Skate thinks him a bad writer and King a good one.

"Alas, Poor Maling" (1940)

2742 Hythe, Wesby
Head of the Hythe Company; an invalid.

2743 Maling
"Poor inoffensive ineffectual Maling" (402), secretary of the Simcox newsprint company, has "borborygmi" (stomach rumbles) which cause him great embarrassment. His stomach picks up "notes"--music and other sounds--and plays them back after meals. This amusing form of indigestion proves disastrous at a board meeting involving the directors of the Simcox and Hythe printing firms. Maling's stomach sounds the air-raid warning (it is September 3, 1940, first anniversary of the war and a day on which a major attack by Hitler is feared) and drives the directors underground for twelve hours, during which time he says nothing. The companies are "amalgamated" in the end and Maling's firm, to which he is devoted, ceases to exist.

2744 narrator
Former employee of Simcox to whom Maling confessed his condition. Having learned of the Simcox-Hythe meeting second-hand, he will "always believe [Maling] crept away to die of a broken heart in some provincial printing works" (402).

2745 Simcox, Sir Joshua
Head of Maling's firm.

"The Case for the Defence" (1939)

2746 Adams
A heavy man with bulging eyes, on trial for the murder of an old
woman found beaten to death with a hammer. His wife testifies
that he was with her when the murder took place.   He is
acquitted when witnesses linking him with the crime cannot
distinguish him from his twin brother, whose dramatic appearance
in the courtroom brings the trial to a hasty conclusion.
Immediately afterward, one of the brothers dies when he is
accidentally pushed into the street by the crowd and struck by a
bus. The survivor--no one knows whether it is the guilty man or
the innocent--looks menacingly at Mrs. Salmon as the story ends.

2747 Adams, Mrs.
Each of the Adams twins has a wife who will testify that he was
with her at the time of the murder.

2748 Adams's brother
See Adams.

2749 Crown Counsel
Public prosecutor.

2750 MacDougall, Henry
A witness who, driving home late, nearly ran into one of the
Adams brothers close to the scene of the crime.

2751 narrator
A reporter who has covered many murder trials.

2752 Parker, Mrs.
The murder victim.

2753 Peckham
An area of south London. Newspapers called the murder the
"Peckham murder," but the narrator points out that Northwood
Street, where it occurred, is not really in Peckham. (It is in
nearby Forest Hill.)

2754 Salmon, Mrs.
A witness whose manner conveys "honesty, care and kindness"
(408), she identifies the defendant Adams as the man who
dropped the hammer in Mrs. Parker's garden; but later she cannot
be certain that it was not Adams' twin brother.

2755 Wheeler, Mr.
Man who lives next door to Mrs. Parker; he was awakened by a
noise on the night of the murder.

"A Little Place off the Edgware Road" (1939)

2756 Craven
Lonely, deranged protagonist whose obsessive sense of the foulness
of his own body leads him to pray that his body, at least, will not
be resurrected. Weary from walking the streets of London, he
enters a cinema off the Edgware Road and is soon accosted by a
strange man who sits next to him and talks of knowing about
murder. After the man leaves, Craven discovers that the stranger
was covered with blood; he telephones the police, only to learn
that the man who spoke to him was not a murderer but a murder
victim. The incident unhinges Craven, who begins screaming in
the telephone booth until a crowd gathers and the police come to
get him.

"Across the Bridge" (1938)

2757 Calloway, Joseph
A seemingly gentle, silver-haired Englishman living alone in a Mexican border town where he has come to escape extradition and prosecution for defrauding shareholders of an investment trust company in England. Lonely, and frustrated because he cannot speak the language and has nothing to do, he vents his feelings by kicking his dog, not in anger but as if in revenge "for some trick it had played him a long while ago" (422). As a millionaire, he longs for luxury, culture--something on which to spend his money. After two detectives who are pursuing him steal the dog, he goes to the American side, perhaps to alleviate his boredom, perhaps to look for the dog; no one knows for certain. As he starts back across the bridge, the dog sees him and runs toward him, followed by the detectives, who in their attempt to avoid hitting the dog with their car hit Calloway instead.   In his dying gesture he raises his hand, which falls across the dog's neck in what may be either a caress or a blow.

2758 detectives
Two detectives come to the border town in search of Calloway but fail to recognize him even when they talk to him.   Equally unsuccessful in obtaining extradition papers, they bribe a peasant to smuggle Calloway's dog across the bridge into the U.S., and finally kill Calloway with their car rather than run over the dog.

2759 Lucia
An acquaintance of the narrator who spends a short period in the border town waiting for a ride to the American side.

2760 narrator
An unnamed observer, a somewhat aimless man who has remained in the border town after a ride to the Yucatan failed to materialize. Although he does not know Calloway well, he talks

to him, is present at his death, and believes that he may have contributed to that death by revealing to Calloway that the townspeople all speak English.   Nevertheless, his view of the action is essentially detached and ironic.   He concludes that Calloway's accidental death was comic, and that if the dying man actually expressed affection for the dog at the end it was merely an example of humanity's "baseless optimism" and "capacity for self-deception" (432).

2761   Rover
Calloway's dog, "very nearly an English setter" (420).   He hates it for its imperfection, for it reminds him of his life in England, where he bred setters.

"A Drive in the Country" (1937)

2762   Cohen, Alf
Musician heard on the radio in Mike's car.

2763   Cortez
Fred feels that, having stolen a car, he is now like "the fellow who burnt his boats" (444), Spanish explorer Hernando Cortez (1485-1547).   Cortez burned all but one of his ships at Vera Cruz, in Mexico, to prevent his men from deserting him.

2764   Fred
The protagonist's boyfriend, a brooding, impecunious man of about thirty whose mind has an "odd reckless quality" (435).   Blaming his parents for not giving him money, and the world for not providing him with a job, Fred confronts the protagonist with his plan for a double suicide to escape a world he says is not worth living in. His craziness has always attracted her before, but now she is horrified and leaves him to die alone.

2765 girl, thin
Seen briefly in a car at the roadhouse with Mike, whose love she
rejects.

2766 Joe
Mentioned as someone loved by the red-headed girl.

2767 Mick
The friend who has given Fred a membership in the roadhouse
where Fred plans to take the protagonist.

2768 Mike
Young man whom the protagonist asks for a ride from the
roadhouse to her home in Golding's Park. He lets her off at
home after half-heartedly attempting to get her to go off with him.

2769 protagonist (daughter)
A young woman whose vaguely defined rebellious attitudes lead
her to view her thrifty middle class family--especially her
father--with contempt. She sneaks out at night for a rendezvous
with her boyfriend, expecting a romantic or at least a passionate
fulfillment, only to find that he wants her to complete their
rejection of the world represented by her parents by joining him
in a double suicide. She abandons him to his own death and
returns home with a greatly changed attitude toward her father
(Fred now seems a man, her father a Man) and a measure of
understanding, gained through Fred's fatal despair, of what it is
that her father locks out at night.

2770 protagonist's father
Clerk at an export agency, a hard-working man who runs his home
with business-like efficiency and presents "the account" to God in
church on Sundays. Proud of having improved his property over
the years, he carefully secures multiple locks every night, as if he
were locking out something his daughter cannot identify. He is
completely unaware of her antipathy toward him.

2771 protagonist's mother
The protagonist feels alienated from her mother as well as her
father.

2772   protagonist's sister
The protagonist's sister is mentioned as "going to the hop tomorrow" (438).

2773   Roy, Harry
Musician heard on the radio in Mike's car.

2774   Weatherall, Peter
Musician heard on the radio, a friend of Mike

2775   weights
Fred spends part of his weekly allowance on "weights," probably weight-for-age races in which the weight a horse carries is determined by its age.

"The Innocent" (1937)

2776   Bishop's Hendron
The fictional town to which the narrator returns is clearly modeled after the Berkhamsted of Greene's childhood.

2777   Cochran, C.B.
Outside his old teacher's house, the narrator hears a tune from one of Cochran's reviews. (See 434.)

2778   dancing teacher
The narrator walks by her house and discovers that she is still teaching according to the schedule used in his boyhood.

2779   girl
An eight-year-old girl in the dancing class was the object of the narrator's intense love when he was a boy of seven. They danced together once a week in winter and saw each other at birthday parties but had no other contact.

2780 Lola
Young woman whom the narrator has picked up at a bar and
taken for an overnight stay at a hotel in his home town, where she
seems out of place in the flood of memories the town evokes.
She does not understand his feelings, and he wishes he were alone
because Lola, who means nothing at all to him, will now become
part of those memories that are important.

2781 man who committed suicide
As a boy the narrator once saw a middle-aged man run into one
of the alms houses, where he committed suicide. (Greene records
a similar incident in chapter two of *A Sort of Life*.)

2782 narrator
The protagonist, a man who returns to his home town for a
one-night stand with a woman he has met in a bar. As he walks
about the town alone, he is stirred by many memories, most
poignantly by those of the girl in his dancing class whom he loved
fervently and hopelessly when he was seven years old.
Remembering that he once left a picture for her in a hole in the
gate at their teacher's house, he nostalgically reaches into the
secret place and finds to his surprise that it is still there and that,
moreover, what he remembers as a beautiful expression of his
feeling appears to his adult eyes as merely an obscene
drawing--painful evidence of how the innocent child is corrupted
by the adult.

"The Basement Room" (1936)

2783 Alice, Aunt
Philip's aunt, who gave him a teddy bear when he was already too
old for one.

2784 Baines
The butler, a kind-hearted man idolized by the boy Philip, to whom he tells tall tales of his manly life in Africa, stories which seem calculated to enhance his own injured self-esteem as much as to impress the child. Trapped in a marriage with a termagant, he carries on a hopeless romance with Emmy. When Mrs. Baines pretends to leave London for several days, Baines brings Emmy to the house, only to be discovered by his jealous wife. In a violent quarrel on the hall stairway he pushes her to her death and then moves the body in the hope of convincing police that she fell down the basement stairs, but he is caught when Philip inadvertently reveals the truth.

2785 Baines, Mrs.
The housekeeper, an unhappy, mean-spirited woman whom Philip recognizes as the embodiment of the witches of his nightmares. In her mistreatment of him, she alternates between tyranny and servility and uses food to tempt her victim into forgiveness. Her deceitful strategy for discovering her husband's affair with Emmy results in her own death when she attacks Baines and is pushed from the top of the stairs.

2786 Bastables
Characters in *The Story of the Treasure-Seekers* (1899) and other popular children's books by E. Nesbit (1858-1924). (See 1862.)

2787 Bo
Town in Sierra Leone. Baines says that the governor had dinner with them once in Bo.

2788 constable, young
Policeman who takes Philip seriously and senses intuitively that some important matter may lie behind the boy's appearance on the street in pajamas.

2789 Down, Cora
Mentioned in the *Daily Mail* as having been married a fourth time.

2790 Emil
Possibly Emil Tischbein, the hero of Erich Kartner's *Emil and the Detectives* (1929).

2791 Emma
A woman seen shaking out mats at a neighboring house.

2792 Emmy
A slender young woman with whom Baines is romantically involved; Philip believes her to be Baines's niece.

2793 Lane, Philip
A boy "between nurses" who is left alone with the butler and the housekeeper during his parents' two-week holiday. Through his love of Baines and fear of Mrs. Baines he is drawn into the adult world of passion, betrayal, violence, and death, a traumatic experience which destroys much of his potential for a creative life.

2794 Mrs. Baines's mother
Mrs. Baines traps her husband and Emmy by pretending to leave to visit her mother, whom she says is dying.

2795 Park, the
Hyde Park in London.

2796 Reed, Sir Hubert
A "withered" Permanent Secretary, who with Mrs. Wince-Dudley is mentioned as among those people whom Philip could laugh at safely.

2797 Rose
A frowsy policewoman whom the sergeant asks to take Philip home.

2798 Sandale, Lord
Seen by Philip and Baines on the steps of the Army and Navy store.

2799 Sergeant
The sergeant at the police court, who has six children of his own,

does not take children's distresses and nightmares very seriously and therefore shows little interest in Philip's case.

2800 Stillwater, Sir Anthony
Governor in Freetown who once dined with Baines and his companions. He is seen riding in Hyde Park.

2801 Undine
The water-spirit who falls in love with a knight in the tragic story *Undine* (1811), by Friedrich von Fouquet (1777-1843).

2802 Wince-Dudley, Mrs.
A family friend who visited once a year from her home in Suffolk. Philip could make up stories about her. (See Reed, Sir Hubert.)

"A Chance for Mr. Lever" (1936)

2803 boy, the
Mr. Lever's African manservant who, along with the carriers, deserts him out of fear of fever in Davidson's village.

2804 chief
Village chieftain who bargains successfully for higher wages for the carriers Lever needs to take him to Davidson.

2805 dash
A present or tip.

2806 Davidson
Englishman overseeing the mining operation in Liberia for a Belgian company. Mr. Lever's mission is to gain Davidson's recommendation for purchase of the new Lucas crusher, but when he reaches Davidson the man is dying of yellow fever.

2807   Eastbourne
Coastal resort city in East Sussex. Mr. Lever plans to take Emily
there for a holiday after his return from Africa.

2808   Golders Green
Mr. Lever's north London home is in Finchley Road, Golders
Green. (See 1177.)

2809   Golz, M.
Executive of the Brussels company to which Lucas hopes to sell
the crusher.

2810   Greh
African village.

2811   Lever, Emily
Mr. Lever's wife of thirty-five years. His worst fear is that the
costly failure of his mission might make it impossible for them to
go on living together. He "had never for a moment imagined that
he could be happily married to anyone else" (498).

2812   Lever, Mr.
An aging drummer who retired from the selling of heavy
machinery only to lose his money in the depression and be forced
to seek new employment. In desperation he takes on the task of
journeying to Liberia to obtain Davidson's endorsement for a new
crusher which can then be sold to the Belgian company operating
the Liberian mines.   When after great difficulty he reaches
Davidson only to find him dying of yellow fever and unable to
transact business, Mr. Lever calls into question the clichés about
honesty, the "solemnity of death," and the like, around which he
has organized his life. He decides that only his relationship with
his wife Emily is of transcendent value.   Thus, he forges the
signature of the dying Davidson and heads back toward civilization,
not knowing that he is infected with the yellow fever which will
bring illness and death after three days of happiness.

2813   Lever's parents
Mr. Lever recalls having seen his parents properly laid out for
burial.

2814 Lucas, Mr.
The man who hires Mr. Lever to sell the patented crusher to
Davidson's firm in Liberia.

2815 Maidenhead
Town in Berkshire, west of London.

2816 narrator
The narrator addresses the reader directly at the conclusion of the
story, testifying that he (like the author) also has traveled through
that drab Liberian forest "where it is impossible to believe in any
kind of spiritual life, in anything outside the nature dying round
you . . . " (509).

2817 Revelation suitcase
An expandable leather suitcase.

2818 Stone's
Well known chop house in Panton Street, in central London, a
favorite of Mr. Lever's.

"Brother" (1936)

2819 customer
The café's only customer practices billiard shots while the action
goes on in the next room.

2820 Faubourg, the
Avenue in central Paris.

2821 Gardes Mobiles
Policemen.

2822 girl
The young woman is so attentive to her companion, holding the
glass of cognac to his lips and placing her forehead against his,
that the proprietor assumes they are lovers. One of the Reds tells
him the young man is her brother. Together they seem terribly
weary, starved, and hopeless.

2823 man, young
A young German Communist whose leg is injured from manacles
in a concentration camp. He limps into the café on the arm of the
girl, and shortly afterward he is killed by the police. Her
comment that he is her brother may indicate literal kinship or
Communist brotherhood, or both.

2824 men, four (Reds)
Shabby revolutionaries enter the café, order cognacs, and refuse
to pay, asserting that since what they have is the proprietor's, what
he has is theirs.

2825 proprietor
Elderly café owner whose café is entered by Communists just as
he intends to close for the night. He is afraid of them and what
they represent (free love; threats to women, life, property, savings),
and he takes comfort in the thought that the police will soon
subdue them. Yet the pitiable quality of the young man and
woman make him feel momentarily as if he belongs to the wrong
party. He feels compelled to speak to them in spite of his
intention to avoid warning the group that police have set up a
machine gun directed at the café windows. After the young man
has been killed, the proprietor says that the man was his
"kamerad," his "brother."

2826 proprietor's wife
The proprietor has sent his wife away because of the danger.

2827 Tuileries
Gardens in central Paris, extending from the Louvre to the Place
de la Concorde.

"Jubilee" (1936)

2828 Amy
A former streetwalker who became a prosperous madam by offering the services of her girls through the guise of a tour company. She wants to help Mr. Chalfont, whom she believes at first to be a former client, but her offer of money and even her hiring of him to enable him to save face merely remind Chalfont of how old and unsuccessful he has become.

2829 Berkeley St.
Fashionable address in Mayfair.

2830 Boob, the
See Merdy.

2831 Chalfont, Mr.
A friendless, aging (fifty) gigolo whose poverty, seen in his frayed cuffs, is carefully masked by his Mayfair manner ("the air of a retired governor from the Colonies") and his freshly pressed tie. Having secluded himself during the Jubilee week for fear of being seen by old acquaintances from whom he wants to conceal his declining fortunes, he emerges only to meet Amy, whose patronizing manner and "bright plebeian spontaneity" (525) destroy his elegant facade and leave him feeling old and exposed.

2832 Jubilee
The Silver Jubilee of King George V (the twenty-fifth anniversary of his reign) was held on May 6, 1935.

2833 King, the
George V.

2834 Merdy
Merdy and the Boob were friends of Chalfont, probably in the
same line of work, who have "long ago vanished from his
knowledge" (521).

2835 Shepherd's Market
Current address of Mr. Chalfont, in Mayfair but less fashionable
than Curzon Street where he once lived.

"A Day Saved" (1935)

2836 Jones
One of the names Robinson uses for the man he pursues. The
other names are Wales, Canby, Douglas, and Fotheringay.

2837 Robinson
The protagonist and narrator, a schizophrenic man who records his
relentless shadowing of an unnamed man who carries something
Robinson wants and has knowledge that Robinson needs. The
tangible and intangible objects of the quest are unknown even to
Robinson himself, as is the other man's identity, yet Robinson is
willing to kill him if necessary to get what he wants. The
obsessive, irrational quality of the pursuit, together with Robinson's
tendency to identify himself with the man he seeks, suggests that
neither the man nor the journey in pursuit has any existence
outside Robinson's mind.

"I Spy" (1930)

2838 men, two
The men who take away Mr. Stowe are not identified specifically, but the bowler hats and mackintoshes they wear mark them as policemen in Greene's fiction.

2839 Stowe, Charlie
A twelve-year-old boy who sneaks into his father's tobacconist's shop at night to steal cigarettes and secretly witnesses an encounter between the father and two men who take him away. Although Charlie has always felt distant toward his father, he senses a kinship with the departed man who "was very much like himself, doing things in the dark which frightened him" (537).

2840 Stowe, Mr.
Charlie's father is not loved by the son to whom he has seemed only "a wraith, pale, thin, indefinite, who noticed [Charlie] only spasmodically and left even punishment to his mother" (534). In what appears to be a permanent departure Mr. Stowe is taken away from his shop at night by two men.

2841 Stowe, Mrs.
Charlie's mother, whom he loves intensely. Her manner of speaking makes him think her everyone's friend.

"Proof Positive" (1930)

2842 Brown, Dr.
Member of the audience who thinks Weaver is seriously ill and
urges Crashaw to make him stop talking. Later he determines
that Weaver has been dead at least a week.

2843 Crashaw, Colonel
President of the Psychical society who assents to Weaver's request
that he be allowed to address the group concerning his
extraordinary experience.

2844 lady, elderly
Member of the audience who distracts Weaver with the flashing
knitting needles that so obviously indicate her lack of interest in
his talk.

2845 Leadbitter, General
Member of the audience who so strongly dislikes Weaver's scent
that he asks whether he may smoke.

2846 Weaver, Major Philip
Tall, thin, dark retired officer of the Indian Army who addresses
the Psychical society at his own request and tells them that his
comments may "alter their whole view of the relative values of
matter and spirit" (539). As the audience loses interest in his
comments he seems to lose vitality and coherence; finally he
collapses and apparently dies, but a physician present says that he
has been dead for at least a week. The "proof positive" he speaks
of with his last breath "had probably meant that the spirit outlived
the body, that it tasted eternity. But all he had certainly revealed
was how, without the body's aid, the spirit in seven days decayed
into whispered nonsense" (542-43).

"The Second Death" (1929)

2847 doctor
Attends the dying man and urges the narrator to see him in the hope of easing the man's troubled mind.

2848 doctor who healed
The dying man recalls that he was once supposed to have been dead and was actually on the way to his burial when a doctor interrupted the procession with the declaration that the man was still alive.

2849 mother, the
Domineering woman who asks the narrator to visit her dying son.

2850 narrator
A friend of the dying man, skeptical at first of the news of his impending death. Throughout their final conversation he tries to get his friend to abandon belief in the supernatural--especially in the idea that he may have died once before--but at the end he is afraid to touch the dead man's eyes because of his memory of a day long ago when he too may have "felt a cold touch like spittle on my lids" and awakened from death to see "a man like a tree" walking away (550).

2851 Rachel
One of many women the dying man has known; the only named character in the story.

2852 son, the
A dying man of about thirty who is deeply troubled by the belief that he experienced death once before only to be awakened miraculously by a wandering "doctor" who was connected with rumors about the healing of blind and sick people among the

poor.   In that earlier experience--or dream, since he is
uncertain--he discovered that death offered no peace but rather
the knowledge that he was surrounded by people who knew
everything about him, even his liaisons with various women and
"that young one who hadn't understood" (548). He believes that
after having seen what punishment lay in store for him he was
given a chance to reform, and that since he did not reform he
now faces a much severer punishment.

"The End of the Party" (1929)

2853   Henne-Falcon, Colin
Boy whose tenth birthday is celebrated at the party.

2854   Henne-Falcon, Mrs.
The hostess, whose name combines fussy motherliness and
predatory terror. She directs the children as if they were "a flock
of chickens" (556).

2855   Joyce
A party guest, an eleven-year-old girl who, unlike Francis, is
permitted to go for walks alone.

2856   Morton, Francis
Nine-year-old boy whose fear of attending a friend's birthday party
is symptomatic of a larger fear of life. After his ominous dream
of a big bird confirms his feeling that something bad will happen
to him at the party, he feigns illness and swears on the Bible that
he will not go, hoping that his nurse will sympathize or that God
will prevent him from breaking such an oath; but in the end he
is too timid to rebel against his destiny. During the game of
hide-and-seek, his brother's touch in the dark frightens him to
death.

2857   Morton, Mrs.
The mother of Francis and Peter, whose ignorance of Francis's
feelings is revealed by her implication that she would have heard
more about his cold if it were not for the party.

2858   Morton, Peter
Francis's older twin, whose "brief extra interval of light" (551) has
given him greater confidence and a protective attitude toward his
fearful brother. He tries to help Francis, first by asking the other
children to play a different game than hide-and-seek in the dark,
then by delaying the game as long as possible. Ironically it is
Peter's touch in the dark, intended to be comforting, that frightens
Francis to death. Afterward, Francis's fear seems to have been
transferred to Peter, who senses that his brother's fear continues
to pulsate even after death.

2859   Nurse
Unsympathetic woman whose response to Francis's feigned illness
is to suggest a walk that will enable the wind to carry off the
germs.

2860   Warren, Mabel
Dreaded thirteen-year-old girl who scared Francis at the last party
by putting her hand suddenly on his arm in the dark.   The
unfavorable portrait, especially the "masculine stride," suggests that
Greene's use of the name for his character in his later work
Stamboul Train is more than coincidental. (See 210.)

Part Four: "THE BEAR FELL FREE" (1935)

2861 baby
Child born to Jane Farrell; the father is Carter.

2862 Baron
Serious friend of Farrell, eight years younger than Farrell but
seemingly much older. Filled with contempt for the waste of
money in Tony's Atlantic flight, he imagines his own future as a
serious politician and social reformer, but in midst of planning he
dies in his overheated bath.

2863 Brigstock
A guest at Farrell's when the reporter arrives with news that Tony
has won the sweepstakes.

2864 Carter
Farrell's loyal but humorless friend who sees the idea of flying the
Atlantic as a heroic adventure and makes the necessary
arrangements for gasoline, charts, weather reports, and the like,
thus pushing Farrell toward his death. A veteran of the trenches
in World War I, Carter is haunted by memories of comradeship,
images of death, and ultimately the sense of terrible guilt after he
sleeps with Tony's widow Jane.

2865 Clayton, Tubby
The Rev. P.T.B. Clayton, an Anglican clergyman who developed
the first Talbot House and founded a second one in London.

2866 Conway
A soldier who died after being stuck on barbed wire on the
battlefield. Carter wept when he saw him.

402

2867 Davis
A soldier killed in the Great War.   Carter is haunted by the
memory of Davis's face in the mud.

2868 Dolly
Farrell paid Carter three pounds a week to look after Dolly,
apparently a horse.

2869 "Events do not happen; we come across them."
The story's epigraph, attributed to Weyl (probably German-
American mathematician Hermann Weyl, 1885-1955), may be
compared with the lines attributed in *The New Book of Unusual
Quotations* (1957) to Arthur Stanley Eddington: "Events do not
come, they are there and we encounter them on our way."

2870 Farrell, Jane
Farrell's unfaithful wife who purchases the teddy bear and puts it
in the plane. After Tony's death she pursues her "lech" for his
friend Carter, becomes pregnant by him, and bears a child.

2871 Farrell, Mrs. (Tony's mother)
Unable to watch her son's takeoff, she runs into the house when
Carter spins the propeller.

2872 Farrell, Tony
Agreeable but not very sensible young man who, having just won
the Irish Sweepstakes on a ten-shilling ticket, announces
impulsively after several drinks that he will use the money to do
a solo flight across the Atlantic. Although he never really intends
to go through with the plan, the earnest assistance of Carter and
the expectations of friends push him relentlessly toward the
takeoff. Even after he is airborne, however, he doesn't really
believe that he will go through with it, and he throws his lifebelt
overboard to provide an excuse for returning. He is caught in a
storm over the Irish Sea, however, and killed when his plane
crashes.

2873 Haig, Foch, *et al*
Tony's late father is described as having had the familiar
distinguished look of famous generals in the peace parade

following the end of the Great War.   The others named are
French, Joffre, Allenby, Gough, Petain, Sarrail, and Plumer.

2874 Hamley's
Famous toy shop in Regent Street where Jane buys the teddy
bear.

2875 Hardy
Named but not identified in the story.

2876 John
A guest at Tony's Atlantic Flight Party.

2877 Kathie
See Wuthering Heights.

2878 Mavis
Mavis and Pim are guests at Farrell's when the reporter arrives
with news that Tony has won the sweepstakes.

2879 Pim
See Mavis.

2880 Talbot House
The name of two rest and recreation centers for soldiers, created
in memory of Gilbert Talbot, the son of the Bishop of Winchester,
who died in the war in 1915.   The first Talbot House was
established in Poperinghe, France, in 1915, the second in London
in 1920.

2881 teddy bear
The teddy bear given to Tony by Jane "falls free" and is recovered
after the crash and brought to her by Carter.

2882 Toc H
In Morse code, the pronunciation of the letters "TH"; thus, a
popular name for Talbot House.

2883 Wuthering Heights
The ghostly image of "Kathie" which Farrell sees against his

windshield shortly before his fatal crash recalls Lockwood's dream, in Emily Brontë's novel *Wuthering Heights* (1848), in which the ghost of Catherine Linton (Cathy, not Kathie) presses her face against the window pane.

CHAPTER FOUR: COLLECTED PLAYS

THE LIVING ROOM (1953)

2884 Browne, Helen
The younger and more forceful of Rose's great aunts, a stout woman of narrow Catholic faith who takes upon herself the responsibility for her niece's spiritual welfare. To destroy the relationship of Rose and Michael she lies to each about the other's whereabouts, convinces her fragile sister Teresa to feel seriously ill, and with fatal success arranges a confrontation between Marion Dennis and the adulterous couple. It is characteristic of Helen's rigid faith that, as her brother says, her inability to believe in God's mercy has inflicted her with an unchristian fear of death; thus, she was the one who initiated the progressive closing off of the house and the abandonment of rooms in which family members have died.

2885 Browne, Father James
Brother to Helen and Teresa, a priest in his mid-sixties who is no longer active in the priesthood. He interprets the paralysis of his legs, the result of an automobile accident, as God's way of chastising him for his fear of death by inflicting him with a condition worse than death. He regrets the loss of his powers of contemplation and meditation but retains a strong belief in God's

mercy; he believes that divine mercy will extend to Rose, a victim of suicide, and to his sisters whose lives are severely constricted because they have inadequate faith in divine mercy.

2886 Browne, Teresa
Rose's great-aunt, a fragile woman in her seventies, gentler and kinder than her sister Helen. Having suffered from an unspecified illness ten years earlier, she allows herself to be made ill through her sister's suggestion and therefore enables Helen to keep Rose at home for a while. After Rose's death, however, she proves herself stronger than expected; by making her bed in the living room, she testifies to her own faith in God's mercy and overcomes the death-fearing superstition of Helen.

2887 Burns Oates
A publisher of religious books.

2888 Debenham's
A large department store in Oxford Street. Helen once saw Beatrix Potter shopping there.

2889 Dennis, Marion
Michael's wife, a bitterly unhappy middle-aged woman, childless since the death of their young daughter. Marion, who refuses to divorce Michael, makes a hysterical visit to the Browne home, where she begs Rose to allow her to keep her husband and threatens to commit suicide if Rose does not.

2890 Dennis, Michael
A professor of psychology at the University of London, chosen by Rose's mother as the executor of her estate because he was a close friend of her late father. Unhappily married at forty-five to a neurotic wife, he seduces Rose on the night of her mother's funeral and begins a passionate affair with her. He resists the interference of her staunchly Catholic relatives, plans a fake marriage with Rose when his wife refuses to grant a divorce, yet is so clearly bound to his wife by love and pity that he shows little real promise of being able to break off their relationship.

2891 Faulconbridge
Philip Faulconbridge, the illegitimate son of Richard the Lionhearted in Shakespeare's *King John*. Rose, discussing with Michael the likelihood that they will have illegitimate children, professes admiration for Faulconbridge, but adds that in her school's performance of the play the nuns hurried over the parts concerning bastards.

2892 Flopsy Bunnies
See Potter, Beatrix.

2893 "funeral bakemeats did coldly furnish forth . . . ."
Michael, commenting on his beginning an affair with Rose on the day of her mother's funeral, quotes from *Hamlet* I,i: "Thrift, thrift, Horatio! the funeral bak'd meats / Did coldly furnish forth the marriage tables. / Would I had met my dearest foe in heaven / Ere I had ever seen that day."

2894 John, St.
James reads passages from "The Dark Night of the Soul," by the Spanish mystic and poet St. John of the Cross (1542-91), a Carmelite friar.

2895 Little Flower
See Theresa, St.

2896 Martha, the anxious
In Luke 10:38, 40-42, Martha is rebuked by Jesus for complaining about her sister Mary's failure to help in preparation of their meal. Greene's stage directions describe Teresa as an "anxious Martha" (13).

2897 Mary
The daily maid, drawn regretfully by Helen into spying on Rose's adulterous relationship with Michael.

2898 Pemberton, Rose
A girl of twenty, at the peak of her youth and beauty, with a sleepy-eyed look suggestive of her innocence. In the few weeks following her mother's funeral her awakening progresses through

the pleasures of love in an adulterous affair with Michael, the executor of her mother's estate, to the pain of witnessing the destructive effect of her affair on Michael's wife Marion. Claiming to be only a "coward" who simply wants "a bit of ordinary human comfort" (49), she tries unsuccessfully to resist those forces that would make her think about things too deeply. Finally unable to reconcile the claims of her love with the expectations of her Catholic family and her compassion for Marion, she despairs of ever finding happiness and takes her own life.

2899   Poe, Edgar Allan (1809-49)
Rose describes the superstitious Browne household as resembling something from the stories of Poe, known for his tales of the grotesque.

2900   Potter, Beatrix (1866-1941)
English writer, creator of *Peter Rabbit* and many other popular children's tales. Helen remarks that Beatrix Potter (whose name was also Helen) was of her generation, and Rose comments that the Brownes all have large ears like Potter's flopsy bunnies.

2901   *The Psychology of Everyday Life*
In claiming to have read this work, Rose probably means Freud's *The Psychopathology of Everyday Life* (1904).

2902   Regal Court
Rose tells Michael that if he asks her to go to the Regal Court she will accept: "It's where people go to make love" (34). Later the two of them meet there several times. (See 915, 2722.)

2903   Rose (the grandmother)
The only one of the three Browne sisters who got married. When she died after giving birth to Rose's mother, the family closed off her room.

2904   Rose's mother
Rose's recently deceased mother surprised the family by choosing a non-Catholic, Michael Dennis, as trustee of her estate.

2905 Ruth
Rose declares her love and devotion to Michael by comparing
herself with the Biblical Ruth, whom she quotes: "Your people
shall be my people." (See 2184.)

2906 Theresa, St.
St. Teresa (also Thérèse) of Lisieux (1873-97), was a watchmaker's
daughter who at age fifteen entered a convent and became a
Carmelite nun. Her hope of serving with the Carmelites in China
was lost when she was stricken with tuberculosis in 1896. Her
autobiographical *L'Histoire d'une âme* (*History of a Soul*)
contributed to her reputation; from its subtitle arose the name by
which she was popularly known in England: "the Little Flower."
Teresa Browne objects to Helen's insistence on reading St.
Theresa to her; the saint is really Helen's "Little Flower," she tells
James, not her own.

2907 Vincent de Paul, St. (1580-1660)
French priest whose life was devoted to the performing and
organizing of charitable works, especially care for the poor and
sick. He was founder of the Lazarist Fathers and the Sisters of
Charity. In response to Helen's offer to get her a holy picture,
Teresa says she would rather have St. Vincent than St. Theresa.

THE POTTING SHED   (1957)

2908 Alexander, Miss
A parishioner whose call in the night Father William Callifer failed
to answer.

2909 Baston, Dr. Frederick
A tired, anxious bachelor in his sixties, formerly the chief disciple
of H.C. Callifer, whose funeral oration he delivers. He reinforces
the family's determination to ostracize James and keep him away

from his dying father--perhaps because Baston himself has a vested professional interest as well as friendship with the dying elder Callifer.   When James discovers the secret of his own past and believes that he was raised from the dead, Baston tries to have him committed for insanity but accidentally reveals, in the heat of argument, that he too believes that James died in the potting shed.

2910 Bentham, Mrs.
A woman Mrs. Callifer plans to hire to make slip-covers.

2911 Butler, Samuel
Baston quotes lines from a sonnet from *Life and Death*, by English novelist and poet Samuel Butler (1835-1902).

2912 Callifer, Anne
John Callifer's thirteen-year-old daughter whose detective-like curiosity and her vow to speak the truth for an entire month make her a catalyst in the process by which her uncle James recovers his past.   Anne cables to James the news of his father's impending death, overhears and tells James about Willis's conversation regarding Mr. Potter, and arranges for Mrs. Potter to visit James.

2913 Callifer, Henry C.
Head of the Callifer family, a once-prominent rationalist philosopher whose reputation declined in his later years even though it was jealously guarded by followers like Baston. After his death the causes of the falling off in his work are revealed and his fraudulent life exposed: he believed in but publicly denied the truth of the miraculous restoration of the life of his son James, who committed suicide in the potting shed; and he rejected James rather than face the consequences, personal and professional, of that truth. Having written a book about the necessity of proof, he saw the proof himself and never published again.

2914 Callifer, James
The protagonist, a journalist who has lived for years in isolation from the family that rejected him and from Sara, the wife he divorced because of his self-acknowledged emotional deadness. Notified by his niece Anne that his father is dying, he returns

home only to be denied a chance to see him. After the funeral he
becomes determined to find out what secret from his past could
explain why his father rejected him completely and why his mother
discouraged him from coming home. From the gardener's wife,
his uncle William, and finally his mother he learns that at fourteen
he committed suicide and was returned to life through William's
prayer and sacrifice. The discovery reconciles him to life and faith
and promises to reunite him with Sara, who still loves him.

2915 Callifer, John
James's brother, father of Anne; a banker.

2916 Callifer, Mrs. Mary
H.C. Callifer's wife of almost fifty years, who has loved him and
guarded his happiness and reputation by acceding to his rejection
of their sons James and William.

2917 Callifer, Sara
James Callifer's ex-wife, who comes to Wild Grove in the hope of
seeing James, whom she still loves. In their marriage she felt that
he lacked real interest in her, although he pretended well and was
kind. She would have preferred to lose him to another woman
than to a bed-sitting room in Nottingham.

2918 Callifer, William
An alcoholic priest, an outcast of the rationalist Callifer family.
Ridiculed for his faith by his older, smarter brother Henry, he
cherished Henry's son James as a substitute for the child he could
never have. When James hanged himself, William offered to give
up his dearest possession--his faith--if God would allow James to
live. The plea was granted, and William suffered as a diligent
but faithless priest for thirty years. In the play his encounter with
James restores his faith.

2919 Connolly, Miss
Father Callifer's long-time housekeeper who chides him for his
failures and bad habits but says she would give her life for him.
She has protected him by dissuading parishioners from writing to
the bishop to complain about him.

2920 Corner
James's colleague on the *Journal*, described by James as that paper's only true reporter.

2921 *The Cosmic Fallacy*
Book by H.C. Callifer.

2922 Councillor Worm
The Nottingham councillor's European travels are reported in the *Journal.*

2923 *The Credo of a Sceptic*
Essay by H.C. Callifer.

2924 dark walk
The dark walk recalled or invented by James in his attempt to reconstruct the experience of the potting shed for Dr. Kreuzer is apparently the laurel walk, also feared by Anne, that leads to the shed. (See 2560.)

2925 *He Was a Man*
H.C. Callifer's book which denied the divinity of Christ.

2926 Kreuzer, Dr.
Elderly psychoanalyst who tries to help James remember what happened in the potting shed incident. He has vowed never to give up on a patient, and because his own son committed suicide he is especially sympathetic to James.

2927 Kreuzer's son
Kreuzer's mentally troubled son refused treatment by other doctors, and when his father failed to cure him he killed himself.

2928 Kreuzer's wife
Kreuzer's estranged wife, whom he had not seen in years, took the news of their son's death very badly.

2929 Lazarus
A friend of Jesus and the brother of Martha and Mary, Lazarus died but was raised from the dead after three days (John 11:1).

2930 Minster, Mr.
Calls the *Rationalist Review* to express concern for the Callifer
family. Mrs. Callifer says they never thought highly of him.

2931 Murphy, Father
Mentioned by Mrs. Connolly as having a more beautiful voice and
more original sermons than Father Callifer.

2932 "Out, out, damned Spot."
Anne, afraid of ghosts and unwilling to carry water for the dog
Spot into the potting shed, thought of Lady Macbeth's familiar line
(*Macbeth* V,ii).

2933 Potter
Former gardener at Wild Grove whose death pleased H.C. Callifer
because Potter had witnessed the miraculous restoration of James's
life after his suicide. Callifer forced Potter to retire for spreading
stories about the event.

2934 Potter, Mrs.
Brought to James's lodgings in Nottingham by Anne, Potter's wife
reveals to James what her husband saw in the potting shed.

2935 Russell, Bertrand
Bertrand Russell (1872-1970), Cambridge professor and
philosopher, author of *The Principles of Mathematics* (1903) and
many other works. His name appears in the guest list at Wild
Grove.

2936 Spot
James Callifer's dog.

2937 Stone, Marcus
Engravings by Stone hang in James's bed-sitting room.

2938 "They scoff at scars who never felt a wound."
Father Callifer slightly misquotes Shakespeare's Romeo: "He jests
at scars, that never felt a wound" (II,ii,i).

2939   Wells
The name of H.G. Wells (1866-1946), novelist, historian, and rationalist thinker, appears in the guest list at Wild Grove.

2940   Willis
The current gardener at Wild Grove, overheard by Anne as he talks about Potter's having seen the events in the potting shed.

THE COMPLAISANT LOVER (1959)

2941   Adams
Mentioned as a boy at Robin's school whose father left the family for a girl employed at the Zoo.

2942   "all for love and the world well lost"
Clive says that in his "school" (for conducting adulterous relationships) there are no lessons in "all for love and the world well lost." The line comes from Dryden's *All for Love, or the World Well Lost* (1678), a version of the story of Antony and Cleopatra.

2943   Binlow, Lord
Mentioned as an old Liberal who also likes to watch the Larkins.

2944   Caton, Lord
Recalled by Victor for his comment that alcohol kills germs.

2945   Clive, Robert (1725-74)
Baron Clive of Plassey, the British military hero who led the overthrow of the French in India and became the colony's first British governor. Root's father admired the famous Clive and named his son after him.

2946 Clive's father
An admirer of Clive of India, to the point of imitation: he not
only named his son after Clive but shot himself as Clive did.

2947 Crane, Jane
The imaginary friend from Northumberland invented by Mary
Rhodes to conceal her relationship with Clive. Mary arranges a
holiday in Amsterdam with "Jane" but meets Root there.

2948 Farquhar
A patron of Howard's bank who invested all of his money in
potatoes.

2949 film-magnate
A film magnate who reads erotica introduced Clive to a
Knightsbridge dealer in black market currencies.

2950 Forsters and Morgans, the
Guests at the Rhodeses' second party who are mentioned but do
not appear. Greene seems to be having fun with the name of
novelist E. M. (Edward Morgan) Forster, whose familiar novel
Howards End (1910) has a Margaret (Schlegel) as its protagonist.

2951 Fuchs
Sir Vivian Ernest Fuchs (1908-), leader of the British
Commonwealth Trans-Antarctic Expedition in 1957-58.

2952 girls in Curzon St.
Prostitutes whom Clive says he has been with only two or three
times, when lonely.

2953 Howard, Ann
Nineteen-year-old daughter of William and Margaret Howard,
bored with her life and oppressed with a sense of the smallness of
England. Longing for a romantic adventure, she offers to begin
an affair with Clive Root, who rejects her because of her
inexperience.

2954 Howard, Margaret
Wife of William and mother of Ann Howard.

2955 Howard, William
A bank manager in his middle fifties, a friend of Victor and Mary
Rhodes.

2956 the Larkins
Television program watched by the Rhodeses and the Howards in
act one.

2957 Macbeth
Robin Rhodes will play the part of the second murderer in a
school performance of Shakespeare's play.

2958 man in Knightsbridge
A black marketeer who deals in currencies and helps Clive Root
to arrange the purchase of diamond earrings in Amsterdam for
Mary Rhodes.

2959 Prime Minister
In 1959, Harold MacMillan.

2960 Redoute's *Lilies*
Clive buys Mary earrings with profits from the sale of this work
by Pierre Joseph Redoute (1759-1840), a French painter of
flowers.

2961 Rhodes, Mary
A restless wife whose passionless marriage has been celibate for
five years, Mary is torn between her romantic adulterous affair
with Clive Root and her lingering sense of obligation toward, and
affection for, her family and her husband Victor. Pretending to
meet an old friend "Jane Crane," she spends a weekend in
Amsterdam with Clive, who subsequently reveals the affair to her
husband, creating a crisis that Victor solves by offering to allow
Mary to remain in the marriage while continuing the affair. With
an optimism not shared by Clive, Mary accepts.

2962 Rhodes, Robin
Twelve-year-old son of Victor and Mary, in love with Ann
Howard.

2963 Rhodes, Sally
Fifteen-year-old daughter of Victor and Mary, away at school.

2964 Rhodes, Victor
A north London dentist in his mid-forties who relies upon practical
jokes and anecdotes to alleviate the boredom of his life and
boasts, ironically, that a sense of humor is the key to a happy
marriage. He loves Mary, his wife of sixteen years, but for five
years has not been intimate with her because he is aware that he
no longer satisfies her physically. When he discovers her affair
with Clive Root he contemplates suicide but decides that it would
be silly; instead he agrees to allow her to continue her affair while
staying within the marriage and the family--not having to choose.
By doing so he undermines some of the ardor and much of the
confidence of his wife's lover.

2965 *Riders of the Purple Sage* (1912)
Novel by Zane Grey, of whom Ann Howard is an avid reader.

2966 Root, Clive
Handsome antiquarian book dealer whose preference for
experienced women has led him by age thirty-eight into four
affairs with married women, all of whom eventually returned to
their husbands. In love with Mary Rhodes, he is jealous of her
husband Victor and cannot feel confident in her love until she
leaves Victor for him. Root carries on successfully a four-day
holiday with Mary in Amsterdam, then sends Victor a letter
intended to force Mary's marriage into a crisis by revealing her
adultery. His strategy backfires, however, when Victor forgives
Mary and decides to allow her to continue her relationship with
Clive while remaining married. Unable to have Mary on his own
terms, Clive now faces an uncertain future.

2967 Swinburne
The poem alluded to is "The Leper" (1876). (See 3075.)

2968 valet
Clive, impatient to bring about a crisis that will force Mary to
leave her husband for him, hires the valet in their Amsterdam

hotel to write a letter to Victor revealing that Mary and Clive were intimate in the hotel.

2969 Van Droog, Dr.
A manufacturer of dental instruments whom Victor meets in Amsterdam and takes to the hotel where he finds Mary and Clive.

2970 Victor's father
Victor recalls that his father always locked all of the doors in his house, even the interior doors, because he believed in "that piece in the church-service. You know--a strong man keeps his house" (164).

CARVING A STATUE (1964)

2971 Adventist
The Second Girl wants to know whether the Father is an Adventist, one who believes that the end of the world and the second coming are near.

2972 bollard
A post, on a wharf or a ship, to which ropes are tied.

2973 Botticelli
Dr. Parker compares the Second Girl to the figure of Venus in the Italian painter Sandro Botticelli's "Birth of Venus" (1478).

2974 Boy
The sculptor's son is a lonely boy of about fifteen, largely ignored by his father. He tries unsuccessfully to reconstruct an image of his dead mother, and he dreams of life as a sailor bound for Valparaiso. The First Girl he brings to the studio is easily seduced by the Father; the second runs out into the street to escape the attentions of Dr. Parker and is killed by a car. Stricken

with grief and disillusioned by the full realization that the Father embodies the very indifference which the Father attributes to God, the Boy threatens suicide but is dissuaded by the Father's confession that his obsessive work and detachment from emotion are ways of escaping pain and sorrow.

2975 Bridges, Joe
The First Girl says she has a date with Bridges.

2976 Burne-Jones
English painter Edward Burne-Jones (1833-98).

2977 Davies
One of the Father's slides shows Davies on the Brighton Pier. Davies, he says, resembles God in that he really did kill his son and was not ashamed of it (as he proved by collecting insurance money).

2978 *Eloi, Eloi, lamma sabasthani*
Christ's words on the cross: "My God, my God, why hast thou forsaken me?"

2979 Father
A sculptor obsessed with the creation of an enormous figure of God, a work he has struggled with for twelve years. Believing that the only fit subjects for sculpture are the Virgin, the Son, and God, he ignores the ordinary concerns of life and becomes completely absorbed in his work in an attempt to define satisfactorily his own concept of God and to escape the pain of living. Like the God he imagines, he seems neither to love nor to hate but merely to communicate; he shows no sadness over the death of his wife years ago, no affection for the dutiful young son whose girlfriend he casually seduces. At the end of the play he admits that the figure of God is outside his scope and realizes that instead he may be able to capture a new vision of the fallen angel Lucifer, who is more accessible to the human imagination.

2980 Girl, First
A flirtatious girl whose apparent toughness probably masks her

vulnerability is brought to the studio by the Boy. She rejects his immature advances but is willingly seduced by the Father.

2981 Girl, Second
A deaf and dumb girl who was lost on the Inner Circle of the London Underground is brought to the studio by the Boy. When the lascivious Dr. Parker tries to seduce her, she runs out into the street, where she is hit and killed by a car.

2982 Grand Duke of Lichtenstein
A work from the Father's abstract period.

2983 Holman Hunt [William] (1827-1910)
English painter. A reproduction of Hunt's "Light of the World" hangs on the wall in the studio.

2984 Hully Gully
The Hully Gully, the Madison, and the twist are dances that were popular in the 1950's and early 1960's.

2985 Inner Circle
Part of the London Underground railway system comprised by the District and Circle Lines. The Boy says he found the Second Girl on the Inner Circle.

2986 Landru
Henri Desiré Landru (1869-1922), French swindler and murderer believed to have defrauded over two hundred women; he was executed for the murders of ten women and one boy.

2987 Lawrence, Sir Thomas (1769-1830)
English painter best known for elegant portraits.

2988 Michelangelo
The Father says that Michelangelo, though ambitious, never attempted to sculpt God.

2989 Moore, Henry
A large photograph of one of sculptor Henry Moore's reclining women hangs on the wall in the studio.

2990   Mother
The Boy's mother died of cancer.

2991   Muggeridge
An acquaintance the Father wanted to use as a model for the statue. Muggeridge proved unsuitable because he could not sit for more than thirty minutes without his cigar. The Boy mentions that Muggeridge recently married for the third time.

2992   Murillo
Spanish painter Bartolomé Esteban Murillo (1617?-82).

2993   Parker, Dr.
The Father's physician who also attended the mother during her terminal illness, likened by the sculptor to God because his patients (or victims) so often die. Parker's attempt to seduce or molest a girl the Boy brings to the studio causes her to run into the street, where she is killed by a car.

2994   Salt, Johnny
A boyfriend mentioned by the First Girl as more interested in motorcycles than in kisses.

2995   Sickert
English painter Walter Sickert (1860-1942). The Father says that he considered following the example of the painter Sickert by using photographs rather than live models.

2996   Tomlinson, Henry
A man the Father considered as a model for the sculpture but rejected when he discovered that Tomlinson was only a cuckold, not a father.

2997   Watkins, Mr.
A banker who has carried on a long-term adulterous affair with Tomlinson's wife. The Father thought of using him as a model, but found the situation too delicate.

2998   "When the Assyrians came down like a wolf on the fold"
The Father quotes from Lord Byron's "The Destruction of
Sennacherib" (1815).

2999   Whitaker, Joseph (1820-95)
Not really the world's greatest poet as the Boy says facetiously, but
publisher and editor of *The Gentleman's Magazine* and founder
of several other well-known publications, including *Whitaker's
Almanac.*

THE RETURN OF A.J. RAFFLES (1975)

3000   Alice
The woman with whom "Mr. Portland" has arranged an assignation
in Lord Queensbury's bedroom for the very time Raffles and
Bunny attempt to carry out their robbery there. Her character is
based on Alice Keppel, a mistress of Edward VII who was
regarded tolerably by his wife Alexandra.

3001   Axminster, Lady
Mentioned teasingly by Raffles as worrying that her jewels have
been stolen.

3002   Bertie
The Prince of Wales, later King Edward VII.

3003   Bertillon, Monsieur
French criminologist Alphonse Bertillon (1853-1914) was one of
the first to use fingerprinting in the identification of criminals,
although he considered the method less important than his own
anthropometric system called Bertillonage.

3004   Betteridge
Smith's predecessor as head porter at Albany.

3005   Botha, General Louis (1862-1919)
Raffles claims to have been interrogated during the South African
War (1899-1902) by Botha, who was Commander of the Boer
forces and, later, prime minister of the Union of South Africa.

3006   Buller, General
British commander jeered at by newspapers for his incompetence
at Spion Kop. The Prince, however, expresses doubts whether he
or Kaiser Wilhelm would have done better.

3007   Bunny
Friend of Lord Alfred Douglas and former homosexual companion
of Raffles, whose death he believes in so completely that he is
easily deceived by Raffles' disguise as a police inspector. During
their robbery of Lord Queensbury he escapes when Raffles is
caught.

3008   century
In cricket, the score of one hundred runs by a batsman.

3009   Digby
A resident of Albany who recently spent a night in jail.

3010   Douglas, Lord Alfred (1870-1945)
Poet, translator, editor, whose relationship with Oscar Wilde led
to Wilde's disgrace, imprisonment, and exile. In the play he plots
with Raffles and Bunny to steal money from his father, the
Marquess of Queensbury, in revenge for the father's withdrawing
of his allowance after the Wilde affair.

3011   Englebeim, Dr. Heinrich
Mentioned as a professor under whom von Blixen studied English
law enforcement.

3012   Grace, W.G.
An outstanding cricket player.

3013   Grosvenor, Mr.
Ninety-year-old resident of Albany.

3014 hat trick
In cricket, the feat of getting three players from the opposing team out on three successive bowls (pitches).

3015 Himmelstuber, Dr.
Mentioned as a professor under whom von Blixen studied psychology.

3016 "I will give you the keys of heaven."
Alice's suggestive love song echoes Matthew 16:18-19.

3017 Jones
Name taken by Raffles in his pose as servant to Lord Queensbury.

3018 Kruger, President
Kruger (1825-1900), leader of the Boer rebellion of 1880, President of the Transvaal (1883-1900).

3019 La Goulue
A woman at the Moulin Rouge, admired by the Prince and, for the purpose of their conversation at least, by Raffles.

3020 Landseer
Sir Edwin Landseer (1802-73), English artist best known for paintings of animals and for the lions in London's Trafalgar Square.

3021 Lobb's
Shoemaker who made Raffles shoes that do not squeak.

3022 Mackenzie of Scotland Yard
Police inspector, a Scotsman dressed in tweeds who has long pursued Raffles and finally catches him, somewhat awkwardly, in the company of the Prince of Wales.

3023 Marquess of Queensbury (1844-1900)
John S. Douglas, a fan of boxing who introduced in 1865 the code of rules under which the sport has operated in modern times. In the play he is a coarse, mercenary man disliked by everyone; when

he falls from the roof of the Burlington Arcade and appears to be dead, even the Prince of Wales expresses pleasure. (See Oscar.)

3024   Mary
Alice's maid.

3025   Newbolt
Sir John Henry Newbolt (1862-1938), a writer mentioned by Raffles as an underrated poet.   The lines quoted are from Newbolt's "Vitaii Lampada."

3026   Nicholas, Emperor
Edward's nephew, the Russian Czar Nicholas II (1868-1918).

3027   "O let him pass /. . . rack of this tough world"
Said of Shakespeare's King Lear (V, iii):   "O let him pass; he hates him / That would upon the rack of this tough world / Stretch him out any longer."

3028   Oscar
Oscar Wilde (1854-1900), Irish-born dramatist, poet, and scholar who became a key figure in the Aesthetic Movement. In the play he is mentioned as in exile in France. Wilde's relationship with Lord Alfred Douglas provoked Douglas's father, the Marquess of Queensbury, to insult Wilde in public; Wilde sued for libel, lost, and was imprisoned in 1895 for homosexual crimes. After his release he spent the brief remainder of his life in France.

3029   Petrovich, Captain Yevgeny
Von Blixen insists that Jones/Raffles is his arch-enemy, the Russian spy Petrovich.

3030   Portland, Mr.
Name used by the Prince of Wales in conducting his affair with Alice.

3031   Raffles
Witty and resourceful thief who is also a champion cricket player. Believed to have died at Spion Kop in the South African War, he returns to surprise his lover Bunny and enter into Lord Alfred

Douglas's scheme for burglary of the Marquess of Queensbury's house. Discovered in the act by the Prince of Wales, he poses as a waiter, serves champagne to the Prince, and through pleasant conversation wins not only the Prince's tolerant forgiveness but also--in exchange for a vow to devote himself to cricket instead of thievery--a pardon.

3032 Smith
Head porter of Albany.

3033 Spion Kop
British forces lost an important battle for the hill Spion Kop during the siege of Ladysmith (1900) in the South African War.

3034 Stephen
The friend Lord Alfred had intended to meet for dinner on the night of Raffles' return.

3035 "That little tent of blue that prisoners call the sky."
From Wilde's "The Ballad of Reading Gaol," Part iii (1898).

3036 Thompson, Francis (1859-1907)
English poet; the lines quoted are from his poem "At Lord's."

3037 Thorneycroft, Colonel
Raffles's commander at Spion Kop.

3038 Villon
Raffles suggests that the English need a poet who, like Francois Villon (1431-1463?), was also a thief.

3039 von Blixen
A captain of the Prussian Hussars, serving in England as a German spy attempting to steal Prince Edward's love letters to Alice.

3040 Willy
Prince Edward's nephew, Kaiser Wilhelm of Germany.

3041 Woodgate, General
Died at Spion Kop. The Prince, who knew him slightly, says he
was lucky to die.

THE GREAT JOWETT (1939)

3042 Adeimantus
A character in Plato's *Republic*, studied by Knight.

3043 Archbishop of Canterbury
The head of the Church of England, who gives a testimonial to
Jowett at a dinner honoring the Master.

3044 Arnold, Matthew (1822-88)
The Victorian poet gives a testimonial to Jowett at a dinner
honoring the Master.

3045 Asquith
Herbert Henry Asquith (1852-1928), 1st Earl of Oxford and
Asquith, was a former student of Balliol who served as prime
minister (1908-16) and helped to create new social welfare
programs including old-age pensions and unemployment insurance.

3046 Balliol
The Oxford college which Jowett served as professor of Greek
from 1855 and as Master from 1870 to 1893. Balliol was also
Graham Greene's college.

3047 book on St. Paul
Jowett's *A Commentary on St. Paul's Epistles* (1855) is the book
Ross finds blasphemous.

3048 Butler
The man who remarked that the Church of England was the only

thing that stood between the English people and real religion was
writer Samuel Butler (1835-1902).

3049 Carmichael, Dr.
A Balliol don whose specialty is Hegel.

3050 Curzon
George Nathaniel Curzon, Marquess of Kedleston (1859-1925), was
a politician, statesman, and writer who served as Viceroy of India
(1899-1903) and became Chancellor of Oxford in 1907.

3051 Davis, Professor
A Balliol don whose specialty is Aristotle.

3052 Foster
Head porter at Balliol College.

3053 Golightly, Dr.
Ross asks Golightly and McBride, members of the Convocation of
Oxford University, to complain to the Vice-Chancellor about
Jowett's religious views.

3054 Green
A Fellow of Balliol who regards Ross's criticism of Jowett as
irrelevant.

3055 Griggs, Mr.
An Oxford guide who thinks Jowett studied Pluto rather than
Plato.

3056 Jenkyns
An earlier Master who once rebuked the young Jowett for wearing
his cap in the dining hall.

3057 Jowett, Benjamin (1817-93)
Known affectionately as "Jowler" by the students, Jowett was one
of the great classical scholars of the nineteenth century; his
translations of many Greek works are still in print. He became
a professor at Balliol College, Oxford, in 1855 and expected to be
elected to the mastership before he was forty years old, but his

enemies who thought his religious beliefs unorthodox prevented the election. He outlasted them, however, and in 1870 was finally elected Master of Balliol, a post he held until his death. Many of Jowett's pupils were important public figures in the Edwardian period.

3058 Knight, Matthew
Jowett's servant, whom he teaches Latin.

3059 Knight, Miss
Jowett's Oxford housekeeper, sister of his servant and pupil. She visits him on his deathbed in London.

3060 McBride
See Golightly.

3061 Mallock
William Hurrell Mallock (1849-1923), a writer whose gentle caricatures of Jowett appeared in *New Republic*.

3062 Melchizedek
King and priest who appears in Genesis 14 and is mentioned in Psalms 90:4 and Hebrews 5:5-7.

3063 Milner
Viscount Alfred Milner (1854-1925), a Balliol man who in 1897 became governor of Cape colony and British high commissioner in South Africa.

3064 Newdigate
A prestigious prize for English verse, given annually at Oxford.

3065 Newman
John Henry Newman (1801-90), a fellow of Oriel College, Oxford, was a leader in the Oxford Movement, which included among its chief goals the restoration of the earlier High Church tradition in Anglican worship. Newman, who argued in *Tract XC* (1841) of his *Tracts for the Times* that the Thirty-Nine Articles were compatible with Roman Catholic belief, left the Church of

England to become a Catholic in 1845. He was made a Cardinal in 1879. (See also Ward.)

3066 Paine
Returning student greeted briefly by Jowett, who asks him about Lady Mary, apparently Paine's mother.

3067 Peel
Fellow of Balliol, a political enemy of Jowett.

3068 Plumer
A student at Balliol whom Jowett greets with an inquiry about Sir Ronald, who is probably Plumer's father. Swinburne considers Plumer a dummy.

3069 Ross
Fellow of Balliol, opposed to Jowett's candidacy for the mastership. Ross disapproves of Jowett's excessive reading of Plato and is afraid to have a Master who might be condemned for his religious opinions. He considers blasphemous Jowett's now highly regarded *Commentary on the Epistles of St. Paul.*

3070 Scott, Dr.
Jowett regarded Scott as a mere "country preacher" and wrongly thought Scott would not be elected Master.

3071 Shelley
The poet Percy Shelley (1792-1822) was expelled from Oxford in 1811 for distributing a pamphlet on "The Necessity of Atheism."

3072 *Si monumentum requiris, circumspice*
"If you seek for a monument, gaze around." The phrase is inscribed in St. Paul's Cathedral, London, and has been attributed to the son of architect Sir Christopher Wren, designer of St. Paul's.

3073 Sparks, Mrs.
Swinburne's landlady, who turns him out and complains to Jowett and Scott about the young man's behavior.

3074 Stanley, Arthur (1815-1881)
Stanley was an ecclesiastical historian and, following his mentor
Thomas Arnold (whose authorized biography he wrote), a leader
of the Broad Church movement. In the play he is a Balliol
colleague who warns Jowett, with regard to the forthcoming
election, that Jowett is up against men who have not religious but
"parsons'" minds (336).

3075 Swinburne
English poet Algernon Charles Swinburne (1837-1909), was
befriended by Jowett. In the play, Jowett encourages Swinburne's
entrance into the Newdigate competition, defends him to the
college Master when Swinburne's drunken behavior brings
complaints from his landlady, and persuades the young man to
leave Oxford of his own accord rather than be "sent down."

3076 Tennyson
The English poet Alfred, Lord Tennyson (1809-92) is said to have
trusted Jowett's judgment.

3077 The Thirty-Nine Articles
Jowett suffered disgrace when the Vice-Chancellor ordered him to
sign these articles, which set forth the Anglican position on various
theological questions.

3078 Toynbee, Arnold (1852-83)
English philanthropist notable for his efforts to improve the quality
of working class life in London's Whitechapel district, where he
helped to create parks, libraries, and better housing. He was
educated at Balliol, where he became lecturer in 1878 and bursar
in 1881.

3079 Vice-Chancellor
Humiliated Jowett by ordering him to sign the Thirty-Nine Articles
or lose his fellowship.

3080 Ward
William George Ward (1812-1882), a former fellow at Balliol
whose degrees were revoked after he was accused of heresy.
Ward converted to Roman Catholicism in 1845 and in his later life

became a controversial writer. Ross urges Smith and Peel to vote against Jowett to protect Balliol from religious controversies like those surrounding Newman (see above) and his follower Ward.

3081 woman, American
A tourist who remarks that the dining hall in Balliol would be conducive to prayer.

YES AND NO (1980)

3082 Actor
A "young and nervous man" (359) who is being coached by the director of a play in which he has a small part requiring him to say "Yes" and "No" a few times. His admitted lack of knowledge of the entire play implies an innocence with regard to its homosexual theme, and his final "no" may be an answer to what he has finally recognized as the director's indirect advances toward him.

3083 Comyns, Cyril
Sir Ralph's character, a man whose homosexual relationship with Cruikshank began in their schooldays.

3084 Cruikshank, Edward
Sir John's character, whose lingering jealousy for Comyns' affection leads him to attempt to destroy any relationship in which his old lover is involved.

3085 Director
A middle-aged man who enthusiastically but sometimes impatiently leads the young actor through a rehearsal of his part, insisting that the few instances of "yes" and "no" are of vital importance to the performance. His explanation of the play's subject as "the homosexual world we most of us live in" (362) and his frequent

confusion of the performers with the characters they portray
suggest that his ulterior motive is the seduction of the actor.

3086 Hobbs, Henry
The character played by the Actor. Hobbs is a young man who
disappears from the play after his homosexual relationship with
Comyns ends in the first act.

3087 John, Sir
The name calls to mind Sir John Gielgud (1904-).

3088 Lord Chamberlain
The Director remarks that thirty years ago a play like the one
being rehearsed would have been forbidden by the Lord
Chamberlain, the government censor.

3089 Michael, Sir
Privett had considered creating a part for a third knighted actor,
Sir Michael, but was convinced by the Director that to do so
would transform a dignified play into a tournament. The name
suggests Sir Michael Redgrave (1908-85).

3090 Pinter [Harold]
English dramatist (1930-) said to have influenced Privett.

3091 Privett, Frederick
Author of the play being rehearsed.

3092 Ralph, Sir
The name suggests Sir Ralph Richardson (1902-83).

3093 René
In the play, a young French acrobat loved by Comyns, whom he
betrays for money paid by Cruikshank.

FOR WHOM THE BELL CHIMES (1980)

3094 Anne, Princess
Chips shows X a picture in which Princess Anne of England
(1950-) is seen with a polio victim. X in turn urges Chips to
wear better clothes in case the Princess shows up at the agency's
Christmas party for children.

3095 Assistant Secretary
The Assistant Honorary Secretary of the RSPCA arrives in
response to a report the agency has received about "a dead bitch
killed under terrible circumstances by someone unknown" (413).

3096 Chips
Nickname for Masterman.

3097 Falconbridge, Mrs.
Chips promises X that for his contribution he will receive a letter
of thanks from Mrs. Falconbridge, a friend of Princess Anne.

3098 Fenwick, Colonel
An elderly man with grey hair and a military bearing, Fenwick
appears as a legitimate agent for the Anti-Child Polio campaign;
he is pursuing Chips, who has been posing as an agent for the
same group. Claiming to be a veteran of the African campaign
against Rommel, Fenwick is determinedly combative, smoking
strong cigarettes in a "war to the death" against cancer, and
insisting that a gentleman would never cheat people for money
but would kill for it in a manly fashion. Convinced that his quarry
is hiding behind the wall, he breaks through it and into the next
apartment.

3099 Ginger
Friend and former homosexual lover of Chips, Ginger is believed dead but turns up as a female police officer, claiming to have undergone a sex change operation. She is said to combine male intellect with female intuition. At the end of the play she takes off her wig and police cap and goes off with Chips.

3100 Hargreaves
A resident of the next block who had no ready cash but gave Chips four silver spoons.

3101 Harwich, Felicity
The murder victim, a fat, ugly woman who was supporting X. She was Branch Secretary of the local RSPCA.

3102 Marbles, Mrs.
A neighbor, over ninety years old, in the flat below Miss Harwich's. X did not know her name.

3103 Marks and Sparks
Nickname for Marks and Spencer, a popular chain of clothing stores.

3104 Masterman, Ambrose
A rather badly worn con man whose current racket is the soliciting of donations for the Anti-Child Polio fund. His petty villainy is overmatched when he asks for a donation from X, who offers him good clothes and a bath, then leaves him in an apartment where the body of X's fiancée, whom X has murdered, is hidden in the folding bed.

3105 Mona
A neighbor on the other side of the wall broken through by Fenwick, Mona does not appear but is constantly talked about by her husband, who fears that Fenwick and Chips plan to attack Mona. During the confusion Mona burns her dinner.

3106 Neighbour
Miss Harwich's neighbor, who is understandably alarmed when Fenwick and Chips break through his wall.

3107 Sergeant
Apprehends X, believing him to be Masterman.

3108 Spike
Friend or acquaintance whose name Chips used, for good luck, on his credentials.

3109 X
Clever, unscrupulous, nail-biting man in his forties who calls himself unemployable and prefers to allow women--preferably fat women--to support him. Having just murdered Miss Hargreaves and hidden her body in a wall bed, he cons Chips out of his clothes and identification and leaves him alone with the body. Caught by Sergeant, he confesses to Chips's crimes and identity, expecting to be jailed on that account. He slips away in the midst of the uproar surrounding the discovery of the body and the broken wall.

CHAPTER FIVE: THE LAST WORD

"The Last Word" [1988]

3110 baker
Mentioned as one of the few people who saw Pope John regularly.

3111 concierge
The concierge at the hotel asks the identity of the special guest;
when told that it is the Pope, he does not know what a Pope is.

3112 doorkeeper, uniformed
Salutes the Pope as he enters the hotel in the foreign country.

3113 General
As current ruler of the world state, the General receives the Pope
ceremoniously as a past head of state and informs him that
Communism, imperialism, and Christianity are dead. Explaining
that his strategy for preventing war is the elimination of
alternatives, the General says that the Church had to be destroyed
because even with its diminished following it represented an
alternative. He executes the Pope to complete the elimination of
Christianity, yet in the very act of shooting he is troubled

by the old man's faith, which demonstrates the possibility that Christian belief may be true.

3114   "He was in the world, and the world knew him not."
The Pope reads from John 1:10.

3115   lady, old
A gossipy woman living on the top floor of the Pope's building. She met him in the street one day and called him John.

3116   man in the street
A nameless guard, changed on alternate days, is posted outside the building where the Pope lives. When the Pope blesses him one day, he turns away.

3117   manager, hotel
Greets the Pope courteously and says he hopes to make him comfortable during his short stay.

3118   Megrim, General
The man, apparently a dictator, who tried to kill the Pope twenty years earlier because he feared the Pope and his few remaining Christian followers.

3119   officer
Takes the Pope to a car at the foreign airport.

3120   officer in uniform
A uniformed officer receives the Pope at the airport, treats him with great courtesy, and orders the stranger to return the Pope's Bible, which he says is harmless now.

3121   Pope John
An old man who lives an isolated, ascetic life in a small apartment, supported by a small pension from anonymous sources. A victim of amnesia as the result of an injury suffered in an attempt on his life some twenty years earlier, he finds happiness in privation but fears that he may have committed some crime in the past.   One day, without warning, a stranger brings him a passport and a visa and dispatches him to a country he never

expected to visit. After his arrival he is given ceremonial robes, brought before the ruling General, informed of his identity as Pope John (possibly John XXIX, but the General is uncertain), and then executed as the only surviving Christian in the world. Before dying, however, he achieves a final victory: with the glass of wine given him by the General he begins a celebration of the Mass that leaves his executioner wondering if Christian belief may after all be true.

3122 steward
The servile steward on the World United flight offers the Pope a drink from an international assortment of beverages.

3123 stranger
An unnamed man who brings the Pope a passport and a visa, tells him Christmas has been abolished, and takes him to the airport.   He threatens to report the Pope's Bible to the authorities.

3124 waiter
A waiter at the hotel serves the Pope breakfast and instructs him to prepare for his visit with the General.

3125 woman, old (in dream)
The Pope dreams of speaking to an old woman and a small girl. The woman looks at him contemptuously as if to say that he does not speak clearly.

"The News in English" [1940]

3126 Bishop, David
An Oxford professor of mathematics who is stranded in Germany after war breaks out while he is there to deliver a course of lectures.   Captured and forced to do propagandistic radio

broadcasts ("The News in English"), he is denounced by the English newspapers as a traitor who expected war to come and left his own country to avoid military service. In the broadcasts, however, he uses a private code, shared only with his wife, to convey intelligence information to the British.   His heroism is confirmed when he sacrifices his chance of escape, and presumably his life, in order to broadcast information about the refueling of U-boats.

3127 Bishop, Mary
David Bishop's wife, who never loses faith in her husband even when the papers accuse him of betraying his country.   At first resentful of her husband and embarrassed to go out in public, she nevertheless tries to persuade reporters that he may have been forced to make the broadcasts. Later she recognizes their private code and goes to the War Office. With the aid of that office, she constructs a plan for David's escape, which probably would have worked had he not given it up in order to broadcast additional information.

3128 Bishop, Mrs.
David Bishop's mother, with whom Mary Bishop lives. She knits khaki socks for soldiers, as she had done in World War I. Having reached the age at which a sense of duty is more important to her than personal ties, she recognizes her son's voice on the radio and insists on identifying him to authorities even though it means that he may be tried for treason.

3129 Colonel
An officer at the War Office who interviews Mary Bishop, confirms her belief that her husband is sending important coded messages, and arranges for the press to continue publishing articles accusing David Bishop of treason.

3130 Crowborough
A town in East Sussex.

3131 Funkhole, Dr.
The derogatory nickname given by English listeners to David

Bishop. His wife and his mother are already familiar with this name when they first hear the program and recognize his voice.

3132 Haw-Haw of Zeesen, Lord
David Bishop's predecessor on German propaganda broadcasts, "Lord Haw-Haw" (the name assigned by a London newspaper) was American-born William Joyce, who was convicted of treason in 1945 and hanged the following year for broadcasting anti-British propaganda from Berlin during the war.

3133 SOSPIC
The message Mary Bishop takes to the War Office, where she learns that it was her husband's warning that the ship *Pic* would be attacked--as it was, with the loss of two hundred lives.

"The Moment of Truth" [1988]

3134 Burton, Arthur
A waiter at Chez Auguste, a Kensington restaurant which sells English food under French names. Rightly suspecting that his recent medical examination will reveal cancer and the need for immediate surgery, he fears facing death alone and longs to share the secret of his condition with someone who would be concerned. He imagines that Dolly Hogminster, a friendly American customer who has asked his advice about the menu and local shopping, will intuit his situation and express, even if silently, her concern. When she gives him an envelope on her last visit to the restaurant, he believes his hope confirmed, but upon opening it in the hospital he finds that it contains only a tip and a friendly note.

3135 Hogminster, Dolly
An American woman who frequents the Chez Auguste with her husband. She is friendly to Arthur Burton, calling him by his first name, but she has only a superficial interest in him; her real

concern is with shopping, and her final message to Arthur is merely a tip with thanks for recommending Jermyn Street shops to her.

3136 Hogminster, Mr.
Dolly Hogminster's husband, who prides himself on having regular check-ups and corrects his wife when she says the restaurant is the Augustine rather than the Auguste.

3137 manager
The manager of the Chez Auguste accuses Arthur Burton of talking to customers when they want to be left alone. On the day Arthur goes for the report on his medical examination, the manager takes over the care of Arthur's favorite customers, the Hogminsters.

3138 surgeon
The doctor who diagnoses Arthur Burton's cancer advises immediate surgery and speaks unconvincingly of hope.

"The Man Who Stole the Eiffel Tower" [1956]

3139 Chester
An American who comes with a girl to the site of the missing Tower. He is disappointed, not because the Tower itself is gone, but because there is now no place to eat.

3140 friend
A friend of the narrator impersonates the Minister of Education at a funeral, one of the diversions used by the narrator to facilitate his return of the Tower to its familiar location.

3141 girl
Accompanies Chester to the Tower.

3142   Mollet, M.
Guy Mollet (1905-75), French socialist politician and statesman
who served briefly as Premier of France (1956-57).

3143   narrator
A man who hired a fleet of 702 trucks to take the Eiffel Tower
into the French countryside near Chantilly to allow it to rest on
its side in the country air. He explains that it was a fairly easy
task because the tourists were easily diverted, and those people
whose livelihood depended upon the Tower would not admit its
absence as long as their paychecks came.

3144   *poujadiste*
A follower of Pierre-Marie Poujade (1920-), a French bookseller
and right-wing politician who led successful campaigns to reduce
taxation in France in the mid-1950's.

3145   taxi driver
Follows the narrator's advice and takes Chester and the girl to
the Tour d'Argent (Silver Tower) where they can eat and enjoy
the view. This response becomes the standard way of dealing
with tourists while the Tower is missing.

"The Lieutenant Died Last" [1940]

3146   Barlow, Major
The local magistrate who grudgingly commends Purves for his
heroism and warns him against poaching.

3147   Black Boar
The only public house in Potter.

3148 Bojers
Purves's name for the Germans, whom he apparently confuses
with "Boers."

3149 Brewitt
Landlord of the Black Boar.

3150 Brewitt, Mrs.
The landlord's wife, who sees the Germans cutting telephone and
telegraph wires but assumes that they are working for the post
office.

3151 Brewitt, young
Mrs. Brewitt's son, the only villager to recognize the Germans
immediately. When a German soldier finds him hiding in the
outdoor lavatory of the Black Boar, young Brewitt tries to run
away but is shot in the legs and permanently crippled.

3152 Drew, Lord
Owner of the large estate which is the principal feature of Potter.
Purves poaches on Lord Drew's grounds.

3153 Driver
The village constable. Purves feels confident that Driver will be
too tired from working in his garden to be on the lookout for
poachers.

3154 gamekeeper
Lord Drew's gamekeeper is mentioned as having vowed to catch
the poacher Purves.

3155 lieutenant
The young leader of the German paratroopers becomes the last
of them to die when, after being seriously wounded, he begs
Purves to kill him out of mercy. In the lieutenant's pocket Purves
finds a photograph of a baby on a rug.

3156 Margesson, Mrs.
Keeper of the post office and store in Potter. She tries to call

the police when the Germans arrive, but her telephone line has been cut.

3157 Potter
Fictitious English Metroland village which German paratroopers invade during World War II in order to sabotage communication and railway lines.

3158 Purves, Bill
An old veteran of the South African War who lives on the fringes of the society in Potter. From time to time, especially on Bank Holidays, he purchases a bottle of liquor and vanishes for the day into Lord Drew's estate, where he sets traps, drinks, and sleeps outside. On one such outing he sees the German paratroopers in pursuit of young Brewitt, kills several of them, and captures the rest at the Black Boar. Although he is now a hero, he still receives a stern warning about poaching game.

3159 undergardener
Criticizes the beer at the Black Boar and blames its inferior quality on the war.

3160 vicar's wife
Mentioned as changing her book in the local library, unaware of the action going on nearby.

"A Branch of the Service" [1990]

3161 boss
The narrator's superior in the special duties branch of IGGR tells him that the doctor he has been observing may indeed be an honest man. Honest traitors, he says, are the most dangerous of all.

3162 Bovary, Madame
Protagonist of Flaubert's novel *Madame Bovary* (1857).

3163 doctor
In his last job the narrator observes a doctor who looks honest
but has become suspicious because of his ties to the chemical
industry. His enormous appetite makes him a difficult assignment,
and he escapes when the narrator is forced to go to the lavatory.

3164 *Education Sentimentale* (1869)
Novel by Flaubert.

3165 Eno's
Eno's Fruit Salt, a laxative and antacid.

3166 Flaubert
Gustave Flaubert (1821-80), French realist novelist whose work is
the subject of conversation between the solitary man and the
woman at the three-star restaurant.

3167 IGGR
The *International Guide to Good Restaurants,* a British publication
(fictitious) for which the narrator works.   Modeled after the
famous Michelin travel guides, it was formerly the International
Reliable Restaurant Association guide but underwent a name
change because the resulting acronym IRRA too closely resembled
IRA (Irish Republican Army). The IGGR serves as a front for
British intelligence agents who spy on restaurant customers.

3168 instructor
Introduces the narrator to the sort of "special duties" (spying)
performed by the IGGR.

3169 MI5
The narrator remarks that MI5, the British Security Service, was
jealous of the work of IGGR because that work overlapped its
territory. (See also 2136.)

3170 man, French
A spy observed by the narrator at a three-star restaurant. The

man pretends to be a literary scholar discussing his professional interests with a woman who shares his interest in the work of Flaubert. He receives from her a cigarette containing information coded in microdots.

3171   narrator
An inspector for the *International Guide to Good Restaurants,* recruited for special duties (spying) following two years of regular service. His narrative traces the course of events in which the loss of appetite forces him to give up his work.   After a brilliant performance in which he obtains a cigarette containing important coded messages, he is assigned to observe a doctor who eats in a small country restaurant. The doctor's considerable appetite forces the narrator to overeat in order to keep the man under surveillance; the narrator is stricken suddenly with diarrhea, has to leave his table, and allows the doctor to escape.   After this blunder he resigns from the service.

3172   narrator's father
The narrator traveled widely with his father, an accomplished chef who worked in several European countries but never achieved recognition.

3173   narrator's mother
Because the narrator remembers nothing about his mother, he concludes that she must have stayed home while he traveled with his father.

3174   Ritz, the
A luxurious London hotel, in Piccadilly.

3175   "There's no problem."
A phrase identified as suspicious, presumably because it is not a characteristic English expression.

3176   waiter
The old man who waits tables at the Star and Garter turns out to be the landlord as well.

3177 woman in restaurant
See man, French.

"An Old Man's Memory" [1989]

3178 Ambassador, French
Represents his country at the English ceremony inaugurating the
cross-Channel tunnel.

3179 Britannia
Great Britain personified as a woman.

3180 IRA
The Irish Republican Army, the terrorist organization suspected
of planting the bomb in the cross-Channel tunnel.

3181 Minister of Defense
Appears with Mrs. Thatcher at the ceremony inaugurating the
cross-Channel tunnel.

3182 narrator
Identifying himself as a old man telling a story in 1995, the
narrator recounts the occasion two years earlier when terrorists
blew up the cross-Channel tunnel on its inaugural day, killing
hundreds of people aboard the English train enroute to Paris
under the Channel.

3183 Semtex
Believed to be the explosive material used in the bombing of the
Tunnel (and in the explosion of a Pan American 747 over
Lockerbie, Scotland, December 21, 1988).

3184 Thatcher, Mrs.
Margaret Thatcher (1927-), British prime minister from 1979 to

1990. In the story Mrs. Thatcher, having recently won her fourth election to that office, presides over the opening of the cross-Channel tunnel at the English port of Dover.

"The Lottery Ticket" [1947]

3185 bank manager
A sweaty half-caste whose scant English, all words with Latin roots, makes him resemble a confused Dr. Samuel Johnson. He is eager to handle Thriplow's lottery winnings, but when he discovers that the Englishman wants to become a public benefactor he insists on taking Thriplow to see the Governor.

3186 beggar
To ease his conscience after winning the lottery, Thriplow gives all of his pocket money, fifty pesos, to a beggar outside the restaurant.

3187 candidate
The rival candidate for the governorship is falsely accused by the ruling party of being a reactionary who receives help from European fascists. He is arrested by soldiers at his home half an hour before Thriplow arrives to warn him. It is clear that he will be executed.

3188 capital
The capital of Tabasco, unnamed in the story, is Villahermosa.

3189 Carnegie
Andrew Carnegie (1835-1919), wealthy American industrialist notable for his philanthropy. Thriplow imagines himself as a public benefactor like Carnegie, who sponsored many public libraries.

3190   Chief of Police
A fat man, dressed in dirty white clothes, who interprets for the
bank manager, telling Thriplow that the Governor is happy with
his gift and will use it for progress--not, as Thriplow expects, for
a school, but to defeat political enemies. The Chief says that in
appreciation a marble seat with Thriplow's name on it will be
placed in the city plaza.

3191   Cortes
Hernando Cortez (1485-1547), Spanish conqueror of Mexico,
founder of Vera Cruz. Thriplow rationalizes his choice of Mexico
as his holiday destination by saying he wants to study the career
of Cortes.

3192   Diaz, Porfirio (1830-1915)
Mexican general who became President of Mexico (1877-80, 1884-
1911).

3193   girl
The girl who catches Thriplow's attention in the square turns out
to be the daughter of the rival candidate for the governorship.
Educated in England, she sympathizes with Thriplow and realizes
quickly that he has been made a fool. To ease his conscience she
asks him for money which she hopes to use to arrange burial for
her father.

3194   girl, small
Sells Thriplow the lottery ticket in Vera Cruz.

3195   Governor
Tabasco's governor, who is in a dentist's chair when Thriplow first
sees him, is in danger of losing the next election because he has
been unable to pay wages to the police and the army. With the
aid of Thriplow's gift, however, he pays the soldiers and uses them
to destroy the rival candidate.

3196   Obregón
Ivaro Obregón (1880-1928), a general in the Mexican revolution
who become an anticlerical, reform-minded president of the

country from 1920 until his assassination in 1928. A statue of Obregón stands in the square of the port town.

3197 proprietor
The elderly hotel owner talks to his guest Thriplow in a mixture of French and English. He laments the passing of happier days under the regime of Diaz, thinks Thriplow foolish for believing the state democratic, and is angered by Thriplow's belief in progress.

3198 Thriplow, Henry
A prosperous English bachelor of forty-two for whom travel is a way of escape from his humdrum life in Kensington. Timid and uninterested in women, he pursues holidays in areas unpopular with tourists and frequently so unpleasant that he returns to London with a new awareness of the comfort and attractiveness of his ordinary surroundings. Stopping in Vera Cruz on his journey to the impoverished Mexican province of Tabasco, Thriplow buys a lottery ticket from a small girl; his number wins 50,000 pesos (about £2500), which he decides to donate to the public good, expecting that the money will be used for education or a similarly worthy cause. Actually the money enables the governor to pay his army, which he then uses to capture and execute the rival candidate and thereby to secure his own dictatorial control over the province.

3199 Thriplow's aunt
Thriplow used to write to his aunt in London but has stopped doing so. She reads about assassinations and related political struggles in Mexico and assumes that her nephew is having an exciting time. Thriplow plans to buy her a serape (colored blanket).

3200 Thriplow's cousin
A cousin in Brisbane is the other person to whom Thriplow used to write. He plans to buy silver ear-rings for her.

"The New House" [1923]

3201 Bard, the
American poet Henry Wadsworth Longfellow (1807-82).

3202 bicyclist
A cyclist passing Josephs' house many years after its completion
remarks to his companion that the vulgar house built by Handry
has spoiled a once-beautiful view. He thinks Josephs unwisely
charitable for giving the design to a small-town architect.

3203 Handry
An architect hired by Samuel Josephs to build Josephs' new house
for a £5000 fee, Handry has worked in the region for almost thirty
years, chiefly as a builder of cottages; but he has longed to do a
great work on Josephs' land and has worked on plans for that
purpose for two decades. His design, a subtle one carefully suited
to the landscape, is rejected by Josephs, who wants a more
conventional, monumental building. Handry first declines the job
as an affront to his dignity, but eventually the needs of his family
take precedence over his pride and he designs the house Josephs
wants. The house is vulgar and inappropriate to its setting, but in
his old age Handry becomes proud of it.

3204 Josephs, Samuel
A wealthy, cigar-smoking newspaper magnate who quotes
Longfellow and prides himself on vision as the key to his success,
Josephs owns over a thousand acres of country land on which he
wants to build a new house of grand proportions, in white stone
with Corinthian columns. He offers the project to the local
architect Handry but rejects Handry's own design and points out
that Handry can ill afford to lose the £5000 job merely to uphold
his artistic principles. After the house is completed, Josephs spends
very little time there.

3205 "Nothing is useless or low"
From Longfellow's "The Builders" (1849).

3206 "O thou sculptor, painter, poet! / Take this lesson to thy heart"
From "Gaspar Becerra," in Longfellow's *The Seaside* (1846).

3207 Vanbrugh
Sir John Vanbrugh (1664-1726), playwright and architect, designed two of the grandest English country houses, Castle Howard and Blenheim Palace.

"Work Not in Progress" [1955]

3208 Bishop of Melbourne
The Bishop of Melbourne, visiting in England, discovers one of the false bishops and sets out to track down the kidnappers but is distracted when he falls in love with the false Archbishop. Unwilling to turn her over to the police, he leaves England.

3209 bishops, Anglican
At the opening of the play, the Anglican bishops sing of thirteen bishops when actually there are only twelve. The pointing out of this discrepancy leads to the discovery of the plot by which a gang of thugs plan to kidnap the bishops.

3210 journalist
Points out to the bishops that they number only twelve, not thirteen.

3211 Leigh, Vivien (1913-67)
English actress best known for her portrayal of Scarlett O'Hara in *Gone With the Wind* (1939). After drinking champagne, the

writer-narrator imagines that the woman ringleader in his comedy
is played by actress Vivien Leigh.

3212 Mona Lisa eyes
See Pater, Walter.

3213 *My Girl in Gaiters*
A musical comedy which the narrator, a writer like Greene, uses
when asked to tell stories to children. In the play, a gang of
twelve thugs led by a woman kidnap thirteen Anglican bishops
for their chasubles, which the thugs wrongly believe to be chalices.
They impersonate their captives until the visiting Bishop of
Melbourne discovers the deception and attempts to track down the
criminals. He does so but falls in love with the woman (who is
impersonating the Archbishop of Canterbury) and leaves the
country because he is unwilling to turn her in. She follows him to
Australia, and the play ends.

3214 narrator's brother
By claiming that his brother is Controller of Overseas Services for
the BBC, the narrator identifies himself with Graham Greene,
whose brother Sir Hugh Greene (1910-87) held that position from
1952 to 1955.

3215 Pater, Walter (1839-94)
English scholar and writer, an Oxford professor who was a major
influence on the Aesthetic Movement. Pater's best known work,
Studies in the Renaissance (1873), contains an essay on Leonardo
da Vinci in which Pater describes that painter's Mona Lisa as
expressive of the profound mystery of woman.

3216 thugs
The kidnappers.

3217 woman
Leader of the kidnapping thugs, she becomes the false Archbishop
of Canterbury until she falls in love with the Bishop of Melbourne
and follows him to Australia.

"Murder for the Wrong Reason" [1929]

3218   Callum, Arthur
See Mason, Detective-Inspector.

3219   Collins
The policeman whom Mason asks Scotland Yard to send to the
scene of Collinson's murder. Collins, however, is not on duty.

3220   Collins, Nellie
Mason whistles a waltz which he once heard little Nellie Collins
(possibly English music hall performer Charlotte Louise Collins,
1865-1910) sing at the Old Bedford.

3221   Collinson, Hubert
The murder victim, a wealthy man who years earlier had become
Rachel Mann's lover. Mason implies that Collinson has tried to
blackmail him, perhaps because Collinson knew Mason's true
identity.

3222   constable
The constable who is first to arrive at the scene of Collinson's
death feels that the case may present his only opportunity to win
praise and advancement. Mason takes pity on him and assures
him of success by confessing to him before the arrival of Groves.

3223   Groves
A police detective sent from Scotland Yard at Mason's request.
By attributing Groves's bulging eyes to exophthalmic goiter, Mason
provides a clue to his own past as a medical student.

3224   Lazarus
An engraving over the mantelpiece in Callum's/Mason's flat depicts
Christ's raising of Lazarus (John 11: 43-44).

3225 Leah
Genesis 29:23 tells of how Jacob, who had done seven years'
service to win the hand of Laban's daughter Rachel, was deceived
by Laban and married instead to a younger daughter, Leah.
Arthur Callum, who once said that he would serve seven years for
Rachel, lost his Rachel without gaining a Leah.

3226 Mann, Rachel
The lovely aspiring actress who rejected the marriage proposal of
poor medical student Arthur Callum, choosing instead the prospect
of fame and glamour as mistress of the wealthy Hubert Collinson.
Before accepting Collinson's first invitation to dinner she offered
to sleep with Callum, who refused. Although Rachel has been
dead for ten years, Callum (now Mason) is still obsessed with her
and sees a vision of her--still young and beautiful--on the night he
murders Collinson.

3227 Mason, Detective-Inspector
A doleful, middle-aged police detective with many years of
experience, Mason begins his investigation of the murder of
Hubert Collinson by announcing that it will be his last case.
When the constable who discovered Collinson's body finds among
the dead man's papers a threatening note from a man named
Arthur Callum, Mason volunteers to visit Callum, whom he says
he has long known.   He hopes that if Callum did murder
Collinson he will have done so for a good reason; a good reason
seems possible, too, since Callum as a poor medical student loved
Rachel Mann, a girl who rejected him to become the mistress of
the wealthy Collinson. Gradually it is revealed that Mason is not
merely someone who shared Callum's interest in Rachel and
jealousy of Collinson; he actually is Callum, and he has never
overcome his jealousy. He feels that if "Callum" had murdered
Collinson, he would have done so for the right reason--jealousy
and betrayal in love. But since "Mason" committed the murder,
it was not done for the right reason but, presumably, because
Collinson was blackmailing Mason.

3228 Saunders
Policeman who will drive the car bringing Groves to the scene of
the murder.

"An Appointment with the General" [1982]

3229 Durand, Jacques
The distinctive, elegant editor of a left-wing weekly magazine based in Paris. He hires Marie-Claire Duval to interview the General.

3230 Duval, Marie-Claire
A successful French journalist with a reputation for probing interviews in which she skillfully controls her subjects. Having recently endured a ruinous quarrel with her husband, she accepts an assignment from the editor Durand to interview a Latin American leader--an unlikely assignment, since she does not speak Spanish and is not even told, in the offer, the name of the country involved. Finding herself unable to control the interview in her usual manner, she asks the General what he dreams of; his answer--death--leaves her hating herself.

3231 Fidel
Fidel Castro (1926-), Cuban revolutionary, premier of Cuba (1959-).

3232 Fouquet's
A famous restaurant in Paris, on the Champs-Elysees.

3233 General, the
The head of a small, unnamed Latin American country, the General grants an interview to journalist Marie-Claire Duval. Described as a revolutionary leader whose socialism is merely superficial, he enjoys a precarious and probably brief rule. He is known to be fond of women, is clearly attracted to Marie-Claire, and seems confident, in the interview, of his power; but when asked what he dreams of, he replies that he dreams of death.

3234 Guardián, Sergeant
Soldier who makes Marie-Claire ill at ease by pretending at first
not to speak English, then serving as the translator in her
interview, during which he refuses to allow her to use a tape
recorder. The General orders him to look after Marie-Claire.

3235 Manley
Jamaican leftist political leader Michael Manley (1925-), prime
minister from 1976 to 1980, re-elected to that position in 1989.

3236 Martinez, Señor
The General's Chief Adviser, who arranged the appointment for
Marie-Claire.

3237 Pinochet
General Augusto Pinochet Ugarte (1915-), Chilean army officer
who led a successful coup against President Salvador Allende in
1973; president of Chile since 1974. Durand expresses doubt that
Marie-Claire could do a lively interview with a Pinochet, who has
become a tired subject.

3238 Schmidt, Helmut (1918-)
Marie-Claire is said to have done a successful (i.e., damaging)
interview with Helmut Schmidt, who was West German chancellor
from 1974 to 1982.

3239 Tito
Josip Broz Tito (1892-1980), Communist president of Yugoslavia
(1953-80).

APPENDIX
EDITIONS USED IN THE PREPARATION OF THIS GUIDE

The Bear Fell Free. London: Grayson and Grayson, 1935.

Brighton Rock. London: William Heinemann and The Bodley Head, 1970 (Collected Edition).

A Burnt-Out Case. London: William Heinemann and The Bodley Head, 1974 (Collected Edition).

The Captain and the Enemy. New York: Viking, 1988.

Collected Essays. Harmondsworth, Middlesex: Penguin Books, 1969.

Collected Plays. Harmondsworth, Middlesex: Penguin Books, 1985.

The Comedians. London: William Heinemann and The Bodley Head, 1976 (Collected Edition).

The Confidential Agent. London: William Heinemann and The Bodley Head, 1971 (Collected Edition).

Doctor Fischer of Geneva or The Bomb Party. New York: Simon and Schuster, 1980.

The End of the Affair. London: William Heinemann and The Bodley Head, 1974 (Collected Edition).

England Made Me.   London: William Heinemann and The
    Bodley Head, 1970 (Collected Edition).

A Gun for Sale.   London: William Heinemann and The
    Bodley Head, 1973 (Collected Edition).

The Heart of the Matter.   London: William Heinemann and
    The Bodley Head, 1971 (Collected Edition).

The Honorary Consul.   London: William Heinemann and The
    Bodley Head, 1976 (Collected Edition).

The Human Factor.   London: William Heinemann and The
    Bodley Head, 1976 (Collected Edition).

It's a Battlefield.   London: William Heinemann and The
    Bodley Head, 1970 (Collected Edition).

The Last Word.   London: Reinhardt Books, 1990.

The Man Within.   London: William Heinemann and The
    Bodley Head, 1976 (Collected Edition).

The Ministry of Fear.   London: William Heinemann and The
    Bodley Head, 1973 (Collected Edition).

Our Man in Havana.   London: William Heinemann and The
    Bodley Head, 1970 (Collected Edition).

Monsignor Quixote.   New York: Simon and Schuster, 1982.

The Name of Action.   New York: Doubleday, Doran and Co.,
    1931.

The Power and the Glory.   London: William Heinemann and
    The Bodley Head, 1971 (Collected Edition).

The Quiet American.   London: William Heinemann and The
    Bodley Head, 1973 (Collected Edition).

Rumour at Nightfall. London: William Heinemann Ltd., 1931.

Stamboul Train. London: William Heinemann and The Bodley Head, 1974 (Collected Edition).

The Tenth Man. New York: Simon and Schuster, 1985.

The Third Man and *Loser Takes All.* London: William Heinemann and The Bodley Head, 1976 (Collected Edition).

Travels with My Aunt. London: William Heinemann and The Bodley Head, 1976 (Collected Edition).

NOTES
CHAPTER ONE

1. Graham Greene, "Henry James: The Religious Aspect," *Collected Essays* (Harmondsworth, Middlesex: Penguin Books, 1970; rpt. 1978), 34.

2. "François Mauriac," *Collected Essays,* 91.

3. *The Heart of the Matter* (London: William Heinemann and The Bodley Head, 1971), 139.

4. Richard Kelly makes a similar comparison with "Dover Beach" in his discussion of *The Confidential Agent* in *Graham Greene* (New York: Frederick Ungar, 1984), 127.

5. *The Poetical Works of Matthew Arnold* (London: Macmillan, 1929), 226-7.

SELECTED BIBLIOGRAPHY

Allain, Marie-Françoise. *The Other Man: Conversations with Graham Greene.* New York: Simon and Schuster, 1981.

Allott, Kenneth, and Miriam Farris. *The Art of Graham Greene.* London: Hamish Hamilton, 1951.

Atkins, John. *Graham Greene.* New York: Roy Publishers, 1958.

Boardman, Gwen. *Graham Greene: The Aesthetics of Exploration.* Gainesville: University of Florida Press, 1971.

Couto, Mario. *Graham Greene: On the Frontier.* New York: St. Martins Press, 1986.

Dear David, Dear Graham: A Bibliophilic Correspondence. Oxford: The Alembic Press with The Amate Press, 1989.

DeVitis, A.A. *Graham Greene.* Boston: Twayne Publishers, 1986.

Donaghy, Henry J. *Graham Greene: An Introduction to His Writings.* Amsterdam: Rodopi, 1983.

Evans, Robert O. *Graham Greene: Some Critical Considerations.* Lexington: University of Kentucky Press, 1963.

Gaston, George M.A. *The Pursuit of Salvation: A Critical Guide to the Novels of Graham Greene.* Troy, N.Y.: Whitson, 1984.

Greene, Graham. *A Sort of Life.* New York: Simon and Schuster, 1971.

Karl, Frederick R. *The Contemporary English Novel.* New York: Farrar, Straus & Cudahy, 1962.

Kelly, Richard. *Graham Greene.* New York: Frederick Ungar, 1984.

Lewis, R.W.B. *The Picaresque Saint: Representative Figures in Contemporary Fiction.* New York: Lippincott, 1959.

Sharrock, Roger. *Saints, Sinners, and Comedians: The Novels of Graham Greene.* Tunbridge Wells and Notre Dame: Burns and Oates and University of Notre Dame, 1984.

Sherry, Norman. *The Life of Graham Greene.* Vol. I: 1904-1939. New York: Viking-Penguin, 1989.

Spurling, John. *Graham Greene.* London: Methuen, 1983.

Stratford, Philip. *Faith and Fiction: Creative Process in Greene and Mauriac.* Notre Dame: University of Notre Dame Press, 1964.

Thomas, Brian. *An Underground Fate: The Idiom of Romance in the Later Novels of Graham Greene.* Athens and London: The University of Georgia Press, 1988.

Wobbe, R.A. *Graham Greene: A Bibliography and Guide to Research.* New York and London: Garland Publishing Company, 1969.

Wolfe, Peter. *Graham Greene the Entertainer.* Carbondale: Southern Illinois University Press, 1972.

ABBREVIATIONS

THE MAN WITHIN	TMW
THE NAME OF ACTION	NOA
RUMOUR AT NIGHTFALL	RAN
STAMBOUL TRAIN	ST
IT'S A BATTLEFIELD	IAB
ENGLAND MADE ME	EMM
A GUN FOR SALE	GFS
BRIGHTON ROCK	BR
THE CONFIDENTIAL AGENT	CA
THE POWER AND THE GLORY	PG
THE MINISTRY OF FEAR	MOF
THE HEART OF THE MATTER	HOM
THE THIRD MAN	TTM
THE END OF THE AFFAIR	EOA
THE QUIET AMERICAN	QA
LOSER TAKES ALL	LTA
OUR MAN IN HAVANA	OMH
A BURNT-OUT CASE	BOC
THE COMEDIANS	TC
TRAVELS WITH MY AUNT	TWA
THE HONORARY CONSUL	THC
THE HUMAN FACTOR	THF
DR. FISCHER OF GENEVA	DFG
MONSIGNOR QUIXOTE	MQ
THE TENTH MAN	TNM
THE CAPTAIN AND THE ENEMY	CAE

MAY WE BORROW YOUR HUSBAND
May We Borrow Your Husband	MWB
Beauty	BTY
Chagrin in Three Parts	CTP
The Over-night Bag	ONB
Mortmain	MM
Cheap in August	CIA
A Shocking Accident	ASA
The Invisible Japanese Gentlemen	IJG
Awful When You Think of It	AWF
Doctor Crombie	DC
The Root of All Evil	RAE
Two Gentle People	TGP

A SENSE OF REALITY
Under the Garden	UTG
A Visit to Morin	VM
The Blessing	TB
Church Militant	CM
Dear Dr. Falkenheim	DDF
Dream of a Strange Land	DSL
A Discovery in the Woods	DIW

TWENTY-ONE STORIES
The Destructors	DES
Special Duties	SD
The Blue Film	BF
The Hint of an Explanation	HOE
When Greek Meets Greek	WG
Men at Work	MAW
Alas, Poor Maling	APM
The Case for the Defence	CFD
A Little Place off the Edgware Road	ALP
Across the Bridge	ATB
A Drive in the Country	DIC
The Innocent	INN
The Basement Room	TBR
A Chance for Mr. Lever	CML
Brother	BRO

Jubilee	JUB
A Day Saved	ADS
I Spy	SPY
Proof Positive	PP
The Second Death	TSD
The End of the Party	EOP
The Bear Fell Free	BFF

COLLECTED PLAYS

THE LIVING ROOM	TLR
THE POTTING SHED	PS
THE COMPLAISANT LOVER	CL
CARVING A STATUE	CS
THE GREAT JOWETT	GJ
THE RETURN OF A.J. RAFFLES	RAJ
YES AND NO	YAN
FOR WHOM THE BELL CHIMES	FWB

THE LAST WORD

The Last Word	TLW
The News in English	NIE
The Moment of Truth	MOT
The Man who Stole the Eiffer Tower	MWS
The Lieutenant Died Last	LDL
A Branch of the Service	BOS
An Old Man's Memory	OMM
The Lottery Ticket	LT
The New House	NH
Work Not in Progress	WNP
Murder for the Wrong Reason	MWR
An Appointment with the General	AWG

GENERAL INDEX

A.B.C., 811 (MOF)
A.C.U., 300 (EMM)
A.D., 1787 (TWA)
A.F.S., 812 (MOF)
A.O., 1402 (OMH)
A.R.P., 813 (MOF)
A.T.S., 950 (HOM)
A chacun son goût, 1788 (TWA)
"A man who starts looking for God," 1522 (BOC)
abogado, 1931 (THC)
Abdul, General, 1789 (TWA)
Abraham, 2267 (MQ)
Absalom, 1 (TMW)
Achilles statue, 211 (IAB)
Acky, 414 (GFS)
Actor, 3082 (YAN)
actor, ex-, 1128 (EOA)
actress, 301 (EMM)
Ada, 1790 (TWA)
Adams, 212 (IAB), 2746 (CFD), 2941 (CL)
Adams, Mrs., 2747 (CFD)
Adams's brother, 2748 (CFD)
Addams, Charles, 1614 (TC)

Adeimantus, 3042 (GJ)
administrator, 1523 (BOC)
Adolph, 45 (NOA)
Advance of Red China, The, 1249 (QA)
Adventist, 2971 (CS)
aflatoxin, 2035 (THF)
Agbo, 2036 (THF)
Agincourt, 2553 (UTG)
Agnes, Mother, 1524 (BOC)
Agnes, Sister, 1403 (OMH)
Agnus Dei, 542 (BR)
"Aimer à loisir, / Aimer et mourir," 302 (EMM)
air raid warden, 1129, (EOA)
Aitkin, 415 (GFS)
Akimbu, Marie, 1525 (BOC)
Aladdin, 416 (GFS)
Albany, 1404 (OMH), 2037 (THF)
Albert, 2220 (DFG)
Alda, 649 (CA)
Aldermaston, 2038 (THF)
Aldershot, 213 (IAB)
Alec, 2429 (MWB)
Alexander VI, 1791 (TWA)

Britannia, 3179 (OMM)
Brixton, 830 (MOF)
Bromley, Teddy, 968 (HOM)
brother, elder, 2556 (UTG)
Brothers, 831 (MOF)
Brown, 969 (HOM), 1630 (TC),
2396 (CAE)
Brown, Dr., 2842 (PP)
Brown, Maggie, 1631 (TC)
Brown, Pinkie, 563 (BR)
Brown, Tom, 2712 (WG)
Browne, 2060 (THF), 2397
(CAE)
Browne, Helen, 2884 (TLR)
Browne, Father James, 2885
(TLR)
Browne, Teresa, 2886 (TLR)
Browne's, 2638 (DDF)
Browning, Mr., 225 (IAB)
Brown's father, 1632 (TC)
Bruce, Robert, 1942 (THC)
Brûle, Père, 970 (HOM)
Brummell, George Bryan, 2061
(THF)
Brutus, 226 (IAB), 1633 (TC)
Bryce's *Holy Roman Empire,*
971 (HOM)
buer, 564 (BR)
Buffy, 2062 (THF)
Bullen, 227 (IAB)
Bullen, Miss, 1363 (LTA)
Buller, 1943 (THC), 2063
(THF)
Buller, Captain, 972 (HOM)
Buller, General, 3006 (AJR)
Bunny, 3007 (AJR)
Burgess, 2064 (THF)
Burgoyne, General, 565 (BR)
Burke, 2557 (UTG)
Burne-Jones, 2976 (CS)
Burns Oates, 2887 (TLR)
Burton, 832 (MOF)
Burton, Arthur, 3134 (MOT)
Burton, Richard, 1944 (THC)

Bury, Lady Caroline, 228 (IAB)
Bury, Justin, 229 (IAB)
Bury, Mr., 2065 (THF)
butcher, 2274 (MQ)
Butler, 3048 (GJ)
Butler, Inspector, 2066 (THF)
Butler, Mrs., 8 (TMW)
Butler, Samuel, 2911 (PS)
Butlin's Camp, 1799 (TWA)
Butterworth, 973 (HOM)
Buzzard's, 662 (CA)
C., 2067 (THF)
C.B., 424 (GFS)
C.B.E., 1151 (EOA)
CC, 1945 (THC)
CD, 1946 (THC)
C.H., 1364 (LTA)
CID, 230 (IAB)
C.T.S., 1415 (OMH)
Cabot, 1257 (QA)
Cadwal, 1416 (OMH)
Caesar Augustus, 425 (GFS)
Caesar, the King's friend, 1417
(OMH)
cafard, 1534 (BOC)
Café Royal, 1152 (EOA)
Calkin, Joseph, 426 (GFS)
Calles, President, 745 (PG)
call-girl, 1634 (TC)
Callifer, Anne, 2912 (PS)
Callifer, Henry C., 2913 (PS)
Callifer, James, 2914 (PS)
Callifer, John, 2915 (PS)
Callifer, Mrs. Mary, 2916 (PS)
Callifer, Sara, 2917 (PS)
Callifer, William, 2918 (PS)
Callitrope, 427 (GFS)
Callot, Anne-Marie, 1800
(TWA)
Callow, 1947 (THC)
Calloway, 313 (EMM), 974
(HOM)
Calloway, Joseph, 2757 (ATB)
Calloway, Lieutenant, 1083

Coral's mother, 148 (ST)
Coriolanus, 984 (HOM)
Cork, mayor of, 2227 (DFG)
Corneille, 2604 (VM)
Cornell, 320 (EMM)
Corner, 2920 (PS)
Cornforth, William P., 985
  (HOM)
coroner, 440 (GFS)
Corpus, 2082 (THF)
Corpus Christi, 2687 (SD)
Corpus Domini nostri, 2280
  (MQ)
corridors of power, 1653 (TC)
Corruptio optimi, 1654 (TC)
Corruptio optimi est pessimi,
  572 (BR)
Cortes, 3191 (LT)
Cortez, 2763 (DIC)
Cosmic Fallacy, The, 2921 (PS)
Cosmopolitan, 573 (BR)
Cost, Mr., 841 (MOF)
Couéism, 986 (HOM)
Councillor Worm, 2922 (PS)
coup de foudre, 1432 (OMH)
cousin, 2083 (THF)
Coward, Noel, 1655 (TC)
Crab, 574 (BR)
Crabbe, 244 (IAB)
Crabbin, 1086 (TTM)
Cradbrooke, the Dowager Lady,
  842 (MOF)
Cranbeim, Mrs., 441 (GFS)
Crane, 50 (NOA), 1267 (QA)
Crane, Jane, 2947 (CL)
Crane, Michael, 93 (RAN)
Crane's mother, 94 (RAN)
Crashaw, Colonel, 2843 (PP)
Craven, 2756 (ALP)
Crawford, Marion, 1809 (TWA)
Crawley, Mr., 2458 (CTP)
Crayshaw, 987 (HOM)
Credo in unum Satanum, 575
  (BR)

Credo of a Sceptic, The, 2923
  (PS)
Creole smuggler, 1433 (OMH)
Crichton, 1959 (THC)
Crikey, 670 (CA)
crime reporter, 442 (GFS)
Crippen, 245 (IAB)
crise de foie, 1656 (TC)
Croesus, 51 (NOA)
Crole, Else, 671 (CA)
Crombie, Dr., 2514 (DC)
Crompton, Father, 1160 (EOA)
Cromwell and shattered statues,
  149 (ST)
Cromwell, life of, 843 (MOF)
Crooks, 844 (MOF)
Cross, Elisabeth, 2714 (WG)
Crosse, Superintendent, 246
  (IAB)
Croupier, 1657 (TC)
Crow, Violet, 576 (BR)
Crowborough, 3130 (NIE)
Crowder, Anne, 443 (GFS)
Crowder, Harvey, 1810 (TWA)
Crowe, 2621 (TB)
Crowle, Janet, 247 (IAB)
Crown and Anchor, 1811
  (TWA)
Crown Counsel, 2749 (CFD)
Crowned Image, The, 1161
  (EOA)
Cruickshank, 2084 (THF)
Cruikshank, Edward, 3084
  (YAN)
Crusoe, 672 (CA)
Cubitt, John, 577 (BR)
cui bono, 988 (HOM)
Cullen, Rose, 673 (CA)
Cundifer, Lady, 444 (GFS)
curate, the, 445 (GFS)
Curia, 2281 (MQ)
Curlew, Melany, 1812 (TWA)
Curlew, William, 1813 (TWA)
Curran, Mr., 1814 (TWA)

Joseph, 1698 (TC)
Joseph, Father, 1564 (BOC)
Josephs, Samuel, 3204 (NH)
José's wife, 768 (PG)
joss sticks, 1295 (QA)
Jossy and Ballard, 475 (GFS)
journalist, 1100 (TTM), 1987
  (THC), 3210 (WNP)
Jowett, Benjamin, 3057 (GJ)
Joyce, 173 (ST), 2855 (EOP)
Joyce, James, 1101 (TTM)
Juan, 106 (RAN), 769 (PG)
Jubilee, 877 (MOF), 2832
  (JUB)
Judas, jealous, 1192 (EOA)
Jude, St. 1457 (OMH)
Judy, 600 (BR)
"Juicy Juliet," 476 (GFS)
juju, 1296 (QA)
Jules, 2366 (TNM)
Jules's father, 268 (IAB)
Jules's mother, 269 (IAB)
Julian, 1844 (TWA)
Jung, 2574 (UTG)
Jupiter, not Venus, 477 (GFS)
justice of the peace, 1699 (TC)
Juventud Febrerista, 1988
  (THC)
K., 701 (CA)
K.C., 702 (CA)
KGB, 2128 (THF)
KLM pilots, 1458 (OMH)
Kalamazoo, 2129 (THF)
Kalebdjian, Mr., 174 (ST)
Kalnitz, Mayor, 2531 (RAE)
Kamnetz, General, 175 (ST)
Kapper, Bertha, 57 (NOA)
Kapper, Joseph, 58 (NOA)
Karl, 59 (NOA)
Kastner, Herr, 2532 (RAE)
Kate, 1459 (OMH)
Kathie, 2877 (BFF)
Kay, 478 (GFS)
Keene, Sir Alfred, 1845 (TWA)

Keene, Barbara, 1846 (TWA)
Kenyatta, Mr., 1700 (TC)
Kerouac, 1701 (TC)
Kibber, Kolley, 601 (BR)
Kikuyu, 2631 (CM)
Kimathi, General, 2632 (CM)
King Charles's head, 1702 (TC)
King Kong, 2411 (CAE)
King Solomon's Mines, 2412
  (CAE)
King, the, 2733 (MAW), 2833
  (JUB)
kip, 602 (BR)
Kipling, 2413 (CAE)
Kips, 2246 (DFG)
Kite, 603 (BR)
Kite, Battling, 479 (GFS)
knacker's yard, 1297 (QA)
Knapsack, The, 2247 (DFG)
Knight, Matthew, 3058 (GJ)
Knight, Miss, 3059 (GJ)
Koch, Herr, 1102 (TTM)
Koch, Ilse, 1103 (TTM)
Kolber, Herr, 176 (ST)
Kraft, Captain, 60 (NOA)
Kreuger, 357 (EMM)
Kreuzer, Dr., 2926 (PS)
Kreuzer's son, 2927 (PS)
Kreuzer's wife, 2928 (PS)
Krogh, 2367 (TNM)
Krogh, Erik, 358 (EMM)
Krueger, "General," 2248 (DFG)
Kruger, President, 3018 (AJR)
Krupp, Herr, 2249 (DFG)
Krus, 2130 (THF)
Kurtz, 61 (NOA), 1104 (TTM)
L., 703 (CA)
L.C.C., 878 (MOF)
La Eterna Martir, 770 (PG)
La Garçonne, 1298 (QA)
La Goulue, 3019 (AJR)
lacrimae rerum, 1703 (TC)
lady, elderly, 2844 (PP)
lady, intense whimsical, 879

manservant, 708 (CA)
Mansfield, Jayne, 2440 (MWB)
Manville, Lord Charles, 2720
  (WG)
maquis, 1722 (TC)
Marbles, Mrs., 3102 (FWB)
Marcel, 1723 (TC)
Marcus, Sir, 486 (GFS)
Margaret, 2482 (CIA)
Margesson, Mrs., 3156 (LDL)
Maria, 783 (PG), 1466 (OMH),
  1854 (TWA), 1994 (THC),
  2577 (UTG)
Marie, 1467 (OMH)
Marie-Chantal, 1573 (BOC)
Marie's father, 1574 (BOC)
Marie's husband, 2547 (TGP)
Marie's mother, 1575 (BOC)
Marina, 370 (EMM)
Marion, Aunt, 1383 (LTA)
Mark, 1031 (HOM), 1468
  (OMH)
Mark, King, 371 (EMM)
Marks and Sparks, 3103 (FWB)
marksman, 1724 (TC)
Marlene, 274 (IAB)
Marlowe, 64 (NOA), 1469
  (OMH)
Marlowe's devils, 1109 (TTM)
Marquess of Queensbury, 3023
  (AJR)
Marquez, 2321 (MQ)
Martha, 2624 (TB)
Martha, the anxious, 2896
  (TLR)
Martha's father, 1725 (TC)
Martin, 1995 (THC)
Martin Fierro, 1996 (THC)
Martin of Lisieux, Señorita,
  2322 (MQ)
Martin, David (Popey), 2707
  (HOE)
Martinez, Colonel, 2418 (CAE)
Martinez, Señor, 3236 (AWG)

Martins, Rollo, 1110 (TTM)
Mary, 2140 (THF), 2578
  (UTG), 2897 (TLR), 3024
  (AJR)
Mary (Wormold's ex-wife), 1470
  (OMH)
Mary (Wormold's sister), 1471
  (OMH)
Mason, Detective-Inspector,
  3227 (MWR)
Mason, Mrs., 487 (GFS)
Mason, Perry, 1997 (THC)
Masterman, Ambrose, 3104
  (FWB)
maté, 1855 (TWA)
Mather, James (Jimmy), 488
  (GFS)
Mather's brother, 489 (GFS)
Matisse, 1576 (BOC)
matron, somber, 1384 (LTA)
Matthews, Flossie, 275 (IAB)
Mau-Mau, 2634 (CM)
Maud, 372 (EMM), 1204
  (EOA)
"Maud," 490 (GFS), 1856
  (TWA)
Maude, Aylmer, 2141 (THF)
Maude, Mr., 889 (MOF)
Maugham, Somerset, 1032
  (HOM), 1205 (EOA)
Maverick, 2694 (SD)
Mavis, 2878 (BFF)
Maybury, Ethel, 1033 (HOM)
Maydew, Miss (Binns), 491
  (GFS)
Mayfair, 65 (NOA)
Mayhew, 492 (GFS)
mayor, 1206 (EOA), 1385
  (LTA)
Mayor, 2323 (MQ)
Mayor of Bourge, 2376 (TNM)
mayoress, the, 493 (GFS)
Mazzini, 66 (NOA)
McBride, 3061 (GJ)

Russell, 1225 (EOA), 2015
  (THC)
Russell and the old *Times*, 1333
  (QA)
Russell, Bertrand, 2935 (PS)
Russell case, 1226 (EOA)
Russian novelist, the great, 287
  (IAB)
Ruth, 2184 (THF), 2905 (TLR)
Rutherford, Lord, 1499 (OMH)
Ruttledge, 288 (IAB)
Rycker, 1596 (BOC)
Rycker, Marie, 1597 (BOC)
Saccus stercoris, 517 (GFS)
Sacher's Hotel, 1118 (TTM)
Sagrin, 2615 (VM)
saint, popular, 2344 (MQ)
St. Ambrose's College, 2725
  (WG)
St. Cyr, 1334 (QA)
St. Pancras (station), 627 (BR)
St. Vitus's dance, 518 (GFS)
Saladin, 2185 (THF)
Salisbury, Lord, 1335 (QA)
Sally, 725 (CA), 2500 (ASA)
Salmon, Mrs., 2754 (CFD)
Salt, Johnny, 2994 (CS)
Salvation Army Leader, 1598
  (BOC)
Salvationist, 289 (IAB)
Sammy, 628 (BR)
Sampson, Sir Nigel, 2583
  (UTG)
Sam's father, 2186 (THF)
San Martin, General, 1894
  (TWA)
Sanatogen, 290 (IAB)
Sanchez, Maria, 1500 (OMH)
Sanchez, Professor, 1501
  (OMH)
Sanchez, Señora, 2016 (THC)
Sancho, 1895 (TWA)
Sandale, Lord, 2798 (TBR)
Sans Souci, 1765 (TC)

Sargent, 393 (EMM)
Saunders, 519 (GFS), 3228
  (MWR)
Saunders, Miss, 2698 (SD)
Savage, 1502 (OMH)
Savage, Miss, 921 (MOF)
Savage, Mr., 1227 (EOA), 2739
  (MAW)
Saveedra, Jorge Julio, 2017
  (THC)
Savory, Quin, 195 (ST)
Schmidt, Anna, 1119 (TTM)
Schmidt, Father, 2637 (CM)
Schmidt, Frau, 2539 (RAE)
Schmidt, Helmut, 3238 (AWG)
Schmidt, Herr, 2540 (RAE)
Schmidt, Mr., 1120 (TTM)
schoolmaster, 801 (PG)
Schopenhauer, 2659 (DSL)
Schultz, Frau, 74 (NOA)
Schwenigen, 1228 (EOA)
Scio cui credidi, 2345 (MQ)
Scobie, Catherine, 1052 (HOM)
Scobie, Henry, 1053 (HOM)
Scobie, Louise, 1054 (HOM)
Scott, 1229 (EOA)
Scott, Captain, 922 (MOF)
Scott, Dr., 3070 (GJ)
Scott, Sir Walter, 1896 (TWA)
Scott's, 2187 (THF)
Scott's Lockhart, 394 (EMM)
Scrubs, 2726 (WG)
sculptor, Sweden's greatest, 395
  (EMM)
"Seafarer, The," 2258 (DFG)
Seagull, 1394 (LTA)
Sebastopol, 923 (MOF)
Second Mrs. Tanqueray, The,
  1897 (TWA)
secretary (club), 1230 (EOA)
Secretary, First, 726 (CA)
Secretary for Social Welfare,
  1766 (TC)
Secretary of Embassy, young,

"You can trust him when the
wind's blowing east," 738
(CA)
"You say I am not free," 2219
(THF)
Yusef, 1079 (HOM)

Yvonne, Tante, 2552 (TGP)
Z., 739 (CA)
Zancas, Enriques, 2352 (MQ)
Zapata, 810 (PG)
Zephyrinus, St., 413 (EMM)
Ziffo, Mrs., 541 (GFS)